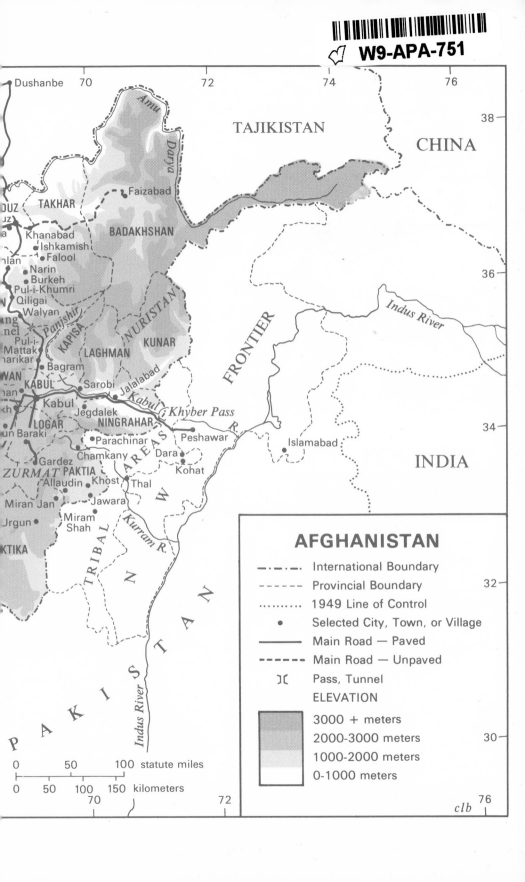

W9-APA-751

Dushanbe 70   72   74   76

TAJIKISTAN

CHINA

38

Amu

Darya

Faizabad

TAKHAR

UZ
uz
a   Khanabad
Ishkamish
lan   Falool
Narin
Burkeh
Pul-i-Khumri
N   Qiligai
ng   Walyan
nel

BADAKHSHAN

36

NURISTAN

Indus River

Pul-i-
Mattak
arikar   Bagram
WAN
an
kh
Kabul
LOGAR
un Baraki

KAPISA

LAGHMAN   KUNAR

FRONTIER

KABUL   Sarobi
Jalalabad
Kabul
Jegdalek
NINGRAHAR   Khyber Pass
Parachinar   Peshawar
Chamkany   Dara
Kohat

34

Panjshir

Islamabad

INDIA

ZURMAT PAKTIA
Allaudin   Khost   Thal
Miran Jan
Jrgun   Miram
Shah
KTIKA

Gardez

AREAS

W

Jawara

TRIBAL

Kurram R.

N

32

A
T
S
I
N
A
H
G
F
A

P

K

I

S

Indus River

AFGHANISTAN

—·—·—	International Boundary
-------	Provincial Boundary
··········	1949 Line of Control
•	Selected City, Town, or Village
———	Main Road — Paved
-------	Main Road — Unpaved
)(	Pass, Tunnel
	ELEVATION

32

ELEVATION

	3000 + meters
	2000-3000 meters
	1000-2000 meters
	0-1000 meters

30

0   50   100 statute miles

0   50   100   150 kilometers

70   72   76

clb

Among the Afghans

Central Asia Book Series

AMONG THE
AFGHANS

ARTHUR BONNER

Duke University Press   Durham and London   1987

© 1987 Duke University Press
Second Printing
All rights reserved
Printed in the United States of America
on acid-free paper ∞
This volume is part of the Central Asia Book
Series, published by Duke University Press.
Photographs by Arthur Bonner.
Maps by Christopher Brest.
Library of Congress Cataloging in Publication Data
Bonner, Arthur.
Among the Afghans.
(Central Asia book series)
Bibliography: p.
Includes index.
1. Afghanistan—History—Soviet Occupation, 1979–
—Personal narratives.   2. Afghanistan—Description
and travel—1981–   .   3. Bonner, Arthur—Journeys—
Afghanistan.   4. Journalists—United States—Biography.
I. Title.   II. Series.
DS371.2.B65   1987   958′.1044   87-22260
ISBN 0-8223-0783-9
ISBN 0-8223-0794-4 (pbk.)

Contents

....

Editor's Note

In transliterating Afghan words into English, the author has relied on those sources that represent a consensus of usage. For transliterations of unfamiliar names and places, simplified spellings have been employed that reflect common pronunciations.

Chronology

....

998-1030	Mahmud of Ghazni, first mention of Afghans
1296–1316	Allauddin Khilji, sultan of Delhi
1451–1526	Lodi (Afghan) Dynasty in India
1613–1689	Khushal Khan Khattak, Pushtun poet
1747	Ahmad Shah Durrani establishes Afghan kingdom
1839–1842	First Anglo-Afghan War
1878–1880	Second Anglo-Afghan War
1880–1901	Abdur Rahman unifies Afghanistan
1893	Durand Line divides Afghan tribal lands
1919	Amanullah becomes king, Third Anglo-Afghan War
1921	Bukhara's Amir flees to refuge in Afghanistan
1921–1922	Enver Pasha tries to organize Basmachis
1929	Bacha-i-Saqao revolt, Amanullah abdicates
1933	Zahir Shah ascends throne
1947, August	Indian independence, creation of Pakistan
1953, September	Mohammed Daoud becomes prime minister
1955, December	Visit of Khrushchev and Bulganin
1963, March	Daoud resigns as prime minister
1965, January	PDPA (Communist party) organized
1965, October	Parliament inaugurated
1973, July	Daoud ousts King Zahir with Communist help
1975, July	Attempted Islamic insurgency
1978, April	Communist Saur Revolution
1979, February	Khomeini seizes power in Iran
1979, July	Execution of young fundamentalists

1979, September	Hafizullah Amin ousts Nur Mohammed Taraki
1979, December	Soviet invasion, Babrak Karmal installed
1980, July	Islamic principles for negotiations
1981, February	Nonaligned nations adopt altered principles
1981, April	UN indirect peace dialogue begins
1982, June	First "proximity talks" in Geneva
1982, June	Staale Gundhur, Norwegian cameraman, killed
1983, January	Philippe Augoyard, French doctor, captured
1983, October	Raffaele Favero, Australian cameraman, killed
1984, September	Jacques Abouchar, French journalist, captured
1985, May	New seven-party coalition formed
1985, September	Charles Thornton, American reporter, killed
1985, September	Reagan-Gorbachev summit in Geneva
1986, March	Gorbachev calls Afghanistan "bleeding wound"
1986, May	Najib replaces Babrak Karmal
1986, May	USSR offers four-year withdrawal timetable
1987, February	UN peace negotiations stalemated

List of Political Parties

....

SUNNI, TRADITIONALIST

Mahaz-i-Milli-i-Islami (National Islamic Front)
Leader: Pir Sayed Ahmad Gailani

Jabha-yi-Nejat-i-Milli (National Liberation Front)
Leader: Maulvi Sibghatullah Mujaddidi

Harakat-i-Inqilab-i-Islami (Islamic Revolutionary Movement)
Leader: Maulvi Mohammed Nabi Mohammadi

SUNNI, FUNDAMENTALIST

Hizb-i-Islami (Islamic Party)
Leader: Gulbuddin Hekmatyar

Hizb-i-Islami (Islamic Party)
Leader: Yunis Khalis

Jamiat-i-Islami (Islamic Society)
Leader: Professor Burhanuddin Rabbani

Ittihad-i-Islami (Islamic Alliance)
Leader: Professor Abdur Rasul Sayyaf

SHIA, ALLIED WITH PESHAWAR SUNNI PARTIES

Shura-yi-Ittifaq-i-Islami (United Islamic Council)
Leaders: Sayed Ali Beheshti, Sayed Jaglan

Harakat-i-Islami (Islamic Movement)
Leader: Sheik Asaf Muhseni

SHIA, ALLIED WITH KHOMEINI FORCES IN IRAN

Sazman-i-Nasir (Organization for Victory)
Leader: Sadiqi Neeli

Sepah-i-Pasdaran (Revolutionary Guardians)
Leader: Unknown

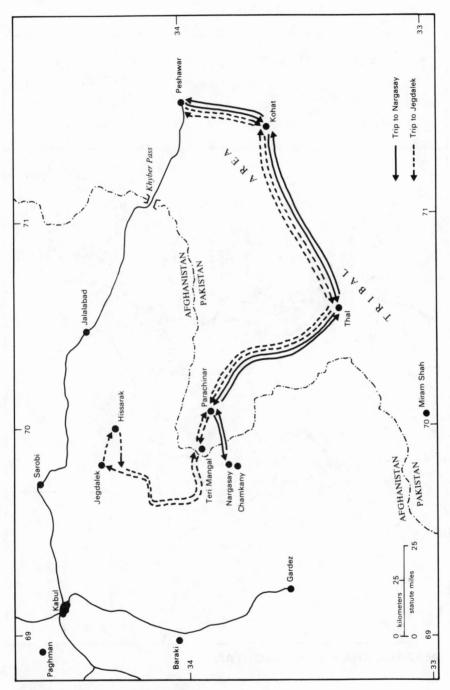

NARGASAY and JEGDALEK

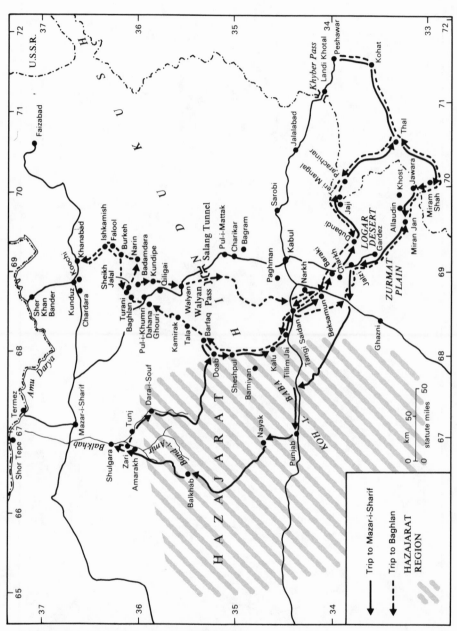

MAZAR-I-SHARIF and BAGHLAN

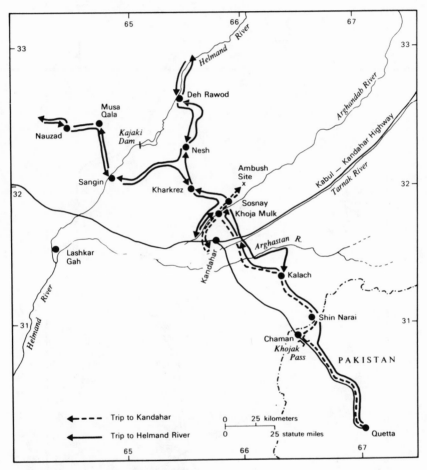

KANDAHAR and HELMAND

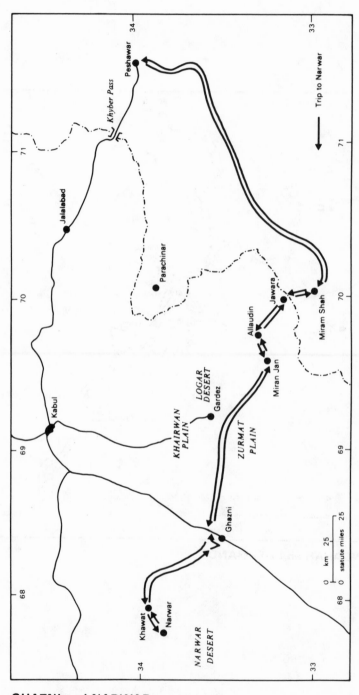

GHAZNI and NARWAR

Among the Afghans

Fluttering pennants over graves of civilians killed by bombs. An ancient civilization with little natural wealth that wanted only to be left in peace is threatened with extinction, and the outside world does not seem to care.

Missiles, MiGs, and Mynahs

••••••••••••

1

My most vivid memory of Afghanistan is a scene in a mujahidin camp in the southwest a few miles from the Pakistan border. A young man walked by with his left hand hanging limply at his side. The hand was livid pink and was dripping fluid. I asked my interpreter what happened. "He was arguing with a friend about who was the bravest," the interpreter replied. "He put his hand into a fire and held it there until it was burned like that. Someone has been called from another camp to put a bandage on it."

Bravery is central to the Afghans. Being brave, or just seeming brave, shapes their attitudes toward life and the people around them. A large part of bravery in Afghan eyes is being able to bear pain and suffering. Honor is also important, and honor to the Afghans means not taking second place to anyone. They don't like to be pushed around. It offends their honor and makes them want to get even. Revenge is another part of what it means to be a man in Afghanistan. The proof of these generalities is that Afghanistan, a poor and mountainous nation, with no technology and only light arms has literally stopped the Soviet Army dead in its tracks.

Since a tiny Communist clique seized power in April 1978, and the Soviet forces invaded in December 1979, a third of the people, mostly women and children, have been driven into exile. Whole villages are deserted, and the remains of their rain-eroded mud walls stand like great African ant heaps. Tens of thousands are dead, and next to every village and along every trail bodies lie under heaps of stones marked by fluttering pennants atop tall poles. There are no parades and no medals.

There are few medics for the wounded, no pensions for the disabled. All that doesn't matter. The Afghans say they are fighting a *jihad*, a holy war, and call themselves *mujahidin*, holy warriors. The old and the young, the strong and even the disabled say they will fight on to the next generation if necessary. Their resistance has been likened to that of the Spartans at Thermopylae and the Jews at Masada.

But such analogies raise questions. Hellenic unity quickly dissolved after the retreat of the Persians, and the squabbling Greek states were effortlessly conquered by Rome, the superpower of the day. Masada ended in mass suicide and a Roman victory. Does the incident at the Afghan camp foreshadow a similar end? Was the man who burned his hand foolhardy, if not plain foolish? If there had been a battle, he had put himself out of action. His bravado also challenged others to turn their sense of honor in on themselves instead of preserving their strength for action against the enemy.

A guerrilla war needs trained and disciplined men, not heroes. It also needs political and social planning. Guerrilla war is about the needs and hopes of people. War is the means, not the end. A reporter who wants to devote himself to what is most significant should spend his time writing about people and social planning, but it is hard to ignore the glittering bravery and endurance of the mujahidin. Afghanistan has not consumed much of the world's attention, and most of what has been written or filmed has been devoted to the war. In many ways this reflects the limits of journalism. Reporters look for the events of a day, and nothing is more topical than battle. It is a foreign correspondent's equivalent of a five-alarm fire—the easiest story and the one most likely to see print. And the process feeds on itself: if others have been reporting battle, battles are news.

When I went to Afghanistan I thought I could avoid this trap, but by chance on my first trip into the country I brushed with battle. I had been in Pakistan three weeks, establishing contacts, trying to understand the story, and trying to get an extension of my one-month visa. Pakistan, like almost all countries in Asia, does not welcome stray travelers, especially nosy journalists and scholars. Tourists can get a one-month visa with little delay, but other applications are referred to Islamabad, the capital, and an answer might take a month or more. Freelance reporters solve the problem simply by getting a tourist visa. They don't intend to stay longer than a month in any case. If they do overstay their visa, the usual government response is an order to leave the country within forty-eight hours.

I was not aware of this problem when I set out to write from within Afghanistan on a nonstaff basis for the *New York Times*. I first went to India on another matter, and then, with a letter of introduction from the *New York Times*, I asked for a one-month entry visa at the Pakistani consulate in New Delhi, figuring it would be faster if I went to Islamabad and applied there for a long-term visa. The Pakistan Ministry of External Affairs received my request with complete graciousness. Nevertheless, the application touched off a series of telexes and phone calls between Islamabad, New York, and the Pakistan embassy in Washington. About six months later, a one-year visa was stamped in my passport. I was accredited as a correspondent in Pakistan. Nothing was said about what sort of reporting I would do. Pakistan insists it has no knowledge of persons who cross through its territory en route to Afghanistan.

Getting There

While I was waiting, I was given a temporary visa that allowed me to stay in Pakistan until things were straightened out. I was not worried, especially since American officials said they had private assurances that Pakistan did not want to prohibit news coverage from Afghanistan. I decided to make a few short trips over the border just to get the feel of things. The problem then became how to get through a heritage of colonial rule in Pakistan known as tribal territory. Two wars and countless skirmishes taught the British that they could not subdue the refractory Afghan tribes along their northwest frontier. Instead they gave the tribes autonomy, along with subsidies to persuade them to keep the peace. Every now and then they sent in punitive expeditions, giving rise to Kiplingesque tales of Afghan ferocity and honor. Civilians were rarely allowed inside tribal territory, and then only with armed guards.

The tribal areas are still closed to foreigners. A journalist must get help from Afghans, who are allowed to wander back and forth across the tribal territories and in and out of Afghanistan without passports or visas. Getting help means seeking out and demonstrating minimal authenticity to any of the seven major Afghan resistance parties headquartered in Peshawar, the capital of Pakistan's Northwest Frontier Province.

I went into Afghanistan with the help of the National Islamic Front, the most Western oriented of the Afghan resistance parties. I was told to wear Afghan clothes: baggy pants with a drawstring at the waist, a shirt that draped down to my knees, and a hat with a rolled brim. A car came to my hotel on February 9, 1985, and took me to the party's Peshawar headquarters where, in the privacy of a courtyard, I was transferred to an ambulance. Actually, it was just a white van with Red Cross markings. It had a long, leather-covered seat in the rear that could accommodate a patient and cloth curtains to obscure the wide windows. There were four other passengers, including Kamaluddin Koochi, who was sent as my guide and interpreter. He introduced me to the others and said they were on a secret mission, so I did not ask them any questions. Kamaluddin said that if we were stopped by a police patrol I was to take off my glasses and stretch out on the bench, with a blanket pulled over me. I was to remain silent, even if someone pulled back the blanket to look at me. As it turned out, the driver merely sounded a tinny siren and waved to the police as he sped past checkpoints. After about six hours we arrived at Parachinar, in a part of Pakistan that extends like a thumb into Afghanistan. I was hustled through an alley between two buildings and into a single-story building facing a small enclosed courtyard. "You must stay here," Kamaluddin said. "There are Pakistani spies everywhere, and if they know you are here they will arrest you."

The house and courtyard bubbled with the excitement of war. Tall turbaned and bearded men, with AK-47 Kalashnikov semiautomatic rifles hanging from their shoulders, talked animatedly of battle, using their hands to indicate machine guns being fired, or a jet plane coming in for a rocket attack. One had a huge handlebar mustache and a gorgeous blue turban tilted to his eyebrows. There were a few beardless boys who seemed hardly fifteen years old. Stacks of olive gray boxes, containing mortar shells, teetered against a wall. A pile of light brown Chinese plastic antivehicle mines filled one corner. Hundreds of large, square tins of ammunition, with Chinese characters on the lids, formed a waist-high wall. A 12.7-mm Dashika heavy machine gun, the standard antiaircraft weapon, was mounted on a high tripod at one side of the court.

Two Defectors

Five young men in baggy gray uniforms and rough boots were brought in and taken to the roof. They were defectors from battles in Paktia Province, just to the north. A commander debriefed them, asking the designation of their units, the names of their officers, and details of their service. They said a Soviet and Afghan government column had been sent from Gardez, the capital of the province, to reinforce the beleaguered city of Khost, about twenty miles inside the border. They also said small posts had been set up at high points in the mountains to protect the route. The interrogator questioned them closely about these posts, trying to get specific locations, but the defectors said they knew nothing of local geography.

As I watched and listened to Kamaluddin's explanation of what was taking place, I recognized an incongruity. Technically, these soldiers were prisoners. A week or so earlier they had guns in their hands that could have been used to kill mujahidin. But there was none of the tension that I would have expected. When a man was questioned, he answered freely and comfortably. His comrades sprawled back against a wall, relaxing in the warm winter sun. Three of them had wristwatches. One took out some Afghan currency notes and counted them.

In other wars—in Laos in the 1950s, and in the former Belgian Congo, now Zaire, in the early 1960s—I had seen men in similar situations. But they had been stripped of their valuables and had cuts and bruises on their faces from beatings. They sat with their eyes down and their shoulders hunched. When questioned, they had fear in their eyes. Now I asked Kamaluddin if I could ask the men some questions. The interrogator brought two men over to sit next to me on a blanket. One appeared to be twenty years old. When I took out my notebook and asked his name and age, he stiffened and his eyes widened. The interrogator laughed and put his arm around the man, saying some comforting words.

"He is afraid," Kamaluddin explained. "You're a foreigner and he does not know why you want to talk with him. If he was back in Afghanistan, and a Russian was asking questions, he might be in serious trouble. We have told him not to be afraid. We said we are his brothers. All Afghans are brothers."

The men were Turkmens, from a northern area bordering the Soviet Union. The Communist regime usually sends men from the north to the south, and men from the south to the north, to make it difficult for them to fraternize with the local people and hence more difficult to defect. The second man was not worried about my questions. Somewhere he had thrown away or lost the visored cap with cloth earlaps that is part of the Afghan Army uniform and had replaced it with a new white turban that looked out of place atop his craggy peasant's face and jagged teeth. Kamaluddin translated my questions into Pushtu, the language of the south, for the interrogator, who then asked the questions in the Turkmen language. The process was complicated, and by the time the answers got back to me in English the results were minimal.

"His name is Ibrahim and he is thirty-six years old," Kamaluddin translated. "He says there were 150 vehicles in the convoy and that many of them were destroyed by the mujahidin. He says the Russians took their own dead from the field, and the bodies of Afghan officers, but left the bodies of ordinary soldiers to rot. That is a terrible thing to do in our country. It is treating a man like an animal. He is from Jowzjan Province, where it is all flat. He says when he was a young man he served ten years in the army and was supposed to be exempt from more service. One day, about three months ago, Russian tanks came to his village and he had no place to hide. They put him in a helicopter and took him direct to Gardez. He tried to incite a revolt but they beat him and transferred him from post to post, surrounded by mines so he could not escape. You see, even if a man does not want to fight for the Communists, he has to shoot to defend himself if a post is attacked. If he does not shoot at the mujahidin an officer will kill him."

I asked Kamaluddin what would happen to the prisoners. "They will be given some money to go to Pakistan, where they can join a mujahidin convoy and return to their villages. Or, if they want to take some money home to their family, they can look for work first in Pakistan."

Afghan Etiquette

There was a sudden chill as the sun set. We went down and joined a large group of mujahidin who had taken off their shoes and sat cross-legged in a room waiting for dinner. I watched to learn the etiquette. A boy brought a ewer of water and a basin shaped like a spittoon, with a wide brim and a perforated tin plate in the center. He poured water over the hands of each man, who rubbed them together, with the water spilling down into the bowl. There was no soap or towel. A long oilcloth was spread on the floor and the men crowded forward to sit shoulder to shoulder around its sides and ends. Two small kerosene lamps were placed in the center. A large flat piece of bread was thrown before each man and then separate platters of rice and fatty meat were put within reach of about three men on each side of the cloth.

They ate quickly, using the fingers of their right hands to scoop up some rice, form it into a ball, and pop it into their mouths. They tore off a piece of meat, wrapped a bit of bread around it, and stuffed that into their mouths too. Water was served in a tall metal cup. Each man emptied the cup when he drank and put it down on the oilcloth, where it was refilled for the next user. The meal passed with little conversation. The men were intent on eating, and in about twenty minutes had finished everything, using pieces of bread to wipe the platters clean. The dishes, scraps of bread, and the oilcloth were removed, and water was brought for washing soiled hands. A towel was also passed around. It was soon soaked with water and grease.

A small glass was set before each man and the boy walked around the circle, filling the glasses with tea. Now the men became communicative, talking, smoking cigarettes, and chewing tobacco, which they spit into a small aluminum vessel shaped like an hourglass with an open top. One by one, or two at a time, with no apparent order, they spread a blanket on the floor, took off their shoes, and prayed; standing, bending, kneeling, sitting on their heels, standing again, and bending, all the while silently repeating the prayer in their minds or sometimes with small lip movements.

The boy came in again with a pile of thin, narrow mats and spread them on the floor, covering almost every inch of space. It was a cold night and the men had only thin blankets to cover themselves. I was favored with a string cot that raised me above the tangle on the floor, was given a quilt, and used the sleeping bag I had brought along as a pillow. The lamps were blown out and soon the stillness of the night was broken only by snores.

With the distant sound of a priest intoning the call to prayer and the crowing of cocks, the room came to life. The men went to the courtyard to a toilet—just a slit in the floor of a room like a closet—and then performed their morning ablutions, washing their faces, ears, arms, feet, legs, and genitals. Only then did they say their morning prayer, the first of the five that a Muslim must say every day. It was still early. The first prayer comes just before dawn. Some of the men went back to sleep. Others sat next to the lamps, which had been relit, and silently read from the Koran. Some of their copies were only palm-sized, to be carried in a man's pocket near his heart. Others were the size of a paperback book.

Breakfast was bread and tea. Three heaping spoonfuls of sugar were put into a small glass, filling it almost a third of the way to the top. Then the tea was poured in. Only some of the sugar dissolved with the first pouring. More tea was added for a second glass, and a third. Often the sugar was not used up until the fifth glass of tea.

"They don't want you to go to the roof today," Kamaluddin said after breakfast. "Some spies might see you from another house and tell the Pakistanis." With nothing to do, I wandered in the courtyard and counted the tins of ammunition (718) and the wooden boxes of mortar shells (107). I examined the Dashika, and although I could not read the Russian on a metal plate at one end, I could make out the date—1944. The guerrillas hardly had the latest weapons.

On the covered walk that ran along one side of the courtyard a man sat on his heels, looking into a small mirror and trimming his mustache with a pair of folding pocket scissors. When he finished his barbering, I asked him to lend me the scissors so I could cut the button hole on the Afghan shirt I had bought in a hurry for the trip. As I moved to return the scissors Kamaluddin took them. "Let me trim your mustache," he said. "It is down over your mouth." I took the scissors and mirror and cut off what I thought was enough.

"That's much better," he said. "But let me do a little more." He took the scissors and snipped away until my upper lip was fully exposed. "You look like an Egyptian or a Turk," he said. Others, who gathered to watch, made comments that seemed to be words of praise.

This was my first brush with what I later learned was an Afghan trait. The Afghans are rigid conformists, and a stranger who comes among them is expected to act as they do. The prophet Mohammed is said to have kept his lip bare and Muslims follow his example. However, elsewhere in the Islamic world there is no pressure to enforce the custom, especially not on a non-Muslim stranger.

But in Afghanistan there is a certain way to dress, to sit, and to eat. If you have exerted yourself and have raised a sweat, you are reminded that you must not drink cold water, which Afghans believe will make you sick. If you drink water from a communal glass, you must finish it or throw the remainder away before putting the glass down for someone else to use. If you let a bit of food fall on the ground, you must pick it up so that no one defiles it by stepping on it. Once I folded up the bottom of my loose trousers to keep them from dragging in mud. I was told that the proper way to raise the bottom was to tuck part of the top under the drawstrings. Afghans often say that they insist on such things as part of the disguise against spies. But no matter how a foreigner acts or dresses, he will stand out. The pressure to make outsiders conform as much as possible is a deep cultural trait. For centuries the Afghans have been isolated from their neighbors. They don't feel comfortable with a stranger in their midst. It appears to ease things if the stranger looks and acts as much like them as possible.

A Story of Torture

The courtyard became crowded and Kamaluddin told me to go into a small room to keep out of sight. He came with me, to keep me company, and brought one of the men who had come with us from Peshawar. He was a stocky man, about five feet six, with a round face, gray hair, a mustache, but no beard. He wanted to be known only as Yusuf because members of his family were still living in Communist-controlled areas. He had a long story to tell, and bit by bit Kamaluddin translated it:

"I was once an Olympic athlete. I lived in Germany for nine years and studied at a police academy. When I decided to return to Afghanistan, I was not lucky. I arrived in Kabul to become a teacher at the police academy nine days before the Communists took over. One day, a jeep came to the gate and I was called out. They told me someone wanted to see me. When I got into the jeep, a cloth was put over my head and I was taken away. I was put in a room and did not know where I was or why. I was kept there two months and eleven days and then was put into a jeep and taken back to the school. They said, 'Sorry, we thought you were another person.'

"I was worried. I left Kabul and went to other provinces but, after a year, friends could not keep me so I returned to Kabul. I was told I had to take up my job again at the academy. I was reckless. I took part in a demonstration and was hit in the leg by a bullet. The wound was not serious, but it marked me as a dissident. A friend asked me to come to his room for tea. I went and soon two jeeps came and I was dragged away to the KHAD [the Afghan equivalent of the Soviet KGB] office. There were five of us in the room. After a while, fifteen men came in and started to beat us. 'Where did you hide the tanks?' they kept asking. They took me to another house and kept kicking me and hitting me with brass knuckles. I became weak and they put me in a cell. I was allowed to rest for two days and then I was brought back for more questioning. This time there was a Russian present, only he was dressed like an Afghan. He had a tape recorder. 'Now tell me,' he said, 'we know you stole many tanks. You must tell us the truth. In what province did this take place? Where did you hide them?'

"I told them I did not know anything about tanks. They hit me again and again. They put me in a chair with my hands tied behind my back and gave me a huge electric shock. My body was thrown back against a wall. When I awoke I had blood on my face and in my eyes. I later learned I had been unconscious for three days and nights.

"They brought me to the room again. 'Brother,' they said, 'tell the truth. When did you sell the tanks? Who did you sell them to? Did the people come for the tanks by helicopter or by mules? Were you paid in dollars or Pakistani rupees?' Like that it went, for two months. Questions and more questions. I was beaten with sticks and a cable. My hands were put under the legs of a table and men stood on it. I was given more electric shocks. My body turned green. Then they took me to another room in a special prison in the prime ministry building. KHAD ran this too. There was more torture. They said a big force was destroyed and I knew all about it. 'Brother,' they said, 'tell us who was in command?'

"'When did this happen?' I asked. They said one month ago. I laughed and laughed. I told them I was in jail at the time so I could not know anything about such a battle. After two months more of torture they sent me to a jail where I was left alone for nine months. But then I was taken back to the prime ministry. Again they tortured me and said I must tell the truth. They put me in the middle between two soldiers and I was forced to stand up with no food or water. After three days I fell down. I was paralyzed with my hands and legs folded in so I was like a ball. They tried to pull me to my feet but I fell down again in a twisted heap. They dragged me to another office and put me in a chair and asked questions for a long while. But I could not even talk.

"Then someone who was like a chief came. 'We know who you are,' he said. 'You are so and so Khan, and you are a leader of the bandits.' I said, 'No, I am just so and so and I have no importance.' 'You must tell the truth,' he said. 'We know you are responsible for an ambush where Russians were killed.'

"I asked when this took place. They said two months ago. Again I laughed until tears came into my eyes. I said I was in a jail cell for the past nine months. With that, they seemed satisfied. They carried me out into the hall and left me on the ground. I was picked up by an officer who secretly was a mujahid. He took me to a room where I was left alone for two nights. Then he brought me to a prison where I was given a job cleaning up piles of dirt and shit in the yard. I did that and then another officer found me. He had been one of my students at the police academy. He gave me a better job, growing plants and cleaning jail cells. After

"Yusuf," left; Agha Mohammed Showhady with Kalashnikov rifle; Kamaluddin, my interpreter; and Ghulam Ahmad Etemadi: on a mission to fire missiles at the Soviet-Afghan garrison at Chamkany.

three years they told me I was free. The secret mujahidin in the jail told me where to go to contact the mujahidin. They brought me to Pakistan. I could have gone to the United States where my brother is living in Illinois. But I decided my duty is here. I must serve the jihad."

During the long narration, a boy brought tea and we were joined by the two other men who had come with us from Peshawar. They were Aga Mohammed Showhady, who had been a colonel in the Afghan Army, and who had been put in prison and tortured, and Ghulam Ahmad Etemadi, who had been a captain in a parachute unit. Kamaluddin said since we would start after lunch he could now tell me about the mission. A cache of 107-mm ground-to-ground missiles had been hidden in the nearby mountains. Aga Mohammed and Ghulam Ahmad were going to fire them at an enemy post. Yusuf's assignment was to report back to the party headquarters on the success or failure of the mission. Earlier, as I was idling about the courtyard, I had seen them searching through a large crate with Chinese markings that was packed with mines and electronic gear for remote-controlled explosions. The only thing they removed was a roll of wire. They said the missiles, each the size of a small artillery shell, had been supplied without a launching device. They planned to prop the missiles up on some rocks, attach the bare ends of the wire to the rear, and fire them with a charge of electricity. I said it seemed a hopeless way of firing missiles, but Aga Mohammed defended the mission: "I served for many years in the artillery. When they send us missiles without launchers and sights we have to improvise."

Entering Afghanistan

Lunch was eggs poached in a sea of cooking oil plus bread and tea. We set off in a small passenger car early in the afternoon, bouncing across rocks, following the wide floodplain of the Kurram River. Before the British developed the road through the Khyber Pass, the Kurram valley was one of the main routes to Afghanistan. Now a single Pakistani policeman stood before a tent marking the frontier. We had a guide with us, a *mullah* (priest) who wore a white turban and had a stringy beard down to his chest. The mullah was from a nearby village and seemed to know the policeman well. He leaned out the window, handed the policeman 200 rupees (at the time, about $13.50), exchanged greetings, and we drove on.

We came to the mountains, left the car and guide, and after walking only two hours arrived at the sound and sights of war. Off to one side of a twisting trail were three ancient trees blackened by napalm. Nearby a large mud house lay in a tangle of rubble. We climbed sharply toward a ridge line. A rocket from a Russian MiG hit the reverse side of the ridge, sending a pall of smoke into the darkening sky. The MiG banked in a whining scream above us and turned away. We topped the ridge and descended through a mass of rocks to what seemed to be a deserted village at the upper end of a small valley.

The Afghans are an effusive people. About two dozen mujahidin flocked from the houses for handshakes, hugs, ritual kisses—a sort of pecking over the shoulder, right, left, and then right again—the murmur of good wishes, and questions about the health of family members. I limited myself to handshakes, sometimes just the touching of fingers, other times a full, double-handed grip. Either way I had to greet each and every man.

It was soon dark, and a fire could be started without the smoke inviting shelling or an air attack. We crowded into a room with the windows covered so as not to show light, where a tin stove took the chill from the air. The mujahidin sat in the deep shadows cast by the single lamp, wrapped in blankets with their weapons cradled between their knees.

The commander was Jan Gul, twenty-nine, a clean-shaven man with a sharp chin, long straight nose, and a direct, inquiring look. During the greetings outside I had noticed that he seemed to stand lightly on his feet, like a boxer ready to move in an instant. He said we were in a small valley on the eastern side of the Kurram valley. Over a small ridge, Soviet forces had established a post at Chamkany to block the route to the interior. Jan Gul drew a crude map, showing Chamkany and the Pakistan border about three miles to the south. We had walked much farther than that because we had started from a point to the east and had traveled in a semicircle to get around a mountain. Jan Gul made eight "X" marks around Chamkany, on both sides of the Kurram valley, to show it was nearly circled by resistance camps. He said five of the camps were associated with his party, the National Islamic Front, and the others were linked with three separate parties.

Afghan Hospitality

Water was brought for washing, and a long strip of begrimed cloth was unwrapped and spread on the dirt floor. It already had broken scraps of bread on it. Kamaluddin explained that it was impossible to cook fresh bread, because the smoke from an oven would invite attack. He said resistance camps throughout the region were running short of food and the men were eating moldy bread. Some had no food at all and the men had gone back to their villages or to Pakistan.

Hospitality means a lot to Afghans. I sat next to Jan Gul. As the host, he picked out the largest piece of bread and put it before me. Then bowls of other food were brought. The dish set before me contained a chicken. "Look," said Kamaluddin. "They knew we were coming so they cooked a chicken." The men ate bread soaked in hot water flavored with cooking oil and onions while we visitors divided the scrawny chicken, chewing and sucking at the bones and tossing them onto the cloth.

As we waited for tea Jan Gul showed samples of some of the mines that the Afghan Army sowed in thick fields around Chamkany. One was a serrated, oval-shaped piece of metal, somewhat bigger than a fist. It was placed atop a wooden peg set in the ground and connected to similar mines by thin wires that were hardly visible even by day. A man who walked into the field and hit a wire would trigger several mines and would be killed or seriously wounded by large pieces of shrapnel. Another mine was a round metal box about four inches across and two inches high. A piece of rubber-like material covered the top. Beneath this was a plate and a spring connected to an explosive charge. This mine was hidden just beneath the surface of the ground. A slight pressure on any point of the covering material would tilt the plate and touch off the explosive charge. Fragments from the metal box could destroy a man's leg.

It was cold. Soon after the final tea I slipped into my down sleeping bag, with all my clothes on except my jacket. There were no mats for the men to sleep on. They just bundled themselves in their blankets and were soon asleep on the cold, dirt floor.

A thin blanket is an integral part of the Afghan costume and has many uses. Generally a man folds it during the day and carries it on one shoulder. When the air is chilly, he wraps the blanket around his shoulders. If it is extra cold, he drapes it over his head to keep his ears warm. Under a hot sun he folds it into a thick pad and places it on top of his head to keep it cool. He spreads it on the ground as a clean area for prayers. He drapes it over his back like a curtain when he goes into an open field to relieve himself. If a man has a number of things to carry, he wraps them in the blanket and knots the ends in front of his chest so that it becomes a sort of pack. If he sits on the ground he folds the blanket under him as a cushion and also to keep his trousers from getting dirty. But its main use is to keep him warm.

At six in the morning, before dawn, a fire was started in the stove to warm the room and heat water for tea. After prayers the long cloth was spread on the ground, still with the same scraps of bread from the night before and the chicken bones too. Bread soaked in tea would be the only hot meal until the night, when a fire could be started again. The men dispersed to their posts in the hills. Yusuf, Aga Mohammed, and Ghulam Ahmad went off to prepare the missiles, which they said would be fired in the afternoon.

"A Village without People Is Ugly"

Jan Gul took Kamaluddin and me on a tour. He had a Kalashnikov over his shoulder and an olive-green, canvas ammunition holder strapped to the front of his chest. He had worn it all the previous evening, taking it off only as he lay down to sleep and then putting it under his head, along with his gun, as a pillow. The other men took the same precautions. The canvas holder had three large pockets for metal clips that held thirty rounds of bullets, and small pockets for grenades and whatever else a man might want to keep handy. The pockets were closed by loops with wooden clasps, a telltale sign of Chinese origin.

As we walked I asked Jan Gul how long he had been fighting. "I went to school through the twelfth grade. I knew the Communists were atheists even before Taraki came to power," he said, referring to Nur Mohammed Taraki, who led the first Communist government after the coup of 1978. "I knew they hated Islam and would kill our mullah. When they began to arrest our village elders I took my gun and got some friends and we began to fight." We were in a village named Nargasay. Jan Gul took us past houses with corners blasted off and sides collapsed, two bomb craters deep enough for a tall man to stand in, pockmarked and burned fields, and trees mangled into grotesque skeletons. The ground was littered with fragments of bombs and rockets.

"Sometimes the Karmalis come over that hill at night," he said, pointing to a hill on our right. The term Karmali was a reference to Babrak Karmal, who was then the head of the government in Kabul. The Afghans have a language code for their war. They reserve the name Afghan for mujahidin and their sympathizers. Those who side with the government are called Communists, or any other name, like Karmali, that is regarded as derogatory. Another code name is martyr. If a mujahid or a villager dies in the war, he is referred to as a martyr. If one of the enemy dies, the mujahidin say he is killed. "It is the word we use for animals," Kamaluddin once explained. "Animals are killed but those who fight in the jihad are martyred."

A deep gully of a dry river cut through part of the small valley. We stopped at its edge, looking across to rising tiers of mud houses on the steep opposite hill. They looked remarkably like a Hopi Indian village in the American Southwest. The houses were deserted, with the twin windows on the second stories like sad faces looking across at the desolation. We walked back the way we had come, disturbing a now feral cat, the only remaining sign of domesticity. "I saw this village a year ago," Kamaluddin said. "It was beautiful. Now it is ugly. A village without people is ugly."

The Battle Begins

Suddenly, there was a burst of rifle shots from the hill we had passed about ten minutes earlier, where Jan Gul said the Karmalis came down at night. Then came more and more shots, extending like a string of firecrackers along the top of the hill, almost the complete length of the valley. Jan Gul jumped down into the gully, pausing for a moment to tie his blanket over his right shoulder and under his left arm, like a warrior in a samurai movie tying back his wide sleeves before a sword fight. We followed him into the gully for protection against possible shots from the hill. He moved up the valley at a brisk walk, shouting directions to mujahidin who had come out from cover, eager to join the fighting. Soon they were up on the small hill and out of sight again, hidden in bushes and behind rocks. A steady crackle of rifle fire told that a fight was raging. A helicopter appeared and began to strafe and rocket the top of the hill.

An elderly mujahid came to guide Kamaluddin and me. He took us up the gully to a point where we had entered the valley the night before, thus placing us on an escape route should the enemy overrun the valley. A whoosh and an explosion shook the side of a steep hill near us. A column of smoke and dust rose about 200 yards away. Another explosion hit, the echoes reverberating from the hillsides, and then a third. We were under mortar attack. The guide decided things were getting too hot. He took us back down the gully and across to the tiers of abandoned adobe houses on the opposite side. From there we could see where the Kurram valley entered Pakistan. He told us our new escape route lay in that direction should we need it.

The high ground was like the rear tier of an amphitheater, looking across to the battle on the hill above Nargasay village. A pair of MiGs appeared. Twin white vapor trails in the blue sky signaled that a pilot had fired a pair of rockets. They slammed into the hill and the pilot pulled out of his dive, banking over our heads for another run. Soon the second MiG rocketed and banked away. A helicopter gun ship approached. It hovered over the hill, raining bullets down on the mujahidin among the rocks. Mortar shells whooshed and exploded with a thumping sound. A pall of smoke and dust drifted over the valley.

The staccato of Kalashnikov shots, and single shots from rifles, gradually subsided, and the MiGs and helicopters flew away. Silence returned, but the mujahidin remained hidden in case there was another attack. The dust settled. Two small cows appeared from somewhere and nibbled tiny shoots pushing up from an abandoned field. Mynah birds hopped alertly at their feet, hoping for an upturned insect.

We had been sitting under the cover of a grove of trees. I had a cold, and my head felt stuffed. After an hour I left the shade to sit in the warm sun, to see if that would help clear my nose. Out of nowhere, a rocket slammed into the ground about 150 feet in front of me. Another struck with a crash and a shower of stones. Shocked, I ran back to the trees. Kamaluddin and the guide had seen the helicopter in the distance and had dropped to the ground as the first rocket hit. I joined them there.

The day droned on. Then there was a shout from across the gully. A wounded man had been carried down from the hill. We ran over to try to help. He lay on a smooth space before a ruined house, covered with a blanket, with just his face showing. He had a thick black beard and long eyebrows and eyelashes. His dark face was smeared with blood. His eyes were half open, but he was unconscious. A light bed, made of wood and strings, was taken from inside the house, which the mujahidin used as night post. The man was placed on it and covered with two blankets. Another of the all-purpose blankets was twisted into a rope and used to tie the wounded man to the bed. Four men then lifted it by its legs as a sort of stretcher and jogged off in the direction of Pakistan. A fifth man followed, carrying the wounded man's boots and rifle. The guide said he would be taken to another camp and kept there until night, when it would be safe for a vehicle to come and take him to a Red Cross hospital in Parachinar. I was later told that he did not survive the jolting walk and the long wait.

As the hours passed the cows moved somewhere else, leaving the mynahs to forage for themselves. Another mujahid came down the hill. He was about twenty years old, happy and laughing, and he told us that the fight was about over, but that the mujahidin had been told to stay in position until late afternoon. As if to amuse us, he pulled up one leg of his loose trousers, rolled down a sock, and showed that he had a plastic leg to his knee. He said he had lost his leg when he stepped on a mine four years ago. He rested a while and then picked up his rifle and walked off, with only a hint of a hop to show his loss.

We walked back to the cluster of houses where we had spent the night. It was half past four and still full light, but the men walked around in the open, feeling that the danger had passed. Their bodies seemed to glow with the adrenaline of battle. They hugged and kissed and exchanged stories. A boy, perhaps thirteen, showed a grenade that had

Mujahidin on Nargasay ridge overlooking Chamkany: only dried bread to eat, chewing snow for water. The mujahid, right, holding a piece of bread, is blind in his left eye. All, except one, are armed with British World War I bolt-operated rifles.

been thrown at him but failed to explode. An older man fondly tweaked his chin. Another man produced two small cans of Bulgarian mutton and rice: field rations taken from the kit of a dead enemy soldier. He gave me one, which I gratefully accepted and ate immediately. It was cold and tasteless, but I was too hungry to care.

The guide led us up a hill to a post from where we could see the ground-to-ground missiles being fired at Chamkany. The post was a pit that could hold a half dozen men on sentry duty, with a hole dug nearby as a place to rest. The men had been there all day without food or relief, and were munching on dry bread and chewing snow for water. The ground was strewn with cartridge casings from repeated fights. The mujahidin said the attack had been centered on this post, and that one of their men had been martyred. They said seven of the enemy had been killed, and that four bodies lay nearby. They offered to take me to look at the bodies but I demurred, giving the excuse that I was tired.

They told me to go to the front of the pit but to keep my head as low as possible. If I looked down, they said, I could see part of Chamkany and some Russian tanks parked in the open about 300 yards outside the garrison. They warned me to take off my glasses, because an enemy mortar post was nearby, and any reflection of light from my glasses might invite shelling. I had binoculars and peered down at the tanks. The mujahidin, always curious, immediately demanded the binoculars and handed them around, commenting and laughing. An older man, with broken teeth and a stringy beard, spurned them. Kamaluddin explained: "He says foreigners are always weak. He can see perfectly well without any glasses or binoculars and he has only one eye." The man pulled back the lower lid of his left eye and showed he had a glass eye and they all laughed at the joke.

The Missiles Are Fired

Then there was an excited cry. A pair of missiles whooshed overhead. I got back the binoculars and saw that the missiles had fallen short, raising tall, white columns of smoke on the flat plain well in front of Chamkany. Within minutes, a mortar shell rocked the ground near the post. Then there was another whoosh of missiles overhead. The aim had been corrected. The missiles landed within the rear portion of the garrison. The tank drivers started their motors and scurried to safety. Another two missiles sailed over and landed in the same area, sending up black smoke.

The guide said we had better leave quickly. We skipped down the steep path as six mortar rounds fell on the slopes. Once the guide flinched as a bit of shrapnel or a piece of stone fell a few inches from his foot. It was almost dark when we reached the houses. Jan Gul said we must leave right away because the enemy might try a night attack to seize the area where the missiles were launched. There was no moon. With no air pollution and no ground lights, the vast sky was bejewelled with stars, but I had little chance to enjoy it. I kept stumbling in the dark. The mujahidin would not allow the use of flashlights that might reveal our presence, not that they needed them. They seemed to have 20/20 vision by night as well as day. One gripped me under the arm and guided and dragged me through gullies and up and down hills.

The trails near the border come alive at night with mujahidin supply convoys. We were pushed aside as trains of camels or donkeys claimed the path as their own. Shadowy men, muffled to their eyes, passed without greetings or idle conversation. Each group had its own mission and avoided unnecessary disclosure. At about nine o'clock we arrived at a house for dinner and sleep. We were told that Yusuf, Aga Mohammed, and Ghulam Ahmad had taken another route and were at a village nearby. In the morning we walked for an hour and met them just as a pair of MiGs high overhead dived and banked in bombing runs.

"They think we are still back at Nargasay and want to punish us for the missile attack," Yusuf said.

Aga Mohammed was excited. From the color of the smoke he was sure they had hit a vehicle storage area. He wanted to be sure I understood the implications of what I had witnessed. "You see," he said, "we are trained officers. Maybe we never used a weapon like that but we can learn. Now we have reached over their mine fields and hit them inside their garrison for the first time. Give us long-range mortars and missiles, and modern weapons against their MiGs and helicopters, and we'll destroy the garrison at Chamkany."

Yusuf planned to return to Nargasay to make contact with an informer inside the garrison and get an exact report on the damage. We walked back to the village where we had been set down. The mullah had a car waiting to take us to Parachinar, where the ambulance was summoned to take Kamaluddin and me to Peshawar on February 13th.

I ran into Yusuf about six months later and asked what had happened on the day of the attack. He said that, indeed, the missiles had struck the target. They brought in more missiles and hit the town so often that the Soviet and government forces withdrew. But the mujahidin could not hold the town and government forces reoccupied it. "We are not strong enough and don't have antiaircraft weapons to hold a base on an open plain like Chamkany," Yusuf said. "But neither are they strong enough to chase us from our bases in the mountains."

The Afghans

....

2

Afghanistan is the only place in the world where Soviet soldiers are dying in combat. With the United States supplying the Afghans with guns and bullets, it is also the only place where the superpowers are in bloody, if indirect, conflict. And yet the war is sparingly reported.

Obviously, the war itself is a deterrent. I was a bit over sixty years old when I first planned to go there. Wondering if I was up to it, I took a long bike tour of the Hebrides and hiked for twelve days across the cold and rocky Hardangervidda Plateau in Norway. I was pleased that my knees and lungs took the strain. While cycling across Germany to Amsterdam to complete the trip, I met a young man at a hostel. When he learned that I was a journalist he said he had just finished college, with training in how to make film documentaries, and asked how he might get started. I suggested that he travel where no one else wanted to go and make a film about something that had not already been reported extensively. I said a television station or network would certainly look at anything from Afghanistan.

"Go to Afghanistan?" he asked. "I might get killed."

Other wars in distant lands have been covered extensively, the Vietnam War for instance. But in Vietnam jeeps and helicopters ferried reporters to a battle zone where someone explained, however inadequately, what was happening. There were facilities to get the story out quickly, and reporters were certain they had a good chance to make the front page or the network news. In recent years reporters have also traveled secretly with the rebels in El Salvador and Nicaragua. They are assured of a large and receptive audience and can expect to be back in a capital city having a bath and a good meal in a week or two at the most.

But interest in the Afghan story is minimal, and for regular news organizations, the story is not worth the costs or the risks. The most chilling discouragement came late in 1984, when French journalist Jacques Abouchar was captured in Kandahar Province and tried as a spy. An Agence France-Presse reporter in Islamabad asked Soviet Ambassador Vitaly Smirnov for a comment.

"I warn you and all your journalist colleagues to stop trying to penetrate Afghanistan with the so-called mujahidin," Smirnov replied. "From now on, the bandits and the so-called journalists—French, American, British, and others accompanying them—will be killed and our units in Afghanistan will help the Afghan forces do it." Abouchar was sentenced to eighteen years in prison but, after the Communists had milked the story of its publicity value, was allowed to return home.

Afghanistan also poses the hardships of travel and the cultural shock of living among people who, among other things, do not use toilet paper. In my case, I was not overly concerned about being in a war zone. I had some experience in Indochina and knew how to take cover. I also experienced no cultural shock. I had been a radio and television reporter and magazine writer in South and Southeast Asia for eight years in the 1950s, and had brief assignments in Africa and South America in the early 1960s. After years of a television desk job in New York, I wanted to be a foreign correspondent again. Afghanistan was a place where others did not go, leaving an opening for a geriatric journalist. At the age of sixty-two I took early retirement and headed east.

A Hermit Kingdom

I first saw Kabul in December 1955, when Afghanistan was beginning to shed its reputation as a hermit kingdom. About half a dozen reporters were allowed to cover the visit of Soviet party chief Nikita Khrushchev and President Nikolai Bulganin. The city at that time was a honeycomb of houses behind high brick or mud walls with a population estimated at 200,000. It had a few paved streets, thanks to Soviet aid, and a few taxis and rickety buses, but most of the traffic consisted of horse-drawn carriages and carts pulled by camels.

In the new, two-storied, Western-style hotel, most of the rooms were vacant and we were constantly looking for someone to feed wood into the inadequate stoves in our rooms or to serve us a meal, such as it was, in the restaurant with its grease-spotted tablecloths. Most of the people were obviously poor but the rich did not seem to live in splendor. When we were ushered into the palace for a reception, it seemed, as I wrote at the time, "to resemble a second-class French hotel that had refurbished its lobby." At least the palace had radiators and central heating. A conference room in the prime minister's office and the main reception hall of the officers club had iron stoves with tin pipes jutting up and across to flues in the walls.

The wives of a small corps of Western diplomats assigned to Kabul said they were appalled at the sight of Afghan women shrouded from the top of their heads to their feet in an ugly and often ragged garment with a woven lattice at face level. The wives told stories of girls desolately sobbing when they first had to wear the *burqa*, as the costume is called, and of a servant running up the stairs of an airplane to deliver a burqa to some official's wife returning from abroad.

Afghanistan, it seemed, was a primitive land with an insubstantial culture. Yet the Afghans have challenged a superpower and have fought on, year after year, amid slaughter and desolation.

The Islamic Factor

A common simplification is to assume that the resistance began with the Communist seizure of power in 1978 or, more specifically, with the land and marriage reforms later mandated by the new regime. This can lend credence to a charge that the resistance movement is led by ultraconservative priests who oppose not only the invading Soviet forces and their puppet government but also modern education and economic and social reforms.

In fact, the resistance movement can be traced to the middle 1950s, long before the Communists seized power and before a Communist party was even organized in Afghanistan. Resistance leaders say they have an agenda for reform, but it is not a copy of ideologies or practices imported from the West. "When we say we want a government on the model of the early Islamic pattern," wrote Professor Burhanuddin Rabbani, the head of one of the seven major resistance parties, "we believe those principles are applicable in national and international affairs today as much as they were at that time. . . . Islam is not an impediment in the way of knowledge, science, technology, peace and justice."

Islam does not bend or change easily. It says its revelations come directly from God (as distinct from Christianity, in which the words of

Christ are retold by the Apostles). Islam imposes similarities of thought and action on generation after generation of believers. Its freedom includes the right to direct others in how they should act. The ties of kinship, tribe, and community are believed to stem from religion and are reinforced by rituals that take place at birth, circumcision, marriage, and death.

Western sympathizers may call the mujahidin freedom fighters, but that confuses their motivations. What puts Islam on a higher plane than other religions is its stronger emphasis, as a sincere Muslim sees it, on morality and truth. He believes God's morality is more important than life. "Jihad" derives from an Arab verb that means to strive or exert oneself for some praiseworthy aim, ranging from promoting the cause of Islam to a struggle against bad inclinations. To be killed in a jihad is a glorious death that assures felicity in the next world. Thus the struggle against the Communists is both a war of freedom and a test of the moral commitment of the Afghan people. Since social virtues and religious virtues are the same, a vast complex of values—wife, land, village, honor, motherland, and religion—are packed into one to confront the invading nonbelievers, or *kafirs* as they are generally called. To an Afghan, the term has a special repugnance. Kafirs are reviled for idol worship and the filthy practice of eating pork. They are also immoral, as evidenced by the fact that their women "flaunt their charms before the world," to use one of the milder expressions for unveiled women.

The concept of jihad is critical to the present struggle because it helps unite people who are normally divided. About 85 percent of the Afghans are Sunnis, in the mainstream of Islamic culture. The others are Shia and look to Iran for inspiration. Among Sunnis, the closest to any form of religious authority is provided by heads of esoteric Sufi brotherhoods, the Naqshbandiya and the Qadiriya, who are regarded as living saints. Jihad also binds different classes, ranging from educated and comparatively well-paid university graduates to the rural and urban masses. But like "stars and stripes" and "king and country," jihad is an all-embracing concept subject to abuse.

Where Empires Collided and Conquerors Tread

Afghanistan is about the size of Texas or France and is mostly deserts and mountains. The crumpled peaks of the Hindu Kush, which range up to 25,000 feet, run like a spine down the center of the country. It is the homeland of people who are separated by language, culture, and geography, many of them locked away in their valleys for months on end by the deep snows of winter. Until as recently as fifty years ago most Afghans were nomads or seminomads and most trade goods were carried on the backs of camels over trails that were already thousands of years old when Marco Polo passed this way en route to China.

The isolated valleys were little worlds, with their own blacksmiths, weavers, potters, millers, carpenters, shoemakers, and tailors. An urban economy and the beginnings of a university and a modern banking system did not develop until the early 1930s. There has never been a survey of land ownership or an adequate census. At the time of the Communist coup in 1978, population estimates ranged as high as 18 million people. The commonly accepted figure is 15 million.

Afghanistan, with its mountains and deserts, is not an inviting place, but its geographic position has long prompted invasions. Empires and cultures have collided here since the dawn of Asian history. It has felt the tread of conquerors from the Greeks of Alexander the Great, through the Kushans (a Scythian empire that extended from Central Asia to the Ganges in the first three centuries of the Christian Era), White Huns, Mongols, Turks, and Moguls, to the modern-day British and Russians. Like Switzerland, it bears the stamp of its multiethnic heritage. The region north of the Hindu Kush, bordering the Soviet Union, is the home of Turkmens, Uzbeks, and Tajiks. The mountains of central Afghanistan, known as the Hazarajat, are the home of the Hazaras, who are popularly (although inaccurately) said to be descendants of the Mongols of Chinggis Khan. The south is the home of tribes known to the British as Pathans but who call themselves Pukhtun in the southwest and Pushtun in the east. Also like Switzerland, Afghanistan shares its languages and cultures with neighboring countries. Many more Turkmens, Uzbeks, and Tajiks live in Soviet Central Asia than in northern Afghanistan; many more Shiite Muslims speaking Persian (or Dari, as it is called in Afghanistan) live in Iran than in western and central Afghanistan. The Pushtun tribes of southern Afghanistan consider the northern regions of Pakistan as part of their homeland and patrimony.

Afghans are a tough people who can live on bread and goat's milk, and most who have known them have commented on their extraordinary personal dignity and love of freedom. The Afghans believe that the greatest of all virtues are revenge and hospitality. They never forgive an injury, yet paradoxically they do not turn away a guest even if he is a tribal or personal foe. These qualities are particularly associated with the Pushtuns. The romantic image is of a tall, bearded tribesman striding along a rocky path with a rifle on his shoulder and a fierce glint in his eyes. His land is everything and his home, with its thick mud walls, stout gates, and watch towers at the corners, is his castle. His prestige and honor depend on his ability to defend them against a foreign invader, against another valley—or against another branch of his family. It sounds gloriously heroic, but from the cold view of politics it amounts to ordered anarchy.

The origin of the Afghans is unknown. They may be descendants of White Huns who intermarried with local people while retaining a sense of separateness. They first appear in history when the name Afghan (we do not know what the word first meant) was applied to a people living east of Ghazni around the year 1000. Mahmud, a Turkic conqueror, established his capital in Ghazni, in what is now southern Afghanistan, around that time. He raided repeatedly into India, sacking its temples, enslaving its peoples, and founding a dynasty famous for its wealth, splendor, and learning.

Allauddin and the Qazi

In 1290 a warrior named Allauddin Khilji (or Ghilzai as his Pushtun tribe is now called) seized the throne of Delhi and established a brief dynasty. He was illiterate, bad tempered, hardheaded, and bloody minded, adjectives that would be bestowed on his Afghan avatars for centuries to come. When he was told that Mongols, who had settled on the outskirts of Delhi, were planning a revolt, he had thousands of men slaughtered and turned their women and children adrift to live or die as fate might decree.

Once Allauddin summoned his chief *qazi*, or legal officer, and put to him a series of questions. The dialogue is part of a debate that has echoed through Islamic history from the earliest days to the contemporary fundamentalist movement. Among other things, the sultan asked if war booty was his personal property or if it should be given to the public treasury for the benefit of the entire Muslim community. "The time of my death is at hand," the qazi replied. "If I answer your question honestly you will slay me and if I do not tell the truth I will go to hell." He replied that according to Islamic law all the treasure won by the armies of Islam belonged to the public and not to the sultan, and that if he wanted to follow the example of enlightened caliphs, the early rulers of Islam, he should take no more from the treasury than he needed for himself and his family.

"Do you not fear my sword when you tell me that all my great expenditure on my harem is unlawful?" the sultan demanded.

"I do fear Your Majesty's sword and I look upon this turban as my burial shroud, but Your Majesty questions me about the law and I answer to the best of my ability. But if you ask my advice from a political point of view, then I say that whatever Your Majesty spends upon your harem no doubt tends to raise your dignity in the eyes of men and the exaltation of a king's dignity is essential to good policy."

Modern Islamic fundamentalists are not surprised that the first part of the qazi's reply sounds like Marxist socialism: "From each according to his talents, to each according to his needs." They say economic justice is at the core of Islamic beliefs. They also are not surprised at the qazi's willingness to overlook or find excuses for the lapses of an autocrat. The fundamentalists say it is just such servility on the part of the traditional clergy—their willingness to sell out to authority—that has brought on much of the degradation of Islam. For that reason they often battle mullahs as well as atheists.

The dialogue continued with Allauddin's reply: "You have declared my proceedings to be unlawful. Now see how I act. When troopers do not appear at the muster, I order three years' pay to be taken from them. I place wine drinkers and wine sellers in the pits. (Literally: he had deep pits dug and threw drunkards into them.) If a man debauches another man's wife I effectually prevent him from again committing such an offence and the woman I cause to be killed. Rebels, good and bad, old hands or novices, I slay; their wives and children I reduce to beggary and ruin. Extortion I punish with the torture of the pincers and the stick, and I keep the extortioner in prison, in chains and fetters, until every halfpenny is restored. Political prisoners I confine and chastise. Will you say all this is unlawful?"

"My Liege, send your unworthy servant to prison or order me to be cut in two, but all this is unlawful and finds no support in the sayings of the Prophet or in the expositions of the learned," the qazi replied. Allauddin rewarded him richly for his brave honesty but said he had no intention of taking his advice: "Although I have not studied the Science or the Book, I am a Muslim of a Muslim stock. To prevent rebellion, in which thousands perish, I issue such orders as I conceive to be for the good of the state and the benefit of the people. Men are heedless, contumacious, and disobedient of my commands. I am then compelled to be severe to bring them to obedience. I do not know whether this is lawful or unlawful. Whatever I think to be for the good of the state or opportune for the emergency, that I decree." These words, from a thirteenth-century Afghan autocrat, read like a guide for the policies of Afghan rulers in the nineteenth and twentieth centuries.

For the next 250 years or so, Afghans ruled small kingdoms, principalities, and fiefs throughout northern and central India. To the other ethnic groups of India, they were turbulent barbarians: clannish, whenever possible excluding from power all who were not fellow tribesmen, and at the same time forever quarreling among themselves, with each Afghan considering himself equal to any other and superior to all non-Afghans.

Another Ghilzai clan, the Lodis, clawed its way to power in Delhi in 1451. The first king of the dynasty, Bahlol Lodi, placated his rapacious and unruly nobles by sitting on a carpet in front of the throne and inviting the chiefs to sit there with him. His grandson, Ibrahim, tried to institute regal pomp and made the chiefs stand before him with folded hands. The inevitable discontent led to revolt, and the disunited kingdom fell to a new invader—Babur, the first ruler of the great Mogul dynasty.

Martyrdom and Honor

Although Ibrahim was not wise or strong enough to rule as an Afghan, he knew how to die as one. At the historic battle of Panipat that won India for the Moguls in 1526, the Afghan troops were routed and an aide urged Ibrahim to flee. "Look here, my nobles, my companions, my well-wishers and friends have partaken the cup of martyrdom," he replied. "My horse's legs are dyed with blood up to his chest. While I was king I governed the empire as I pleased. Now that perfidious fortune has sided with the Moguls, what pleasure is there in life? It is better that I should be like my friends, in the dust and blood." Ibrahim and his closest retainers charged into the heart of the battle and "obtained martyrdom."

With that the Afghan chiefs left the stage of Indian history, but the tribes never ceased fighting the Moguls, whose empire included Afghanistan as well as most of India. In 1587 the Yusufzais destroyed an entire army, killing 8,000 Moguls. In 1672 the Afridis killed 10,000 Mogul soldiers and captured 20,000. In 1673 the tribesmen cut another Mogul army to pieces and destroyed another force a year later.

Khushal Khan Khattak, the greatest of the few poets produced by Afghan culture and a tribal chief, tried to form an alliance against the

Moguls during these years. As always, the Afghans demonstrated that they could fight but not unite. Their honor spurred them to battle, but they could see nothing beyond that ideal. Khushal Khan admitted that honor was everything. He wrote:

> I despise the man who does not guide his life by honor,
> The very word honor drives me mad.
> What madman cares whether he gains or loses a fortune.

The Mogul emperor Aurangzeb eventually settled the endless battles by distributing liberal subsidies and inciting intertribal feuds. He paid some chiefs to keep the peace and others to reopen old feuds. He encouraged sons to depose their fathers and brothers to contend against brothers. The policy produced anarchy in Afghanistan and security for the frontier of the Mogul empire. It was copied exactly by the British and now the Soviet Union is trying to see if it will work for the USSR too.

By the early 1700s Mogul power disintegrated. A Ghilzai seized the throne of Iran and was in turn overthrown by a Turk, Nadir Shah, who went on to conquer Delhi. His empire did not survive him. One of his lieutenants, a Pushtun named Ahmad Shah Abdali, retained a portion of the wide conquests, including the plains of what is now northern Pakistan. Out of this he stitched together autonomous tribal fiefs and, in 1747, created the first nation to be called Afghanistan. In the process he changed his tribe's name to Durrani. Various branches and septs of the tribe would rule the nation he created until the Communists, under a Ghilzai, seized power in 1978.

In 1757 the British established a toehold at Calcutta, on India's east coast, and rapidly extended their rule across the subcontinent to the gates of the Hindu Kush. They then saw a threat from the armies of the Czar pushing south into Central Asia. In 1839 they used this as an excuse to send an army into Afghanistan for what came to be known as the First Anglo-Afghan War. It was a fiasco, etched on the minds of British imperialists by a later painting of a man on a woebegone horse, the only survivor to return alive to British lines.

The challenge and response to the steady advance of Russian power in Central Asia, which came to be called "The Great Game," gave the British the excuse to intervene again in 1878 for the Second Anglo-Afghan War. The unexpectedly prolonged and expensive war was unpopular with the people at home, and the British sought to excuse their ineptitude by maligning the people they had ostensibly sought to help. "They are a vile race, and we shall never make anything of them. The more I see of them, the more hateful does their character appear," wrote Lieutenant General Donald Stewart, who commanded the British forces. In February 1880 the British viceroy, Lord Lytton, wrote to the new head of the mission in Kabul that his first duty should be "the preparation for us of a way out of that rat trap."

Two Kings: An Iron Hand and an Evening Dress

The British solved their problem by putting the tyrant Abdur Rahman on the throne. He reigned for twenty-five years and created the first centralized government in Afghan history. His name can be translated "The Slave of the Merciful," a misnomer if there ever was one. "I must say," he once wrote, "that I am fully aware that people who do not know me well call me cruel, a lover of money and a man of most suspicious nature. Others have said, and justly said, that though the Amir rules with an iron hand, it is justified, because he has to rule an iron people." An Englishman who was living in Kabul during Abdur Rahman's rule listed some of these iron methods: burying, blinding, cutting off hands, starving, and boiling and skinning alive.

With the support of the complaisant religious leaders in Kabul, Abdur Rahman declared a jihad against the Shias of the Hazarajat, inviting Pushtun tribesmen to join in the battle and the now-sanctified loot. The Hazaras were slaughtered and their best lands were seized. He then mounted another jihad against the people living in what was then called Kafiristan, who had still not been converted to Islam. They became Muslims and the name of their lands was changed to Nuristan, or Land of Light. Similarly, he persecuted the Tajiks, Uzbeks, and Turkmens of the north, settling their lands with Pushtun nomads from the south. In this way Afghanistan became a nation and hatreds were created that would be stored in memories for generations to come.

In 1893 the British forced Abdur Rahman to sign away Afghanistan's claims to the hills and plains west of the Indus River and south of the mountains that rise to become the Hindu Kush. The new border— called the Durand Line after Sir Mortimer Durand who demarcated it—suited imperial convenience and ignored Pushtun ethnic and cultural realities. The settlement echoed through Afghan history until it facilitated Soviet domination of Afghanistan.

Abdur Rahman's grandson, Amanullah, succeeded to the throne in 1919 and promptly declared a jihad to redeem the lost lands. He failed, but the treaty ending the Third Anglo-Afghan War, as the six-week conflict was called, granted Afghanistan the right to handle its own affairs, although in fact the British continued, through bribes and other machinations, to impose their will on Kabul for generations to come. Amanullah called himself king, instead of amir, to symbolize his break with the past, and was full of the ideas of democracy, secularism, and the liberation of women that were sweeping the Islamic world. However, his government was too corrupt and mismanaged, and his rule too arbitrary and oppressive, to achieve social reforms. Instead he had to deal with a succession of rural revolts by local *khans* (landowners with large families and a circle of retainers and dependents).

Eventually, what did him in was a simple picture. In 1928 Amanullah took his queen, Soroya, on a grand tour of Europe. She was photographed wearing an evening gown with bare arms. The picture was circulated in Afghanistan (and Afghans to this day say it was the British who did it to destroy Amanullah) to show that the king had allowed his wife to appear "naked" before the world. Religious leaders declared a jihad to remove Amanullah from the throne. Tribal revolts mounted and he fled to Italy. Kabul was captured by a Tajik peasant named Bacha-i-Saqao, "son of the water carrier."

Nine months later the British arranged for another branch of the Durranis to assume power under Nadir Khan, a general who had been exiled to Europe. There was no more talk of unveiling women as Nadir placated the tribes and religious leaders and, with British money and German advisers, rebuilt the army and reestablished royal authority, using tactics reminiscent of Abdur Rahman. Nadir was killed in 1933 at the culmination of a series of the assassinations and vendettas that typify the family cliques and clans of Afghanistan. He was succeeded by his nineteen-year-old son, Zahir, with actual rule in the hands of three uncles who jockeyed for authority.

At the end of World War II, when Britain left India, Afghanistan turned to the United States for help in building an elaborate system of dams and irrigation works in the Helmand and Arghandab valleys in southwestern Afghanistan. In 1949 Afghanistan accepted $21 million in American aid. Soviet publications were full of warnings of imperialist maneuverings, but the concern was premature. The time bomb of the lost lands south of the mountains was ticking away.

During the process of the British withdrawal, Afghanistan had protested the inclusion of these territories in what became West Pakistan. They called for the creation of a new state, to be named Pushtunistan, that would include not only Pushtu-speaking territories but other regions, including all of Baluchistan, and thus give Afghanistan an access to the sea. The demand amounted to nearly half of West Pakistan and included several million people who had no linguistic or cultural affinities with the Afghans. Moreover, the purported homeland of the Pushtuns did not include five million Pushtuns who lived in Afghanistan.

When its protests were ignored, Afghanistan in 1947 voted against Pakistan's entry into the United Nations. The stance was widely opposed within Afghanistan, both by religious leaders who welcomed the formation of an Islamic state, and traders who believed it would be easier to deal with fellow Muslims than with Hindus. But public opinion was easily ignored by the rulers of Afghanistan and, despite the absurdity of it all, from 1948 onward books and maps printed in Afghanistan and Kabul radio referred to events in the mythical state. In 1951, after Mohmand tribesmen raided into Pakistani territory at the instigation of Kabul, Pakistan closed the border, cutting Afghanistan's exit to the sea. Moscow was quick to grant alternate transit facilities, bartering petroleum products, cloth, and sugar for Afghan wool and cotton. In 1953, when Afghanistan received another $20 million loan from the United States, it also received Soviet aid for grain storage facilities, a bakery, oil storage tanks, and street paving in Kabul.

Mohammed Daoud: Opening the Door for Moscow

In the same year a cousin of the king, Prince Mohammed Daoud, who for years had been manipulating the royal entourage to achieve power, was named prime minister. Bald, bullet-headed, and ruthlessly ambitious, he had admired Adolf Hitler and Benito Mussolini in his youth; later he found inspiration in Gamal Abdel Nasser of Egypt. His Afghan role models were iron-fisted Abdur Rahman and Amanullah, the anticlerical would-be reformer. Daoud promised to bring about Islamic democracy, the rule of law, and economic growth. Instead he ruled as an autocrat, manipulating foreign aid to strengthen the central government and attempting to build an army loyal only to himself. He had no interest in easing the plight of the poor. He did build schools throughout the country, in what was largely an attempt to create and win over an elite made up of the articulate, the skilled, and the enterprising—including Westernized military officers, government employees, academics, and businessmen. All of this could be justified as the tried and true formula for ruling such a turbulent people, except for his embrace of the

Soviet Union. Several people close to the royal family warned him of the dangers, but he insisted, "I know what I am doing."

Soon after taking office Daoud asked for military aid from the United States, but that was turned down. He linked his request with a demand that the United States guarantee Afghanistan's security. Both the U.S. Joint Chiefs of Staff and the National Security Council decided this was impossible because, with a common frontier separated only by a river, Moscow could gobble up Afghanistan at will. Moreover, the United States had started giving military aid to Pakistan and, in view of the Pushtunistan issue, it would have been awkward to send weapons to both countries.

In 1954 Moscow orchestrated a Czechoslovak offer to build a textile mill and a cement plant. By early 1955 several hundred Soviet and East-bloc technicians were working in Afghanistan. They were still far outnumbered by Americans employed in the Helmand and Arghandab river schemes and by the expanding U.S. technical assistance mission in Kabul. But in mid-1955 everything changed, when the separate provinces of West Pakistan were joined into a single unit to balance the single province of East Pakistan. Daoud took this as an affront to Pushtunistan and made an inflammatory speech. The next day mobs, apparently with the government's approval, sacked the Pakistani embassy in Kabul. A retaliatory attack on the Afghan consulate in Peshawar came a few days later. When Pakistan closed the border, Daoud quickly arranged for new trade routes through the Soviet Union. A few weeks later Bulganin and Khrushchev arrived and offered a long-term, low-interest credit of $100 million and, while they were at it, announced support for Pushtunistan. In April 1956 a military mission went from Afghanistan to Prague to purchase arms. The shipment arrived in September. The next month jet aircraft arrived. Then young men were sent to the Soviet Union for training and, in 1960, Soviet and Czech instructors began to teach at the Kabul military academy.

Daoud's Downfall

Although in his personal life Daoud was a sincere Muslim, who prayed regularly and obeyed the injunction against alcohol, he never forgot how the clergy had destroyed Amanullah and his reforms. "This Vatican is retarding our progress," he once said. In August 1959 he ordered government officials to bring their wives unveiled to a major reception. Many of those who objected to exposing their women were forced to retire. When a group of religious leaders protested, he arrested many of them and a few later died in jail. A full-scale revolt broke out at Kandahar in southwestern Afghanistan. Troops were sent to restore order.

In September 1961 Daoud inflamed the Pushtunistan issue by recklessly sending troops to occupy a bit of Pakistan soil. Once again Pakistan closed trade routes and the results were disastrous. The embargo lasted for eighteen months. Fruit rotted in warehouses as exports dropped by 70 percent. Food prices doubled and foreign reserves were almost depleted. The troubles gave the feckless Zahir Shah courage to dismiss Daoud in March 1963. In 1964 a new constitution was drafted granting popular government, including legal political parties. But Zahir, always afraid of opposition, refused to sign the enabling legislation. Moderates, who could not bring themselves to illegal activities, were handcuffed, and politics was captured by Communist and Islamic conspirators.

Between 1950 and 1965 the number of schools and students increased fourfold. Kabul University's enrollment increased tenfold. At this time students were marching and shouting throughout the world, mainly against the U.S. role in Vietnam. Islamic students were also enraged about Israel, and in Pakistan constant student rallies demanded democratic rule. It all was front page news for Kabul papers, read by thousands of young men with only the slightest knowledge of parliamentary or democratic traditions. They became cannon fodder for a new class of ideologues.

The Rise of the Communists

The first traces of radicalism had appeared soon after World War II, when a few Kabul intellectuals gathered informally for discussions, calling themselves Awakened Youth. One of them was Nur Mohammed Taraki, a Ghilzai Pushtun from a seminomadic family. He was born in 1917 and was sent to Bombay in the 1930s as a clerk for a trading company. There he may have been influenced, if not actually converted, by Indian Communists. In any case he returned home and appears to have been a secret Communist by the 1950s when he published, in Pushtu, four books dealing with class struggle, exploitation, and poverty in Afghanistan. Another participant was Mir Akbar Khyber, an instructor in the military and police academies who was identified as a Communist in a report of the British secret service. A third, Babrak Karmal, whose father was a general, came from an elite family. Karmal, born in 1929, entered Kabul University in 1950 and immediately foreshadowed his destiny by establishing a student association. It was outlawed ten months later.

The government suppressed the Awakened Youth on the eve of parliamentary elections in late 1952. In the election itself, about twenty would-be reformers were defeated. When their supporters demonstrated to protest alleged ballot rigging, several leaders of the protest were arrested. Karmal then brought a student delegation to the royal palace to demand their release. They were asked to send in a smaller group to meet King Zahir. Only Karmal went and he was promptly arrested.

Mir Akbar Khyber, meanwhile, had been arrested in 1950 and sentenced to ten years in prison for making impolitic remarks against the monarchy in a discussion among army officers. Karmal, as the son of an elite family, was given a comparatively comfortable cell and allowed books to continue his studies. He was also permitted to meet Mir Akbar Khyber, and it was probably in jail that Karmal became a Communist. The two of them helped pass the time by sketching plans for party work once they gained freedom.

Nur Mohammed Taraki, despite the social consciousness evidenced by his books, carefully stopped short of direct provocation and avoided jail. Instead, in early 1953 he was sent to Washington as a press attaché in the Afghan embassy, a favored method short of jail or execution for removing someone from the scene. He resigned in less than a year and for the next several years his movements are obscure. It is known that he traveled extensively in Europe and the Soviet Union. For a man from a poor family with no obvious resources, this strongly suggests that Taraki was a paid agent of the Soviet Union, if not the KGB. His care in avoiding a confrontation with the monarchy may have stemmed from his commitment. He later established a translation bureau in Kabul and did work for both the American embassy and the American foreign aid mission, which might also be taken as evidence of KGB diligence, as well as of American naiveté.

The U.S. contribution to the Communist explosion in Afghanistan was Hafizullah Amin, the biggest fuse of them all. Like Taraki he was a Ghilzai Pushtun, and like Karmal he was born in 1929, but he lacked Karmal's social advantages. Amin's father was a government clerk who died when Amin was young. His elder brother helped him through school. He gained a Kabul University degree and went on to become principal of Ibn Sina High School, a leading school for boys from the provinces. Amin received a scholarship to New York's Columbia University, where he got an M.A. in education in 1957. Back home, he became principal of Darul Mualimeen Teachers College in Kabul. He returned to Columbia University in 1962 for his Ph.D. but soon lost interest in further studies. On his own admission he was converted to Communism while on work-study programs at the University of Wisconsin. He was elected president of the Afghan students' association at Columbia in 1963 but then dropped out to return to Afghanistan via the Soviet Union.

Amin was still abroad on New Year's Day 1965 when twenty-seven men gathered at Taraki's home as founding members of the People's Democratic Party of Afghanistan (PDPA), the name the Afghan Communists have used ever since. Taraki was named head of the Central Committee and Karmal, who had been released from jail by Daoud in 1956, was chosen as his deputy. The selection of Taraki and Karmal for the first and second positions pointed ahead to a difference that would soon split the party in two.

The Rise of the Islamic Resistance

The rise of the Communists was paralleled by the growth of the Islamic resistance. In 1951, during the brief liberal period after World War II, religious activists had organized a plot against the monarchy. Some were arrested and remained in jail for about fifteen years. The plot was supported by the Mujaddidis, the most distinguished religious family in Afghanistan, although none of its members were among those arrested. The Mujaddidis claim descent from the second caliph, Hazrat-i-Umar, and also trace their ancestry to a renowned Indian seventeenth-century Naqshbandiya Sufi called the "Renewer of the Second Millennium" (*Mujaddid-i-alf-i-thani*) of Islam.

The Mujaddidis intermarried with royalty and considered public affairs part of their ritual obligations. Sibghatullah, the eldest son, was a student at Al-Azhar University in Cairo at the time of the plot. He got an M.A. in 1953 and returned to teach Islamic studies at Kabul University. When Bulganin and Khrushchev visited Kabul in 1955, Sibghatullah organized a small protest and was jailed for four years.

The Mujaddidis, with their authority based on the traditional structure of Afghan society, represented one of two sources of Islamic resistance to communism. The other source was the fundamentalist ideologies that developed outside of Afghanistan. The father of Afghan fundamentalist resistance was Ghulam Mohammed Niyazi. Niyazi also attended Cairo's Al-Azhar University, where he became a convert to the Muslim Brotherhood, a violent and conspiratorial society that helped Nasser unseat Egypt's King Farouk in 1952 but then turned against Nasser and tried to kill him. Nasser threw the Brethren into desert concentration camps, but the movement thrived on persecution. (It was the Brethren who assassinated Nasser's successor, Anwar Sadat, in 1981.) Niyazi returned to Afghanistan in 1957 and became dean of the Faculty of Theology of Kabul University.

Fundamentalism has been a growing force in Islam since the Wahhabi movement in Arabia in the middle of the eighteenth century. It gained new strength in the 1950s, when Egyptian radicals reached back to a thirteenth-century thinker, Ibn Taymiyya, who wrote that Islam must be cleansed from within before it could meet the challenges posed from without. The formulation gives precedence to the internal Islamic revolution even before the struggle against imperialism or communism. It was this concept that led the Brethren in their attempt to kill Nasser and their assassination of Sadat.

It would be more exact to describe the fundamentalists as revolutionaries. They compare the superpowers to the blades of a pair of scissors cutting the roots of Islam. In their eyes, while the Russians have a history of exterminating Muslims in Central Asia, the Americans are no less guilty of supporting what they view as Israel's violation of the rights of Muslims in Palestine and supposedly conspiring against the Islamic revolution in Iran. The Islamic revolutionaries believe the existing *ulama*, or religious teachers, are too servile to kings and despots and that Islam is encumbered with the dross of saints and trances. They seek to establish on earth what they are convinced is the will of God: to tear down idols, unseat tyrants, and gain victory for the oppressed and the deprived. But their political and social goals are often obscured by their asceticism. They denounce modern pluralistic, permissive society and rail against drinking, gambling, obscene literature, indecent films, vulgar songs, immorality, and the display of female beauty. A seventeenth-century Calvinist would feel right at home with their ideas of propriety. But these Islamic revolutionaries deny that they are calling for a retreat to the past. They say a return to the pristine ideals of the Koran will make Islam strong enough to thrive in a modern world of democracy, equality, and technology.

At Kabul University in the late 1960s, Ghulam Niyazi established small, anti-Communist discussion groups and gathered a cadre of teachers and students into a pyramid of secret, five-member cells, with a committee of ten men at the head. Three of the men trained or inspired by Niyazi now lead major resistance parties based in Pakistan: Professor Burhanuddin Rabbani, Abdur Rasul Sayyaf, and Gulbuddin Hekmatyar.

What was critically important about the fundamentalists at Kabul University was their atypical ability to create coalitions—and their foreign connections. In addition to their links with the Egyptian Brethren, they had ties with the late Sayed Moulana Moududi, an Indian (and later Pakistani) scholar who made important contributions to fundamentalist thinking and who founded the Islamic Society (*Jamaat-i-Islami*) of Pakistan. With foreign connections, the fundamentalists, like the Communists, could find advice, money, and refuge if necessary beyond Afghanistan's borders. Furthermore, they were sufficiently flexible to coordinate their campus activities with reformist scholars within the traditional Islamic structure, including Sibghatullah Mujaddidi, who was released from prison in 1959. Two others who joined the university fundamentalists in their public opposition to the Communists were Yunis Khalis, a teacher and religious publisher from Ningrahar Province, and Maulvi Mohammed Nabi Mohammadi, from a widely respected scholarly family in Logar Province. These three also now lead major resistance parties based in Pakistan.

Democracy and Discontent

Thus both the Communist and Islamist opposition were in place when the 1964 constitution presented a new opportunity for agitation. The Communists, with a clearer understanding of the way politics work, moved first. Babrak Karmal and three other members of the newly organized, but secret, PDPA were elected to Parliament as a tiny vanguard of the Left amid 300 representatives of the landed and religious elite. Taraki and Amin, who by this time had returned to Kabul, were both defeated.

Karmal later explained that the Communists supported "the revolutionary use of Parliament's tribunal on behalf of advancing party goals." What he meant by this was demonstrated within days of the opening of the new House. He demanded that Dr. Mohammed Yussuf, who had been nominated as the first prime minister, produce a list of his assets. When Yussuf refused, Karmal and a few supporters shouted charges of corruption and nepotism and later instigated student riots during which three people were killed when the police opened fire on the mob. The annual anniversaries of these riots were the excuse for demonstrations that became a feature of democracy, Afghan style.

The formation of the PDPA only papered over a division in Communist ranks that became apparent in the spring of 1968, when the party was divided into two parts, each with its own Central Committee and membership roll. The parties were named after newspapers they were briefly allowed to publish. The party of Taraki and Amin was called *Khalq*, or Masses. The party under Karmal was called *Parcham*, or Flag. Khalq was predominately Pushtun, more rural oriented, and more revolutionary. Parcham represented the non-Pushtun, Dari-speaking one-third of the population and favored a gradualist confrontation with the monarchy.

The split brought the number of illegal Marxist parties to four. The third was a Maoist group called Eternal Flame (*Shu'la-i-Jawed*) that drew its support from both ends of the social spectrum: on one end, doctors, lawyers, and other highly educated professionals, and on the other Shiite Muslims and Hazaras, who pulled hand carts and did other hard labor on the streets of Kabul, and the northern Tajiks, Turkmens, and Uzbeks. The atrocities of Abdur Rahman still rankled in the north. The fourth Marxist party, called Against National Oppression (*Setem-i-Meli*), was a splinter from the PDPA.

With the four parties stirring demonstrations and strikes, the Kabul University fundamentalists were convinced that they had to stop a headlong rush to communism. Previously, under the name of the Islamic Society (*Jamiat-i-Islami*), they had limited themselves to secret discussion groups. When Ghulam Niyazi was arrested in 1972 he was replaced by Burhanuddin Rabbani, but individual identities were still kept secret. The fundamentalists now formed a militant faction, called Young Muslims (*Jawanan-i-Musulman*), under the charismatic leadership of a young teacher named Abdur Rahim Niyazi (who was not related to Ghulam Niyazi). They came into the open with a series of rallies and protests. The largest and best-remembered rally was called to protest an article in *Parcham*, the Communist paper. It included a picture of Lenin and the words "*daroud* (praise) to Lenin." Daroud is a term used in Afghanistan only in the context of praise for the Prophet Mohammed. Niyazi took this as blasphemy and called his followers into the streets. Such were the seeds of discontent in Afghanistan.

By the parliamentary elections of 1969, the government was thoroughly frightened and manipulated ballot boxes; among the Marxists, only Karmal and Amin managed to win seats. However, the fundamentalists by now had also learned how to manipulate the process. The Young Muslims claimed that many of the religious figures who won seats owed their victories to the group's support.

Abdur Rahim Niyazi died of leukemia in 1970. He was succeeded as leader of the Young Muslims by Gulbuddin Hekmatyar, then a second-year student at the School of Engineering. Hekmatyar was arrested in 1972 after a Maoist student was killed in a fight with Young Muslims. He spent eighteen months in prison.

At the end of the 1960s there were five times more Soviet civilian and military advisers in Afghanistan than the combined total of Westerners. A lethargic bureaucracy had attempted to implement a series of five-year plans, 75 percent of which were paid for with foreign aid. The bulk of the funds went for white elephant projects such as the Helmand and Arghandab irrigation schemes, the Kandahar International Airport, and hydroelectric works near Kabul and Jalalabad. There were also extensive road and telecommunications projects, including a long tunnel through the Salang Pass, built with Soviet aid to shorten and make easier the land passage across the Hindu Kush. The tunnel is now a vital part of the Soviet occupation infrastructure.

Meanwhile, the rural and urban poor were hurt, some severely, by steadily rising prices and the competition of goods imported (or, more often, smuggled) from Pakistan. While receiving one of the highest per capita amounts of external assistance in the developing world, Afghanistan descended from being a food surplus area, to subsistence, and finally to being a food deficit area. Two successive droughts, the worst in memory, caused a famine in 1972.

For rural Afghans, the only real benefit of all the foreign aid was the expansion of secular education. By the mid-1970s more than 800,000 students were attending 4,000 schools and over 600,000 had completed some formal education. But this too proved an empty blessing. The job market was saturated by the late 1960s as foreign aid, particularly from the United States, declined. The educated unemployed were fuel for the street demonstrations that marked the period from 1968 onward.

Daoud Seizes Power

His opponents thought they sealed the defeat of Mohammed Daoud with Article 24 of the constitution, which prohibited a member of the royal family, as Daoud was, from becoming prime minister. But the mounting discontent of the late 1960s and the famine of 1972 gave Daoud an opportunity for the revenge that ranks so high in Pushtun psychology. While he was in office, Daoud's toleration of the Left and antipathy to the clergy went hand in hand with his friendship with the Soviet Union. His antireligious attitude appealed to Karmal's Parcham Communists. When Daoud turned to the Parchamis for support in overthrowing the monarchy, they adopted the slogan: "Daoud's friends —our friends; Daoud's enemies—our enemies." At the time, the Khalqis had lost membership and were dormant. Although they too were in touch with Daoud, more often it was Karmal who was received by Daoud or his men.

Daoud struck in July 1973, while the king was in Italy. As a former general who invited the foreign aid that made it possible to enlarge the officer corps and equip new regiments, he had the automatic support of most officers of the military. The Communists guaranteed the vital support of military officers who were secret party members. They also supplied students with red arm bands, who patrolled the streets of Kabul to insure public neutrality. Not that they were needed. The public was apathetic and the coup was virtually bloodless. The Soviet Union was the first country to recognize Daoud. Only four days after seizing power, he held a large public rally for Pushtunistan.

About half of Daoud's first cabinet were Communists. Together they began to suppress the only organized opposition, the Islamic intellectuals. Ghulam Mohammed Niyazi was at first released from jail but was rearrested in June 1974 and never seen alive again. The brunt of the repression fell on the Young Muslims. About 300 were rounded up. Some were executed outright; others were kept in prison, including Abdur Rasul Sayyaf, who had been one of the most active of the Young Muslims. Hekmatyar, who by then had been released from jail, managed to go underground. He fled to Pakistan in 1974 where, a year later, the fundamentalists began their insurgency.

Pakistan's Prime Minister Zulfikar Ali Bhutto was alarmed at Daoud's revival of the Pushtunistan campaign. He allowed the fundamentalists to train several thousand men in secret camps near Peshawar. They infiltrated back into Afghanistan and, in July 1975, attempted to provoke a general uprising in four provinces. However, the young intellectuals had no rapport—indeed, no contact—with largely illiterate farmers or their traditional leaders. The attempt was a complete failure, except in the Panjshir Valley where the insurgents, under Ahmad Shah Massoud, were able to capture a police station before reinforcements were summoned and forced them to flee. Still, the incursions were enough to frighten Daoud. He diminished Pushtunistan propaganda and, after the Afghan and Pakistani leaders exchanged visits to one another's capitals, Pakistan reined in the Afghan exiles on its soil.

Nevertheless, the Afghan exiles were still among friends, particularly the fundamentalists. Qazi Hussain Ahmad, a Pushtun who was then amir of the Islamic Society (Jamaat-i–Islami) of Pakistan, and later secretary general of the party, had visited Kabul and other places in Afghanistan several times from 1970 onward.

In Kabul, Daoud tried to gain control, dismissing Communists and paying visits to Iran, Egypt, and Pakistan, where General Mohammed Zia ul-Haq ousted Bhutto in a 1977 coup. But he was floundering in quicksand. Hafizullah Amin later candidly admitted that the 1973 coup had been an eye-opener that showed that "it was possible to wrest political power through a shortcut . . . working extensively in the armed forces." While Babrak Karmal and the Parchamis worked and negotiated with Daoud, Amin focused his undoubted skills as an organizer to gain recruits in the military.

The Great Saur Revolution

Debate has long centered on the extent of Moscow's involvement in the overthrow of Daoud and the PDPA's seizure of power. A consensus has developed that, although the Soviet Union may not have instigated the action, it was aware of what was happening and lent tacit approval. The key evidence is a series of articles that began to appear in 1976 in Communist party publications in India, Iraq, and Australia, deploring the rift in Afghan Communist ranks and calling for unity. The articles were obviously planted by Moscow. Outsiders, even Communists, had never heard of Afghan Communists. Responding to the prodding, the rival Khalqis and Parchamis formed a joint Central Committee in 1977, although each held tight to its own members. Neither of them had many to hang on to. Their combined strength was just 5,000 to 6,000.

Amin later revealed that at least ten rehearsals were held for a coup that first was planned for August 1978. The date was moved up after Mir Akbar Khyber, who all this while had been living quietly as the Parchamis' chief theoretician, was murdered on April 17. By whom, no one has revealed. An estimated 11,000 people attended his funeral two days later. Daoud reacted by putting some Parchamis and Khalqis in jail, including Taraki and Karmal. But Amin was only kept under house arrest and managed to smuggle out notes ordering army and air force regiments under Communist officers to seize power immediately. They did, on April 28, the month of *Saur* on the Afghan calendar. The Communists titled the coup the Great Saur Revolution.

Daoud and his entire personal bodyguard, in true Pushtun spirit, fought to the death. Also in the Pushtun spirit, about 200 other guards who surrendered were later executed. In all, perhaps as many as 3,000 people were killed. The Russians, with advisers in every regiment and air force unit, did nothing to prevent the coup, and may actually have helped it by restraining military units who were loyal to Daoud. Moscow rushed to recognize the new government on a Sunday in the midst of preparations for the May Day celebrations.

The Afghan public shrugged off the coup as just another of the convulsions among the elite and things were quiet for the next few weeks. Perhaps emboldened at the ease with which they seized power or, more likely, utterly unaware of the sensitivities of the masses of the people, the PDPA began to send Parchami and Khalqi activists to the countryside to round up, arrest, and kill village leaders and mullahs.

Government in Afghanistan has always been a matter of personal ties; a village was led by a chief who was linked with someone higher up the ladder. The Communists snapped these links when they removed local leaders. Villagers felt no obligations to the new emissaries from Kabul. When the Communists also moved against village mullahs, the regime was clearly perceived as anti-Islamic. From then on the Khalqis and Parchamis sent to usher in the new order were either driven away or killed, and uprisings, uncoordinated and unrelated, spread throughout the country.

Instead of drawing closer to meet these challenges, the Communists fell to fighting among themselves. The winners were the militant Khalqis, with Taraki as president but with Amin, as prime minister, wielding the real power from behind the scenes. Karmal and the other leading Parchamis were sent abroad to serve as ambassadors while lower-ranking Parchamis were arrested and executed. The removal of the more moderate Parchamis, and the rise of the radical Amin, were made manifest in a series of decrees on land tenure, rural debts, equal rights for women, and the price for brides.

Actually, this tinkering with social mores was not as shocking as it has been made to seem. Land tenure, marriage reforms, and the rights of women had been on the liberal agenda for Afghanistan since 1953, when Daoud first became prime minister, and for that matter even back to the days of Amanullah in the 1920s. But other symbolic actions stirred passions profoundly: Government statements were no longer preceded by a dedication to God, and the Afghan flag, which contained symbols representing a prayer niche and the Koran, was replaced by a red flag modeled after those of several union republics of the USSR.

In January 1979 all the men of the Mujaddidi clan who could be found were secretly assassinated in one night, and all the Mujaddidi women and children who could be located were rounded up and sent to the infamous Pul-i-Charki prison, which had become a slaughterhouse for thousands of alleged class enemies and saboteurs, along with intellectuals, priests, and out-of-favor Communists. Many Parchamis were also thrown into prison, but they enjoyed some protection from the Soviet Union and their lives were spared.

Most of the mass executions went unnoticed, but one was too shocking to be kept hidden. The fundamentalist Young Muslims who had been imprisoned by Daoud were transferred from the old Deh-Mazang prison to Pul-i-Charki. At dawn on June 4, 1979, they were executed. Their final invocations of Allah and their curses against communism are part of the lore and the strength of the jihad.

Now the uprising against the atheists and their kafir masters spread to every province, and the army dissolved through repeated mutinies and wholesale desertions. The guns of the defectors strengthened the resistance. Moscow was understandably alarmed. In April General Aleksey Yepishev, the head of the Political Directorate of the Soviet army, arrived with a full military team for an inspection tour. Ominously, Yepishev had visited Czechoslovakia just before the Warsaw Pact invasion of that country in 1968.

Moscow apparently thought it would be advisable to try first for a political shuffle in Kabul. Taraki went to Havana at the end of August for a meeting of the nonaligned heads of state. He returned by way of Moscow, where he met both CPSU General Secretary Leonid Brezhnev and Babrak Karmal. It appears that plans were laid to get rid of Amin and bring back Karmal. But Amin learned of the plot, and a few days after Taraki returned he was arrested and strangled on Amin's orders. It was mid-September. The jails held 30,000 men, women, and children. At least 12,000 Afghans had been executed and 385,000 refugees were registered in camps hastily established in Pakistan.

The Soviet Invasion

In August, even before Taraki's removal, a secret fifty-man Soviet delegation had arrived, headed by General Ivan Pavlovskiy, who had commanded Soviet forces in the invasion of Czechoslovakia. Two combat battalions of Soviet troops were flown into the Bagram base in the first weeks of December. It is believed that Amin made some sort of request for additional aid to suppress the resistance. He got more than he asked for. Soviet troops began to land in overwhelming force on Christmas Day, 1979, and on December 27 took over the country. Amin and his bodyguard all died fighting when Soviet soldiers stormed the presidential palace.

The Soviet invaders brought with them Babrak Karmal, who blamed Amin and promised to set things right. He released 14,000 prisoners and restored the traditional black, green, and red colors of the Afghan flag (but not the religious symbols). He said he supported private ownership of land, and did away with mandatory coeducation and the unveiling of women. Once again government announcements were preceded by the invocation of God. Karmal insisted that his government was the true champion of Islam but also stressed the regime's social goals; in short, the prophet Mohammed would have to cohabit with the prophet Marx. The USSR built up its forces to about 118,000 men, with another 30,000 in support across the border in Soviet Central Asia. Cynics said the "Great Game" had ended and the Russians had won.

But the Afghans had reserves of strength that were not easily comprehended by outsiders. With the Soviet invasion, the jihad became an obligation that no one could shirk without losing honor. Twenty-five years of struggle, beginning with the first term of Prime Minister Daoud, had created a viable and effective anti-Communist movement. The resistance also had a proven sanctuary in Pakistan's Northwest Frontier Province and its tribal territories. Through the Islamic Society (Jamaat-i-Islami) of Pakistan, the Afghan resistance was linked to Pakistani fundamentalist activists and, through them, to General Mohammed Zia ul-Haq, who was using conservative Islamists to bolster and obtain legitimacy for his martial law government. Moreover, the overthrow of the shah of Iran by the Ayatollah Ruhollah Khomeini in February 1979 opened another sanctuary. And the fact that the entire leadership of the resistance movement bore the stamp of Islam, both traditionalist and fundamentalist, assured sympathy and support throughout the Islamic world—in particular in Saudi Arabia and the Gulf States, which had every reason to fear an extension of Soviet power in their direction.

What the early resistance movement lacked was large donations of weapons and ammunition, which only the United States could supply. Jimmy Carter was president when the PDPA staged its coup. He accepted at face value Taraki's claims to be a mere leftist reformer and continued American aid programs, despite a specific law that aid must be suspended when Communists seized a government. The United States did not cut off aid until February 1979, when U.S. Ambassador Adolph Dubs was killed. The ambassador was kidnapped and held hostage for a few hours in a hotel room. Afghan police recklessly stormed the room, killing the ambassador as well as his abductors so that their identities and motivations are unknown to this day. Aid projects were then ended and the embassy staff was reduced to a minimum, headed by a chargé d'affaires. A few months later the CIA began its first tentative efforts to supply weapons to the resistance.

As Moscow sent reinforcements, the U.S. State Department issued low-key statements expressing the hope that all parties would respect the principle of nonintervention. Similar statements continued to be issued as the Soviet generals made their inspection tours and Soviet troops assembled at take-off points, suggesting the United States was well aware of what was about to happen. However, after the USSR seized control President Carter appeared to be taken by surprise, and said his "opinions of the Russians had changed more drastically over the past week than in the previous two and a half years."

Carter then embargoed American grain shipments to the Soviet Union, boycotted the Moscow Olympic Games, and ended the attempt to ratify the proposed SALT II restrictions on nuclear weapons. The United States also issued a series of specific warnings that any extension of Soviet power beyond the borders of Afghanistan would be considered a direct assault on American interests.

Carter was the first to refer to the mujahidin as "freedom fighters." Aside from rhetoric and acts of pique, the United States developed a carefully limited attitude toward the Russians in Afghanistan. The USSR was invited to attend the next Olympics in Los Angeles (it refused), and the grain embargo was lifted by President Ronald Reagan. The SALT II agreement, though never ratified, was accepted for many years as a fact of international life. The heart of U.S. policy was implicit in the repeated warnings against any extension of Soviet power beyond Afghanistan. The United States is following the same policy outlined by the

Joint Chiefs of Staff in the early 1950s—recognizing that sheer power and geographic proximity put Afghanistan in the Soviet sphere of influence, and the United States cannot protect Afghanistan's independence.

The shipment of covert arms increased dramatically with the Soviet invasion. The arms were easily dispersed throughout Afghanistan because a mechanism was already in place. About 100 groups had sprouted in Peshawar, the capital of Pakistan's Northwest Frontier Province and gateway through the Khyber Pass to Afghanistan. There was a rapid shakeout and then a succession of mergers, alliances, and partitions, ending with seven major organizations. Six were headed by men active in the opposition to Daoud and the Communists. The seventh leader, Sayed Ahmad Gailani, had been close to the royal family and was Westernized to the extent that he owned a Peugeot dealership in Kabul. The Gailani family took no part in politics until it formed a small, moderate, opposition group to protest Daoud's ouster of the king. The Gailanis did not migrate to Pakistan until the winter of 1978, months after the Communists seized power.

Overall the parties cover a spectrum of attitudes and egos and are generally grouped into two wings, traditionalist and fundamentalist.

Traditionalist Parties

National Islamic Front (*Mahaz-i-Milli-i-Islami*) is the party of Pir Sayed Ahmad Gailani. The Gailani family claims descent from Abd al-Qadir-al-Jilani, a scholar who founded the Qadiriya order of Sufi mystics in Baghdad during the twelfth century. There are many branches of the Abd al-Qadir family throughout Islam and some have long settled in Afghanistan. However, Sayed Ahmad Gailani's father did not come to Afghanistan from Baghdad until the early 1920s, for which reason detractors say he is an Arab and not an Afghan. Nevertheless, the charismatic attraction of the Gailani family is second only to that of the Mujaddidis. The initial strength of the National Islamic Front came from the Pir's extensive religious network in southern Afghanistan and from tribes and groups associated with the Durrani royal family. The party also gained important support from Westernized regional chiefs and former army officers who were uncomfortable in fundamentalist surroundings.

National Liberation Front (*Jabha-yi-Nejat-i-Milli*) is the party of Sibghatullah Mujaddidi, who in his sixties is the oldest of the resistance leaders. After 1973 he toured Islamic countries to organize opposition against Daoud. The Libyan leader Colonel Muammar el-Qaddafi helped him establish an Islamic center in Denmark for missionary activity in Scandinavia, including the construction of several mosques. He came to Pakistan in 1978. His following is largely restricted to his family's widespread religious following in southern Afghanistan, plus tribal leaders and other regional chiefs. His party is the smallest of the traditional group.

Islamic Revolutionary Movement (*Harakat-i-Inqilab-i-Islami*) is the party of Maulvi Mohammed Nabi Mohammadi. He remained in jail four years following his arrest in 1973. He migrated to Quetta, in Pakistan's Baluchistan Province, shortly after the Communist coup and then was invited to Peshawar to head one of the earlier attempts at unity. He founded his own party when this broke up. His party has active units in almost all provinces and is the strongest of the traditionalist parties.

Fundamentalist Parties

Islamic Party (*Hizb-i-Islami*) is the party of Gulbuddin Hekmatyar, a Pushtun of the Kharot tribe from the northern province of Badakhshan. Hekmatyar has often been called a spoiler. The repeated attempts to unify the resistance groups in Peshawar, and to establish cooperation among the commanders inside Afghanistan, have generally failed because Hekmatyar and his followers refuse to compromise or shed any part of their identities. Hekmatyar did not have the strength that automatically accrued to the traditionalists. Instead, he developed a cadre of educated, ambitious, and daring veterans of the Young Muslims, and together they recruited young refugees who were eager to return to their villages for revenge. His followers are accused of attacking other groups and of seizing their arms to assert superiority. Whatever the truth, there is no doubt that most of the deadly battles between rival groups, with cumulative casualties in the many hundreds, have involved Hizb-i-Islami fighters.

Islamic Party (*Hizb-i-Islami*) (Khalis) is the party of Mohammed Yunis Khalis, a Pushtun of the Khogiani tribe of the southern province of Ningrahar. Khalis and Hekmatyar founded one party originally and, when their alliance split, each kept the name. To avoid misunderstanding Khalis's name is usually added to the party designation. His party is an amalgam of regional strong men with weak ties to the party's center.

Islamic Society (*Jamiat-i-Islami*) is the party of Professor Burhanuddin Rabbani, a Tajik from Badakhshan. His is the most moderate and pragmatic of the fundamentalist group. It is strongest in the north, with a large following among the Tajiks, Uzbeks, Turkmens, and Heratis. Ahmad Shah Massoud, the Islamic Society commander in the Panjshir Valley, has attracted international attention.

Islamic Alliance (*Ittihad-i-Islami*) is the party of Professor Abdur Rasul Sayyaf. He was arrested in 1974 and spent about five years in Deh-Mazang prison. Thus he was isolated from the 1975 insurgency and the succeeding growth of resistance groups. He was released from jail—after the Communist coup, surprisingly enough—and escaped to Pakistan in 1979. In May 1982, at the insistence of Saudi Arabia, a united front was formed with Sayyaf as its leader. Sayyaf kept much of the money donated by the Saudis for himself, with no apparent objection from the Saudis, who consider him their principal agent in Afghanistan. Sayyaf used the funds to form his own party when the alliance disintegrated and used the liberal funds at his disposal to win over commanders in many parts of the country.

The Pathology of Disunity

Disunity—an almost pathological inability to unite for any goal—is a disease of Afghan society. The unity achieved during the long struggle against the Communists began to dissolve when the Kabul University intellectuals were forced into exile by Daoud's coup in 1973. The first signs could be seen in the disagreement between Hekmatyar and Rabbani in 1975 over whether the time was ripe for insurgency. When the traditionalists appeared after the Communist coup in 1978, Khalis and Rabbani wanted a broad-based coalition but Hekmatyar was opposed. Later there was a bitter public disagreement over whether the exiled King Zahir might be used as the figurehead leader of a government in exile. The fundamentalists blamed Zahir and the traditional elite for all the troubles the nation suffered before and since the Communist coup.

There were further differences and jealousies about the distribution of foreign aid. The fundamentalists arrived in Pakistan first and were able to move into the refugee camps to recruit soldiers. They also had direct connections through the Islamic Society of Pakistan to General Zia ul-Haq. This put them first in line to get the foreign weapons that were funneled through the Pakistan army. They also received almost all of the money handed out by the Arab states.

The parties also have a basic disagreement on the very concept of Islam. According to the traditionalists, Islam is a religion: a world of ethical behavior, prayers, and ceremonies. It is something an individual holds within himself and is essentially separate from government and politics. To the fundamentalists, Islam is the entire world and the only world: a world of technology as well as prayer, of the glory of the first caliphs as well as the coming glory of modern technology.

Ultimately the disunity of the resistance movement arises from the nature of the movement itself. It swept the Communists from the countryside because it represented existing alignments. Thus it reflects the ethnic, linguistic, communal, and social tensions of Afghan society and is a struggle for local values and Afghan individualism. The self-sacrifice inherent in the concept of jihad is found side by side with the crudest egotism and selfishness.

For God and Country

·············

3

In February 1985, while I was still waiting for a permanent visa, I decided to go into Afghanistan for about a week and then return to Pakistan for the bureaucratic paper chase. For help I went to Massoud Khalili, a member of the political committee of the Islamic Society (Jamiat-i-Islami). Massoud's father, Khalilullah Khalili, was a poet of international reputation and a civil servant and diplomat for thirty years before resigning after the Soviet invasion. Massoud was always willing to help a reporter make a trip into Afghanistan.

He asked if I would like to go to the Kabul area, a round trip of a week or ten days. I said yes, and with that—although it took me a long time to understand what I was seeing—I started to explore the jigsaw puzzle of the resistance political structure. I later realized that the Peshawar-based parties were coordinating agencies for partly autonomous regional commanders, who directed or coordinated smaller groups. The relationships between the parties and the commanders varied from time to time, place to place, and individual to individual. The basis of some relationships was tradition, as with Pir Gailani, or ideology, as with a fundamentalist like Hekmatyar. The basis of others was more generalized, a matter of personal philosophy about what was best for the jihad. Often it was simply a matter of which party was able to give the most money and guns. Another factor was grassroots maneuvering: a man would choose one party because his rival was associated with a different party.

Massoud suggested I visit the camp of a commander in the Jegdalek valley, southeast of Kabul, named Mohammed Anwar. He was a graduate of the University of Kabul and had taught literature there for just half a term before the Communist coup of 1978. After the coup Anwar, who had been active in student anti-Communist politics, fled to Pakistan and joined Jamiat. Massoud had high praise for Anwar, saying he was eager to establish what he called a "unity" between several resistance groups in the Jegdalek area. Massoud told me to wait in my hotel room and someone would come to me to arrange the trip.

Hotels in Peshawar ranged from the lower rung of Western luxury (the Khyber Intercontinental), to going-to-seed British colonial (Dean's), down through a succession of Pakistani establishments with prices as low as a dollar or two a night. Newspeople without expense accounts, of whom I was one, and other foreigners, such as French doctors and nurses going to or returning from clinics in Afghanistan, usually stayed at Green's Hotel on Saddar Road, the main street of the modern section of the city, which was still known by its British designation, the cantonment. Prices at Green's ranged from $12 to $20 a night. The hotel seemed to be in a perpetual state of languid modernization and had a restaurant where the service was atrocious and the food only tolerable.

A man called Mohammed Gul, in his middle twenties, thin, with no beard and dark, sad eyes, arrived at Green's the next day. He said he would be my interpreter and guide. I showed him that I was already outfitted, and said I had made one trip and felt I could stand up to whatever hardships might be entailed. He said I should wait for another call in a few days. This, I learned, was routine. The mujahidin assumed that spies were everywhere and that foreigners were glaringly obvious targets. To take one somewhere was not only to risk the life of the foreigner, but also to lay a trail that would endanger the movements of the mujahidin. Their defense was to disclose as little as possible, simply to show up, take the foreigner, and drive off.

Mohammed Gul came by a few days later and said we would start that evening. I checked out of my room at four in the afternoon and sat in the lobby. Eventually I had dinner and then sat some more. I knew I had to be patient, but this seemed to be going too far. I had no number to call Mohammed Gul to ask about the delay, and when I called Massoud there was no answer. At ll P.M., I checked back into the hotel and went to sleep. The next morning Mohammed Gul showed up in a jeep with two other foreigners, an Italian named Luigi and his companion, Soledad. Both spoke English and appeared to be in their middle twenties. Luigi said he was a filmmaker. Soledad was a small, attractive, Per-

Green's Hotel, Peshawar. It was in a perpetual state of languid modernization.

uvian woman. She wore a man's baggy shirt and trousers that hardly hid her figure and tucked her hair up under a rolled-brim woolen hat.

There were always young people like Luigi and Soledad around Peshawar, with little money and a lot of time, looking for interesting things to do. Many stayed at the cheapest hotels, but some could afford Green's and sat for hours drinking tea in the dining room, talking to one another and trying to meet people who could tell them what was happening around them. Some called themselves journalists or photographers and wanted to visit refugee camps or, if they were really adventurous, to go into Afghanistan. I later discovered that the Jamiat used Jegdalek as a milk run for just such neophytes—a place where anywhere from two to a dozen could be bundled off for a week or more with little danger and little expense. Most visitors expected everything to be free.

Mohammed Gul explained that the night before the plan had been for me to spend the night in Anwar's house—though this was the first I had heard of it. Anyway, we drove there now. Tea was served, as is customary when a guest arrives, and Anwar came in to shake my hand. He said he was not going with us. He had been invited to Tokyo and would be taking off in a few days. A half hour later, without other ceremony, the trip began. It was February 21. This time there was no ambulance or hiding under a blanket. Ten of us, including Mohammed Gul and six mujahidin, were crammed into an ordinary ramshackle van used as a minibus on the streets of Peshawar.

The leader of our group, who was going to Jegdalek to serve as overall commander in Anwar's absence, was called Farouk. Afghans frequently use only one name. He was thirty-five, and was wearing thick glasses and a karakul hat. He said he had been a businessman in Kabul and was now in business in Peshawar but was also fighting the jihad because his family was from Jegdalek and he admired what Anwar was doing there.

The decrepit minibus was sufficient disguise to get us to the border with only one slight incident. A single policeman at the edge of a small town waved the van to the side of the road. Soledad pulled a blanket over herself and pretended to be asleep. Luigi, who had a small, dark beard, could pass as a young Afghan. I took off my glasses and slumped in a corner. The policeman only glanced briefly at us. As Mohammed Gul later explained, the policeman said he needed some help. He did not say what for. Farouk, accustomed to demands for bribes, replied that we were poor Afghan refugees and had no money. The policeman said he was poor too, but did not press the point and let us proceed.

The Bazaar at Teri Mangal

We drove straight through Parachinar, and after an hour and a half on a miserable, rutted, and rocky road arrived at Teri Mangal, on the Afghanistan border. Once this was a thriving village, with an economy based on lumber cut from the tall, thick deodar cedars of the mountains of southern Afghanistan. The village dwindled away to almost nothing when the Afghans, in the early 1970s, tried to conserve and develop their forest resources. The Germans built a lumber and furniture-manufacturing complex at Jaji, just across the border inside Afghanistan. All this has been destroyed, and with no government to exercise control lumber cutters are despoiling the remaining stands of Afghan deodar to feed the furniture factories of Pakistan.

Although stacks of thick, hand-hewn planks marked the outskirts of Teri Mangal, its main commerce when I passed through was in guns, ammunition, and supplies for the mujahidin. A single street, about a half mile long and only ten feet wide, was lined with shops made from raw, rough-cut wood. Some of the shops were barely six feet wide, just big enough for a merchant to sit inside surrounded by his goods.

A drug shop displayed dozens of prescription and patent medicines, mostly vitamins, aspirins, sedatives, and cough drops or syrups. A clothing shop had gloves, sweaters, underwear, socks, and the complete range of headgear: karakul hats, fox-fur hats, rolled-up hats, and turban cloths, either simple lengths of cotton or finely woven and decorated silk or rayon. There were hardware shops, food shops, candy shops, and trinket shops with bangles, rings, needles, and thread to take home to a wife or daughter. One store featured sunglasses, including tinted ski goggles with a rubber strap. The mujahidin, most of them illiterate boys on their first trip away from their villages, love novelty. A few were always in front of the store, trying on the goggles. If anyone bought a pair, he did not remove the label from the lens. That was part of the display of imported authenticity.

In comparison the gun shops were dull: arrays of light machine guns, Kalashnikovs, rifles, and pistols; boxes and tins of bullets, grenades, and shells; and heaps of bandoliers and canvas ammunition holders all looked alike. The more costly items, like mortars and shoulder-fired, rocket-propelled grenade antitank weapons, called RPG-7s, were kept out of sight in the back of a store. The weapons did not come cheap. A Russian-made Kalashnikov cost the equivalent of $1,700 to $2,000, depending on its condition. A Chinese version of the same semiautomatic rifle cost $1,200 to $1,400. The Egyptian version could be bought for as little as $900 if it appeared to be in poor condition. A bolt-driven Enfield 303 rifle, made by the ingenious gunsmiths of Dara, in tribal territory about fifteen miles outside Peshawar, could be picked up for $35 or $40. Once, before the flood of modern weapons, when both Pakistan and Afghanistan had tried hard to limit the weaponry available to tribesmen, a good 303 made in Dara sold for upward of $1,000. Whatever the price, there was no lack of customers. A burst of rifle fire from the open area in back of the shops, and even the sharp explosion of a shell, was testimony that something had been bought and was being tested.

Our van patiently honked its way along the street to a gun shop, where Luigi, Soledad, and I were told to go through to the rear and keep out of sight. The shop was owned by a Jamiat supporter. Just before dark we were taken farther up the road to the man's house, where we had dinner and passed the night. It upsets the routine of an Afghan's family life if strange males are within the compound, because women must be kept out of sight. We left right after a breakfast of tea, bread, and fat-soaked eggs to minimize the inconvenience, and were again parked in the rear of the gun shop while the mujahidin went to the bazaar to hire horses for our trip.

The supply of horses fluctuates from day to day, depending on how many men and animals arrive from Afghanistan and what condition the horses are in. The price also fluctuates. If many parties with large amounts of supplies want to travel to Afghanistan, the price can seem prohibitive compared to what they paid for an earlier trip. The field is ripe for disagreement. Buying, selling, or renting a horse is a serious business for an Afghan—a chance for a full display of bargaining and guile. It is the stuff of life, to be leisurely savored. We waited and dozed off, and were cheered when word was brought that two horses had been hired. They had to be fed, however, and that would take more time.

Fear and Panic on Horseback

Finally, at eleven o'clock, our mounts arrived. Soledad had a horse with a saddle. I was given a packhorse and was supposed to perch, without stirrups, atop our baggage. I am Brooklyn-born and Manhattan-bred and up till then had ridden a horse only once, many years earlier on a half-day excursion in Kashmir. The mujahidin, assuming as usual

A Soviet tank stripped for scrap metal. A reminder of when the Russians thought they could easily sweep the resistance from Afghan soil.

that all foreigners are incompetent in the important things of life, such as shooting guns and riding horses, rightly took it for granted that I had to be boosted up and watched carefully lest I fall off.

At the end of Teri Mangal is a steep hill, almost like a cliff, with a trail winding to the final Pakistani checkpoint at the top. As we went up, squeezing to one side, a train of camels came down from Afghanistan, each carrying four large, roughly squared sections of deodar trunks. There was little doubt that despite our attempts at concealment the Pakistanis knew of our arrival and activities at Teri Mangal. Still, the mujahidin insisted that we play the game to the end. Mohammed Gul told Soledad and me to put our blankets over our heads, leaving only our eyes exposed, and we passed the post without incident.

The trail descended the other side of the hill past a destroyed Afghan border post, the hulk of a tank that had been stripped of its wheels for scrap metal, and the concrete remains of the German lumber mill and furniture factory, through the deserted remains of a village, and out to fields, where the skeletons of seven tanks and armored personnel carriers were spaced along a front about a half mile wide, like driftwood left by a high tide. All this was a reminder of the first furious months of the Soviet invasion, when Soviet forces thought their might could sweep the resistance from Afghan soil. At best, the mujahidin had only RPG-7s, and men often had to stand up, out in the open, with the rocket grenade launchers on their shoulders, and face the cannon and machine guns of an armed vehicle. The hulks by the road and in the fields testify to their bravery.

We rode the rest of the day, with a brief halt for tea and bread for lunch. I was exhausted by the constant fear of slipping off the horse. As we mounted higher into the mountains, through defiles and over rocks, Soledad too was obviously uneasy. A mujahid walking behind her slapped her horse to make it go faster. It bolted forward and she turned to him and shouted in Italian to leave her alone. She could speak English, but Italian apparently was her language of emotion. Fifteen minutes later another man did the same thing, and she shouted at him too. He just grinned. The fact that she spoke in Italian, an unknown language, was not the problem. It was just that Afghan men do not take orders from women. But then they also ignored Luigi, who kept asking Mohammed Gul to order a rest halt. The mujahidin apparently had some sort of timetable that could not be altered. Besides, they were happy to be back in the mountains and clear air of Afghanistan and were enjoying themselves. When we came to patches and drifts of snow, they romped in fights, throwing snowballs and trying to smash large clumps of snow on each other's heads. They also stopped to test their marksmanship by shooting birds, again drawing furious Italian protests from kindhearted Soledad.

After a while Soledad got down from her horse, saying that she preferred to walk. I got down too. My legs ached from being spread out over the packs. But when I slowed down because of the increasing altitude and the unrelenting pace, the mujahidin insisted that I ride. By then Mohammed Gul was riding the saddle horse and no one was on the packhorse. I said I had trouble balancing on the pack and asked Mohammed Gul if I could ride the saddle horse instead. He agreed and dismounted to walk for a while. For me the stirrups and the possibility of gripping the horse with my legs came just in time. For now we began to climb a mountain, and the trail became no more than two feet wide; as far as I could see just wide enough for the horse to put down his hooves. We turned and twisted along the mountainside, and the horse's neck seemed to extend out into the void, with a dizzying drop below. What was best? I wondered—to close my eyes, and try to shut out the danger, or keep them open, to be prepared when we fell over the side, as it seemed certain we must sooner or later?

But the horse was surefooted and we didn't fall. The reverse side of the pass turned out to be buried in snow. The mujahidin, showing off as usual, took a short cut straight down, plunging through the snow with gales of laughter. I followed the path, with Mohammed Gul behind me, then Luigi, still on foot, and then Soledad, now on the pack horse. It grew dark and a quarter moon shed little light. The horse's legs sank into the snow. For a while I almost panicked. I could not see Mohammed Gul. Could he see me? More crucially, could the horse see the trail? I couldn't. In the dim, ghostly light of the moon the snowy landscape all looked the same and I worried that the horse might wander off to be lost in the dark. But the horse did recognize a trail of some kind and came to a small grove where the snow disappeared. Now my main worry was being knocked off the horse by an unseen branch. I put up one arm, to act as a sort of trip wire to tell me when to duck, and let the horse do the rest. I heard Mohammed Gul say something behind me, then Luigi shouting when he found himself wading through water and mud that he had not seen in the dark, and knew I was not lost after all. Finally we reached a teahouse and I slipped off the horse and almost collapsed to the ground. Inside, trembling with cold, I sat as close as possible to a hot tin stove.

At an Afghan Teahouse

An Afghan teahouse, alas, bears not the slightest resemblance to a clean, austere, tatami-matted Japanese teahouse. Afghans sometimes call their teahouses hotels, which is what they really are: places to eat and sleep. But the word hotel, even at the worst, implies a modicum of comfort and service. Such qualities are lacking in a teahouse built to serve the impoverished mujahidin. It usually consists of a large, low, bare room, with a dirt floor covered by squares of canvas and flea-infested mats. A few small windows, often with translucent plastic in place of glass, let in a bit of light. A smoky wood fire in a tin stove serves for heating and boiling water for tea. Cooking is done outside, at a mud fireplace or over rocks spaced wide to hold a large pot. The crockery is chipped and cracked; aluminum or enameled plates are dented. Washing

An Afghan teahouse. The tall metal container in the center served both for heating in cold weather and for boiling water for tea.

consists of swishing cups, glasses, and plates in cold, soon-dirty water. Fastidious customers rinse a glass or cup in hot tea before filling it to drink.

The owner's most time-consuming task is to gossip with the guests and supervise the small store that is usually attached to the teahouse. Guests can buy cigarettes, matches, candies, biscuits, dried raisins, and a few other staples, including barley for the horses. Housekeeping, such as it is, is left to a servant boy, who might be only eight years old. Once a day the boy will use some branches to sweep out the most obvious leavings of scores of guests, raising clouds of dust that soon settle back to the floor. He seldom has the time or inclination to do more. He must fetch water from a stream, chop wood for the stove, make and serve the tea, clear away and wash the dishes, and do anything else the owner can think of. Most of the time the owner's wife and children live nearby, out of sight. They may bake the bread that is the staple of every meal; otherwise that is another of the servant's duties.

Bread is baked in a cone-shaped, mud-walled pit next to the teahouse. First brushwood—often dry desert roots and branches that flare up in a quick, intense blaze—is burned in the bottom of the pit. That heats the sides and forms a bed of glowing embers. The servant has already kneaded flour and water into balls about the size of a large fist. When the pit is hot and the flames have died down, the boy pats a ball of dough into a flat oval about twelve inches long and five inches wide. He puts this on a dampened cloth pad of about the same size, reaches quickly into the pit, and slaps the bread on the side of the oven wall, where it sticks and bakes. He repeats the procedure until he has filled the circular sides of the pit within his reach. By that time some pieces of bread are ready. He reaches in with a long thin rod that has a hook at one end and pulls them out. It's not easy to get it just right: If you make part of the bread too thin, or leave it in the oven too long, it comes out burned and charred. Other parts may not be baked enough.

In the old days in Kabul baking bread was an art, and each piece came out thick and baked just right, with a delicious aroma and taste. The best that can be said for teahouse bread, even fresh from the oven with the burned or underdone parts picked out and thrown away, is that it is edible. Unfortunately it quickly goes stale. Sometimes it has to be taken along as emergency rations when the journey will be long and there will be no time for rest. Then it's pure cardboard.

It was eight o'clock when we arrived at the teahouse, too late for any food to be cooked. We had tea and bread for dinner. Afghan men are not used to being in a room with an unrelated woman, especially when it's time to sleep. Our teahouse had more headroom than usual, and the owner cleared some junk from an overhead storage platform where Luigi and Soledad spread their double sleeping bag.

We were up and off by a little after seven o'clock. At an altitude of more than 5,000 feet, the ground was hard with frost. I was on the packhorse and by now had learned that if I relaxed I would not fall off. At two in the afternoon we stopped at a teahouse for a lunch of bread and greasy potatoes. The Afghans like fatty food. They spoon out huge globs of white, solidified oil, which they buy in two-, three-, or five-gallon cans, heat the oil, add onions and salt, let that simmer a while, and then throw in whatever they want to cook, in this case potatoes.

We were soon under way again. Sometimes I walked to ease the constriction in my legs, but the mujahidin invariably insisted that I ride, saying I slowed them down. When we came to the top of a steep rise they said Jegdalek was near, just down at the bottom of the valley. I was too much of an amateur to doubt them. Only later would I learn that when a mujahid says some place is near, he merely means to be encouraging, and the destination is usually still hours away.

Night fell and clouds obscured the moon. We went up another mountain, the darkened trail narrower than it had been the day before. I was aware of the abyss yawning at my side, but I kept telling myself to trust the horse. At a plateau Mohammed Gul told me to dismount, saying the horse would be taken by another route. Some mujahidin turned on penlights, but my flashlight was stowed inaccessibly in my pack. A mujahid with a light took my hand and led me along. He found this funny. He rocked our hands back and forth, as if he were walking a child, and began to sing what I took to be a children's song. I found it funny too. Then we started down an almost vertical slope. He had to hook his arm under mine and practically lower me down. Suddenly we were on a narrow ledge with a door leading into a room in a mountain hut. I stumbled in and lay on the ground, numb from the journey: thirteen hours on foot and horseback, with an hour's break for lunch, capped by the final half-hour rush in the dark over rocks and down the cliff.

At a Mujahidin Base

They were expecting us. In short order platters heaped with rice and hidden chunks of mutton were placed before us. Nourished and revived, I began to make plans. The only interpreter was Mohammed Gul, and Luigi and I had different objectives. During brief chats in English along the way, he said he wanted to make a documentary film about the war, the people, and the destruction. That seemed ambitious, since he had only two small cases of equipment, but that was not my business. To me, the important thing was what we would do tomorrow. Luigi said he planned to rest a few days and had no objection if I worked with Mohammed Gul.

It turned out that Farouk, who came with us as Anwar's representative, was a sort of executive. The local military commander was Mohammed Omar Tandar. At age twenty-five he was already growing bald, and had a large mustache, no beard, and a gap between his upper front teeth. I asked how he started in the jihad. "I was a farmer when Taraki did his coup," he replied. "A mullah said to me: 'He is not a Muslim and those people are not honest. They are Russian servants and you should fight them.' I, and some others like me, began to fight the government."

Jegdalek is famous in British Empire lore. Before the British built

their military roads, the easiest route east from Kabul to the city of Jalalabad and on to India passed through the Jegdalek valley. The last
slaughter of British soldiers and civilians in their disastrous retreat from
Kabul in the First Anglo-Afghan War took place in Jegdalek. Then it
was bypassed by history and now consists of a central market town and a
string of villages twenty-seven miles southeast of the capital. Mohammed Omar said ten resistance groups from five political parties were
camped in the long valley. He said they had a combined roster of about
400 men, but half of them were generally on rotation in Pakistan. Although they lived in separate camps and had separate supply lines, they
joined for battle under his direction. He said the various commanders
would meet to plan the action and each group would send a number of
men to take part. Their usual targets were convoys on the Kabul-
Jalalabad highway, about eight or nine miles away, but that they sometimes also attacked the Sarobi power station, about twelve miles from
Jegdalek, which supplied most of the capital's electricity.

I asked if he was planning an action. He said that nothing was defi-
nite: any action would require serious consideration because both sides
of the highway were cleared of people and sowed with mines. Helicopters regularly flew overhead to hit anything that moved. In addition, defending forces could be dispatched on short notice from a series of Soviet, Afghan Army, and militia posts along the highway. Moreover, back
from the highway a line of lesser posts, surrounded by mines and manned by Afghan troops, served as trip wires. The men inside, even those
who might be sympathizers, fired on infiltrators to protect themselves,
alerting the main posts along the road. He said it could take as many as
three nights just to slip small parties of men through the outer defenses
to get them into position for an attack on the highway.

Rather than face an indefinite wait for military activity, I thought it
best to talk with commanders in the area and return to Pakistan. Early
the next morning Mohammed Gul and I began our tour. By daylight I
could see where I was. The hut, which was built about halfway up one
side of a deep and narrow ravine, was made of the same rocks as the cliff
itself and blended into the mountain with natural camouflage.

There are no servants in a mujahidin camp. The youngest fighters,
eager to be accepted in the jihad, cheerfully do the chores. Khan Aga,
sixteen, had tilted his Kalashnikov against the cliff side and was helping
another youth make bread. "I never went to school," he said. "When I
was small, I walked around and watched what the Communists were

doing and told the mujahidin. When I was twelve my father showed me how to use his gun; how to put the bullet in, how to aim, and how to shoot. Then, when I was thirteen, the Russians captured my village and I joined the mujahidin and took part in an attack on the highway. My commander said I was a good mujahid and gave me money to buy a Kalashnikov in Teri Mangal."

At the bottom of the ravine about thirty men were preparing a meal. Their commander was Nuruddin, whose huge shoulders, long black hair, and beard made him look like a bear. He had a bandage on his left hand and said he had fallen from a horse. Then he raised his shirt to show where a bullet had passed through the side of his chest and exited from the back. He showed another bullet scar on his left arm, more on both legs, and finally, one on a finger. He said he had been wounded three years earlier. He had been sitting with an ambush party along the Kabul-Jalalabad road when they were spotted. The Soviets used helicopters to surround them with airborne commandos. They fought all day, and five of his men were killed, but when it grew dark the survivors managed to drag him to safety. I asked how long he had been fighting.

"For more than seven years," he replied. "My home was in Kunar Province. The Communists came and killed mullahs and burned the Holy Koran and when we began to fight them they bombed our houses and killed women and children."

I said many people had told me such things. It seemed everyone believed in the jihad. Why then were there so many different groups? I repeated what Mohammed Omar had said, that in Jegdalek alone there were ten groups belonging to five parties. "We should have unity," Nuruddin replied. "In all of Afghanistan, all parties should join and make unity. I belong to Jamiat and Professor Rabbani tells me to help my brothers. He tells me to join with other people of all groups, with all mujahidin, to fight the Communists. But there are some who don't think like that. There are some who stop other groups and take their weapons. They are Hekmatyar's people," he continued, referring to Gulbuddin Hekmatyar, the leader of the Hizb-i-Islami. "We want to make a unity with them, but if we go near they will kill us and take our weapons and ammunition. He thinks he is more important than anyone else. Hekmatyar tells his mujahidin it does not matter if they are killed. It is only important for him to become president of Afghanistan."

Mines like Toys

We walked to the mouth of the ravine and turned to follow the bed of a small river that flowed past Jegdalek. The town, which once had a population of about 5,000, was deserted and in ruins. Mohammed Gul pointed to one house that he said belonged to Anwar's family. The ground was littered with the debris of war, from large containers that held cluster bombs to fragments of missiles. I noticed a small green plastic object that looked like a vase. Mohammed Gul said it was the remains of an antipersonnel mine, and that there were others that looked like clocks, watches, or pens. He said the Russians dropped them from helicopters, hoping that a child would pick one up as a toy and be injured. However, he said, children were aware of the danger and threw stones at them, as a game, to make them explode.

I discarded the piece I had picked up, an act I later regretted. The mines are frequently cited as an example of Soviet atrocities in Afghanistan, but few people have ever produced samples. I never again came across one, although I frequently asked about them.

We came to two craters, twenty feet in diameter and fifteen feet deep, with pools of stagnant water at the bottom, covered with a green growth. Mohammed Gul said a nomad family had camped there about five months earlier. He said MiGs appeared the next morning and destroyed them, killing many people and hundreds of sheep. Because of such incidents, few people moved about during the day. At the sound of a plane overhead, Mohammed Gul stopped in a grove of bomb-twisted trees. Once it must have been a desert-dwelling Muslim's vision of paradise, filled with the flowers and apple, pomegranate, almond, and mulberry trees, and a grape arbor beside an irrigation canal. Now it was just a place to hide from death.

"It's a spotter plane," Mohammed Gul said, looking through the dead branches to the sky. "They send them over several times a day. If they see something, the MiGs will be here in a short time."

The plane droned into the distance and we continued our walk, coming to a building with a veranda that must have been a government office of some kind. A mujahid guard sat on a wide seat taken from a bus. Mohammed Gul spoke to him and the guard went off to a collection of small houses on a hillside. "This is a Sayyaf group," he said, referring to the Islamic Alliance of Professor Abdur Rasul Sayyaf. "I asked to see their commander." Although Mohammed Omar had said all the groups worked together, they kept their distance from one an-

Mujahidin with abandoned buildings of Jegdalek in the background: a valley where the debris of war included mines like toys.

other and guarded their secrets. Thus we did not simply walk into the Sayyaf camp without permission.

A man came down the hill wearing an incongruous, black, imitation-fur-and-leather winter hat, with the flaps turned down over his ears. He said he was Sadullah, twenty-eight, and had fifteen men in his group and others in Pakistan. I asked my standard question: How had he gotten started? "I was in school in Sarobi," he said. "They sent Communist teachers and about ten out of every hundred students in the school became Communists. They were all sons of rich families. The middle-class families were good Muslims. Six months after Taraki came to power the teachers told us we should not go to the mosque. They burned a Holy Koran. We did not like that. We attacked and burned the school as a Communist center. The Communists put me in the army and sent me to the north, to Khanabad in Kunduz Province. I was there eleven months. Most of the soldiers were good Muslims. We made contact with the mujahidin, and one day we went to join them. We took with us thirty-five weapons and an artillery piece. Then I went to Pakistan, and now I have come back to fight here."

I asked why he joined Sayyaf. "He is a good Muslim," Sadullah replied. "And I am an experienced soldier. I know I can be a good commander and Professor Sayyaf gave me the weapons to organize this front."

We went on and climbed a long hill to the end of a ravine, where some men were excavating a cave, chopping out the earth with pickaxes and carrying away the soil on the backs of donkeys. Mohammed Gul said this was another Jamiat group. A man in his middle forties was supervising the work. He had a neatly clipped mustache, good clothes, and what seemed to be an air of authority. It turned out that he had been a comparatively wealthy landowner. He said his name was Akhtar. "Do you see those trees?" he asked, pointing down to a series of elaborate terraces, built of stone, filled with earth, and planted with trees. "I had that land prepared and I planted those trees when Daoud was in power. We all know where our farms and gardens are. And our children know too. We are not afraid of the Communists and the Red Army. They will not take our land away."

Obviously, word had been sent ahead and the men at the Jamiat camp were prepared for our arrival. A large, red-and-white-striped canvas was spread on the ground, with a fine view of the wide valley. It was mostly desert, with a few patches of pale green amid the gentle blending of browns. The sky was blue, with white clouds like sheep, and the sun was pleasantly warm. We had a pilau of chicken flavored with raisins and apricots. At another time or place we would have relaxed and gossiped, but now we talked of war.

There were six of us, including Akhtar's cousin Yassin, who was about thirty years old and was the local commander. Yassin said there were eighteen men at his base, and many more on rotation to Pakistan. He said his men took part in an ambush on the Kabul highway once or twice a month, and sometimes went to Sarobi to cut the pylons that carried electricity to the capital. "When Taraki came to power," he said, "the Communists called our village leader to their office. They said they wanted to talk to him. His name was Gafur Khan and he was a mullah. They arrested him and the village leaders all over Jegdalek district. They knew exactly who the important men were. Someone had told them: 'this man has power; this man can control people.' They were all killed. We sent our families to Pakistan and we went to the mountains to fight. We did not have weapons and we went to several parties. Professor Rabbani gave us weapons and now we are Jamiat."

After lunch Yassin took us to a cliff, where a ladder led up to a platform that had been hacked out of rock. On the platform was a Dashika antiaircraft heavy machine gun. "We put that there, and are digging a new cave, because they have discovered us," he explained. "They send su-25 bombers to try to destroy us. Last week a helicopter came and fired flares to mark our location. Then a plane dropped four bombs. Three exploded far away, but the fourth went right over our heads and landed there without exploding." He pointed across a ravine to the tail stabilizer of a bomb buried in the soil. "They were probably Afghan pilots. They are afraid to come in low enough and their aim is terrible. No one was killed and nothing was damaged." That was a joke and they all laughed.

Akhtar said the families of the mujahidin were in refugee camps in Pakistan. He said the mujahidin themselves visited their families on a rotation basis, living with them for two or three months and working, generally as masons, painters, or in some other construction trade, to earn extra money. He said Pakistani officials cheated the refugees of their rations and charged for medicines that should be free. Or else, he said, the camp pharmacists gave old or adulterated medicines so that a refugee had to buy medicines in the Peshawar bazaar. Such complaints are often heard from refugees. Pakistani and United Nations officials, who supervise the camps, admit that corruption is inevitable, but they deny that it is as pervasive as the refugees claim.

"Go to Afghanistan. Fight the Jihad"

I asked why, if life in the camps is bad and money is short, don't the men stay in Pakistan to support and care for their families? Akhtar was shocked. "We want our country to be free," he exclaimed. "Our wives, our children, our parents would say to us: 'Go to Afghanistan. Fight the jihad against the Russians.'"

Mohammed Gul and I walked back in the direction we had come, but instead of going down along the valley floor, we went across a series of hills to a group allied to the National Liberation Front of Sibghatullah Mujaddidi. The commander was Mohammed Daoud, who had narrow eyes, black hair reaching down to his shoulders, a heavy black mustache, but no beard. When he said he was twenty-one, I asked how such a young man could become a commander. "I have been fighting for five years," he replied. "I was a small boy when Taraki came to power. A mullah told me he was not a Muslim and did not have a law. Then the Russians invaded our country and bombed our villages. My family decided it was not safe and I left school and we moved to Pakistan. When I was sixteen, I was old enough to go back to fight. My uncle knew Professor Mujaddidi before the war. He gave guns and mines and we went to the highway with another group and blew up a bridge. We attacked the highway many times and, after two years, the men decided I should be their commander."

Mohammed Daoud was obviously well respected. His was the largest of the ten groups in the Jegdalek valley, with fifty men. He said ten of his men had been killed, four by butterfly mines that are sown from helicopters and litter both sides of the highway. They are plastic mines, called "butterflies" because they have a flat surface on one side that looks like a wing. They explode only when someone kicks or steps on a fuse in the center.

Next we climbed high up on a cliff side to an isolated camp linked to the Islamic Revolutionary Movement, or Harakat, of Nabi Mohammadi. The commander was Atiqallah, twenty-five years old, dressed in black with hair even longer than Daoud's. Long hair seemed to be a fashion with the younger commanders of Jegdalek. Atiqallah and a few of his men sat on a narrow ledge before a cave hacked out of the mountainside, with a light machine gun on a tripod just above their heads. They were cleaning their Kalashnikovs, and had the parts spread out on a cloth before them. Atiqallah said his family owned a small piece of land near where the Sayyaf group now had its camp. "I was in school when

Atiqallah, twenty-five, left, with karakul hat, and his men above Jegdalek. In front of Atiqallah is an RPG-7 rocket-propelled grenade launcher. The lookout has a 12.7-mm Dashika heavy machine gun, the main mujahidin antiaircraft weapon.

Taraki came," he said. "A Communist teacher told us about him and spoke against Islam. I left school and helped the mujahidin, telling them what the Communists were doing. Then I went with my family to Pakistan. Some of us decided to come back here to fight. We went to one party but they would not give us weapons. Then we went to Harakat and we got guns and ammunition and now we have been fighting for about six years."

I asked him if Harakat also gave them money. "No, we have no money," he replied. "If a man has land near here, he tries to work it. My father is in a refugee camp and he can take care of my mother. I will plant some of my family's land, but I can't plant it all because we have no fertilizer. We also had a fruit garden, but the trees have all been destroyed. If a man is like me and has land he will stay here longer. The others must go back to Pakistan to work to support their families and to buy food to bring here."

On our way back to our base we stopped at a final Jamiat camp on a low hill overlooking the valley. The commander, Sayed Hassan, twenty-four, spread a mat on the ground and brought a large dish of dried mulberries that tasted as sweet as candy. The exercise had raised my appetite and I ate them by the handful. Hassan pointed far across to the opposite side of the valley, to the ruins of a village with three houses to one side. "The one in the center was built by my grandfather. My parents built the other two. We had lands, a garden, and 120 sheep. But then the planes came and bombed our houses and burned our fields. The helicopters came and shot at anyone who walked. Twelve people from our village were martyred. Over there you can see the graveyard." He pointed to tall poles and fluttering pennants on a hill above the village.

He said all the men in his group came from villages in that part of the valley, and those with land would start planting potatoes and vegetables when the weather grew warmer. The others would remain in Pakistan for several months. Fortunately, they had established a connection there with a brick factory where the owner rotated jobs among members of his group. When he spoke of how hard they had to work to care for their families, I asked the same question I had asked Akhtar earlier in the day: Why didn't they stay in Pakistan?

"Pakistan is not my country," he replied. "We know our country will be free some day and we will be able to come back. We will not be discouraged. We will fight until we have an Islamic government in Afghanistan."

With that, I felt I had learned as much as I could in Jegdalek. I told Mohammed Gul I would like to return to Peshawar as soon as possible, even the next day if that could be arranged. He said that was impossible, because the man who supplied the horses that brought us had already left. But as we talked he noticed a man with a loaded packhorse walking the valley floor. Afghans are able to shout to someone far away and understand the faint sounds of a reply. Mohammed Gul called to the man, who replied that he was delivering wheat to the camp of Mohammed Omar Tandar and that he would return with us to Pakistan. It was like hailing a taxi.

We walked back to our camp. Luigi and Soledad had been moved to the privacy of a nearby storehouse. Luigi was asleep and Soledad said he had something wrong with his back and had taken a painkiller. They did not have dinner with us. The room was crowded and the men were in high spirits, telling elaborate stories and jokes that I did not understand but, judging by their huge and deep laughs as they rolled over and held their sides, must have been funny indeed.

Farouk seemed to feel that I was neglected and asked a few questions about my day: Had I met all the commanders I wanted? Was I feeling tired? I took advantage of his hospitality and asked a few provocative questions. I said I was impressed with how eager everyone was to fight, but it seemed to me that, even with their coordinated actions, they were too weak to defeat a superpower. Farouk had a ready answer: "Our God will help us fight the Russians. Everyone belongs to God. He likes honest and good people, and does not like the Russians."

"That's all very well," I said. "But God does not distribute arms. You must get weapons from the political parties in Peshawar."

Daoud, the young Mujaddidi commander, was among those in the room. He had been leading the jokes and had opened his shirt and obviously was feeling in top form. "We don't fight for the Peshawar leaders. We fight for God and our country and for our country's freedom," he said passionately. With a smile he added: "And you say God does not help us. Then how is it that we have only Kalashnikovs and RPGs, and the Russians have MiGs and helicopters and tanks and modern missiles, and they still cannot capture Afghanistan?" There were nods of approval at his wisdom.

Farouk delivered what appeared to be the final dictum: "If only one mujahid is left alive, he will fight the Russians."

My bags had been put in the house with Luigi and Soledad and I went there to sleep. Luigi still complained of a pain in his back and remained in bed the next morning, and Soledad stayed near to care for him. Mohammed Gul had disappeared. I guessed that he wanted to rest before the return journey. I went down to the valley where there was an irrigation canal, stripped to my underwear, and washed myself with soap and a hand cloth. Afghans are shy about taking off their clothes in public, and I knew this was a slight to their sensibilities, but along with a layer of dirt I had picked up a few fleas. I turned my shirt and trousers inside out while waiting for the sun to dry me and saw two of the little beasts hop away. I went back to the camp, found a warm rock to sit on, and composed my notes and my thoughts.

The Lessons of Jegdalek

Both the Afghans and the Russians obviously had their strengths and weaknesses. The Russians had the firepower to spread death and desolation at will. But they had failed in the more crucial task of developing either a surrogate army or civilian cadres to seize and hold the ground they laid waste. The mujahidin had unflagging zeal. But their courage and enthusiasm were hardly enough to overcome their lack of heavy weapons and adequate food supplies.

More important, the mujahidin lacked a strategy. The men in the Jegdalek valley were not fighting for the liberation of their country or to achieve some national ideological goal. No matter what they said about freedom and an Islamic government, they were fighting for their own land and their own families. There was no military structure to link their struggle with a struggle in the next valley or the next province. They had links with the political parties in Pakistan but, for the most part, these links were just for arms or because of some family or personal tie.

The unity they were so proud of in Jegdalek was of little military importance. They were without an offensive spirit. They were part-time soldiers and had to take care of their families as well as fight. In their camps they spent almost all of their time doing nothing. Their attacks were limited to nearby targets of opportunity. They were wasting their strength and their blood in pinprick raids that did nothing to sap the strength of the enemy.

Mohammed Gul appeared for lunch along with Luigi, who was still complaining of pain in his back. Luigi said he hoped to stay in Jegdalek for a month, and didn't mind if Mohammed Gul went with me, leaving him without an interpreter, although he asked that someone else be sent as a replacement as soon as possible. Mohammed Gul said the man with the horse wanted to visit his family in Hissarak—in Ningrahar Province a few hours away—before returning to Pakistan, and that we would start in the afternoon after the second prayer.

The ride to Hissarak was a four-hour, uneventful journey. The difference between the two regions was startling. The Communists destroyed Jegdalek, and monitored events in the valley, because it was a resistance stronghold and part of a natural route to Kabul. The Hissarak district of Ningrahar was isolated, of no strategic importance, and had no concentration of mujahidin to attract Soviet bombs. It was green with early budding fields watered by a working irrigation system. The houses were intact and people walked about openly.

The commander of a small Gailani band learned that we were in the area and gave us dinner and a place to stay for the night. We spent the next night in the same teahouse where we spent the first night on our journey to Jegdalek. That meant we were able to go up the snow-covered mountainside by daylight. We were back in Teri Mangal in the early afternoon, and I waited in the same gun shop and had dinner in the same house of the Jamiat supporter. Mohammed Gul, telling me to keep my glasses off and do nothing to attract attention, put us on a regular bus for Parachinar, where we got a minibus back to Peshawar on February 17. Pakistan was hot, and so was the welcome shower at Green's Hotel.

The Refugees

....

4

When the Communists first seized power, it seemed that the Afghan resistance could hold out no longer than weeks, or months at the most. But the mujahidin fought on. As the anniversaries of the April 1978 coup and the December 1979 Soviet invasion piled up, people marveled at their determination. What motivated their struggle? Religion? The easy availability of foreign arms? Or something intangible, having to do with Afghan attitudes toward honor, life, and death? There were many questions but few answers.

One question that intrigued many reporters was the extent of American military aid and what happened to the money in the process of distribution. According to an estimate of the International Institute for Strategic Studies in London, covert aid from the United States, other Western countries, and friendly Islamic nations from 1979 to 1984 amounted to $600 million. By 1987 the total was reported at $1.3 billion.

However, there were no indications of a marked increase in the weapons reaching the mujahidin or in their fighting abilities. Massive corruption seemed the only explanation. Some reports said 30 percent of all aid was stolen or misappropriated; other reports put the estimate as high as 75 percent. I asked a long-time observer in Islamabad for his opinion. He said half the military supplies that arrived in Pakistan were diverted by the Pakistanis and another 25 percent were siphoned off by Afghan exile groups or individuals at the border.

Despite the almost universal charges of massive corruption, official sources in Washington made no response. This in itself is significant.

Congressmen and special interest groups watch with hawk eyes covert aid to the contras fighting the Sandinistas of Nicaragua. There are constant demands that aid to the contras end. But no one seems to be upset at covert aid to the mujahidin and what might be happening to it.

I asked another experienced political observer in Islamabad for an explanation.

"Nicaragua is a debatable proposition," he replied. "There are many who think the Sandinistas are not all that bad, especially in comparison with the contras. But no one in Washington, London, Paris, Bonn, or even Stockholm doubts that what the Russians are doing in Afghanistan is utterly evil. You simply can't go crossing a frontier to attack a peaceful neighbor and expect to get away with it. So aid to the mujahidin is sacrosanct. Sure, there is a lot that could be faulted. In any cross-border operation a lot will be lost on the way. But everyone—conservatives and liberals alike—believes the mujahidin must be helped and no one wants to do or say anything that will hurt their cause."

Afghan Leaders: Questions, Few Answers

When I raised the subject of military aid with some of the resistance leaders in Peshawar, they said I should make such inquiries in Washington. When I asked about the charges of corruption, they said that whatever help they received from friends abroad was used correctly.

In fact, they added little to my knowledge on any subject. The party leaders are not like American politicians, who must curry favor with the media to enhance their chances in the next election. Rather, they are like American corporate executives, who do not depend on public opinion for their positions and feel that a reporter can do little to help them but a great deal to harm them. They are also religious figures and, like their counterparts in the United States or any other country, they have a bland ability to cloak their thoughts in what appears to be ideological certitude. Instead of giving explanations, Afghan leaders often settle for speeches reiterating well-established positions. An interview is rarely newsworthy.

One of those I interviewed was Pir Sayed Ahmad Gailani, leader of the National Islamic Front, or NIFA as it is often called. Gailani had put aside the Gucci shoes of his cosmopolitan past and now wore a turban and robes and had the aura of a traditional Qadiriya saint. His eyes were wide and moist; his beard long and neatly combed. The gates to his house were blocked by devotees eager to kiss his hand or just to catch a glimpse of him through closed windows as he was driven by in a car.

I asked him whether in view of all the reports of quarrels among the seven major parties there was a hope for unity. He replied with a speech: "The door is left open for everybody to participate in the Grand United Front. There should be a fair representation of freedom fighters, tribal chieftains, the refugees, intellectuals, former high civil servants, and all the existing parties. Those who reject the whole concept will be responsible to the nation and to the world. They themselves will pay for it, because they will be deprived of support."

I asked whom he meant by the rejectors. He ducked the question, saying in effect that everyone knew who they might be, so he did not have to single anyone out. He did say at another point that actual clashes had occurred with what he called "extremist" organizations, but added, "the clashes are not of significance to have any major effect on our movement."

I asked him to estimate the number of mujahidin fighting the Communists. "From one point of view, the entire nation is participating actively in our resistance," he said. "As far as the armed mujahidin are concerned, they are in sufficient numbers, but I would not like to state how many in specific numbers."

I asked how long he thought the struggle would last. "We are ready to sacrifice our lives. We have a firm determination to continue till the last living soul," he replied. "But our ability to continue the struggle will depend on our Muslim brothers and also the free world; how much they can support us. Despite the shortage of weapons, and weapons of a poor quality, if we have been able to achieve and accomplish what we have accomplished in the past six or seven years, you can imagine what we can achieve with proper weapons and what will be the effect of that on our struggle."

Mohammed Nabi Mohammadi, the leader of the Islamic Revolutionary Movement, or Harakat, was an even more imposing religious figure. I saw him at his house, a gaudy, orange-tinted building standing out from the pale, dusty browns of the surrounding mud walls and scrub desert on the western outskirts of Peshawar. He wore a thick, pale blue turban with a white tail hanging down the back. Under an elaborately worked shawl he wore layers of woolen sleeveless jackets. His black beard, turning white in spots, reached down to his chest. His eyes, large, brown, sorrowful, and deep set, were usually half-closed, as if he was in constant meditation. He sat relaxed, without tension, and spoke slowly in a deep, low voice, resembling a biblical sage painted by Rembrandt.

I asked him about outside aid to the mujahidin. "The help is in two kinds, military and economic," he replied. "On the military side, we are told the political situation does not allow us to get more help. We accept this and keep ourselves quiet. But on the economic side, the help we get from Islamic countries as well as from the others is not enough. We are not able to support one percent of Afghan families in a complete way. There is heavy fighting inside now, with a lot of snow and cold, but the mujahidin have no good jackets, sweaters, shoes, socks, or sleeping bags. In that respect, the help we get from the outside we can say is zero percent. We cannot care even for the mujahidin. How can we also care for the widows and orphans?"

Mohammadi did cast a little light on one aspect of foreign aid: He said that the fundamentalist parties received a great deal of help from the Arab countries, but that such aid did not come to his party or the other parties labeled as traditionalist. He said it would be welcome if the United States could arrange for direct cash payments to the traditional parties, to be spent to help widows, orphans, and refugees.

When I met Professor Burhanuddin Rabbani, the leader of the Jamiat-i-Islami, he was dressed in a simple brown shirt and trousers, a khaki military-style jacket, and a gray turban. His face was young and unwrinkled but his black beard was heavily laced with gray. He wore a gold wristwatch and his hands were small and neat. As he talked in a soft, unhurried voice, he fingered pale yellow prayer beads.

"Basically, there are no differences in our beliefs," he said of the political parties. "Still, there are limited differences between the personalities of the jihad. Each has his own freedom of choice and judgment and his own ideas. Some of our differences go back even before the jihad. Some are personal and some are tactical."

"Are you saying that those who use the labels fundamentalist and traditionalist are wrong in suggesting there is a difference in ideology?" I asked.

"I think these views arise from a lack of understanding of the nature of the jihad. These views are superficial. It's not that one is Islamic and another is not Islamic. There are differences, but they are not so basic that we should divide them into two lines."

"Do you think that a unity of command for all of Afghanistan is possible?" I asked.

"Why not?" he asked in return. "We think the day will come when all the forces in Afghanistan will be united."

I knew that Rabbani's Jamiat and the Hizb-i-Islami of Gulbuddin Hekmatyar disagreed in their perception of the United States. Hekmatyar hewed to the fundamentalist idea that there is no real difference between the United States and the Soviet Union in their treatment of Islamic nations. I asked if this view would hurt the Afghan independence struggle. Rabbani answered without a specific reference to Hekmatyar.

"In my view, there is a big difference between the East and West," he said. "We cannot just talk emotionally. There are two worlds: the world of God worshippers and the world of atheists. We believe the enemy fighting in Afghanistan belongs to the other world, the world of atheists, who are against God. On the other hand, we have the world of God worshippers, who have common points with us. These common points bring us closer."

He spoke, as did all Afghans I met, of their determination to fight no matter what the odds against them: "It is a fact that the war will be prolonged. The Russians are launching hundreds of offensives all over Afghanistan. Sometimes very large ones. But we inflict more losses on the enemy than they inflict on us. We have losses of buildings and property, but the real loss of manpower is higher among the enemy. If we had better weapons and could attack larger bases inside Afghanistan we could make the war very expensive for the enemy. Then they might want to leave."

I met the most controversial of the party leaders, Gulbuddin Hekmatyar, at a small, somewhat shabby old house in University Town, a section of Peshawar favored by foreigners and upper-income Pakistanis. Hekmatyar was trimly built, about five feet six, and wore a simple gray Afghan shirt and loose trousers, a khaki jacket over a gray woolen sweater, and a striped brown turban. He had a black beard and a thin, unwrinkled face. He too fingered prayer beads, but while the others tended to project a religious calm, Hekmatyar had an alert, sharp look as if he knew the answer to a question before it was completed. I asked if in view of Soviet strength the war could be won.

"It's true the Russians have won control of the major cities," he said, "but even while they are supported by hundreds of tanks and helicopter gunships, it's not safe for them to pass from one city to another. They are afraid of each and every person in the country. They consider them their enemies."

"But in the process Afghanistan is being destroyed. How long can the people suffer?" I asked.

"With all our sacrifices and sufferings, the nation is still strong," he said. "Instead of asking how long can this nation suffer, we should say this nation cannot be subjugated. Our people know how to live in hardship and how to fight against aggressors."

"Other nations with proud and warlike histories have had to surrender to the Russians," I said. "The Hungarians and Poles, for example. Why should Afghanistan be an exception?"

"A comparison between this nation and others would take a long time to explain. I will just say that our nation considers death the starting of a new life. We believe in God and think that martyrdom is the highest of aspirations. Most of my mujahidin, when they leave for the front, ask me to pray for them to be martyred."

I asked about the differences between his party and the parties of Gailani, Mohammadi, and Mujaddidi. Where others had glossed over differences, Hekmatyar did not hesitate to say why they could not unite: "They belong to the stratum of the nation that was once the rulers. They belong to the stratum that ruled brutally and caused all these calamities. Now the mujahidin have got power. This leadership has been selected by the entire jihad force in Afghanistan. The people you ask about are now going toward extinction. I do not say this from a feeling of grudge or jealousy but this is a fact. They have been tested once and they have failed. It is like a night that cannot return."

Since Hekmatyar, refreshingly, stated his position clearly, I wanted a clear understanding of what he thought of American aid. I said American newspapers told of large amounts of secret aid but the mujahidin did not appear to have sufficient weapons or clothing. I asked how he accounted for this.

"This is also a big question," he said. "What does all this propaganda and these rumors mean, and what is the motive behind them? As you say, you do not see any evidence of this assistance. For our part, we feel the negative influence of these rumors on our jihad. It has proved very detrimental. These rumors mean that our resistance loses its originality, an originality that has attracted the sympathy of the whole world. The world so far has accepted that this jihad is a battle between a small and downtrodden nation against a superpower. But if the world is told that somebody else is involved, and this nation is not fighting by itself, we will lose this sympathy. The condemnation that the Russians receive from the world will be gradually diminished. With all these rumors, the

Russians are justifying their illegal occupation of Afghanistan. They can justify their presence even to their own nation and their own soldiers. They can say, 'Well, the Americans are involved and you have to fight. This is your duty.'"

"Some people have said that you are anti-Western or anti-American. How do you reply to that?" I asked.

"I am a Muslim," he replied. "I have gone to prison to fight for the independence of my people. My aim is a free, independent, Islamic Afghanistan; an Afghanistan which, while keeping its national interests, would have independent relations with other nations with no strings attached. I long for a happy, independent, and vigorous Islamic Afghanistan. All those who respect our independence and territorial integrity, our ideology and our rights, we do not want animosity with them. I am opposed to ignorance, oppression, exploitation, and the enslavement of other nations by any one people."

I persisted: "Americans are terribly shocked by Ayatollah Khomeini's revolution in Iran. He takes a very strong anti-American position. People wonder if there is any relation between your ideas and those of Ayatollah Khomeini."

"I started my struggle when there was no revolution in Iran," he replied. "Our struggle was in the stage of hopefulness before the Ayatollah Khomeini came to power in Iran. You can judge then if we are the same."

Finally, I asked him about the refugees in Pakistan, saying the presence of so many Afghans raised fears among Pakistanis that they would be dragged into a struggle that was not their own.

"There are some who want to trouble the waters to create misunderstandings between the local people and the refugees," he said. "The Russians would like to deprive the refugees of this sanctuary. But those in Pakistan who believe in independence and territorial integrity, and understand the threat posed by the Russian presence in Afghanistan, accept the burden. It is not easy for a nation with its own economic problems to accept millions of refugees. But as far as we have seen, this nation has accepted the refugees with open arms. We are assured the situation will remain the same and are satisfied and grateful for the assistance being provided by the Pakistani nation."

The Camps

According to the Pakistani government, more than three million Afghan refugees are scattered throughout the country. This figure has been used for about five years. The United Nations High Commission for Refugees (UNHCR) puts the number of registered refugees at 2.7 million but concedes that many others are not registered. Thus "more than three million" appears to be a reasonable estimate. About three-quarters of the refugees are in camps in Pakistan's Northwest Frontier and Baluchistan provinces and in tribal territories, crammed as close as possible to the Afghanistan border. This is the largest concentration of refugees anywhere in the world.

Another 1.9 million Afghan refugees are in Iran. In addition, hundreds of thousands of internal refugees have been driven from their village homes to the comparative safety of Soviet-dominated cities. For instance, the Communist government in Kabul estimates the city's population at 1.4 million, as compared to a prewar estimate of 800,000.

The number of casualties is unknown. Many speak of a million killed. The Jamiat uses a figure of 500,000. Some European observers put the figure at 200,000 killed.

The refugees are housed in 350 camps built and administered by the Pakistani government with aid from the UNHCR, the United States, a dozen other countries, and eighteen private agencies. About 25 percent of the refugees are males, mostly elderly men; about 28 percent are women; and the remaining 47 percent are children. Only those registered with the UNHCR are entitled to housing, food, and other assistance. To be registered a family must live where the UNHCR tells it to live. The UNHCR and the Pakistani government want to spread the refugees over as wide an area as possible, because some locations—for instance near Peshawar, with its job opportunities, bazaars, and medical facilities—are saturated with refugees. Similarly, some tribal areas now have more refugees than original inhabitants, leading to fights about grazing rights and water.

Many thousands of refugees, perhaps too stubborn or simply too frightened to pack up and move, have been in Pakistan for years and are still not registered. Under the best of circumstances a family must wait for months to be registered even if it tries to comply with regulations. In fact, Afghans say it is impossible to get registered at all without paying a bribe.

Refugee tents on barren land without adequate water or sanitation facilities. One-third of Afghanistan's prewar population has fled to Pakistan and Iran.

If a family is registered it receives a tent, which it soon transforms into a mud-walled hut, and is entitled to food, water, blankets, and medical attention. Weekly rations include eight pounds of wheat, a half pound of edible oil, a half pound of powdered milk, five ounces of sugar, and less than an ounce of tea. However, according to foreign medical and humanitarian workers, while the refugees generally receive the wheat and oil, they seldom, perhaps never, get the milk, sugar, and tea. They are also supposed to get a monthly allowance from Pakistan of 50 rupees per person, with a family ceiling of 350 rupees. (In 1985 the Pakistani rupee was worth close to seven cents. In 1986 its value had dropped to less than six cents.) This is the principal Pakistani expenditure on the refugees. The foreign observers say the refugees might actually receive only one or two monthly allotments over an entire year.

The refugee camps are located on barren wasteland. The refugees are supposed to get about six and a half gallons of fresh water per person every day, but more often than not there are no, or too few, tube wells, and trucks that are supposed to bring water come too late or not at all. Instead, the families get water from a river or an irrigation canal, just as they do in Afghanistan. But back home women from only two or three families use a particular spot, while in a refugee camp hundreds of women compete for the water. A canal may run through a camp containing tens of thousands of people and thousands of horses, donkeys, goats, and other animals. It soon becomes a sewer of waste, germs, and parasites.

Even if the authorities dig latrines, they become foul and the people choose to use the fields, just as they do at home. But empty ground is scarce around the camps. The same ground is also used to dump rubbish from houses. There is no natural drainage, and wastewater collects in stagnant and muddy pools. When there are heavy monsoon rains the pollution washes into the ditches.

The refugees are wracked with diarrhea, tuberculosis, malaria, measles, tetanus, typhus, whooping cough, impetigo, skin parasites, respiratory infections, the eye disease trachoma, anemia, and just about anything else a doctor can diagnose. One foreign relief committee found a 21 percent incidence of malaria in a single camp. Perhaps a quarter of all infant deaths are the result of measles. One out of every five children born alive is dead by the age of five.

Women: Suffering and Despair

Most of the women in the camps—estimates range as high as 90 percent—suffer from depression or some other mental illness. A refugee camp is particularly hard on an Afghan woman brought up under the *purdah* system. She must not be seen by any male except a member of her family. In Afghanistan even the poorest family will have several rooms in a walled compound, so that a woman can wander around and sit in the sun. There is another family nearby to whom she probably is related, offering a chance to exchange visits. There is a secluded place by a stream to wash clothes and enjoy the company of other women. Above all, there are men nearby to protect and comfort her and to buy food from the bazaar or deal with tradesmen. But in a camp a woman is alone, confined most of the day in a stifling hut. Her men may be in the jihad or working in Peshawar, or perhaps far away in the oil fields of the Gulf States. Worst of all, her husband, brothers, and perhaps her father may be dead. It is not unusual for one man to care not only for his own family but for the family of one or two brothers as well.

It is impossible for a foreign male to plumb the depths of the suffering and despair of Afghan women, whether in the refugee camps or amid the shattered society of their homeland. An American nurse, Diane Price of Grand Forks, North Dakota, was trying to help. She heard of Dr. Robert Simon of Los Angeles, who had organized the International Medical Corps to aid the Afghans, and volunteered to travel into Afghanistan to work in temporary clinics for women. A year later she returned to Pakistan to teach at a recently established school for paramedics that Dr. Simon had established near Peshawar. I met her there.

Diane, twenty-nine, was a nurse practitioner—a registered nurse with two years of added training in diagnosis and treatment. She had dark hair, pale skin, and direct, animated eyes that seemed to project the intensity of her thoughts. "When I found out what was going on in Afghanistan I had to come," she said. "People are having to crawl to the border to get medical care and many die before they get it. I think it's one of the most desperate situations in the world."

Two nurses made the trip. The other was Jane Orlando, from Dallas, whose husband was a retired Air Force colonel. Before starting into Afghanistan the nurses visited women in the refugee camps. Diane Price found the horror even worse than she had expected. "Women would sit before us and tell us stories of seeing things that were atrocious. Mujahidin in a village put between two Russian tanks and pulled apart. Mothers and children pulled out of their homes. When the mothers wouldn't tell where the mujahidin were, the Russians would pour kerosene over the child and set the child on fire. They would shoot the mother later. Story after story like that. Often, they said, the Russians would bayonet pregnant mothers in the abdomen. The mujahidin brought us one woman who could no longer speak or react emotionally. She told us about five women who had been taken up in a helicopter by the Russians and raped numerous times. Three of them were thrown out of the helicopter while it was still high in the air. The others were brought back to their village as a warning not to help the mujahidin."

"Do you think the mujahidin were steering people to you to tell those atrocity stories?" I asked.

"No, these were very poor village people," she replied. "What we heard was from their hearts. I have no doubt about that. They were not making up these stories. It was as if the women now had another woman they could verbalize with. It seemed the main help we could give was psychological. The women had no one to talk to, no one to really turn to."

It took Diane and Jane four days of riding on horses and a camel, but mostly walking, to reach an area in Afghanistan's Paktia Province where they began their work. "When a tent was put up for a clinic, and we set the medicines out, we were just amazed," she continued. "We started seeing between 110 and 150 women and children every day. Many of them had walked a day and a half to see us. Some were barefoot. Many had a baby in their arms and another holding their dresses. Many had diseases that were beyond treatment. They were spitting up blood; they were passing blood vaginally; they had pains in their abdomen. When we went to examine them we didn't even have to feel their abdomens. We saw the huge masses of tumors. We would assume they were either uterine or ovarian cancers. At that point the only thing we could do was to refer them to Peshawar, but we knew they would never make that journey. It's a difficult journey and many times there were no men to take them along. They couldn't travel by themselves.

"We were seeing respiratory diseases, many cases of tuberculosis, malaria, and a lot of skin diseases. We were just appalled. I think the worst thing was the malnutrition of the children. The first child we saw made us entirely speechless, mainly out of frustration. The grandmother brought the child, a little girl, three years old. She had never had solid food in her life—breast-fed the whole time. She had no reflexes. Her pupils would not react to light. She couldn't swallow any more. It was very sad. We had no oral dehydration salts with us. We had one bottle of multivitamins left. We gave that to the grandmother and we sent that child home. To die.

"There's such a desperate need there for women medical workers that it's almost incomprehensible. The women need someone to examine them and they can't have male examiners. If the women were treated earlier, the cases that were turning up as fatal might have been cured or arrested. We were seeing women in their twenties with blood pressure of 180 over 120. The normal blood pressure is 120 over 70. Women were coming to us and saying, 'My husband has been killed.' They would tell us of things they had seen and say, 'I don't sleep at night.' Women who were in their twenties or early thirties looked like they were sixty. I'm sure it's a very rough life, even without war. But the war has exacerbated the whole conditions of living for them. We could feel a bit of what they went through all the time. We would often be put in a dark room, in a corner, and left there. We worked from six in the morning till nine at night. Then we would go to a room. It would be full of men who would stop talking. We would go over and sit in a corner and then they would start talking again. They would turn around and look at us and then turn back and talk to one another.

"On the other hand the women were so kind to us. They would bring us walnuts and pinole nuts that they had to climb in the high mountains to get. They were so glad we were there, just thankful someone was there to listen to them. They would ask me sometimes, 'Don't the Americans care, don't they know what's going on?' I was at a loss. I could say: 'Yes, we care,' but I knew there was so little we could do. When you have a woman with a child who is starving to death in front of you, asking for your help, and you can't do anything it is so frustrating. I don't know if there is any answer, but I do know we can't stop trying."

The worst camps are the ones where the refugees are not registered, meaning they cannot draw rations or seek what little medical attention there is. One such camp is called Kachagarai. It is on the outskirts of Peshawar, just off the main highway leading to the Khyber Pass, and across a smaller road from a registered camp of the same name. Foreign dignitaries are often taken to the Kachagarai registered camp for a look at a symbolic hospital. No one visits the unregistered camp across the road. Foreign medical workers say that in winter as many as a dozen children may die in a single night there, in the huts. The heat of summer is as deadly as the cold of winter. As many as a dozen a day may die of diarrhea and dehydration.

The site is close to the International Medical Corps training center where Diane Price helped teach medics for service in Afghanistan. In her spare time she used to go into the unregistered camp to do whatever she could. "What I am seeing," she said, "is that many organizations are trying to bring medical care to the area, but most of the care has been for the men. In the refugee camps you have 75 percent women and children and a lot of times they are not being treated. There isn't money to buy medicines. There isn't medical personnel, especially female medical personnel. It's of epidemic proportions, what's going on with women. It's like the women are a forgotten culture. I find this very, very disturbing."

The Official Rebuttal

Officials of the UNHCR and some of the voluntary organizations have an explanation for the failings of the refugee programs. Off the record, they say they cannot give the refugees greater services than those available to the population at large. They also point out that infant mortality in the camps, as bad as it is, is about the same as for all of Pakistan. The United Nations and private officials admit that conditions are horrible in the unregistered camps, but they say the only way to pressure the refugees into dispersing is by withholding help.

Moreover, many of these officials are international bureaucrats, with sufficiently broad experience to convince them that corruption in the camps is no worse than it is in Pakistani society as a whole. They say Pakistanis too must pay bribes for almost any government service. They also say the refugees themselves cheat by holding double registration cards and by selling some of their aid on the black market. They say many refugee families are better off than they pretend to be, with their men working in urban areas or in the Gulf States, while their women and children are cared for at the expense of the United Nations. One UNHCR official frankly admitted that rations and supplies actually received by the refugees were below subsistence levels. He said that this was to prevent welfare dependency and that the refugees have to be kept discontented with life in Pakistan because they must accept the fact that they have no permanent home there. Someday, he said, they will have to return to their ruined villages.

One UNHCR official advanced what he appeared to regard as conclusive evidence that the assistance program was going along pretty well, and that criticism by outsiders had little justification: He pointed out that there had never been a riot or demonstration about food or living conditions in the camps. As evidence that an even balance had been achieved between the needs of the refugees and the sensibilities of the Pakistanis, he cited the fact that there had never been a clash between refugees and the local population. There had been many fights and killings, he said, but those arose from the usual passions of Afghan society—women and honor. It was not, he said, a matter of "us against them."

What he said about the lack of tension was true. In the United States there are perpetual animosities, jealousies, and quarrels between refugees from Cuba and the people of Florida. In Thailand refugees from Cambodia are kept behind barbed wire. In Lebanon Palestinian refugees are blamed for touching off the civil war that has devastated the country.

Why is the situation of the Afghan refugees different? For one thing, their leaders are aware of the need to maintain good relations with the Pakistanis and hesitate to press even valid complaints to the point of confrontation. Then there is the nature of the refugees themselves—their elemental hardiness, their ability to get along on little, and their ability to bear pain. They don't make great demands on the host society. Their pride as individuals makes it an affront to their honor to stand with their hands out as beggars. An Afghan sees his capacity to take care of his family and the families of his relatives as a test of his manhood. Finally, there is the inspiration of the jihad. Men, women, and children have an inner assurance that their hardships are part of a greater goal.

Sacrificing for God

At the end of 1985, when I returned to New York for a rest, four Afghan children were flown in for medical help. They were two girls, Zarmina, four, who lost her right leg when her village was bombed, and Utmarkhail, ten, whose right arm was destroyed by a shell from a tank; and two boys, Safihullah, seven, who had lost a hand, and Mozafar, ten, who had lost an arm. The Free Afghanistan Alliance, a privately financed voluntary group of Americans and Afghans based in Cambridge, Massachusetts, had brought the children to the United States to receive artificial limbs.

Charles Brockunier, an import-export merchant who had come to know and admire the Afghans in their days of peace, had made many trips to Pakistan, searching the refugee camps near Peshawar to find children who needed special help. He had patiently dealt with the paperwork involved in getting these four on a plane to start what the alliance hoped would be a continuing program. I met him and the four children at Kennedy airport with a *New York Times* reporter, Sara Rimer. "We want the West to see what is happening in Afghanistan," Charles said. "Our only motive is to stop the war and end the suffering. There are thousands of children like these in the camps."

The children were accompanied by an uncle of three of them and by Dr. Hashmatullah Mujaddidi, a younger brother of Sibghatullah Mujaddidi, head of the National Libertion Front. "The children are here as part of the jihad," he told us. "Whatever we have, we sacrifice for God. When a man loses a son, he sends a second son. When he loses that one, he sends a third son. When he loses that one, he sends the next son. And the next and the next and the next. We have a lot of people who have lost all their sons. Only the mother and father are left in a refugee camp." Dr. Mujaddidi said ninety-four members of his own family had died in the decades-long struggle, most in the slaughter of the Taraki-Amin regime.

We went to a house in a residential section of New York that had been converted into a community center and mosque for Afghans living in the city. There was not a whimper from Zarmina as her uncle carried her from the plane swaddled in his blanket, took her in the car to the mosque, and gave her something to eat. The other children were equally stoic. After they had rested, Ms. Rimer asked them what they knew of the jihad. Utmarkhail said all Afghans must return to their country to fight. "The people who did this to me are unbelievers," added Safi-hullah, pulling up the sleeve of his baggy white shirt to show his missing hand. "I have lost my arm," said Mozafar, "but I can fight with my other arm. The Russians did this to me. I want to go back and fight them."

Convoy to Mazar

··········

5

At the end of March 1985 I received a police permit to remain in Pakistan for six months and a temporary press card to use while my long-term visa worked its way through the bureaucracy. I felt free to plan a long trip and told representatives of several parties I wanted to go somewhere north of the Hindu Kush. Only Massoud Khalili of Jamiat-i-Islami offered help. He said a large convoy of men and arms would leave for Mazar-i-Sharif, near the Soviet border, as soon as word was received that the snows had melted, opening the route across the mountains. That, he said, was expected in a few weeks.

To help pass the time I found someone to sponsor me at the British Council Library in Peshawar, where I discovered a cache of British histories of the Afghan wars, studies on Afghan society, and old accounts of travelers. Later, as I joined those ranks of travelers, I was impressed at how, now that the modern overlay of factories, schools, hospitals, roads, telecommunications, and government offices has been stripped away by war, the Afghanistan that has persisted for centuries is revealed underneath. The continuity of small customs and attitudes seems to indicate that there was always a special Afghan nation and always will be one.

In 1856 an English translation was published of the *Caravan Journeys and Wanderings* of Joseph Pierre Ferrier, a French traveler who meandered through Afghanistan in about 1846. A meal, he wrote, "consisted of black bread, sour milk, and an uneatable ragout—grains of maize cooked and crushed, with small pieces of bread, floating in boiling and rancid grease." Although I had not come across a dish with the same ingredients, I found food floating in grease all too familiar and equally inedible.

Ferrier also wrote:

One of the greatest annoyances in traveling over these immense solitudes is the complete uncertainty which always exists as to the distance that must be accomplished before the next halt. The inhabitants . . . divided the time in their own manner; from one prayer to another; from one meal to another; till time to sleep, or time to rise; and as every one calculates distance by the power of his own legs, or the speed of his own horse, it followed that there exists no fixed idea either of time or distance. I have often travelled five or six parasangs when the Afghans had assured me that it was only a short gallop to the place to which I proposed to go.

This was an echo of my own trip to Jegdalek, with the mujahidin telling us our destination was near. Subsequent journeys would reinforce what Ferrier had observed 140 years ago.

He continued:

Scarcely had I succeeded in settling myself in my tent when these ragged warriors crowded in upon me, close as herrings in a tub. . . . I was persecuted by a continuous cross fire of the most stupid and impertinent questions. "What are you? Where are you going? Where do you come from? What is your rank? What do you want to do? Are you rich? Is your country more fertile than ours? Have you good melons there?" . . . These fellows never for a moment considered they were annoying me. It was a duty of hospitality to keep me company.

Another echo. Many a time when I wanted to be alone to think, admire the scenery, or write my notes, I would find myself surrounded by similar "ragged warriors." But at least I was spared most of the questions. The interpreters who accompanied me did not want to be bothered with the endless repetition and simply stored my first answers, repeating them to the next group without involving me.

Almost anyone who has written about the Afghans has commented on their inveterate petty thievery, saying nothing is safe and one must always be on guard. One might be tempted to dismiss this as the excessive fears of rich foreigners among people who are mostly poor and sometimes hungry. But it is a failing to which the Afghans readily admit and against which I was warned. Ferrier discovered the same thing:

"After all, the Afghans, to do them justice, never pretend to be the possessors of great virtues—they never praise themselves for anything but their courage; and if they hear of a bad action or a great crime, they claim at once, with the consciousness of their own sentiments, that is Afghan work."

In 1857 Henry Walter Bellew, a British civil servant, was sent on a leisurely tour of Afghanistan to observe political and social conditions. His recollections were first published in 1920.

During his visit, a delegation of mullahs charged that the visiting English were defiling the country with their presence and demanded that the local chief get rid of them. The chief replied that the British "although undoubted heretics were nevertheless 'people of the Book' and as such deserving of consideration." That was the same reasoning Professor Rabbani had used in explaining to me why the Western nations were not to be equated with the Soviet nonbelievers.

Bellew entered Afghanistan through the Kurram valley, the route now blocked by the Communist position at Chamkany. He spoke of Afghan soldiers sent ahead to keep the road open for his party:

> The men seemed none the worse for the exposure to the cold during the preceding nights, and as we passed their little parties we found them in merry converse and high spirits round blazing camp fires. . . . The hardiness of these soldiers is really astonishing. With scanty and threadbare clothing, poor and flimsy tent accommodations, and no commissariat whatever, they seldom fail to make themselves comfortable in their own fashion and in their bivouacs, and they are always found ready for the work required at their hands.

He might very well have been writing about the mujahidin 127 years later.

On my trip to see the missile attack on Chamkany I first experienced the effusive way the Afghans greet one another and their mumbled exchange of ritual phrases. Bellew described the same scene:

> Wali Mohammed of Ghazni . . . expressed great delight at meeting us again, declared that he had never ceased to pray for our safety and welfare, and was most pressing in his inquiries after our present health. When he gained breath after a dozen repetitions of, "Are you well? Are you quite well? Are you perfectly well? You are welcome," which he gabbled over with the greatest volubility to each of us, never waiting or caring for a reply, he told us the Sardar . . . and a new escort were encamped at the next stage.

Also abiding through the years is the Afghan taste for great quantities of sugar in tea. Bellew found the tea "very refreshing, although its delicate flavor was marred by an excessive addition of sugar."

At Nargasay, at my first meal with the mujahidin in the field, I was struck by the bedraggled cloth on which the food was served and the chicken bones that still adorned it next morning. A similar sight had impressed Bellew: "Once on a time . . . this cloth, it is presumed, gloried in a snow white and spotless surface of purity. On the present occasion, however, its dust begrimed, dirty, foot impressed, greasy fingered, spotted and stained surface gave ample evidence of its long continued service and utter guilelessness of the restorative effect of soap and water." I was to meet the incarnation of that cloth, and be reminded of the Afghans' disdain for any scientific theory of germs, at many a meal.

Travelers have often noted what appears to be the firm Afghan conviction that all foreigners are doctors with medicines to cure all illnesses. Among the first to make this observation was Charles Masson, a deserter from the East India Company army who traveled in Afghanistan in the 1830s and 1840s: "I asserted my ignorance of the art of healing, but was not credited; and finding it impossible to avoid prescribing, or to be considered unkind, I took upon myself to recommend such simple appliances as might be useful, while they could not harm. I particularly enjoined cleanliness, which in all their maladies seemed to be neglected from principle."

When I went to Jegdalek an old man coming in the opposite direction along the trail stopped me and held out his wrist. Mohammed Gul, the interpreter, laughed and said the man wanted me to diagnose his ailments and prescribe medicine. Doctors throughout Asia diagnose a patient by feeling his pulse, hence the man extending his wrist to me. During our interviews with Jegdalek group commanders, I was twice asked for medicines.

Preparations

While preparing for the trip to Mazar-i-Sharif, I asked a British doctor at one of the private refugee organizations to suggest medicines to take along. He said he would have no part in civilians giving way to the Afghan importunities for medicine and advice, but I assured him I did not want to play doctor and was thinking only of myself. We agreed, realistically, that if I were wounded or seriously injured, with bones broken, there was nothing to be done short of trying to get to a doctor, however long that might take. All we could do was put together an elementary medical kit. He wrote a note of supplies and instructions. First and most important were three varieties of pills for diarrhea: Lomotil, "as a symptomatic treatment with one tablet to be taken every hour"; Septran D.S., "a general antibiotic also good for chest infections, with one tablet to be taken twice a day"; and Flagyl, "for bloody diarrhea and diarrhea failing to respond to Septran, with two tablets three times a day for five days." Next came Penicillin V tablets for skin infections, in case I fell and got some bad cuts. There was also an antibiotic skin ointment for cuts and bruises, along with bandages, Mercurochrome, and aspirin.

He also suggested I take along a good supply of chloroquine and take two tablets a week as a preventive dose against malaria. Here he was willing to relax his injunction that I should not try to play doctor. If I saw someone who seemed to be having a bad attack of malaria, he said, someone shaking severely as if he were freezing, I might give him four tablets to be taken at once.

On April 9, 1985, Massoud Khalili came to Green's Hotel to tell me that the convoy was ready to go. He would return shortly to pick me up. My bags were packed; my medicines were ready; and I had even had the foresight to cash travelers checks in case, as it turned out, I received notice after the banks were closed. I had told Massoud that I would pay all my expenses, including the cost of an interpreter, but he insisted that my trip was a matter of Afghan hospitality and that Jamiat must pay. We did make one exception; I would pay for the horse. I had cashed dollar checks for about 15,000 rupees, enough for the horse and what I thought would be many times more than my needs for incidental expenses. If there were extraordinary costs, I knew I could reimburse Jamiat on my return.

All that remained was to store my clothing, books, typewriter, and other excess gear with Green's. I also called an American official asking him to do me the favor of sending someone to the hotel the next day to return some books to the British Council Library. I had already informed another official where I might go and with which party, but not when, since I did not know myself. It was not a question of the officials' approving or disapproving, but we knew there would be inquiries from Washington if something happened to an American in Afghanistan. It would make things much easier for the American consulate in Peshawar if it had some clues as to my whereabouts should a search be necessary. I really did have books to go back to the library, but I also knew that my phone request and remark that I would be away for about eight weeks would be passed along as notice of my departure.

Nothing in Afghanistan goes as expected. It was not until 10 P.M. that Massoud came to Green's and took me to his office for final instructions to Shafiq, the young man who would be my interpreter. He said he wanted to be sure that Shafiq, whom I had met briefly a few weeks earlier, fully understood what was expected of him. Shafiq was clean shaven and looked even more boyish than his eighteen years. He had learned some English in Mazar-i-Sharif, where his family lived, but left school just before he turned sixteen, conscription age. Zabihullah, the former Jamiat commander in Mazar, as the Afghans call both the province and the city, had sent him to Peshawar to perfect his English so he might serve as a guide for journalists who traveled north. Shafiq had done remarkably well in his studies at a Peshawar school organized by the American Center, a U.S. government institution.

The choice of an interpreter is the most crucial part of planning a long trip into Afghanistan. I told Massoud I hoped to find someone who would do more than just translate my questions and the replies. My earlier trips had left me with a feeling of isolation in an alien environment. I needed someone who would tell me without being asked what people were saying around me, where we were, and what we were to do. Massoud, with his usual helpfulness, had searched the Jamiat organization and found Shafiq, who he thought was just the man. Massoud spoke to Shafiq and all seemed well. As it turned out, Shafiq had entirely different plans and would eventually leave me stranded in Mazar-i-Sharif.

Departure

Shafiq, I, and a young man who was the representative in Peshawar for Jamiat commanders in Mazar left in an enclosed jeep. I was told to stretch out on one of the seats, cover myself with a blanket, and not budge or say a word. We kept the lights off and went along for hours without being stopped. Finally, inevitably, the back door opened, a flashlight flickered around, and there was a lot of talk. Shafiq reached under my seat for my rucksack and a small leather bag that contained my camera. Eventually a bribe was offered and accepted and we sped on. Shafiq said that the two police were impressed by the camera and wanted to keep it but were persuaded to give it back. I looked in the camera bag and discovered they had taken a large flashlight I had bought for the trip. When I asked Shafiq how much the bribe was he said it did not matter and would not say more.

About three in the morning we turned off to a large camp of tents to sleep. At dawn we climbed into a huge, open-backed trailer truck and were taken to another camp. This apparently was the main Jamiat base in tribal territory. Scores of mujahidin clambered over the sides of the truck, almost crushing me beneath them, and we drove for hours, stopping briefly for pieces of bread to be thrown up to us for breakfast and again to fix a flat tire. The mujahidin, for all their hardiness, are not used to cars and trucks and the motion often makes some of them sick. Several threw up over the sides and one inside the truck, next to me. "We have problems in our jihad," Shafiq said, "but we accept everything for Allah."

Late in the morning we arrived at Miram Shah, a large market town that had developed, like Parachinar, as a transportation hub and supply point for mujahidin entering and leaving Afghanistan. I was hustled, as usual, into the courtyard of a house. The mujahidin scattered to prepare for the trip and soon returned with bundles of rags and old clothing that they tore apart and sewed into packs for themselves. I joined them on a wide, flat roof. They cut, folded, and stitched, laughing and sharing advice. One proudly showed off his handiwork. What had been a man's European tweed jacket was now a pack with a flap on top and shoulder straps. After lunch they disappeared and returned carrying plastic bags. Apparently the Jamiat commissariat had issued them a suit of long johns, socks, and Pakistani boots.

Buying a Horse and Getting a Name

Shafiq returned to say my horse had been bought and took me to inspect it. I looked at it, patted it, and said it seemed fine, not that I had the faintest idea of what a good horse should look like. I asked its name and Shafiq said it had none. The Afghans do not humanize animals. In their eyes, only humans are linked to God: to view or treat animals like humans is a form of sacrilege. Still, they bedeck their animals with charms and gewgaws. Blue and red woolen pompons hung under my horse's ears, and a double strand of coral-colored beads were looped around his neck. I decided to call him Coral Beads.

The mujahidin said the horse cost 5,000 Pakistani rupees, at that time about $310, and that it needed new shoes, which would cost the equivalent of another $2.20. I gave them the money plus another 5,000

Once I was given the Afghan name of Ghulam and later learned it meant "servant" or "slave." Happily, on subsequent trips I was known as Jan, meaning "Dear," and Gul Mohammed, meaning "Flower of Mohammed."

rupees, which they exchanged for 39,000 in Afghan currency, called Afghanis. As we stood there Shafiq said he would have to think of an Afghan name for me. I said it would be hard for me to respond to some new name, but he said it was necessary because the mujahidin could not pronounce my name, even if they could remember it. Besides, he said, it would often be necessary to call out to me and yet risky to advertise the fact that I was a foreigner. With an Afghan name, as well as an Afghan costume, I would blend in better with my surroundings. Several mujahidin who had gathered around came up with suggestions. But Shafiq said he had a good name: Ghulam. Almost all Afghan names mean something. They are chosen by parents as being auspicious and are generally linked to God. For instance, Mohammed Gul, the name of my previous interpreter, meant "Muhammed's Flower," and was considered a particularly lovely name. I asked Shafiq what Ghulam meant, but he said it had no meaning.

From then on I was Ghulam. Mujahidin called out that name as I passed. Months later, when I returned to Peshawar, I happened to mention to an Afghan scholar that I was known as Ghulam in Afghanistan. "What else?" he asked. "Ghulam means servant and is used with another name, such as Ghulam Mohammed, meaning the servant of the Prophet. Such a name is used to dedicate a newborn child to the service of God. Ghulam is never used alone." Someone else suggested that "slave" was a better translation of the name. So there I was, all during the trip, being called slave.

Dinner was rice and stew. I took some rice with three fingers of my right hand and, before raising it to my mouth, shook my hand a bit to drop off the loose bits. Shafiq, sitting next to me, said he would have to get me a spoon. He said it was bad manners to drop anything that my fingers had touched back into the dish. Then he asked about Americans and Europeans who, so he heard, drank beer and wine with their meals. He said this must be bad, or the Koran would not have forbidden alcoholic drinks. I said it depended on the kind and quantity of the drink, and that in some cultures drinks served a nutritional function. He repeated that the Koran said it was bad. He was beginning to annoy me but I let the matter drop.

After dinner everyone went to the roof for group prayers, standing, bowing, kneeling, and touching their foreheads to the ground in unison, with one of the mujahidin leading them as mullah. Obviously, this group took the practices of Islam seriously. Later I asked Shafiq about something that had been troubling me. I knew that in about four weeks the Islamic month of Ramazan would start, the time when Muslims refrain from eating or even letting a drop of water pass their lips from sunrise to sunset. During an entire lunar month much of the Islamic world comes to a halt, with people drowsing most of the day to escape the pangs of hunger and thirst. It would take us three weeks to reach Mazar. I asked Shafiq what would happen then. "We will stay there, of course," he said. "The mujahidin will want to spend the holy month of Ramazan with their families in their villages." I had hoped to stay just two weeks and then return, for a total journey of eight weeks. If Ramazan meant I could not travel the journey would stretch to about three months.

After lunch the next day I saw some of the men with Kalashnikovs and other rifles. I had been allowed to leave the seclusion of the house the day before to inspect the horse and thought my movements would not be as restricted as in Parachinar and Teri Mangal. I got my camera and went to take pictures of the distribution of arms.

Distributing World War I 303 Enfield rifles at Miram Shah. An Afghan commander accused the Pakistanis of substituting these old guns for modern weapons paid for with covert American aid.

A Question of Guns

Although the transfer of foreign arms is technically covert, it has been going on so long and involves such quantities that the process is well known to diplomats and journalists in Pakistan. Most of the supplies come from China and are flown to Pakistani military bases. Other supplies arrive by sea and are received by the Pakistani military without the intervention of civilian officials. The supplies are retained in Pakistani military warehouses and once the Pakistanis decide which party will get what—that part of the process has never been clarified—the delivery takes place at a designated point.

In Miram Shah the men were called two or three squads at a time and lined up in a field. Apparently the plan was to call them forward one at a time to get a weapon handed out from a small brick building. But as soon as the first name was called a whole squad would rush forward, pushing, shoving, and grabbing what it could. The commanders and squad leaders pushed and shoved back, amid shouting, loud complaints, and laughter. The melee decided who got what. The most prized weapon was the Chinese-made Kalashnikov semiautomatic rifle. Others got old 303 Enfield rifles. Some were given a plastic Chinese mine that they would have to carry all the way to Mazar-i-Sharif.

I was surprised to see the bolt-operated Enfields and took one from a mujahid for close examination. A stamp of the British crown was under the bolt, along with an inscription stating that the gun had been manufactured in 1914. I looked at others and found dates of 1915, 1916, and 1918. In short, they seemed to be weapons from World War I. But possibly they were copies of old weapons. The Pakistani gunsmiths in Dara are famous for their ability to duplicate any gun, down to the British crown and date of manufacture. The steel they use, however, is never as hard as in the original weapons, and after a thousand or so rounds the barrels deteriorate and their accuracy diminishes. Whether well-worn World War I British rifles or Dara imitations, they were equally bad guns.

This was an illustration of the puzzle of American and other foreign military aid for the Afghans. How could reports from Washington tell of millions of dollars in aid and yet, here in Miram Shah, the weapons being put into the hands of the mujahidin include such antiques?

Abdul Wahab, the commander of our group, spoke no English, but through Shafiq I was able to ask how he explained the distribution of such poor weapons. He blamed it on the Pakistanis: "They keep the good guns and give us these old things from their warehouses. We take them as protection for our convoy on the way north. But they are useless in fighting the Russians."

An Army without Ranks

Abdul Wahab was thirty-one, five feet nine, slim, with a small black beard and a prominent nose. Most of the time he had been away from the courtyard, but when he was there he was always busy, conferring with the squad leaders or doing paper work with clerks. He was the epitome of a tough, resourceful, mujahidin commander. In another army he might have had the bars of a captain on his shoulders, but the Afghans, with their intense individuality and their inability to tolerate superiority in others, have organized their army without a show of uniforms or a clear designation of rank. A man is called a commander if he has ten men under him or 100. He may be called a general commander if he has a number of groups under him, but this too is hazy. A general commander of one party might control many groups in a large valley, but someone else of the same party above him can also be called a general commander. Leaders are distinguished not by symbols on their shoulders but by how they act and what they are able to accomplish—in battle or, as with Abdul Wahab in Miram Shah, in getting a large number of unruly Afghans armed, fed, and across the mountains to Mazar.

Back at the house Abdul Wahab took my camera, saying he would return it after we passed the last Pakistani checkpoint. We were all in a sudden rush, but I managed to send Shafiq to the bazaar to buy a little Chinese-made flashlight before we crowded into the back of a Toyota pickup truck and started off. Shafiq took my glasses and gave them to a mujahid to carry until we crossed the border. By now I knew the drill: I should be as inconspicuous as possible and not say a word to reveal my identity. We drove across a plain to the final Pakistani checkpoint where there was an open parking space. As we got out nobody said anything to me, and I just stood looking around to see what was happening.

I Am Discovered

A man with a large mustache but no beard came up and said pleasantly, in English, "Hello. How are you? Do you like our country?" I didn't reply but I knew what was happening. He was a Pakistani plainclothes officer. Was my long-planned, long-awaited trip going to be aborted now?

"You're not Afghan," the Pakistani said. "Why are you here?" I did not speak. "Come with me," he continued. "We will have some tea and talk." I did not move. "Come with me," he said more peremptorily, taking me by the wrist and pulling me. I twisted my arm free, still silent.

Abdul Wahab intervened. As he and the Pakistani walked away, Shafiq whispered to me, "Sit on the ground." By now there was a lot of commotion. The plainclothesman had seen some bags under a blanket. He pulled the blanket part way back and began rummaging through one of them. It was Shafiq's. Mine, a red German mountain climber's ruck-sack, was still underneath. He pulled off the rest of the blanket and began searching it. Shafiq, standing nearby, told me not to worry. I noticed what appeared to be other border officials in the distance, and mujahidin commanders earnestly talking to them. The first policeman found something in my bag and went into a hut, with Abdul Wahab following. Shafiq told me to get up and sit on the ground at the side of the field. Four mujahidin took up positions in front of me. Through their legs I could see the original policeman coming toward me. Now he had a Kalashnikov in his hand, a pistol at his waist, and two bandoliers of bullets draped over his shoulders. He started to circle around the mujahidin to reach me. They shifted to face him.

Anyone familiar with the mujahidin knows they mean business with guns in their hands. When confronted, they shoot to kill—and they believe in getting in the first shot. Apparently the policeman was well aware of this. As he walked away, Shafiq told me to get up and walk toward the border, marked by a low chain across the path. I did, and soon there were mujahidin on all sides of me. We stepped across the chain and, for the first time, I looked at them. They were grinning broadly: Great fun.

I was still tense as we piled into another Toyota pickup and drove along a dry gravel riverbed with low cliffs on both sides. Shafiq began to criticize me: I should have dyed my hair black and used contact lenses to change the color of my eyes. I should not have left my press card in my bag—a bad mistake, because the policeman found it and it proved I was an American. He said the policeman had demanded a bribe of 5,000 rupees and they had to bargain, eventually paying 1,500 rupees, or 500 for each of the three policemen at the post. That was a great deal of money. He said I should repay it to Jamiat.

I was too drained to argue, though I thought they should not have left me standing there to be so easily picked out. But I did explain that it is never correct for a journalist to disguise himself. I said we were often

Chinese plastic antivehicle mines being tied in rope nets to be carried by pack animals.

accused of being spies or CIA agents, and the use of subterfuges might be taken as proof that we were not what we claimed to be. In fact, I said, I deliberately used a red mountain climber's rucksack, as evidence, should I be accused of being a spy or a combatant of some sort, that I was just a plain and simple civilian. That was true. Many years earlier I had been taken prisoner by a guerrilla force in Central Africa. I happened to be wearing canvas jungle shoes. One of the guerrillas pointed to them as evidence that I was a foreign mercenary and demanded that I be shot on the spot. Fortunately less impetuous heads prevailed, but it was a lesson I could not forget.

We came to a low, narrow canyon with several teahouses and scooped out caves where the vehicles could be hidden. This was Jawara, the most important mujahidin base for offensive operations against Khost and Gardez in Paktia Province, and for the general defense of supply routes into central Afghanistan. I was given tea but otherwise ignored as Abdul Wahab and his men busied themselves for the journey. From the trucks that had followed us came tin containers of ammunition, wooden boxes of mortar shells, dozens of Chinese mines, plastic tubes enclosing antitank grenades, bundles of rocket charges for these grenades, mortars, several Dashika heavy machine guns with large tripod mounts, a shoulder-operated recoilless rifle (actually a small cannon), and bales of rough gray blankets and khaki jackets. Some of the men divided the unloaded supplies into portions and tied them into pairs of wide-woven rope nets that could be lifted up and slung over the back of an animal, with an even balance on either side. Others opened some of the ammunition tins and packed the clips of their Kalashnikovs and the belts and feeder boxes for light machine guns.

Zabihullah's Unexplained Death

Shafiq introduced me to Alam Khan, a general commander for all Jamiat forces in Balkh Province, bordering the Soviet Union. Balkh is part of the region that the Greeks, after the incursion of Alexander the Great, called Bactria. Mazar-i-Sharif is the provincial capital. My visit came at a troubled time for the Jamiat in Mazar. Their commander there, Zabihullah, one of the great hopes for the resistance in the north, had been killed the previous December when a mine exploded under his jeep. The Jamiat command in Peshawar did not believe his death was an accident of war. Zabihullah, whose real name was Abdul Qadir, had been in his early thirties and was once a student activist with Professor

Rabbani and the Young Muslims at Kabul University. After Daoud seized power Zabihullah fled to Pakistan in the general exodus and joined the abortive insurgency of 1975. Like other young men trained by Rabbani, he worked for the unity of all parties. He also started schools and other programs to help civilians.

The Jamiat command charged that the mine that killed him was planted by members of the Revolutionary Movement (Harakat-i-In-qilab). Professor Rabbani, trying to ease the friction, issued a statement saying that the Harakat in Mazar was a loose organization that had taken in many disparate groups and that it had been infiltrated by members of the Fatherland Front, an organization set up by the Kabul government to recruit non-Communists.

The mystery was not solved and amid the dissension and suspicion following Zabihullah's death the Soviet forces attempted to press their military advantage. There was much fighting and the Jamiat was running low on ammunition. Our convoy, with more than 700 men and hundreds of animals, was the first resupply mission. I was with the advance guard, which had relatively few pack animals, and would probe for any obstacles along the route. Alam Khan would follow in about a week with the bulk of the supplies. A third group would leave a day or so later to defend the rear.

We started before dawn. My horse was brought with an ancient saddle that had a broken horn and no stirrups, making it difficult to mount without help. My rucksack and Shafiq's bag were tied to the back, making it even harder. But I was determined to be as self-sufficient as possible. I managed to climb onto Coral Beads alone by maneuvering him near a rock, clambering up the rock while holding the reins, and then making a little leap onto his back. It was a minor triumph, but I felt it got me off to a good start.

"God Will Protect Us"

A half moon above us bathed the white gravel of the riverbed with silvery light, broken by the soft shadows of men muffled in their blankets against the morning cold. There was little talk, mostly just the shuffle of feet and hooves and an occasional low shout and sharp clap of a stick against hide as a man urged on one of the animals. We advanced for fifteen minutes and then came to a halt. The men gathered around and a mullah chanted a prayer and made a little speech. When we started again I saw Shafiq and kicked my horse forward to ask what the mullah had said. "He repeated the promises of the Holy Koran that those who die as martyrs will not feel pain or suffer in hell and said we should not trust our lives to our guns and bullets," he replied. "He said God will protect us more than all our weapons. He pointed out that the Russians had many weapons and could not win and that showed that God alone would give us victory." It was a sort of message the mujahidin had heard many times before. I had noticed that almost a third of them had the Koran, wrapped in cloth or leather packets, slung over their shoulders, almost as if it were a weapon.

Shafiq passed on instructions from Abdul Wahab: "If you hear a MiG, tie your horse to a tree and run to the mountains." He also said he was sick with stomach cramps and diarrhea and asked for medicine. I gave him a dozen of my Lomotil tablets and told him to take one every hour. We crossed a pass and stopped for tea and bread at midmorning. Shafiq sat on the ground, clutching his stomach. He said he had not taken the Lomotil because his stomach was empty; Afghans believe medicines must only be taken with food.

We took only an hour's rest. We had come to a wide and empty desert plain. The men were divided into groups of ten and sent forward at ten-minute intervals as a precaution in case of an air attack. I was put with some pack animals in the middle of the column. At my side was an unarmed, elderly mujahid, with a scruffy gray beard and broken teeth, wearing an old European overcoat that was pale green with bright orange stripes. He pointed to himself and said his name, "Ahmad." Back in Miram Shah, Shafiq had said a man would be assigned to feed and care for my horse and to provide any help I required. Apparently we had been separated at the start of the day, but now Ahmad was there.

We started across the plain under a clear blue sky. We heard no enemy planes, but the need for caution was soon apparent. We came to a large pile of rocks with fluttering pennants: a grave. Ahmad pointed to it, made a circling motion over his head to indicate the rotor blades of a helicopter, put his two hands together and shook them, saying "Dat-dat-dat-dat" to imitate a machine gun, and finally pointed to the rocks and said, "Mujahidin." I noted that there were no trees to tie the horse to and no mountains to hide in to escape a sudden air attack. So much for Abdul Wahab's instructions.

We arrived at another teahouse late in the afternoon, just as it began to pour torrents of rain. We had been traveling for eleven hours, with only an hour's rest for tea and one piece of bread. We now had the first meal of the day, a greasy meat soup and bread. Shafiq said Abdul Wahab ended the day's journey so soon only because of the rain. To make up for lost time, we started again well before dawn under a cloud-flecked moon, stopped for tea and bread after dawn, and started again up a long rise to the top of another pass.

"Ruskies, Bang Bang"

My legs were cramped from sitting in the saddle. I dismounted and made a sign of walking to tell Ahmad I would walk down the steep side of the mountain. Shafiq was nowhere in sight. Ahmad went ahead with the horse while I waited for the circulation to return to my legs, admiring the sweeping view of the thinly wooded mountains under a now clear, azure sky, with the first snow peaks in the far distance. By now the convoy was strung out along the trail and I was sitting alone. Two men came and started down and I followed them, but when they stopped to rest I went on alone.

As I went, feeling free in the fresh mountain air, jumping over stones and roots, I noticed that no one was in front of me. I looked back and could see no one behind. I quickened my pace to catch up with those I knew to be ahead, but still saw no one. I began to panic, wondering if I had missed a turn somewhere among the trees. I came to what seemed to be the bottom of the valley, but there were hills ahead and no clear view. One trail seemed to go around a hill to the right and another seemed to go up a hill to the left, where a man with a rifle was sitting. I was relieved, thinking he was one of our men. I went quickly up the hill, but when I reached him I did not recognize him. Afghans use the English word "group" to describe a number of men in a single party. I said to the man, "group," and pointed first to one path and then the other, to ask which way the group had gone. He pointed to the other path, but without much conviction. Then there was a shout from down the slope. A man was motioning to me to come down. I did, and he took me firmly by the arm. He cocked a finger and thumb like a gun, pointed at my head, and said, "Ruskies, bang bang." Still holding my arm he took me up another slope where there was a teahouse I had not noticed earlier. A carpet of wood chips covered the ground. It was a lumber cutter's camp. My companion motioned to me to sit on a rough-cut log. In a few minutes the mujahidin I had passed earlier finally arrived, motioning me to come with them. Just before I left the man pointed to his stomach and made a wry face, with the usual Afghan assumption that all foreigners are doctors. Grateful, I gave him some aspirin.

We came to a wide valley and a cluster of teahouses, with a rug spread outside one of them and bolsters to lean against. I stretched out and had tea. There had been reports of famine in Afghanistan and I asked about food supplies. Mussa Khan, forty, said he owned this teahouse and another back along the trail.

"We get some grass from the fields to feed the animals, but there is no food here," he said. "We depend on the woodcutters to bring us what we need when they return with their camels after they bring lumber to Pakistan. There used to be 500 families but no one can live here. This is a main trail and they bombard us all the time. Nine families are left who run tea shops. If we cannot fight with weapons, we can help the jihad by serving food to the mujahidin, preparing tea for them and having a place where they can sleep."

A Stranger Questioned

We ate, fed the animals, and rested from morning till late afternoon. Suddenly, there was angry shouting from one of the teahouses. We walked closer and saw Abdul Wahab and his two main aides, Martin and Ziahullah. They were in their early twenties, the equivalent of lieutenants. Ziahullah was roughly searching a stranger, reaching into his pockets to remove his wallet and coins, feeling the collar of his jacket and the shoulders and hems of his garments for hidden papers. He found something wrapped and sealed in plastic and tore it open. It turned out to be a charm such as many Afghans carry, a bit of paper with words from the Koran written on it. After a while Ziahullah punched the man hard on the arm. The stranger gathered his wallet and papers and left.

I asked Shafiq what had happened. "That man was sitting next to Abdul Wahab and asked him what party he was with," he replied. "Ziahullah thought he was a spy. He asked the man his party and the man said Harakat. Ziahullah was very angry. He said Harakat had killed Zabihullah. He told the man to go away and not come near any of our men or we will kill him."

A short while later two men came from another teahouse, walking slowly and smiling gently as if to show they wanted reconciliation. They talked with Abdul Wahab for a while and went away. "They said they were a small Harakat group from Logar Province and they do not know what might have happened in Mazar," Shafiq said. "They said all the parties should cooperate and they were sorry their man had upset us. They also said he was a new man with them and they would watch him closely—we should not be concerned. If they find he is a spy they will kill him themselves."

The mountain ranges of Afghanistan run east and west, so a journey to the north means going over a pass, dropping down to a valley, and then going up over another pass, each higher than the one before it. We crossed a pass and went down to a wide swift river. By now I was at ease with Coral Beads and confidently nudged him across to the small town of Allauddin, on an asphalt road that snaked to the west along the steep, narrow valley. The houses, rising steeply in tiers on the mountain side, appeared mostly uninhabited.

A Ride on a Rutted Road

Until then I had assumed, from what little I had found to read about conditions in Afghanistan, that the road transport system had been entirely destroyed. I was surprised to see a few buses and trucks moving along the road. Shafiq said we would hire vehicles here to take the men and equipment for an hour or so along the road so that the men and animals could get some rest. Even as he was speaking a small donkey loaded with ammunition began to wobble from side to side and then slumped to its belly from exhaustion.

The buses, which had three rows of seats in front and an empty area in the back for cargo, were relics of rural roads that had existed ten or twenty years ago. One of the trucks was an International Harvester. Two others were Russian. It was an hour before the tail of the convoy straggled in. Martin and a few mujahidin were sent ahead with the unloaded animals, and the rest of us waited another hour for the bargaining over how much would be paid as fare to the drivers of a bus and truck.

It was dark when we started, zigzagging through bomb holes and the craters left by mine explosions, bumping over dirt and rocks from landslides, skirting a chasm where a side of the road had collapsed into the valley below and, at one point, inching our way across a concrete bridge with a huge gap torn from one side. All along the way were the ancient hulks of Soviet tanks and armored cars. Shafiq and I were squeezed into the front seat of a truck, along with the driver and his helper. I tried to count the hulks but gave up because the truck's weak headlights barely picked out a few feet of the road ahead. The driver, who had a stubble of beard and a missing tooth, said his name was Haji Nur, and that he had been doing this five years.

"There are many ways to get petrol," he explained. "A driver might tell the Russians he is going on a long trip on one of the controlled roads. He is allowed to fill up a big drum but he sells it to someone else. The best source of petrol is a Russian tank. Their drivers will let us siphon off fuel if we give them enough money or hashish." Then the lights failed completely and Shafiq refused to ask Haji Nur any more questions, saying that the driver had to concentrate. Haji Nur apparently had memorized all the obstacles and was able to zig and zag at the right time in the dark. But after a while he stopped and tinkered with the generator and got the lights working again. He soon had to stop again to replace the fan belt. Then we came to a destroyed bridge and everyone got out as the bus eased down a 60-degree slope, sloshed through a stream, and groaned up the other side. It was almost nine when we reached Miran Jan at the end of the passable road. The teahouse was up a flight of stairs, over a shop. We were now at an altitude of more than 5,000 feet. I huddled close to the wood stove.

Hajibullah, the owner of the teahouse, said that the wrecks along the road were from fighting when the Russians first entered Afghanistan and that the invaders were so badly mauled they never again attacked by land.

"Once 7,000 to 10,000 people lived in Miran Jan," he said. "They have all left because of the bombs and only merchants and some mujahidin are left. If we go the Russians will put a base in Miran Jan. This route is used by all parties going north to Paktia, Logar, and Wardak provinces and we must defend it. But it is hard. They send a plane every morning to try to catch the trucks on the road and we don't have enough guns to protect ourselves."

Martin arrived about two hours later and reported that two donkeys had been lost in the dark. Abdul Wahab said someone would have to go back at daylight to find them. He woke us before dawn and sent the convoy on without breakfast. He stayed behind until the missing donkeys were found and also to care for two sick men. By now I was resigned to the fact that Shafiq had no intention of staying anywhere near me. He had been given a horse and preferred to stay at the rear, where Ziahullah acted as sweep man, making sure that stragglers did not rest for too long.

Along a Valley, over a Pass

With Ziahullah in the rear, Martin guided the van and I went with him. Martin sounded like a foreign name, but Shafiq said it was a standard Afghan name. It was pronounced Mar-teen, accenting the second syllable. The lieutenant was about five feet seven, with a round face, short black beard, and even, white teeth that flashed when he laughed, as he often did. When Shafiq and I talked with him he said his full name was Abdul Martin, that he was twenty-two years old, and that he had studied through the eighth grade. Zabihullah had sent him and Ziahullah to Iran to study the Khomeini revolution, but they did not like what they saw there. On his return from Iran, and while waiting in Pakistan for this convoy to Mazar, he had been taught how to prepare and lay mines.

Martin heard the noise of a distant helicopter and signaled me to get off the horse and crouch close to rocks at the side of the valley. Perhaps it was the daily attack on Miran Jan that Hajibullah had mentioned the night before. We waited until the sound ended and moved on. Martin walked on higher ground at the side of a long valley and I rode with the pack animal, following a riverbed, crossing and recrossing a swift stream, feeling fresh, and enjoying the pellucid air, the pale blue sky, the subtle browns of the bare mountain sides, and the sun glistening on the rushing water. Then we left the river and began to mount higher into the valley. My legs were stiff. I left the horse with Ahmad and walked with Martin. We had no breakfast, and when we came to a small populated village Martin bought a large bag of raisins and nuts. At the end of the village a man stood by the path with his hand out, begging for something. We passed him and came to a little girl, also apparently begging. Martin gave her a coin. They were the only beggars I ever saw in Afghanistan.

Now a straight wall of mountain rose 1,000 feet ahead. We had been gaining altitude all day. We passed patches of snow as we climbed to reach the saddle between two snowcapped peaks, at about 8,000 feet. I was surprised at how well l felt. We rested a bit, dropped precipitously down a boulder-filled gorge, and came to a pair of teahouses where Martin said we would spend the rest of the day.

Rest at a Teahouse

There were four tall poles at the corners of one of the low buildings and two other poles beside the trail, all topped with the heads of wild mountain sheep with thick, curved horns. The mujahidin and the men who run the teahouses shoot everything in sight and are depleting the wildlife of the mountains just as the woodcutters are stripping away the trees.

We arrived well ahead of the others. I took off my jacket, shirt, shoes, and socks and washed myself in the freezing water of the stream that rushed down the gorge. Martin said that was a bad thing to do; that I should never put cold water on myself when my body was warm.

There were several small teahouses along the gorge. The men were distributed among them in order not to overburden the facilities. They ate, rested, and busied themselves with needles and thread, repairing rips in their clothing and homemade packs. An elderly mujahid, who acted as mullah for the group prayers, had apparently received some first aid training. He opened a large sack of medicines and bandages and gave the men ointments for their bruised and blistered feet.

A man arrived with the two missing donkeys and said Abdul Wahab was still in Miran Jan with the sick men and would come the next day. The teahouse was packed that night, so I spread my sleeping bag on its flat roof and studied the thousands of stars. But such simple pleasures were not unalloyed. I had hoped my wash in the stream would rid me of most of the fleas that had long since found a home next to my skin, but they felt as numerous as ever. In the morning, the sun's rays inching over the mountain turned the snowy ridge in front of me into a tourist's picture postcard of whites and pale pinks. I turned my sleeping bag inside out and set it in the sun to see if that would rid me of some of my hungry lodgers. It didn't.

About twenty unarmed men came up the valley from the north with a string of donkeys. They said they were carrying raisins to sell in Pakistan to support themselves until they could get guns to return to the north. Then came a civilian caravan, with women on some of the horses swaddled in bright red clothes and carrying children, and donkeys piled high with tin trunks and bedding. An old man in the party said they were refugees from Kunduz Province, bordering the Soviet Union, and had been driven from their villages by heavy bombing. He did not pause for other questions. Then an elderly man and a boy came down the valley, from the direction we had come. They were carrying and wheeling a new bicycle, with the frame still wrapped in bits of cardboard. "We bought it in Miram Shah," the man said. "It is for the mujahidin in our village. They will use it to deliver rice, tea, sugar, and other small supplies to groups outside the village."

Abdul Wahab arrived at noon with the two men who had been sick and also with two more horses and two men to act as guides. Shafiq said the next leg of the journey would be across the wide Zurmat plain, in sight of the provincial capital of Gardez. He said Russian air patrols constantly flew over the plain and we would have to cross it quickly and at night. The extra horses had been hired to lighten the load on the animals, and the guides were to make sure that we did not lose our way.

Since morning a few of the men had been making bread, but not in the customary oven. They inverted a large, round-bottomed iron pot that looked like a Chinese wok over a fire, patted out a ball of dough into the shape of a small pizza shell, and put it on the hot iron to cook. Each piece took only a few minutes. They removed it, folded it in quarters, and cooked another, until they had several large piles. Others busied themselves untying some of the nets of weapons and ammunition and making new bundles to redistribute the loads. Some stripped and cleaned their guns. As always among the Afghans, when it came to the business of war everything took place with no shouting of orders and no apparent grumbling. But then the men were told to form up, and were counted off by Abdul Wahab and sent down the trail in squads of ten. With the open imposition of order and discipline, signs of contrariness appeared. Men objected to a seemingly arbitrary count that separated friends. Abdul Wahab would have none of it. He roughly grabbed men and pushed them into position. Once, when a man protested too strongly, Abdul Wahab punched him hard on the chest. The man meekly did as he was told.

Ziahullah and the mullah stood a little way down the trail. As each man passed they gave him two of the pieces of bread. This would be his only food until the next day. For the first time I was able to get an accurate count of the men and animals. We had 117 men, including Shafiq and myself, two riding horses, four packhorses including the two that were newly hired, two mules, and six donkeys. I was told to ride with Shafiq near the rear of the column.

At the Shrine of Rohini Baba

Shortly before sunset we came to the ruins of what once had been a major pilgrimage site, a *ziyarat* (grave) of a saint named Rohini Baba. Henry Bellew, who traveled through this same area 130 years earlier, saw shrines everywhere: "So prevalent, indeed, is this saint and relic worship amongst the Afghans that it amounts to almost pure idolatry." He was full of what appears to be Protestant Christian scorn: "Many of them, and especially those most in repute, are under the charge of a priest who lives on the premises and generally manages to realize a handsome income from the credulous dupes of his priestcraft and cunning."

The shrine of Rohini Baba, with a half dozen buildings and surrounding lands, had been just such place. Now it was abandoned, and although the grave was still there, a bomb had ripped a hole in the roof above it. Smaller graves and the surrounding rooms and walls were shattered and the ground over a wide circle was strewn with fragments of bombs and rockets. Large, locked, tin trunks had been pried open at the corners, to reveal the remains of documents charred from fires set by the bombs. Nevertheless, the mujahidin were reverent, cupping their hands in prayer before the grave.

As we looked around a dozen refugees came along the trail, the men and boys walking, the women and children on camels and horses. A tall man in the group said they were three families from Kunduz who had walked ten days to reach the Zurmat plain. He said they left their homes because of continued Russian bombing and because the government would never leave them alone, constantly sending militia to spy if they had connections with the mujahidin. Soon another refugee group from Kunduz passed along the trail. A major flight was under way from that province.

The mujahidin were assembled on some terraced fields near the shrine. They were a mixed group of Tajiks, Turkmens, and Uzbeks, as is often the case with mujahidin from the north, and they were lined up according to their language and also according to their districts within Mazar. Abdul Wahab made a short speech. "They have been in Pakistan a long time and maybe there are spies among them," Shafiq explained. "Some are deserters from the Communists and perhaps KHAD has sent them as agents. They all will be searched for hidden papers."

Squad leaders went to each man and felt his clothing, but only perfunctorily. At first I thought this exercise was pointless: the men knew

Women and children refugees from Kunduz Province. They left because of Russian bombing and constant spying to see if they helped the mujahidin.

one another well. But then I realized that Abdul Wahab was actually trying to instill more discipline. Simply giving orders seldom worked. If the men could be made to think of themselves as bound together to preserve security they might be more ready to act in unison in an emergency.

Across the Zurmat Plain

We started across the plain after sundown. Soon the lights of Gardez were clearly visible a few miles off to our right. Every now and then parachute flares rose into the air and slowly fell to the ground, an orange glare lighting the perimeter of the city to deter a mujahidin night attack. The moon would not rise for hours and all was blackness and silence, except for dogs that barked when we passed through villages that still had some population. Once headlights suddenly switched on in the distance and came in our direction. I wondered if they signaled an enemy tank or armored car on patrol, but Abdul Wahab apparently did not think so, because we kept to our route, although he stepped up the pace so the mujahidin were half running and half walking. The headlights actually swept across our column but then turned in another direction.

We kept going, never seeming to put any distance between ourselves and Gardez. But finally a sliver of moon outlined the silhouette of the mountains on the opposite side of the valley and the lights of Gardez receded. When we started into the mountains our guides lost the way. Tiny flashlights were switched on to examine the ground for tracks. I was cold and my legs were numb. I got off the horse to ease the strain. But when the guides found what appeared to be a trail, a mujahid boosted me up. I was so stiff I slipped off the other side of the horse and had to be boosted up again. We continued, only to stop for another inspection of the ground. This time instead of getting off I crooked one leg in front of me and closed my eyes for a brief nap that was unceremoniously interrupted: Coral Beads made a sudden movement, and I fell off. Again I was lifted and pushed back into the saddle, with no bruises, luckily. At half past three, Abdul Wahab called a halt. I had been on the horse nine hours. We slept until seven.

The next day we went across dry, rocky hills spotted with a dozen varieties of small desert plants and an occasional bush coming into a pink bloom, topped a low pass, and quickly crossed the barren Khairwan Plain to the village of Jalzi. A small fortress with high walls and towers with gun slits guarded each family's domain. The narrow streets were deeply rutted and muddy from water draining from the houses. The whole village was foul with the smell of human and animal waste.

The convoy camped next to a crude mosque, out of sight from the air amid a grove of trees. Abdul Wahab bought a small calf for the equivalent of $30. One of the men cut its throat and let the blood drain onto the ground as the mullah said a short prayer. Soon it was butchered and the liver and heart were fried and distributed as a sort of appetizer while we waited for the main meal. One of the men showed me that he had cut his finger while slicing the meat. I got my packet of medicines, poured water over the cut, put Mercurochrome on it, and wrapped it with a bandage. Immediately another man showed me a blister on his foot and wanted me to treat that too. A third came and pointed to his head. Shafiq saw what was happening and told them I was not a doctor; they should go to the mullah.

A Yusufzai Chief

The village chief was Haji Shah Wali, a Yusufzai tribal chieftain who invited us for tea in his house, which was freshly plastered with a smooth coat of mud. We climbed narrow stairs to the guest room in the outer wall overlooking the high entrance to his fort. Rugs covered the floor, and pillows, embroidered with elaborate floral designs by the women of the house, lined the walls for us to lean against. Haji Shah Wali was a small man, with no beard, a neatly trimmed mustache, and clean, ironed clothes. "Jalzi was attacked twice by the Russians right after they came to our country," he said. "We drove them off and we had 120 martyrs. There used to be 1,000 families here. Now there are only 400. But with the help of God we can live here."

I asked about food supplies. "We are not able to grow much here. We depend on wheat we get from the Zurmat plain and from Pakistan. There is enough food if people can afford it. But many go hungry. Sometimes they have no food for two or three days. They are poor and there is no work. Before the Communists came to power we had everything we wanted. Rugs and furniture. Some even had cars and trucks. Now the Russian planes and helicopters have destroyed our houses and belongings and killed our horses and cows."

"Then why don't the people go to Pakistan?" I asked.

"We must stay to defend our country and our village," he said. "The Communists tried very much to make this place empty. If we leave the jihad will fail. Our country will be lost."

We traveled only two hours the next day. As we entered a village, a man came and began to speak excitedly. Shafiq said the man was complaining that so many people would attract Russian bombers and was demanding that we leave immediately. The village was spread out, with no trees, and Abdul Wahab told the commanders to scatter their men as widely as possible. Shafiq and I and a few men went to a small store that sold provisions and also had a tin stove for making hot tea. The shopkeeper, Gul Agha, was thin and neatly dressed.

"This used to be a rich town and merchants came from Ghazni and Kabul to buy our wheat and fruit," he said. "Now there is enough to eat but nothing else. If someone becomes seriously sick he must be taken to Pakistan."

At his remark I suddenly noticed a young mujahid sitting close to the stove, shivering. He had a smooth, Central Asian face: flat, with narrow eyes and high cheekbones. He had no jacket and wore only a thin shirt and matching loose trousers made of a bright blue cloth. Recalling what the doctor had said about a severe attack of malaria, I searched my rucksack and found the chloroquine. I told Shafiq the man should take four of the tablets immediately. The mujahid did, and as we sat for a while he stopped shivering and fell asleep. Shafiq was impressed and said it was very good medicine.

Two Deserters

I asked Shafiq if we could talk to some of our mujahidin who had deserted from the Communist ranks. We found Mohammed Aslam, twenty-eight, a short, stocky Uzbek from Mazar. "The first time the government took me I was twenty-two years old," he said. "They brought me to Kandahar but I escaped in a short while and got a bus back to my village. Last November, a Russian and Kabul army force surrounded the village and took me and another man on a truck to Mazar. The other man was sent to Herat. They put me on a plane and took me to Kabul. I was given a military uniform and put in the Rishikor garrison outside the city, but I was there only fifty-five days. Six of us escaped at night and went to a nearby village where some people led us to the mujahidin. They sent me to Peshawar where I found men from Mazar who led me to Abdul Wahab."

An older man heard our conversation and volunteered his story. He was Mohammed Eshaq, thirty-nine, from a village near the city of Balkh. "I served for two years under the shah and they were not supposed to take me again. But I knew they would try and I had a hole under my house to hide when they searched our village. Then last October the Kabul troops surrounded a wheat mill where I worked. We were very busy. I did not go home that night and they found me while I was asleep. They put me in a jail for two days and then took me in a tank to Mazar, where I was put on a plane and taken to the Rishikor garrison and put in jail for two months. Then I was assigned to a motor company. After five days I volunteered to be a mullah and lead the prayers. Twelve days later I got up early, gave the call for the morning prayer, walked through the gate, and escaped. Some mujahidin gave me a pass saying I had deserted from the Kabul government. I joined three other men and we walked to Pakistan."

Earlier we had seen Abdul Wahab and an Uzbek commander, perhaps a dealer in animals, trying to buy a donkey from a villager. The commander felt its legs and back, jumped on its back, prodded it into a trot, and came back. The villager asked for the equivalent of $150. Abdul Wahab offered $50. There was a lot of talking back and forth but no deal. Later we saw the same routine elsewhere. Still no deal. "They know one of our donkeys is sick and are trying to take advantage of us," Shafiq said. I said I had often been told that the entire nation was enthusiastic for the jihad, yet here people first tried to get us out of the village and now made it difficult to buy a donkey at a reasonable price.

"You are mistaken," Shafiq said. "These are just a few selfish people. All Afghans support the brave mujahidin." Still, I said, I wanted him to help me ask questions so I could learn more about how people felt. He said he had to wash in preparation for the midday prayer. I found him later and he put me off with another excuse. I said it was important that I talk with people.

"I'm not your servant," he replied angrily. "I'm a free mujahid and I don't take orders from you."

"It's not being a servant," I said. "Massoud Khalili arranged for you to come with me as an interpreter."

"I came because I am returning to my family in Mazar," he said. "If sometimes I help you it is because it is our custom to be kind to guests." I couldn't tell whether he was annoyed at my earlier expression of doubt about support for the jihad or this was just another indication of the Afghan refusal to accept any situation that smacked of an inferior position.

We started at six without dinner but went only four hours before stopping for the night at a village mosque. The next morning elderly villagers came with large kettles of tea, bread, and plates of eggs poached in fat. It was the traditional hospitality. Shafiq was still asleep. Outside, I saw a large truck and bags of what appeared to be wheat being unloaded from it. I returned to the mosque and called to Shafiq, saying there was some sort of activity and I needed his help. He said he needed more sleep. I insisted, saying it was important for me. Abdul Wahab said something and Shafiq stirred. "I haven't had tea," he said. I said I would come back in an hour.

Whatever Abdul Wahab told him worked. When I returned Shafiq was awake and pleasant. We found Haji Mohammed Yar sitting on the tailgate of a fairly new German truck. He said he ran a wholesale food distribution route: "In Ghazni, I buy wheat, tea, sugar, and whatever else might be needed. Old men can go to the bazaar to buy supplies, but a young man would be arrested as a mujahid. The Communists know everyone is against them. Even we have to be careful. They say, 'You are taking supplies to the devils.' That's what they call the mujahidin. I buy a little at a time from merchants I trust and I leave the city at night. I travel for ten or fifteen days. The roads are bad. If the mujahidin work on a road the Russians will bomb it and if the government tries to fix a road, the mujahidin will stop them."

He said dealers bought used vehicles like his in Pakistan and drove them via the Khyber Pass for sale in Kabul, and that was how he obtained his truck. He said he could get tires or any parts he needed either in Kabul or Ghazni. It must have been a good business. He had a warm jacket and a gold wristwatch.

Abdul Wahab bought two sheep for $48 to be slaughtered for lunch. Shafiq said that was very expensive. He also said the villagers would not sell us feed for our animals, claiming they did not have enough for their own. Eventually someone was persuaded to sell, but again Shafiq said the price was high. And Abdul Wahab finally bought a donkey. Shafiq said he did not know how much it cost.

Crossing the Kabul-Kandahar Highway

We were approaching another danger point: the main highway from Kabul southwest to Kandahar. By day it was used by Soviet military convoys, Afghan Army and militia units, and civilian trucks. At night it was deserted, but there were many defense posts, and the enemy, well aware that resistance supply routes crossed the highway, could be waiting in ambush.

We traveled for five hours and stopped just before nightfall for bread and tea. Along the way I passed the man to whom I had given the chloroquine. He had no pack or gun and seemed to be walking in his sleep. We started again, with no moon and flashes of lightning in the sky ahead, crossed the two-lane concrete highway, and went up a slope on the other side. People peered out of the windows of two-story houses at the silent, ghostly procession passing through their lanes. Clouds had obscured the sky and it was pitch black. Sometimes I felt that I was all alone, and then suddenly I would seem to be surrounded by men and animals. I had rolled down my hat to cover my ears and wrapped my blanket around my body and legs, but still I was cold and stiff. We went over a pass and finally came to a sleeping village. At the door of a mosque we hammered and someone let us in. It was a little after one in the morning. I had been in the saddle for about eleven hours, with only an hour's rest.

The next morning one of our mules was discovered on its side. One of the men found that it had a bruised knee. Two men kicked and prodded the animal up on its feet and walked it in circles for half an hour, still kicking it repeatedly to keep it moving, until the mule remained standing on its own.

We were in a small village in Wardak Province. I told Shafiq I wanted to talk to people and he found a village elder who showed us a house that had been destroyed by bombs a few weeks earlier. There was a huge crater and nearby the tail fin of an unexploded bomb stuck out from the powdery gray soil. The elder said the village had no school or clinic, but a hospital staffed by French doctors was about four hours away by foot. As for food, he said, they did not grow enough locally but could get wheat from Ghazni. An old man who had been listening spoke up: "I am a poor man. I have a wife and five children to feed and have no land to grow food. Before the war I worked in Pakistan and we had land in the north. Now we have nothing." At first I didn't understand. If he had land in the north, why was he now in the south? "Our lands were in Turkistan," he explained. "The people drove us out." After more questions it became clear that by Turkistan, he did not mean the Soviet Union but the northern regions of Afghanistan, inhabited by Turkmens, Uzbeks, and Tajiks. Starting with Abdur Rahman, the Pushtun rulers of Afghanistan had settled Pushtuns like this old man and his family in the non-Pushtun regions on the other side of the Hindu Kush. Now local people were taking advantage of the war to drive out the ethnic intruders. I had read that ancient grievances were being avenged in the midst of the jihad, but this was the only concrete example I would find during any of my trips into Afghanistan.

Into the Hazarajat

We resumed the journey after the midday prayer, entering the Hazarajat, the central mountainous region of Afghanistan. We spent the next few days winding through valleys at an altitude of about 9,000 feet. This region was seldom bombed. Some said the Soviet invaders, following a policy of divide and rule, were deliberately favoring the Shia Hazaras to encourage their separation from Afghanistan's Sunni majority. Others said the relative peace was merely tactical; that there were no well-traveled mujahidin routes through the Hazarajat, and no strong resistance bases, and so no need for the Soviets to waste bombs on it. In any event, we could now travel by daylight without fear of attack from the air. But there was a different danger for me. Groups loyal to the Ayatollah Khomeini of Iran were extending their influence over the Shias, and they were vehemently anti-American. "Abdul Wahab says that if anyone asks about you, we will say you are French," Shafiq told me.

The days settled into a routine. We rose early for prayers, had tea and bread, traveled at a leisurely pace, had lunch, and stopped at nightfall. It was spring. Men were ploughing fields to plant potatoes, the main crop of the mountains, and apple and apricot trees bloomed pink and white. In villages houses and garden walls were being replastered with mud after the damages of winter. Children came running furiously to watch us pass, giggling and laughing at the sight of a foreigner. Little girls with babies on their hips ran to hide if I pointed a camera in their direction, while little boys stood boldly. My glasses were a special fascination. A child would form thumbs and fingers into circles, look through them, laugh, and point at me. But the best show of all was me getting on or off Coral Beads. To dismount I had to raise a stiff leg over the saddle and sort of slide down the horse's side. To mount I would have to find a low wall or rock to stand on and then try to spread my leg to get it over the pack on the back of the horse. Sometimes Ahmad would have to pull my leg to get it into position. This made the children's day. The boys would convulse with laughter and even the shy girls would jump up and down and shout.

We entered Bamiyan Province, where the vast, spectacular wall of the central massif, known here as the Koh-i-Baba, came into sight. For much of one unforgettable day the long file of men and animals snaked past a panorama of snowy peaks glistening in the clear desert air, castles and parapets formed by eroded hills, and huge, bold swaths of green, purple, black, and rust-colored minerals mixed with the browns of silt deposited by an ocean long before dinosaurs walked the earth. Unfortunately, my enjoyment of the tableau was somewhat impaired by a cold and a fever. We had traveled recently through a few hours of rain and a sprinkling of snow and sleet. The long-expected diarrhea had belatedly arrived and at times I had to jump suddenly from the horse and run to the rocks. It was especially troublesome if I was sleeping indoors and had to get up at night. Abdul Wahab took military precautions, giving the men a password as they took turns standing sentry during the night. I would get up and try to pick my way through the carpet of men by the light of my little flashlight. The sentry would wave at me to go back but I would persist. When I left the building he would have to come with

Beneath peaks of the Koh-i-Baba range. When we crossed a high pass the irrepressible mujahidin romped and threw snowballs.

me, because dogs let loose in the streets of the villages at night attack strangers.

I lost my appetite. Meals generally consisted of soup with a thick layer of grease floating on top. Afghans eat it by breaking up the bread, putting the pieces into the soup until all the liquid is soaked up, and then scooping up the globs. I restricted myself to a bit of bread, dipping it into the liquid to moisten it so I could swallow it. Abdul Wahab was sympathetic and sometimes found hard-boiled eggs for me. Once I noticed the man with malaria sitting in the room and not eating. The doctor in Peshawar had not said anything about giving medicine after the first four pills. I made my own diagnosis: Several days had passed and it was time for another dose. I gave him two tablets this time.

Late one day the trail merged with the rutted and eroded remains of a road lined with telephone poles, some with wires dangling to the ground. A truck belching smoke and ploughing through a sea of mud signaled that we had reached a village on what had once been a main dirt road that ran all the way from Kabul to Herat in the west. We were in the middle of civilization again, such as it was, and I was told to go inside a large store and teahouse and keep out of sight. It was just as well. It was cold and damp outside and I sat in an alcove looking out a window with real glass.

Apparently this was a hub on the major mujahidin route to the south. Groups coming from the north could get vehicles here to take them east in the direction of Kabul and then south through a much easier route in the direction of Teri Mangal. In only a half hour, while it was still daylight, I saw three separate groups arrive, with a total of 118 men going to Pakistan for weapons. The supply of recruits for the jihad seemed inexhaustible. Abdul Wahab intended to hire vehicles to take us in the opposite direction, but he had trouble finding drivers at what he considered a reasonable price. Shafiq said there had been fighting between Shia groups and the drivers wanted extra money for the added hazard.

In Khomeini's Shadow

The Hazarajat, with its Shia majority, was one of the first regions to declare itself independent after the Communist coup of April 1978. Leadership came from the United Islamic Council (Shura-yi-Ittifaq-i-Islami), headed by Sayed Ali Beheshti of Waras. Its military commander was Sayed Mohammed Hassan, usually known as Sayed Jaglan, a former major (*jaglan*) under Zahir Shah. Mosques and other buildings where the Shura is strong are decorated with pictures of Beheshti, bearded with thick glasses, and a young Mohammed Hassan wearing a long-outdated military uniform.

After Khomeini seized power in Iran in February 1979, echoes of his call for a total social and economic revolution reached the Shias of Afghanistan, who numbered about 2,250,000, or 15 percent of the pre-war population. Their young militants complained that their best lands had been seized by the Sunni Pushtuns; that they were left with no roads, electricity, schools, or hospitals; and that many Hazaras seldom ate pure wheat but had to subsist on a mixture of wheat, corn, barley, and lentils.

Sadiqi Neeli, a deputy to Beheshti, had demanded that the Shura fight against Pushtun as well as Communist oppression. When Beheshti refused, Sadiqi in the summer of 1982 turned to the Iranians and with their help formed the Organization for Victory (*Sazman-i-Nasir*), generally known simply as Nasir. But the Shias too share the Afghan spirit of disunity. Just as four Communist parties bloomed in the time of Zahir Shah, and seven major resistance parties took root in Peshawar, the Shias of the Hazarajat began to replicate. In 1983 another Khomeini-inspired group—the Soldiers of the Revolutionary Guards (*Sepah-i-Pasdaran*), usually referred to as Sepah—was formed as a rival to Nasir.

Complicating things even more was a fourth party, the Islamic Movement (*Harakat-i-Islami*), separate from the Shura but also opposed to Nasir and Sepah. The confusion of names in Afghanistan is unbounded. It is necessary to distinguish between the Shia Harakat-i-Islami and the Sunni Harakat-i-Inqilab-i-Islami based in Peshawar. There are other Shia parties, but they are too obscure to warrant much attention.

Thus the Hazaras were divided into four groups: the Shura and Harakat-i-Islami, with ties to the Sunni parties in Peshawar, and Nasir and Sepah, with ties to Iran.

Nasir and Sepah attracted many of the better-educated Shias and sent them to Iran for military training, as well as indoctrination in Khomeini's Islamic socialism. On their return they executed alleged reactionary landlords, redistributed land, and attempted to reorganize the economy, with price controls in the bazaars, a ban on interest payments (forbidden by Islamic beliefs), and limits on marriage expenses.

The Hazarajat was swept by a brushfire civil war—all the more reason for the Russians to ignore the region and put their planes and tanks to better use against the mujahidin elsewhere. Nasir and Sepah drove Beheshti and Sayed Jaglan from Waras, in the heart of the Hazarajat, to the Nawar region northwest of Ghazni.

In October and November 1983 two Dutch journalists tried to enter the Hazarajat with a convoy from Pir Gailani's National Islamic Front. The convoy was repeatedly stopped and bit by bit its arms were taken away by Nasir and Sepah for their war against Shura. Other groups also had their guns taken from them.

Bill Cross, a young American journalist who tried to penetrate the region in 1984, had to leave hurriedly when his interpreter and guide heard reports that Nasir wanted to capture him for display as evidence of CIA involvement on the side of Shura.

Who Is a Friend?

Abdul Wahab could not find transportation at a price he was prepared to pay. It wasn't prudent for me to be conspicuous, so a room in the rear of the teahouse was cleared of farm utensils and piles of dried brushwood to make a place for me, Shafiq, and a few others. In the morning I asked for a pail of hot water and, for the first time in more than a week, took off my shirt and socks and washed.

A few days earlier a stranger, riding a white horse and carrying a Kalashnikov, had joined our convoy. He was a survivor of a group that had recently been ambushed. When I first noticed the man and asked why he was with us, Shafiq replied: "There are thieves and spies and greedy men all along the way. How can you tell who is a friend and who is an enemy? He has to sleep sometime. Maybe he would be safer if he did not have a horse and a gun. People will kill to get those things. You are only safe if you travel with a group."

The man was nearby and Shafiq called him over. He was thin, with wide eyes and a triangular face ending in a pointed beard. He said he was Nazar Mohammed, twenty years old, from a village near Mazar, and associated with the Islamic Alliance of Professor Sayyaf. "Five months ago we left for Pakistan to get weapons," he said. "Then twelve days ago we departed from Pakistan by way of Teri Mangal with 110 men, two horses, four mules, and six donkeys. We were on the road only six days, going at night in a place where there were no people. Suddenly, hidden tanks opened fire on us. They must have been told we were coming and were waiting in ambush. We fired back but we were not strong enough and we all ran into the hills. In the daytime helicopter gunships came and attacked us with missiles and machine guns. All day it was like that. At night I stood up and could not see anyone near me. I could not see any martyrs either. I don't know where the rest of the group went. I walked all night in the mountains. Then I paid a man to show me the way to a village and I bought a horse and found Abdul Wahab."

Running the Shia Blockade

We left early in the afternoon in a truck and a bus that, like the earlier ones, had a few seats in the front and cargo space in the rear. I was put in the second row to be less conspicuous. After riding for a while we saw an armed man in the middle of the road, who held up his hand for us to stop. Abdul Wahab got out with two men to act as his bodyguards. We sat quietly for twenty minutes until he came back. As we started again Shafiq asked what had happened, and was told we had been stopped by a Harakat-i-Islami group who asked for guns and ammunition. "They said we have so much and they only want a little to help them fight Nasir and Sepah. Abdul Wahab told them we are near the Russian border and need the guns more than they do. They told us to go and warned us Nasir was just ahead."

They were right. In a half an hour several men stopped us, and another sat by the road with a light machine gun pointed at us. This time it was a full hour before Abdul Wahab came back. "They said they had Dashikas set up above us and could disarm us if they wished but they said they did not want to shed blood," Shafiq said after hearing the report. "They said they were respectfully asking for weapons and ammunition because we received guns free from foreign nations. Abdul Wahab replied that we only came this way because we were told there was a cease-fire and all groups were helping the jihad. They were only a small group and let us go. They said the main Nasir force is ahead."

The next time we were stopped, after twenty minutes, there was a light machine gun mounted directly on the road ahead. A well-dressed man came out of a building and, smiling as if this was something of little importance, walked to our bus, stepped up, and looked in. He examined us carefully, pausing when he saw me. Then Abdul Wahab got out to talk to him. "He recognized you as a foreigner," Shafiq said in a low voice. "We told him you are a French doctor."

It was almost an hour and a half before Abdul Wahab returned. "They wanted us to stop to eat with them," Shafiq explained, "but Abdul Wahab thought it was a trick to get us out so they could examine our ammunition carefully. Then they said he must have tea with them. That is why it took so long. They insisted many times that we must give them supplies. Abdul Wahab said Alam Khan will come along in a few days and he has a great deal of ammunition. He gave them a letter to give to Alam Khan, saying Alam Khan should give them guns. But it is a lie. He will give nothing."

Only fifteen minutes beyond we came to another Nasir post, one of two on either side of the main headquarters. We were there only a few minutes. It was dark and the men said they did not want to detain us any longer.

Shafiq said there was a Sepah post ahead. The pills I was taking for the diarrhea were causing me bladder trouble and I was in acute distress. I had hoped we would stop as usual for the sunset prayer but we kept going. If the next stop is a long one, I thought, I can leave the bus under the cover of darkness. After about forty-five minutes the head-lights picked out a young ragged man with his Kalashnikov in both hands before his chest, ready to fire. Four others, similarly alert, stepped from the shadows and glared up at us. After Abdul Wahab got out, Shafiq looked out at the menacing figures and said: "If we have to, we will fight them. They are rebels. If they die they don't become martyrs, because you are not martyred fighting against Muslims. But in our Is-lamic Holy War, we can fight against both rebels and the Russians. In either case, if we die we are martyrs." As I considered that possibility my bladder distress was forgotten.

Abdul Wahab was away for a full hour. "At first they tried to threaten us very much," Shafiq said after hearing the report. "They looked at the letter of identification Abdul Wahab carried and said the signature was false. They asked many times for ammunition but Abdul Wahab would not give anything to them. Finally, they said they did not want any bad feeling with someone from the Zabihullah front and they would let us go."

Late in the evening we reached a village where Khomeini's picture was displayed at the entrance to a teahouse. The next morning Sultan Mohammed Hussain, an old man with a wisp of a beard, high cheek-bones, and narrow eyes, said someone had put the picture there and it had no political significance.

"We can get food and we are not bombed because we are in a nar-row valley," Hussain replied, when I asked him about supplies. "But we have no doctor or medicines. If we get sick or are badly injured we get well or we die. It is God's will."

We were off again through low hills of a bleak, treeless plateau. A tire went flat and, with no spare, we had to stop, remove the wheel, and add another patch to a tube that already had a dozen others. As we waited I talked with the driver, Sher Mohammed, who said he some-times drove a truck all the way from the outskirts of Kabul to Herat near the Iranian border and could make the journey in about ten days. "We carry anyone who wants to ride, along with wheat, sugar, and other sup-plies that are bought in Kabul and shipped to merchants along the way. We also get our petrol in Kabul. You can buy anything there if you have money."

Late in the afternoon we arrived at Punjab, a town with a small airport, high school, and a hospital, all now in ruins. We dismissed the vehicles and waited all the next day for the animals to arrive, feed, and rest.

Across the Koh-i-Baba

I was sick and feverish when we set out early in the morning, despite the day's rest. We passed along a valley with high cliffs on the side then up sharply to the snows of the Koh-i-Baba range, where the animals sank almost to their bellies and sometimes fell over and had to be unloaded. It was easy to see why convoys had to wait until April to cross the mountains. But for the irrepressible mujahidin the snow was fun rather than a challenge. They romped and pelted one another with snowballs and laughed and clowned as they dragged the animals to their feet and pulled them to firmer ground. Going down, the incline was steep and slippery with thick mud and I dismounted to walk. The pass was at 12,000 feet. I had a fierce headache, perhaps from the altitude. When we stopped at about six o'clock, I tried to eat some bread but vomited and crawled into my sleeping bag. The mullah thoughtfully gave me a bottle of medicine from his kit for an upset stomach and with that I was soon asleep.

I felt better in the morning. Shafiq said there had been a change in plans. Abdul Wahab had planned to take a short cut across another mountain, but a message had come during the night from the Sepah commander in Nayak, the next large town, requesting that we pass his way. We arrived in midmorning and left in the early afternoon. Shafiq said the Sepah commander demanded weapons and they gave him a letter for Alam Khan, asking Alam Khan to make the delivery, but the letter was signed with a false name. They all laughed at the deception. I walked with Abdul Wahab at the end of the convoy and asked why Jamiat did not do something about the extension of Khomeini influence over the entire central region of Afghanistan, with a potentially hostile force astride one of the main mujahidin supply lines.

"It is the Russians we must fight," he replied. "They have been trying to seize our country for more than sixty years, but we never had a war with Iran. Border troubles, but never a war. When we defeat the Russians and have our Islamic government then we can deal with people like Nasir and Sepah. They are only in the center of the country and the mujahidin control all the provinces around them, including the border with Iran. We can cut off their guns and food. When we have our freedom, the people of Afghanistan will find one leader and they will not permit foreign influence, from Iran or any other country."

We came to the man with malaria sitting by the road. I had given him two more chloroquine tablets the day before and while he had seemed better then, now he could hardly walk. Since I was not riding, I suggested that he take my horse for a while and Abdul Wahab told him to mount. But about an hour later we came to him again and he was walking. He said he felt much better and did not need the horse.

We continued all that day across a wide saline plain. That night I slept outdoors and in the morning found a thin layer of ice on my sleeping bag. The next day we headed toward what looked like a solid cliff side and then entered a gorge twenty-five feet wide at the bottom but with the walls rising several hundred feet over our heads. We followed a small white water river that raced over boulders, crossing back and forth over rickety bridges made of logs, branches, flat stones and mud, most of them so weak the animals had to be led across a few at a time.

As the countryside opened out, the stream became a wide, swift river. The mujahidin looked at it and joyfully shouted "Mazar, Mazar." They had been away from their homes and families for almost six months. They knew this was one of the many branches of the Band-i-Amir River. The waters would eventually fall into the Balkh River and nourish the rice lands and gardens of their villages before emptying into the Amu Darya, the river that formed the boundary between Afghanistan and the Soviet Union.

The encouragement was needed. By now almost all the men were limping from blisters on their feet. Coral Beads had lost a shoe and trudged along with drooping head. I walked most of the time to spare him further distress. Late one morning we reached Balkhab in Jowzjan Province.

A Bazaar and a Bath

Balkhab was controlled by Sepah, with pictures of Khomeini everywhere and notices posted on shops to warn against cheating and overpricing. Since Balkhab was close to the Sunni areas of Mazar, Sepah had to cultivate good relations with other groups and Abdul Wahab thought it was safe to allow me to wander in the bazaar. It was a living fossil of the Central Asia of fifty or one hundred years ago, stretching for three small city blocks along a muddy street fifteen feet wide. Vehicles might have reached Balkhab before the war, but now there were only horses and other animals to impede the way. A blacksmith had a forge to make horseshoes and small farm implements. A butcher shop displayed whole sheep and goats swarming with hornets and flies. Men strolled in quilted robes, green with thin white stripes, reaching almost to their ankles. The sleeves touched their knees. They wore the garment over their shoulders like a cloak.

There was also a rare luxury: a bath house. Water, heated in a boiler outside, was piped to a row of faucets about six inches above the cement floor along one side of the steamy room. The etiquette was to squat near a faucet and use a large metal cup to pour the hot water over yourself. For the first time in twenty days I was able to strip to my shorts to wash both myself and my filthy clothes. The mujahidin wrapped clothes around their waists, scrubbed themselves and one another with cloths, massaged each other, and shaved under their arms. I was later told that it was the custom in those parts for men to shave under their arms and their pubic hair as well every twenty days or so.

For such hardy men, bare chested they seemed all bones and skin, with thin arms and legs and flat stomachs.

A Burial

The next day was May Day. After breakfast of the usual tea and bread, I toyed with a transistor radio at the teahouse and found Radio Moscow, with an announcer telling of preparations for the day's parade and the Soviet Union's contributions to world peace. He spoke of non-interference in the affairs of other nations.

We started, but soon shots from back in Balkhab signaled a halt. Abdul Wahab sent someone to ask what had happened and, when he returned, Shafiq said the man with malaria had died. The column turned back, the animals were unloaded, and the men scattered to the rooms where they had spent the previous night. The burial took place two hours later.

The body was wrapped in a cloth and placed on a narrow wooden bier with two handles at each end and two at each side so it could be shouldered by eight men. Noiselessly, except for the shuffling of feet through the bazaar, the body was carried to a mosque on a side street, the men walking quickly behind in a tight group, trading off to share the burden. The mosque was wide but not deep, so that most of the men had to stand outside on the steps. The priest intoned, "God is Great"

(*Allah Akbar*) three times with short intervals in between. In less than a minute the bier was picked up again and hurried back through the bazaar, down a steep gully, and up the other side to a bare, rocky hill where the grave was still being dug.

It was completed as the men sat watching, chatting quietly. The body was taken from the bier, the outer cloth removed, and it was lowered into the grave. Large flat stones were removed from other, forgotten graves strewn over the hillside and placed on the sides and over the body. Small stones were used to fill the cracks and finally all was covered with a packing of mud, making a sort of chamber for the body. The men now gathered around, taking turns shoveling earth into the grave or pushing the dirt in with their hands. Someone had brought along a branch. Bits of green cloth were tied to one end and the other was inserted at the head of the grave and held upright by the packed earth. A priest intoned a long prayer as water was poured on the filled grave and it was stamped into a smooth mound. Finally, stones were put at the head and feet, a string was tied the length of the grave between the stones, and all the men stood silently for another prayer. Then the men returned to their rooms and were told the march would resume after lunch.

I wanted to ask about the dead man and Shafiq took me to a group from Shor Tepe, a region of Balkh Province just across the Amu River from Soviet Tajikistan. The unit leader was Lal Mohammed Khan, a tall, solemn man with a long black beard. He said the dead man's name was Allah Berdi. Shafiq explained that it meant "God's Gift," and was a common name given by Turkmen families to a firstborn son.

"His grandparents were refugees from Russia when the Communists suppressed Islam," Lal Mohammed said. "His parents died when he was young and he had only one brother. Then his brother died and a year ago the Kabul government captured him and sent him to Chamkany. After six months he escaped and took with him two Kalashnikovs and a machine gun. A mujahid commander gave him only 750 Pakistani rupees ($50) for them. They were worth at least 75,000 ($5,000). But he did not complain. He was happy with us in our camp in Pakistan. He said he had no parents and we were his real family. He said he wanted to be with us and fight the Russians and the Communists."

I asked about the time Allah Berdi had gotten off the horse. "He was ashamed," Lal Mohammed replied. "He said that was not the mujahid way. He said if he rode he would remain weak and he wanted to be strong to fight in the jihad." Others in the room said Allah Berdi had not eaten for four days. A man in Balkhab who had six months of medical training in Iran had been called the night before and had given him an injection of Novaljin, a painkiller. They said Allah Berdi had stirred when the call came to resume the march but fell back and died.

We started out again at a little after noon and I looked across the gully to the distant mound and limp green pennant on the hillside. The Afghans are stoic. As far as I could see, no one else took a last glance at the grave of the man known as Allah's Gift.

We mounted a series of ridges, higher and higher into the mountains, under a cold, bleak sky, with a strong wind blowing gusts of snow and sleet against the bare hands and exposed ankles of the thinly dressed mujahidin. The trail dropped sharply down the other side. It was dark as Coral Beads picked his way along a cliff path with a sheer drop on one side, a raging stream hundreds of feet below.

We spent the night at a small village. The next day Coral Beads was snorting and wheezing and his head drooped with weariness. He was, as I was soon to discover, no longer surefooted. In the afternoon, after going all day without rest, we followed one side of a wide, swift irrigation ditch. As we crossed a little bridge made of branches and mud, Coral Beads's rear right leg fell through and he fell over on his side into the water.

I tried to pull myself away but couldn't move. The weight of the horse was on me as he kicked and thrashed in the water. Two men jumped into the stream and pulled the horse up but then lost their grip and Coral Beads fell back on me. Thoughts flashed through my mind. My ribs would be crushed. The horse struggled more. My leg would be broken. The men pulled at the horse. What about me? Was the horse more important? The men pulled again and again at the horse, and finally someone gripped me under the arms and pulled me out. He left me on the bank and went back to help to get the horse on dry ground.

I lay stretched on the ground, soaking wet, and the mujahidin walked by, laughing and pointing at me as they always do at something out of the ordinary. I picked myself up and followed them along the trail. It turned out that our destination was only ten minutes away—a Jamiat base at Amarakh where we were received with the customary effusive hugs and mumbled greetings. I was given some dry clothes and, still in moderate shock, went to sleep. My camera bag had been soaked and the next morning I found the camera inoperable.

I had a pain in my arm and wrist as we set out, passing through another narrow gorge. At Zari I was greeted by Dr. Paul Ickx of Doctors Without Borders. He examined my arm and found no broken bones. It was May 3. Twenty-four days after Massoud Khalili told me to get ready, I was in Mazar.

Return to Peshawar

·············

6

Paul Ickx was thirty-two, very thin, about six feet tall, with cropped black hair, a drooping mustache, a three-day growth of beard, and small, metal-rimmed glasses. He had last served as a replacement doctor in an emergency room in Antwerp, Belgium. Three nurses were also at the hospital at Zari, about 100 miles south of the Soviet border: Rudy Senaeve, an X-ray technician from the small town of Izegem in Flanders; Beatrice Fraiteur, from Brussels; and Marie Basuyan, from Lille, France. The four lived in a small room with their possessions scattered on a dirty floor, with no chairs, tables, beds, or even shelves to allow a little more room on the floor for sleeping bags. Their toilet was an outhouse over a hole in the ground about thirty feet away. Drinking water came from a nearby irrigation canal. If they had time they would allow a bucket of water to settle, decant it into a large thermos, and add purification tablets. But usually they were busy or tired so they drank water from the canal just as the Afghans did. The night after I arrived we sat on the floor eating rice and meat, which Paul tried to enhance with spices bought in a bazaar. I asked him about the work.

"We have about 200 patients a day, half and half men and women," Paul said. "When there is a bombing nearby we might be flooded with seriously injured patients, but now most of those who come complain of pain everywhere—in the back, chest, knee, or head. They don't know what a medicine can do. Many times just the consultation and a few vitamins make them feel well. But, of course, many are really sick with tuberculosis, bone diseases, worms, lung infections, and many eye infections. They prepare for their prayers by washing their eyes five times a day in dirty irrigation canals so it's no wonder they have so much eye trouble."

I asked how much he and the nurses were paid and how long they serve.

"We thought we would be here four months but already it is almost six months," Paul replied. "We are not really paid. We will receive about $300 for each month of service to tide us over until we get reestablished in jobs in Belgium."

"Why do it?" I asked. "Is it idealism, politics, or what?"

"Idealism is a big word," he said. "I believe everyone has a right to medical treatment. Political? Of course. We are always on a side that is the weakest, and usually against the government. But political in the sense that I am anti-Russian? No. In fact, I volunteered to serve with the rebels against the Americans in El Salvador but something happened at the last minute. I was asked to return to Afghanistan, where I had been before, to save this hospital, which would have been closed. Besides, I like this country and its people. I speak the language and I can get to know them well."

"Perhaps you might want to escape from something in Belgium," I suggested.

"Sure, sometimes you ask yourself, 'Why am I here?'" he replied. "But for us there are enough sick people in one day to provide the answer. I am not running away from anything in Belgium. People who are escaping cannot do a good job in the third world. You have to know how to adjust to the world around you, and if you can't adjust at home you certainly will not be able to adjust to a country like Afghanistan."

Beatrice Fraiteur, twenty-seven, had a round face, a ready smile, and an assured, at-ease manner. She began as a medical volunteer in 1979 and served in Somalia, Bangladesh, and Thailand. "In Africa, you live in a white ghetto," she said. "In Asia you are something special, 'Dr. So-and-so' or 'Miss So-and-so' and bring along your own culture and comforts. But they don't look up to you here. The Afghan idea is 'Mine is the best country in the world, my province is the best, and my village is the best. And the best man in the world is my father.' You are just someone called a doctor and no better than anyone else. You are not even a Muslim and maybe only a woman and have to cover your head in the presence of men. You eat their food and sleep on the floor as they do and when you ask for something you have to say why you want it, not just that you want it."

A year earlier Paul Ickx, Beatrice Fraiteur, and Rudy Senaeve had

Dr. Paul Ickx, left, with Beatrice Fraiteur, Rudy Senaeve, and Marie Basuyan at the Doctors Without Borders hospital at Zari. "Idealism is a big word," Dr. Ickx said.

worked at a hospital at Jagori in the Hazarajat. A Belgian reporter visited them and wrote a glowing story about Beatrice. He later submitted her name in a contest sponsored by Belgian newspapers to select the country's Woman of the Year. She won, and returned home in May 1984 to find herself greeted with roses and television cameras and invited to three meetings with King Baudouin.

Rudy Senaeve was also twenty-seven. He had learned some of the songs of the Afghan resistance and played the melodies on a five-hole wooden pipe. "There is idealism," he said. "There is an overconsumption of medicine in our part of the world. It is a kind of business. But the biggest part for me is adventure. I love to travel and see a lot of things. I like my work and want to make it interesting. If you are a tourist you only look and collect pictures. I want to live with people and learn from them. Here you are taking and giving. Sometimes I am angry there is so much work. But then sometimes, when you walk in the mountains, with no cars and no radio—just silence such as I have never heard in my life— you are in paradise."

Marie Basuyan, twenty-five, previously served in Thailand. "I want to learn about Islam," she said. "Life is hard here for a woman. She must always go about covered to her ankles and never talk to a man who is not of her family. But that's why we are needed here. The women are so pleased to see us and give us presents of eggs or fruit and sometimes beautifully embroidered pieces of cloth. The men never think of giving anything."

"And sometimes the women apologize because they have nothing to give," Beatrice said. "The mujahidin at the nearby village know the women are bringing food. They stop the women and demand eggs, raisins, nuts, and other things. They say the doctors are rich and don't need the food."

Hospitals That Are Targets

The Paris-based Doctors Without Borders (*Médecins sans Frontières*) grew out of the experiences of doctors who worked in Biafra during the Nigerian civil war in the 1960s. The organization was created in 1971 as a rapid-deployment organization to send medical teams to places in severe need of assistance, particularly those not served by the Red Cross. Its first teams arrived in Afghanistan in May 1980, just five months after the Soviet invasion. They promptly discovered that being among people who were fighting the Communists here was completely different from being among those fighting against other governments.

Naively, Doctors Without Borders marked its first hospital in Afghanistan with the Red Cross symbol. That turned out to be like putting out a bomb marking. Soviet planes promptly attacked it. Within about a year four Doctors Without Borders hospitals were destroyed, along with two others established by a another French organization, International Medical Aid (*Aide Medicale Internationale*). Service in Afghanistan is undoubtedly the most difficult volunteer medical mission in the world.

At Zari, high canyon walls on both sides were a protection against air attacks, and caves were dug into the cliff as shelters. The previous December, during the Soviet offensive following the assassination of Zabihullah, Zari was occupied for ten days by Afghan Army forces, who scratched a warning into the mud wall of the hospital: "Foreign doctors, we know you are here. This is your unlucky day."

It took Dr. Ickx and the others forty-seven days just to reach Zari from Pakistan. Doctors Without Borders follows a system of sending one team for four months, then another team to relieve it, with about a week's overlap to allow time for briefing the newcomers. The previous team was overdue for relief so Paul's team had to be sent in winter.

"We left Peshawar in November 1984," Paul said. "We rode for thirty-six days and walked for eleven days. The plan was to use trucks to save time but we had four bad trucks and only two good trucks. Every day some of the trucks broke down. We wasted as much as one or two full days just in making repairs. And then they had no chains and the trucks had to be pushed and dug out of the snow. Worst of all, a full-scale war was raging between Nasir and Sepah and the Shura of Sayed Jaglan. Once we were held up for two days when Nasir demanded ammunition. We gave them money instead, paying tribute though we had 200 mujahidin in our convoy. At another time we heard there was an ambush and set up a Dashika when we came to the top of a hill. The convoy went down the hill and up the other side under the protection of the gun. Then another Dashika was set up on the other side to bring through the rear of the convoy. Both sides also asked for medicines for their wounded. That, we gave them. We got rid of the trucks and bought donkeys at Nayak. But we could only get enough animals for the ammunition and we had to leave the medicines behind. When we reached Balkhab we learned the Russians had occupied Zari. The other team had been evacuated back to Amarakh. We relieved them and set up a clinic in Tunj, a more secure valley—actually a hidden valley—four hours' walk away from here."

"That was the hardest part," Beatrice said. "We stayed there almost four months, from January to April, shut off completely from the world. We didn't know how the war was going. We only saw the casualties. We had only one room to live and work in. If we had to do an operation we had to persuade a villager to give us a room. The supplies we left behind in Nayak didn't reach us for three months. Before that we had only leftover supplies. We even ran out of blood serum. Finally we came here and found that sign on the wall."

They had been at the hospital for only about a month before I arrived, which perhaps accounted for the disorder of their living quarters.

"When we arrived there was no door on this room," Beatrice continued. "The mujahidin would wander in and out and sit down and stare at us. We kept saying we needed privacy and needed a door on our room but it was weeks before they put one up."

"They don't know to leave you alone," Rudy said. "If you want to read they come over to examine your book. They don't read themselves except for the Koran so a book is a curious thing to them. They want to take it from your hands and examine it. If you just want to sit alone and think they come and ask if you are sick."

"Doesn't it bother you that you try to help them and they don't show any signs of appreciation?" I asked.

"They have no conception of why we are here," Rudy replied. "Doing something for someone who is not a relative is completely against the Afghan mentality. Last year, when we were in Jagori, I asked some people if they knew why we had come. They thought about it and said we had committed a crime in our country and were sent to Afghanistan as punishment.

"The hospital at Jagori is a good example. It was the first ever established in the Hazarajat. We found Hazaras who had learned some English while working in hotels and restaurants in Kabul that catered to foreigners. Our aim was to train them to do as much of the work as possible. That's why I was sent there. I am an X-ray technician and my assignment was to teach Hazaras to do the work. They were eager and quick to learn. One young man could make excellent plates. All the while Sayed Jaglan, who was the chief of Jagori, asked for money and supplies. We gave him some small things. Our hospital was doing so well an official of Doctors Without Borders came from Paris to inspect it. Sayed Jaglan asked for a lot of money. At least, for him, it was a lot of money. But it was not too much in terms of French francs. The official said he would give the money. But Paul and the rest of us said no; once you gave in to a demand like that in Afghanistan you have no peace. They keep asking for more and more, thinking there is no end to your riches. We refused to work there under those circumstances and the hospital was closed."

The Hospital at Zari

The nonmedical administration of the hospital at Zari was in the hands of a young commander who bought food and other supplies required by the doctors. Rudy, who acted as bookkeeper, reimbursed him. The hospital was by the side of a wide, mostly dry riverbed, a short distance from the living quarters. The work began at about 9:00 A.M., but patients began to arrive soon after dawn, waiting in male and female groups on the river bank, with an armed sentry guarding the final path to the hospital. The local commander spent most of his time in this area, maintaining order and mediating the incessant arguments over who would be next.

The hospital had a central corridor with three small rooms on each side. One was a ward for men, with a few patients on the floor; another room was used by the mujahidin as their quarters; and a third room was currently occupied by a woman and her two-year-old daughter. They had been injured by bomb fragments and both wore casts. The woman remained in the room with an elderly male relative who cared for her and took the child out. The rooms on the other side of the corridor served as consulting and treatment rooms for men and women, with a dispensary and medical storage room between them.

"What we need desperately is a table for operations," Rudy said as he showed me around. "It was the first thing we asked for when we came. But they don't use tables themselves and so we can't just buy one. One has to be made. They keep saying next week. As far as they're concerned tables are not necessary, and so we're having all this trouble."

Rudy soon left me to join Paul in the men's clinic. Beatrice and Marie worked by themselves with the women. Sometimes they would ask Paul a question about a patient but, with their years of experience, they generally diagnosed and prescribed medicines on their own. They stopped for about an hour for lunch, then worked at the clinic until about four in the afternoon. They rested and did a few chores like washing clothes until dinner. This was also the time when they could ask for a pail of hot water from the kitchen and take a bath in a small room off their living quarters, pouring water over themselves with a large tin cup and letting it drain out through a hole in the floor.

At dawn the day after I arrived there was a commotion outside. "A man has been shot," Paul said. Paul and Rudy hurried out and returned for a breakfast of eggs, bread, and tea about an hour later. "A bullet went through his face and out the side of his cheek. It was messy but his brain was not touched so he will recover," Paul said. "They say it was a spy who did it, someone from the Fatherland Front who infiltrated the mujahidin camp. They blame everything on the Fatherland Front. I think it was one of their own men who did it. They quarrel and shoot one another all the time."

Dawdling to Shulgara

I was worried about the next part of my program. Massoud Khalili and I had estimated that the journey north would take about three weeks, that I would spend about two weeks looking around, and that the return journey would take another three weeks, for a total of eight weeks. Shafiq said he planned to visit his parents, who lived near Mazar-i-Sharif. In view of his earlier statement that he did not feel obliged to me as an interpreter, I assumed that would be the last I would see of him. He said a convoy might be returning to Pakistan in two or three weeks, and that in the meantime I was to continue with the convoy by truck to the district center of Shulgara, another day's journey to the north. He said my horse would be taken back to Amarakh, where there was grass for it to eat, until I needed it for the return journey.

We left Zari at four in the morning, packed into two old Soviet vehicles for a long, dusty ride through a maze of curiously rounded, treeless hills—like huge balls cut in half and strewn over the ground. After a few hours the trucks halted and the men scattered at the sound of a plane high overhead. They did not seem to be in any hurry to start again. A group of us wandered along the trail and came to a nomad camp of low, black tents and hundreds of sheep, goats, camels, and donkeys. We were hungry, having had nothing to eat before the early departure, and the nomad men brought us earthen pitchers of slightly sour goat's milk mixed with water and large, round, flat bread, like the bread that the mujahidin had cooked several weeks earlier using a round metal pot inverted over a fire as a stove.

After several hours the trucks came racing up, there were urgent calls for us to get back in, and we sped away, reaching Shulgara late in the afternoon. Shafiq took me to a substantial house on the edge of town that was Jamiat headquarters. Shulgara had been captured by the mujahidin about four years earlier. Government buildings were in ruins and many of the houses and offices owned by the former elite were now used by the mujahidin.

We had dinner with Maulvi Abdullah, a small, chubby man with a white turban. *Maulvi* means teacher. It is a title bestowed on men who have completed higher religious studies but it is sometimes used loosely as an honorific. In this case it was earned. Shafiq said Maulvi Abdullah was the second in command and the chief judge for the Jamiat in Mazar. As he said this someone who apparently understood a bit of English drew a finger across his neck, as if to say that the Maulvi had the power to sentence someone to death. Sitting next to him was a man with very fair skin and blue eyes, who turned out to be an Arab from Syria. He carried a Kalashnikov and spoke halting English. He was a bitter foe of Syria's President Hafez al-Assad, calling him "Hafez al-Devil." When I asked what he was doing in Afghanistan he said he was fighting for the Islamic revolution.

"The whole world will become Islam," he said.

A Bazaar and a Rose Garden

The next morning Shafiq took me to the back room of a teahouse in the bazaar, saying the headquarters was vulnerable to air attack. He said I must remain there for the rest of the day. After an hour of sitting, sipping tea, I said I had come all this way to see things and I must go out. At first Shafiq insisted that it was too dangerous, but then he said he wanted to make arrangements to visit his family. He called an armed mujahid and let me go back to the headquarters with the man as a bodyguard.

My protests against seclusion had some effect. The next morning we strolled through the bazaar. The original brick and concrete stalls had been destroyed in the fighting and now the bazaar was a line of shacks along a muddy lane, stocked with things such as Japanese radios, Russian cooking oil, matches and household utensils, Borden's powdered milk from Ireland, aluminum cans of an orange drink from Holland, woolen socks from North Korea, and pink toilet paper from China via Pakistan. The imported goods came by way of Mazar-i-Sharif, about twenty miles to the north. A Toyota pickup truck in fairly good condition served as a passenger bus for regular trips between Shulgara and Mazar and there was also a regular truck service for goods.

From the bazaar we went to a large garden with rose bushes where the mujahidin had a fire to boil water for tea. When I joined them, they spread blankets under ancient trees and shook down sweet, juicy mulberries for us to eat. The most distinguished man in the group was Abdullah, a big man with a huge black mustache who belied his bear-like appearance by sniffing a bright red rose plucked from a bush. "There is the Karmal government," he said, waving the rose toward the top of two hills. He said about 350 Karmal troops were entrenched there behind a wide mine field. I was surprised that enemy posts could exist surrounded by mujahidin-controlled territory.

"Why don't you attack and destroy the posts?" I asked.

"We have a cease-fire with them," he replied. "We don't shoot at them and they don't call in helicopters to destroy our bazaar." Abdullah, which was the only name he used, said the Afghan troops lived in deep tunnels and underground rooms, supplied several times a week by helicopters.

Shafiq said Abdullah had been a commander of urban guerrilla forces in Mazar, but after the enemy offensive of the previous December he was withdrawn to help protect Shulgara.

"The Russians have large forces in Mazar," Abdullah said when I asked him about life in the city. "They destroyed many buildings to make straight roads for their convoys and brought concrete slabs from Russia to build new houses for themselves and their families and for the Karmalis. Some schools are open and they have telephones. But they always have to be on their guard. There are two small factories and a technical school. A Russian will carry a Kalashnikov even to a class and put it on the desk in front of him. On Fridays, special security forces are deployed around the bazaar so the Russian families can come to shop. At night all the shops are locked and the streets belong to the mujahidin."

I asked about urban guerrillas. "Sometimes they are boys, nine or ten years old," he said. "Let any Communist walk alone and the boys will kill him. All the city is with us, except a few spies." He told stories of a room blown up while it was crowded with Afghan officers, and of dozens of vehicles destroyed by mines. He said the bravest man of all was Sulfiq Amin, who had been killed the previous January. "Some spies must have told the Russians where he was. They were waiting when he came out of a house with a companion and blocked both ends of the street. Sulfiq Amin and his companion found some cover and fought until they used up their ammunition. They did not want to be captured so they stood up and were cut down by many guns. The Russians put their bodies on a tank and paraded them through the streets in celebration. But the people were not frightened. They knew Sulfiq Amin and his companion were martyrs and had gone to paradise."

Bullets for Sale

When we returned to the headquarters for lunch we found that two men had arrived with a donkey and heavy saddle bags, which they emptied on a floor, spilling out thousands of cartridges. "The Karmal government tries to win people over to the Fatherland Front by giving them guns and ammunition," Shafiq explained. "The militia in Kunduz sold this to these men who have now brought it to us." After several mujahidin counted the cartridges, Maulvi Abdullah, who was supervising, paid the men the equivalent of about 18 cents for each cartridge. "Last winter, when we could not get supplies from Pakistan, we spent more than ten lakhs to buy ammunition from the militia and the Fatherland Front," Maulvi Abdullah said. A lakh is 100,000 Afghanis and ten lakhs amounted to $8,350.

Someone outside heard the sound of helicopters and shouted to us.

We left the house and went quickly to a man-made cave 100 feet away. The house lay at the foot of a hill on which a Dashika was mounted and sentries were posted to warn the headquarters of air attacks. Soon someone shouted from the hill that the helicopters were bringing supplies to the enemy posts near the bazaar and there was no danger.

The shelter of the hill, along with the antiaircraft gun on top of it, meant that the trajectory of bombs aimed at the headquarters had to be high and that the bombs would pass overhead and hit buildings farther away. And many had been hit. We inspected the damage, picking our way around craters and over the ruins of twenty or thirty buildings, finally coming to some of the mujahidin who had traveled with us from Miram Shah. They had set up camp in what was once a two-story building and had torn out windows and doors to fuel cooking fires.

Shafiq said about a dozen people had been killed in the bombings. I asked if they had bomb shelters; he said no. I asked if Jamiat did anything for the villagers whose homes were destroyed by bombs aimed at Jamiat headquarters; he said they were too busy with the jihad.

That night I told Maulvi Abdullah I wanted to go as close to Mazar-i-Sharif as possible or, alternately, I wanted to go to the Soviet border at the Amu River, only about seventy miles to the north. He said it would be too dangerous for me to go close to Mazar and that a trip to the Amu would take a week just to arrange, a week to get there, and a week to return. Why it would take so long he did not explain. Since I was still hoping to return to Pakistan in about two weeks I gave up on the Amu.

The next morning Shafiq left for three days to visit friends. I sat in the headquarters, arranged my notes, ate, took long naps, and dredged up old songs from my youth to help pass the time. When Shafiq returned I asked if the mujahidin were planning any attacks. He said the battles were too far away and there was no one to take me. After two more days of sitting around, Shafiq informed me that he would leave the next day to visit his parents. I told him I wanted to return to Zari, where I would at least have the company of the French doctors while awaiting a convoy back to Pakistan. Maulvi Abdullah said they could not spare men to take me to Zari.

I felt I had to be more firm. I said Professor Rabbani had approved my trip and Jamiat was not living up to its responsibilities. A meeting of several commanders was called later. After what appeared to be sharp disagreement, Shafiq told me the decision: I would be given an escort and animals and would be taken by back routes used only by shepherds, but the route was very dangerous and I would have to assume full responsibility for myself.

Return to Zari

I left within an hour. A mujahid walked with me to a mosque, where bread and milk were brought and I was surrounded by a group of elderly men, obviously complying with their duty to give me food and keep me company. Shortly before dusk a younger man armed with a Kalashnikov arrived with two horses. We went through dark hills to a village where he left me. I had no interpreter so I just had to sleep and wait until something happened. At about three in the afternoon two men arrived with two donkeys. We traveled the rest of the day and into the night. I tried to ride one of the donkeys. They gave me a sharpened stick and signaled that I was to jab it in the animal's neck to make it go. I couldn't bring myself to do that, but neither could I make it move fast enough with prodding, so most of the time I walked. We slept several hours at a shepherd's camp, started again at dawn, and by noon, weary, thirsty, and covered with dust, I was back in Zari. I gave each of the men 1,000 Afghanis ($8.35) for their time and the use of their donkeys. They appeared pleased. I saw them later in the men's group waiting to see the doctor. Sick or not, a chance to be examined was an opportunity not to be missed.

The medical replacement team had arrived the day before, and my hopes were raised that a convoy would be organized to take Paul, Beatrice, Rudy, and Marie back to Pakistan. But Rudy had a cast on his arm—he had suffered a slight fracture in a fall from a horse—and could not make a long trip until the cast was removed. Marie was staying in Zari with him, while Paul and Beatrice were going on a promised trip to the Amu River to end their stay in Afghanistan. So no convoy was in sight.

The new medical team consisted of Dr. Christoph Bernoulli of Switzerland, a Norwegian male nurse, and two young female nurses from France and England. We were invited to a welcoming dinner with Mohammed Daoud, the Jamiat commander for Zari. Tall, well built, with a full black beard, he looked remarkably like the young Fidel Castro, a resemblance he rejected with disgust when I mentioned it. He was called Engineer Daoud, signifying that he was an alumnus of Kabul University, although not necessarily a graduate. He apparently had read some history. "Do you know any other country that has fought the Russians as we have?" he asked. "Look at Czechoslovakia, Hungary, and Poland. They were defeated by Russian tanks, but we are free. We cannot be conquered even if we have to fight forever."

The next day Christoph took over the work at the hospital and Paul had time to talk. I recalled Daoud's boast but said the mujahidin did not seem as strong as they claimed, citing the many warnings about the dangers of their Fatherland Front and duplicity from Harakat. I told him the story about the Sayyaf commander who had been ambushed and was afraid to travel even though he was well armed. "Are the Communists stronger than they admit or are they fighting among themselves?" I asked.

"It is a combination of both," he replied. "In the first six months of the war, when they fought the Russians directly, they were all together. But as soon as the Russians pulled back into the cities and the direct pressure was off they began to quarrel among themselves as they have for 200 years. The local mujahidin are controlled by the khans and maliks who have always ruled the countryside. The Communists have been driven away and now each man is content to guard his isolated valley. There was a village I knew in the Hazarajat where two brothers argued over a piece of land. The village leaders sided with one brother. The other went away and returned with a few dozen mujahidin from Hekmatyar's Hizb-i-Islami. Now that brother has the land and rules the village. I know villages in the Hazarajat with buildings stuffed with weapons. It's not to fight the Russians but to fight each other, or at least to defend themselves from a traditional enemy."

"Who Killed Zabihullah?"

"Why can't they settle this quarrel with Harakat? They are destroying themselves. Look at the death of Zabihullah," I said.

"Who killed Zabihullah?" he asked rhetorically. "They say Harakat. Perhaps. Harakat here is a loose organization made up of many different factions. Possibly the mine was planted by Communists who had infiltrated Harakat. But maybe it was not that way at all. I meet many people at the clinic—commanders, village elders, and ordinary mujahidin—who tell me things they don't tell others. Reputable men have told me Zabihullah was not on a mission against the Russians when he was killed. Several of his top aides were with him and they too were killed. Actually, they went out in the evening to try to catch someone they thought was their enemy. Maulvi Abdullah was with them, in another jeep I think. They were planning to arrest the man, try him on the spot with Maulvi Abdullah as the judge, and execute him. The man was not at home when they arrived. They left and planned to come back at about two or three o'clock in the morning to catch him while he was asleep. They returned the same route they went the first time. Only now someone had planted three mines along the road, in a triangular pattern so the jeep would be sure to run over one of them. Who planted the mines? Was it someone from Harakat, a hidden Communist, or simply someone who hated Zabihullah as a rival? He had made many enemies. He tried to stop villagers from selling food to the Communists in Mazar. His family was not important before the war and now he had grown very big and powerful. The Afghans have always tried to tear down anyone who becomes strong."

Paul stopped a while, thinking about what he had said. "But I don't want to exaggerate," he continued. "I like this country and its people. I'm ready to come back, not in a few months but maybe in two or three years. Never forget that their weakness is also their strength. They are so divided there is no target for the Russians to aim at. There are no communications for the Russians to intercept. Each valley will defend itself against the Russians as well as all others. If a hundred men are killed, a hundred others will rise to take their place."

Two days later Maulvi Abdullah arrived and with him Maulvi Alam, who had replaced Zabihullah as the Jamiat leader in Mazar. Ramazan would begin the next day and they planned to spend the first few days of it in Zari. Maulvi Alam, who appeared to be in his early forties, had a smooth face and a long, neatly combed beard. With Rudy acting as interpreter, I asked if he had ever tried to meet the leaders of Harakat.

"Certainly, we want to speak to Harakat," he replied. "But they refused. They have seven different leaders and each says he is the big chief. We don't know who to speak to." I mentioned the isolated enemy posts in Shulgara, and Abdullah's statement about a cease-fire. I said there did not appear to be much fighting and I wondered why they did not try to capture Mazar-i-Sharif.

"It is difficult for us to assemble many mujahidin," he replied. "This commander says my place is important and that commander says his place is important. They all say they cannot spare men. If we did assemble the men, it would be difficult to attack. They have big lights on the roads and many defense posts. Besides, our mujahidin have families in the city and property there. Their relatives would be killed and their houses destroyed. Even if we did capture the city it would be possible for us to hold it only a week, maybe a month. Afterward what would happen? The repression of the Soviet Union would be terrible. If we fight face to face many mujahidin would be killed. If we kill 500 people they will send 500 more and more weapons. It is better to fight slowly with guerrilla tactics."

"How long will the war last?" I asked.

"Maybe fifteen years, maybe longer," Maulvi Alam said. "The Holy Koran says when unbelievers are in your country you must fight them. God will help us save Afghanistan."

There was a stirring before dawn as they had their last meal before the start of the Ramazan fast. When I got up much later I was surprised to find Coral Beads hitched nearby. Some mujahidin told me I would leave the next day for Amarakh, where men were assembling to go to Pakistan to receive weapons. I was to learn that they were simply marking time.

A School at Amarakh

Inwardly marking the day as the first of my return trip to Pakistan, I set off with Maulvi Mamur Hashem, Jamiat's educational director for Mazar. He rode a donkey and we had two mujahidin as escorts. It was a pleasant morning. As we went through the narrow, straight-walled canyon that I remembered from my arrival almost three weeks earlier, a gentle light sifted down from the streak of blue sky above and all was silent except for the twittering of birds. Then we pressed our way through a nomad's large flock of sheep and goats, and their baaing and bleating echoed off the canyon walls.

Maulvi Hashem, a small, pleasant, soft-spoken man, could speak a few words of English. We stopped at a nomad camp where a ragged boy brought bread and an aluminum bowl of sour milk, although only I ate. Maulvi Hashem untied a bale from the donkey and brought out piles of clothing. He held shirts and trousers against the boy until he got an approximate fit and sent him scampering back to the black tents on a nearby slope. The boy soon returned with his brother, equally ragged, and he too received a shirt and trousers.

At the other end of the valley we wound upward through hills to the same Jamiat headquarters where I had shivered and slept to recover from Coral Beads's fall into the irrigation canal. To my surprise, the compound was virtually deserted, with no signs of an assembling convoy.

The next day Maulvi Hashem took me to see a school. About two dozen boys, ranging in age from five to twelve years, were squeezed on two long benches. On a blackboard in front of them sums were chalked in English rather than Arabic numerals. The teacher, a mujahid from the Amarakh headquarters, who had studied in a Mazar high school, was apparently staging a class for my benefit. Nevertheless, it was obviously a real school and all the children had well-worn book bags with texts, note paper, and pencils. The children stood, one after another, and recited what I took to be paragraphs of a patriotic litany, then sang a familiar resistance song. As a finale, a boy was called to the front and given a Kalashnikov. He expertly removed the clip, pulled back the lever to eject the cartridge, and with the weapon pointed at the ceiling pulled the trigger to show that the gun was empty. He then pointed to and shouted out the names of all the parts.

Maulvi Hashem took me to a school building that had windows and several desks, apparently a survivor of the prewar school system. However, it was empty. He said the villagers did not want their children to be gathered in such an exposed place and he pointed to nearby cliffs, saying classes were held in caves. As we left we came to an old man and a boy on a donkey. Maulvi Hashem stopped to talk to the boy, asking him why he was not in school. He seemed to have an abiding interest in children. It rained a lot in Amarakh from clouds from the northern plains that shattered against the surrounding mountains. I got into my sleeping bag and dozed for the rest of the day. Again I dredged up words of old songs to pass the time. A petty theft added to my depression. When we started from Zari, I told Maulvi Hashem I wanted to buy a saddlebag to sling over my horse's back to carry my rucksack. On the way through the canyon he bought me a decorative, handwoven bag from the nomads. It was colorful and I thought it would be a souvenir to take home. I now noticed it was missing. Someone else had admired it too. All the next day I could only sit and brood.

Finally, three days after I left Zari, Engineer Daoud arrived to take me back there. However, my feelings of utter disappointment were eased when I arrived. Paul said a convoy was being organized in Tunj and I would go there in two days with Rudy and Marie, who were making an inventory of medical supplies stored at Tunj. What's more, there was a possibility that I would have an interpreter.

Alphonse Artico was an Italian whose family had settled in Belgium. Of medium build, stocky with an olive complexion and a thick, black beard, he was indistinguishable from an Afghan. He had volunteered to work at a refugee school in Peshawar but then, in a spirit of adventure, set out with a Jamiat convoy. Before I left Peshawar a woman at the school asked me to inquire about Alphonse, saying he had gone north seven months earlier and they wondered if he was still alive. Paul said Alphonse had been wandering around with the mujahidin, had become fluent in Dari, and was close to battle several times. He also spoke English and, when he learned who I was, he said he too was a journalist and that he had eighty-six rolls of dramatic pictures about life and battle with the mujahidin.

Alphonse had no money and managed to get by because of Afghan hospitality and because he had been allowed to stay and eat at the hospital. Paul and Beatrice, concerned about how he would be received by the new, non-Belgian team, suggested that he return to Peshawar with me. With Shafiq gone, that would be ideal for me. Alphonse was reluctant. But as Paul and Beatrice talked to him he seemed to accept that his time had run out: he would go with us to Tunj and would travel with the convoy at least part of the way to Pakistan, although he wanted to stop off at several places for sightseeing.

An Execution and an Operation

I asked what had happened to the man who had been brought in with a bullet through his face. "When we first saw him we only dealt with the obvious emergency," Paul said. "But later we found abrasions on his neck and a slight fracture of his skull. We asked what really happened and they admitted it was not the Fatherland Front. He had been choked, beaten, and then shot by a companion. He died in two days. The man who did it was tried by Maulvi Abdullah. His fate was sealed: The sentence for a Muslim who kills a Muslim in the jihad is death, and so he was executed."

The next night Beatrice and Marie washed the clinic's floor with a disinfectant and spread a cloth with an aluminum face. The operating table had still not been delivered. They were preparing for an operation on a four-year-old boy with a huge tumor on his right leg. There were no hospital gowns and no one watching dials for vital signs; there was not even privacy. The Afghan commander in charge of the hospital sat watching off to one side as if it were a TV show. The boy was sedated with Ketalan, an anesthetic used only on animals in Europe because it leads to postoperative hallucinations in humans. The operation lasted three hours under the harsh white light of a single Petromax lamp. The tumor, weighing about three and a half pounds, was removed and the incision was closed. Paul stood up slowly, massaging the small of his back from the ache of bending over for so long. The leg was bandaged and the boy lifted like a doll and carried away. It was 8:30 when Paul and the others returned to their room for a meal that had grown cold in the waiting.

The next morning, as Rudy, Marie, Alphonse, and I prepared to leave for Tunj, the hospital seemed bright and cheerful. The boy was awake and alert, and Paul thought that although the tumor was cancerous the boy would live for some years. A man in his early twenties had come for a checkup and Paul called me to see him. He pointed to a scar on the man's head. "You see," he said, "he had a bullet through his head and part of his brain was lost. It was an operation that took a great deal of time and we thought he would be lost. But look now." Paul waved his hands at the sides of the man's face and his eyes did not move.

"You see, he has full movement except for the loss of some peripheral vision. You asked why we came here. This is why. We help people who would have died."

That was the last I saw of Zari. Within six months the clinic would be closed. It turned out that the constant reference to threats from the Fatherland Front expressed a real danger: not from without but from within. Zabihullah had been the cementing force that held the Jamiat together: it was his personal creation. Although it was never known, or at least never proved, who killed him, the beneficiaries were the Soviet invaders and the Communist government in Kabul. By the following November, reports filtered back to Peshawar that Zabihullah's Jamiat had virtually dissolved and that many of his men, as well as defectors from other groups, had joined the "self-defense" forces of the Fatherland Front. The military situation was so tenuous that Professor Rabbani would not permit a new team of French doctors to go to the clinic.

We left on four horses, with six mujahidin escorts. As we went along Rudy explained why they called Tunj a hidden valley. The river canyon was so narrow that it was filled by rushing water for much of the year. Even when the water was low, huge boulders blocked the way and thus Soviet tanks could not get through. There was a similar narrow valley blocking the entrance to the other end of the valley. We were traveling at a time when the water was high, and so we had to climb up and over the mountains. It took us until late in the afternoon. Some of the mujahidin escorts had preceded us to Tunj and the commander, Kol Ibrahim, was standing at the entrance to his house waiting to greet us.

Rudy and Marie knew him from the long months they had spent at Tunj after Zari was occupied by the Karmal forces. The greetings were as effusive as ever but Rudy mentioned that he thought Kol Ibrahim was two-faced and not trustworthy. The remark proved prophetic, but at the time I was too impressed by the other things I saw to think about it.

Please Take Our Son

There were obvious preparations to assemble a convoy. Animals were tethered nearby and dozens of men were in Kol Ibrahim's court-yard. Two clerks were busy with papers. I asked Alphonse to find out what was going on. The clerks read out some of the letters. One read: "We are a poor family and have little land. Please take our youngest son to fight the jihad." Another was from a mullah. It read: "This man is Sadiq, son of Mustafa. He is honest and wishes to serve God." The clerks said that only about one out of every three—those who were the most fit and had experience with weapons—would be chosen. As I watched I thought of the stories told by deserters, who had been kid-napped for military service only to flee at the first opportunity. Where the Communists were perpetually short of men, the mujahidin had more volunteers than they could accept.

The next day I went with Rudy and Marie to a narrow side canyon where a wall had been constructed under a large overhanging rock to create a storage room. It was a hidden storage area for medicine. Rudy began his inventory, checking off items against a list he brought with him. Many of the supplies were still in boxes wrapped in burlap bales and tied into the nets that had been slung over the backs of animals. But some bales had been ripped open and pills and bottles were scattered on the ground. As Rudy checked through the list he found several entire bales were missing. "They take medicine, don't know what they have in it and sell it to some merchant in the bazaar for almost nothing," he said.

Alphonse was waiting with bad news when we returned to the com-pound. Kol Ibrahim had told him that a convoy might not be ready to start for a week, or maybe even three weeks. I felt as if I had been struck. For weeks now the mujahidin had not found any way to employ my time, had teased me with promises of imminent departure, and had misled me with the trip to Amarakh. Now I faced another delay at Tunj. Rudy, Al-phonse, and I went to Kol Ibrahim. I said if I did not return quickly to Pakistan, my friends might start a search for me and that might be em-barrassing for Jamiat. He said he simply did not have the money to start the men on their way. However, he said, there were some poor men who wanted to go to Pakistan to look for work, and if I could pay their expenses and give them a few thousand Afghanis when we arrived perhaps something could be arranged. I asked how much he thought it would cost. He replied that the five men would need 5,000 Afghanis ($42) each to get started in Pakistan.

I still had about 35,000 Afghanis (almost $300) left from the money I had changed in Miram Shah. I said the arrangement was agreeable. But with my easy acceptance, he thought of something else. He said I would need sentries during the night, so I should take seven men. With the expenses of the trip that would bring me beyond my present funds, but I would get more money from the sale of the horse and so I said that too would be acceptable. Then he thought of something else. With seven men there would be more baggage, so I would need at least one mule for the baggage and in case someone got sick. I knew a mule would cost at least 15,000 Afghanis and said I could not afford it.

"Go and Be Damned"

I slept uneasily that night. I realized that Kol Ibrahim would assume that my talk of not affording the mule was part of my bargaining position and that, as an American, I would undoubtedly have much hidden wealth.

By morning I thought of a way out and shook Alphonse awake. I knew he needed money to return to Belgium and said I would pay him as a guide and interpreter to take me to Peshawar. He asked how much a journalist in America would be paid for three weeks work. New York salaries flitted through my mind, but I suppressed them and said $500 seemed sufficient since he was going to Pakistan in any case. He accepted.

Kol Ibrahim was asleep after his predawn breakfast but Alphonse impetuously called outside his room to wake him and we were invited in. Alphonse said we were grateful for his assistance, but that he was perfectly familiar with Afghan ways and we would set off on our own. Kol Ibrahim said that was too dangerous, that he was responsible for our safety, and that we would discuss it further later in the day.

We were called to his room that afternoon. He had with him a young mujahid who spoke some English. I gathered that Kol Ibrahim did not trust Alphonse to translate truthfully. We went over the same ground again, with the young mujahid trying to persuade me to change my mind. Kol Ibrahim said something angrily, which Alphonse translated as "Go and be damned."

We went to pack our bags. Alphonse, listening to the buzz of mujahidin comment around us, said Kol Ibrahim would not let me take my horse. (The horse that Alphonse rode from Zari was borrowed and had already been returned to Zari.) As we left, walking quickly over a bridge across a swift river, a string of mujahidin came up behind us, saying Kol Ibrahim had changed his mind and would send us on our way the next day with five mujahidin, and we would not have to pay any money. I told Alphonse to tell them we intended to go today. After half an hour, as we rested by a village, I looked back and saw men coming toward us, including Kol Ibrahim on horseback. He demanded that we return. When I still refused he ordered his men to seize us. Two grabbed my arms. Two more men picked up my legs and began to carry me. I shook myself loose, stood up, struggled a while as they grabbed me again and then realized it was useless. Alphonse, who had also been struggling, said they might injure us if we continued to resist. I said we would return with them. They brought horses and told us to mount. We all plunged directly into the river, with a mujahid holding the reins of my horse to guide it as it swam. The bank on the other side was steep and the horse lunged and pawed the earth twice before making it up to firm ground. We galloped back to the compound and sat in the room in our half-wet clothes.

We were told we would be kept at Tunj. I asked for my bag to change into dry clothes, and was told that Kol Ibrahim said no. I said at least let me get a towel and soap and my notebooks. That too was refused.

Reconciliation and Departure

As there was no attempt to confine us to our room we wandered in the area to pass the time. On the afternoon of the third day, we walked to the river and met an old man sitting in the shade of a tree with a Koran before him, apparently observing Ramazan prayers and meditation. He said he was the village qazi, or legal officer, and had heard about us. Alphonse talked to him at length and the qazi said Kol Ibrahim had no legal right to detain travelers. It turned out to be a fortunate encounter. That evening Kol Ibrahim called us to his room. He said the villagers had asked why we were being detained and so he had decided, against his better judgment, that we could leave the next day with three poor men who wanted to go to Pakistan and then to Iran to look for work.

By then I had sorted out the affair in my mind. As we had wandered about the area, people came to Alphonse to express their sympathies. They said Kol Ibrahim was the richest landowner in the Tunj valley. He built and owned most of the irrigation canals and ditches that watered the lands. I assumed that the jihad, and the weapons he received because of his alliance with Jamiat, made him more powerful than ever and that our abrupt departure, without his permission, challenged his position as lord of the valley.

I felt that my impatience had precipitated the clash. When he called us to his room I apologized for the trouble we had caused him and explained that I had been eager to start because of fears that a delay would prompt a search for me. The next morning he stood by the path to his compound, surrounded by his followers, and we all shook hands and exchanged kisses in a hypocritical gesture of reconciliation. It was only after we crossed the bridge that I felt sure, twenty-eight days after I arrived at Zari, that I was on my way back to Peshawar.

We went through a twisting narrow gorge, stayed for the night at a house to which Kol Ibrahim had provided a letter of introduction, traveled across a high, treeless plateau, spent the next night as guests of a village, and the following afternoon reached Dara-i-Souf. The town was a spot of green in the surrounding desert, with substantial buildings, many in ruins from earlier fighting, but some being repaired and indicating the current peace and a degree of prosperity.

Alphonse thought Dara-i-Souf was controlled by Jamiat. As we wandered through the bazaar he saw a man followed by two assistants who seemed to be a senior commander. Alphonse showed him a general letter of introduction from Kol Ibrahim which, among other things, identified me as an American journalist. The commander read it, looked at me sharply, said something, and strolled with us to a teahouse. Alphonse then informed me that the town was actually controlled by an alliance of Hizb-i-Islami and the three Shia parties of Nasir, Sepah, and Harakat-i-Islami. This was unusual; elsewhere Harakat-i-Islami was at war with the two pro-Khomeini Shia groups. This commander was Sepah. Smiling all the while, he demanded to know why the United States favored Israel and opposed the Islamic revolution. I ignored the first part of the question and said the United States supported freedom for all people. Alphonse took over the discussion and, as he later explained, told the

Sepah commander that while I worked for an American newspaper I was actually a Belgian. The commander did not press the point and soon left.

Alphonse found a mixed party of Turkmens from Shor Tepe and Tajiks from the Zari area who did not seem to be attached to any group. They agreed to let us travel with them and we left immediately after the predawn meal. We were now two dozen men, none with arms but in sufficient numbers to travel without fear. The Turkmens had three horses, which they alternated in riding. One of our men was sick. I let him ride Coral Beads most of the time and enjoyed the walk. Four days after leaving Tunj we arrived at a small town, whose name I never learned, where Alphonse said we would sell my horse and go by truck.

Goodbye to Coral Beads

Alphonse said we did not have time for bargaining and sold the horse the next morning to the owner of the teahouse, accepting the first price that was offered. I looked at old Coral Beads, with his large, brown, liquid eyes, his head hanging down wearily, his wisps of black hair like bangs over his forehead, and thought I would always remember him. When the mujahidin bought him for me in Miram Shah they told me he was a gentle horse. As I would learn, that meant plodding and sleepy. Even when someone jabbed him in the rear with a sharp stick he could only manage a spine-jolting jog, more up and down than forward. Yet he carried me over deserts, along dry, boulder-strewn riverbeds, through streams with water up to his flanks, wheezing and panting in the thin air of high mountains, picking his way over ice, edging along cliffs, finding his own way on moonless nights, going hungry like the rest of us, and never giving up. The man took off the saddle and walked around him, looking at his ribs showing from too many missed meals, the open sores on his back from the ill-fitting saddle, and the slight limp in his right front leg from going without a shoe since the day before yesterday. He then offered us even less than the figure he first mentioned. As I counted the money—18,000 Afghanis, or about $150—Alphonse kept saying we should hurry. We were 10 minutes along the road when I suddenly stopped.

"Wait," I said. "I must go back. There is a string of beads around the horse's neck. I want to keep them as a souvenir."

"You don't know anything about selling a horse in Afghanistan," Alphonse said. "A man buys what he sees; everything, even ornaments."

We came to a small store, waited for half an hour, and climbed into a wreck of a truck. The fare was 150 Afghanis ($1.25) per passenger. After about an hour we came to a ramshackle bridge of logs and rope over a small river. The driver got out, walked to the other side, climbed down the bank to look at the underside of the bridge, and came back to say it was not strong enough for the truck to cross. When we got out and walked across the bridge he followed and made another inspection. On second thought, he told us, perhaps the truck could cross, but it would be dangerous. He demanded another 50 Afghanis each for the risk. The customary bargaining ensued, with mock-angry shouts and waving of arms and accusations of who was or was not a good Muslim. At the end of it all Alphonse said we would walk for about an hour and get another truck.

However, we had gone for only a short distance when we met two members of an International Medical Aid team, Dr. Christian Scheph and his nurse Annaik Bellenec, having lunch in a grove near the road. They spoke English as well as French and said they had a clinic nearby and were on their way to see the commander of the valley. A truck came to pick them up and we rode to Doab.

Doab, once a tourist center on the way to the huge Buddhist statues at Bamiyan, was like a scene from a science fiction movie of a dead world after an atomic explosion. We were at an altitude of about 6,000 feet and it was chilly, with a bleak, overcast sky. A tourist hotel stood on a slight rise, looking out over the wide bend of a river toward a distant range of purple mountains. The top of the hotel had been blown away, exposing walls of pink and blue and a reception room littered with debris. On a terrace where tourists once admired the view, a carved fountain was dry and flower pots lay scattered about. A year later, traveling with a German doctor in southwest Afghanistan, I would hear the story of why and when the hotel was destroyed.

There was a bazaar on the road to the hotel, with a row of shops with thick walls where tourists once bought rugs, brass jars, heavy antique jewelry, and the gaudy dresses of nomad women. Now the stalls were shattered, their walls pockmarked with holes from bullets and shell fragments. The street was empty and utterly silent, except for the sound of a cold wind that rattled a door hanging loose on its hinges and shifted papers on the ground.

I wanted to continue to Pakistan with the Turkmens and Tajiks, but Alphonse was talking away happily in French and insisted that we stay for a day with Christian and Annaik. A truck took us north to the village of Barfaq, the headquarters of Bos Mohammed Khan, the ruler of a valley that stretched for about twenty miles. There, we found a National Islamic Front group led by Brigadier Rahmatullah Safi that was just ending a mission in Barfaq and would soon return to Pakistan.

"We Are Armed Against Ourselves"

Safi had a round face and nose, no beard, a neatly clipped gray mustache, and reddish cheeks, looking more like a florid Englishman than an Afghan, with an English accent and a pipe in his mouth to reinforce his appearance. We met after dinner for a talk. He mentioned that he had been chief of King Zahir's bodyguard when Bulganin and Khrushchev visited Kabul in 1955. I remembered that dowdy old palace and said we must have been in the same room more than thirty years earlier. He had trained in the Soviet Union, Britain, and as a parachute officer at Fort Bragg in the United States. When Daoud seized power in 1973, and liberal democrats were suppressed, Safi was sent to prison for two and a half years. He went into exile in London after his release and returned to fight when the Communists came to power in 1978.

"We are fighting for Islam but we should be fighting for Afghanistan as well," he said. "If we just fight for Islam the sectarian and ideological differences that separate us will be emphasized, not only the differences between Sunnis and Shias but also the many differences among Sunnis, including the differences with the fundamentalists. We can fight the Russians for quite a long time if the mujahidin fighting inside the country are not afraid of other Afghans. We can only do this if we fight as a single nation. We must also build up the quality of the fighters and professionalize the jihad. To stand up and be killed just to show you are brave serves no purpose. We must make mujahid blood very expensive for the Russians."

I remarked that he seemed to be saying the opposite from what almost everyone else had told me. Others had talked of the Koran and God as almost the sole source of victory.

"It says in the Koran to depend on God but tie the leg of your camel. It is like saying God helps those who help themselves. When I hear a mullah talk about depending on God I want to tell him: 'Fine, here is a Koran. A tank is coming. Go and stop it.' God gave us brains. We must teach the mujahidin how to use a rocket grenade against a tank. We must also teach civilians. Instead of sitting around all day, the mujahidin should be teaching civil defense. Every woman and child should learn that it takes only an hour to dig a pit two meters long, one and a half meters wide and one meter deep. That's enough to protect them from everything except a bomb that falls directly down on them. We keep hearing that we need better guns against the Russian planes. I say: 'Don't give any sophisticated weapons until the resistance learns and practices simple civil defense.' That would save more lives than thousands of antiaircraft guns.

"Above all, we need unity to develop a professional army that is on duty for twenty-four hours, not soldiers who sit around for two or three months, who eat and don't fight. As it is now, we are not united politically and we are losing the jihad. But if we professionalize the jihad it will make it possible to continue the fighting for a long time and it will be a signal to the Russians that time is not on their side. It will increase the pressure on them to come to some sort of political settlement, if that is possible. The Russians are our enemies but we are only doing things that make them happy. Just look at what you see here. If it were just the Russians to be afraid of I could travel alone to Pakistan, without arms. I would put on a turban, ride a horse, and if there was a Russian post I would ride around it. Now I am taking arms and strong force as a protection against my own people. Disunity breeds distrust and fear. We are armed against ourselves."

An Illiterate Warlord

Alphonse, apparently unsure of his ability as a guide, said we would travel from that point on with Safi's party. But Safi was in no hurry and I spent much of the next two days working on my notes. One day I heard screams from an isolated building. Christian said two horses had recently been stolen, the first such theft in recent memory, and that Bos Mohammed Khan, the valley's warlord, had ordered everyone to track down the thieves. Christian said two men had been captured and were being beaten to make them confess. He said they would probably each have a hand cut off, the traditional Muslim punishment for theft.

Christian explained that he had come to Barfaq to make a request of Bos Mohammed. The warlord had assigned a house near the far end of the valley to serve as a clinic and a commander to act as administrator. Christian wanted the commander removed. For one thing, the day after they set up their clinic, a movie camera was stolen from their room. And then the commander had established his own priorities for clinic treatment. Friends, relatives, and certain mujahidin were given immediate access for trivial complaints while ordinary villagers, no matter how sick, were made to wait.

That night Bos Mohammed gave a dinner for his foreign guests, Brigadier Safi, and some of Safi's aides. I prompted Safi to join me as interpreter in asking Bos Mohammed about schools. When the meal ended, I began by saying that Zabihullah had considered schools a vital part of the jihad and asked Bos Mohammed if he thought of starting schools. He replied that no one had raised the subject before, but in any case he was too busy with the jihad. I said there were young mujahidin among his troops who were educated beyond the eighth grade and could teach elementary reading and writing in their free time. He countered by saying that the villagers would not allow their children to be gathered at one place where they would be exposed to bombs. I told him about caves that were dug for classrooms. Bos Mohammed then said there were no books and papers and he did not have money to buy such things. I said that several foreign groups in Peshawar would certainly supply whatever he needed. Bos Mohammed said he did not know how to contact them.

Safi had warmed to the discussion, framing elaborate questions and using (I was later told) slang phrases and colloquialisms to give them greater meaning. When Bos Mohammed said he did not know how to make contacts in Peshawar, Safi said he would dictate a letter requesting help and circulate it among foreign aid organizations. A clerk took down Safi's words and gave the letter to Bos Mohammed to sign. Only then did I realize that the leader was illiterate. The many arguments he raised against starting schools were thus understandable. Education was a threat to his absolute authority.

The manner of his rule became more apparent the next day, when a bus and truck were hired to take us to Doab. Bos Mohammed came with us, with a guard of a dozen men in uniforms of dark khaki shirts and trousers. Suddenly there was shouting. The driver of the truck was on the ground and the men of the bodyguard were beating him with rifle butts. Alphonse said the driver and truck were hired just to take us to Doab but another truck was not ready and he had been told to take us farther. The driver said he had to return to his family. When he argued, Bos Mohammed had ordered, "Beat him." In a short while the driver shouted his agreement, got back into his truck, and took us on our way.

In the afternoon we arrived at Sheshpul, at one end of a gorge where rock slides blocked the road. It had been a tourist spot. High on one side of a cliff were the authenticated remains of a city that had resisted the armies of Chinggis Khan. At one point in the gorge a raging stream plunged underground, to reappear as a gentle river. At another point there was a hot spring in which a group of men was taking a bath. We spent the night at Kalu, on the other side of the gorge. Safi had horses with him, so that when we went by truck we later had to wait for the animals to catch up. Over the next three days we rode in some places, walked in others, waited for the horses, slaughtered and ate a sheep to restore the mujahidin's energies, and then came to Beksamun where we would cross the Kabul-Kandahar highway.

We left by truck in the late afternoon. From the top of a long hill we saw a convoy of tanks on the road and beat a hasty retreat. We waited, hoping the road would become clear, but finally Brigadier Safi decided not to take chances. He dismissed the truck and we walked all night. In the morning Safi found a bus that took us to Baraki, a large market town on the edge of the wide, bleak Logar desert.

Crossing the Logar Desert

I was weak from diarrhea and able to swallow only bread and rice when it was available. I tried to persuade Alphonse to find our own guide and horses, saying that if we went straight across the desert we would be in Teri Mangal in four days, but he said this was too dangerous. As if to emphasize his caution, a small passenger van riddled with machine gun and bullet holes lay by the side of the main street in Baraki. It had been destroyed in an ambush about three weeks earlier and then towed back to the town for salvage of some of its parts. People also said a caravan of twenty refugees had been ambushed and only one woman survived.

Safi could not make up his mind whether to attempt to cross the desert at Baraki or to go by truck to Charkh, a half day to the west, and attempt to cross there. We waited two days and then went to Charkh. Now, he said there was another possibility: he might continue west, cross the less guarded Zurmat plain and enter Pakistan at Miram Shah. This would mean an added five days. I told Alphonse of my brush with the border police and said I could not risk being arrested in Miram Shah and then, perhaps, being deported from Pakistan. Alphonse still refused to separate from Safi's convoy. Later, when I was sitting off to one side of a room, I looked so despondent that Brigadier Safi asked me why I was troubled. I told him I was completely dependent on Alphonse and saw no way to avoid what might be a disastrous end to a long journey. Safi spoke to Alphonse, and when Alphonse began to argue, Safi assumed his most stern military manner and told him he was taking my money and damn well better do as he was told and be polite about it too.

The next morning Safi brought a man who said he would provide two horses and guides to take us across the desert by a secret way that was less subject to ambush. He asked for 22,000 Afghanis (about $185) and, as others later told me, was surprised when Alphonse accepted without the slightest attempt to bargain. We started across the desert shortly before nightfall. The man who had made the bargain and another, both armed, led the way slowly, scanning the horizon, leading us through gullies, and walking quickly where we seemed exposed. We saw two tanks and waited quietly in a gully until it was completely dark. Then everyone ran, with the horses trotting. We crossed the most dangerous point—a two-lane blacktop highway from Kabul to the strategic base at Gardez in Paktia Province. After crossing the road we slowed down, but continued without a pause until we reached hills on the other side of the desert, where the armed men left us.

We went at a leisurely pace the rest of the night, and at dawn reached Dubandi, an area under mujahidin control. We rested that day, and just after dawn two mornings later reached the high hill looking down to Teri Mangal. It was hardly recognizable as the crowded place where Luigi, Soledad, and I had waited on the way to Jegdalek. A fire, started by an explosion in one of the ammunition shops, had burned down the entire bazaar, and the merchants were doing business in tents until they could build new stalls.

It was June 16. We took a bus to Parachinar and another to Peshawar, where I gave what was left of my money to the three men and arranged with Alphonse to settle our account the next day. I checked in at Green's Hotel and called the consulate to report my return. It was the first they had heard from me in eleven weeks. "There have been some strange reports about you," an official said.

I called a friend and he invited me to dinner. I discovered how hungry I was when I found myself asking for a second helping of meat and vegetables and a second piece of cherry pie and ice cream for dessert.

"Some people said you were dead," he said. "But it doesn't seem so, does it?"

"Happily, it doesn't," I replied.

To the North Again

....

7

The journey to Mazar and back lasted eleven weeks and covered 700 miles. The strengths of the resistance were obvious. Going and coming, hardly a day passed that we did not encounter twenty to 200 men returning to their bases with weapons or traveling south for guns. Their arms were minimal and their supplies meager, but their morale was high and so was their stamina. A commissariat and transport system had developed through the combination of religious dedication and a free-market mechanism. When there was a need to feed and house traveling groups, the tea houses sprang up. When animals or trucks were needed, they appeared. The lack of a central organization meant that no papers had to be filled out, no one sat idle waiting for orders, and there was no one to whom responsibility could be shifted for mistakes. If the enemy attacked and destroyed a part of the system, it repaired itself like an ant heap with thousands of workers and fighters genetically keyed to act without further orders. For the mujahidin, of course, it was not genes but the jihad that coded the response.

Ruins and refugees testified to the savagery of the long war, but civilians appeared to have adjusted to a struggle without end. Daily life unfolded amid biblical simplicity. Often, as I wandered past fields of ripening wheat and rice, through orchards of mulberry, apricot, cherry, and pomegranate trees, past flocks of sheep and goats, with no electric poles, paved roads, billboards, or other modern impedimenta in sight, it was as if I had stepped into an illustration for a Sunday School Bible. The image was especially real once in Mazar, when a white-bearded patriarch in a coat of many colors jogged along on the back of a ridiculously small donkey and we exchanged the ritual "Peace be with you" (*Salaam Aleichem*).

The children who swarmed out to inspect the begoggled foreigner were testimony to the fact that the Afghans were not traumatized by the war. Unlike Europeans during World War II, whose birthrate dropped precipitously, Afghan women appeared to be having as many children as in times of peace.

War and Peace

Mujahidin accounts suggest constant battle and a sweeping destruction of the civilian economy, claims that were reflected in a United Nations report accusing the Soviet Union of approaching a policy of genocide. But in my journey across the country I was never bombed.

After I returned to Peshawar I stayed, as usual, at Green's, resting, writing my stories, and catching up on what had happened while I was isolated in the north. Alain Chevalerias, a French writer and photographer, was also at Green's. He was among the most experienced of the small corps of correspondents trying to make sense of the war. Over the previous five years Alain, familiar to many commanders under his Afghan name, Abdullah, had reported from Mazar, Panjshir, and other distant parts of the country. I asked him how he accounted for the fact that so much of the country seemed to be living in peace.

"The Russians want to win Afghanistan, not wipe it out," he replied. "Look, they don't even use bombers, only MiGs and helicopters to hit specific targets. The only exception was in Panjshir in 1984, when they twice used heavy planes for a carpet-bombing attack. They are selective and don't indulge in blind night bombing. Of course, they often miss and kill innocent civilians, but there is no genocide as some people say. If there is mujahidin activity near their bases the Russians will kill without mercy. That's what is happening in Kunduz, where there are large Russian air bases and garrisons and roads and pipelines leading from the Soviet Union to Kabul. The mujahidin are always harassing their bases and sabotaging their supply lines. The Russians want to destroy them and drive out the civilians who give them food and shelter. But they let other areas alone. Instead, they send in agents of KHAD to tell a chief his village will be spared if he refuses to help the mujahidin. If he forms his own self-defense force and joins the Fatherland Front he'll be given money and guns. This war is 75 percent political and only 25 percent military."

A Splintered Jihad

The most obvious weakness of the resistance movement is its lack of unity, not only among the political parties in Peshawar but also within Afghanistan. The country is divided among regional and local commanders, such as Maulvi Alam in Mazar, Kol Ibrahim in Tunj, and Bos Mohammed in Barfaq. In the absence of central authority, power has reverted to local khans and *maliks* (men who represent village, tribal, or ethnic groupings). Other authority, particularly in matters of justice, fair dealing, and right conduct, is in the hands of the ulama.

In one sense, this makes for the most democratic rule that rural Afghanistan has ever known. Those in authority are local people, answering to local pressures. If a man wants justice he does not have to go far or talk to strangers representing some distant authority. The bureaucrats and great khans who drew their power from Kabul have fled or have been swept away.

Afghanistan has reverted to what it always was beneath the veneer of central rule: an amalgam of thousands of small satrapies. Local chiefs by definition are normally concerned only with the defense of their own territory, as Maulvi Alam implied when he said that local commanders would not supply men for a united attack on Mazar-i-Sharif because each considered his own area more important.

The weakness of the jihad is that it lacks a positive political program to meet the needs of the community. Mao Zedong, Ho Chih Minh, and Fidel Castro demonstrated that success in a guerrilla war depends on which side projects the most appealing political, economic, and social programs and not who shoots the most bullets. But in Afghanistan, except for a few schools in Amarakh, I did not see a single program to help civilians. In fact, commanders such as Bos Mohammed in Barfaq had a positive resistance to even an elemental need such as schooling. I also observed during my trip that people in the countryside have become dependent on supplies from the Communist-controlled cities.

The mujahidin claim to have the complete support of the villages. It is difficult for a foreigner who does not speak the language to test their claims, but I saw enough to suggest that such local support is hardly universal. The man who wanted our convoy to leave the village because we might attract bombs, and the mention by the Belgian medics in Zari of mujahidin taking food from patients, suggests that the mujahidin's welcome may, in at least some cases, be lukewarm at best. The mujahidin have brought destruction on the heads of the villagers but, as Brigadier Safi pointed out, they do not teach them civil defense. The ruined buildings next to the Jamiat headquarters in Shulgara were evidence that the villagers also get little or no help in repairing damage.

Live and Let Live

By attacking only the mujahidin and by refraining from random bombing of civilians the Russians have, in effect, offered local cease-fires, and the offers are generally accepted. The mujahidin freely admitted that they did not attack some targets because of fear of reprisals. Maulvi Alam, for instance, mentioned families living in Mazar-i-Sharif as one reason for not attacking the city. Commander Abdullah spoke of a cease-fire involving the government posts overlooking the Shulgara bazaar.

One result is that the Afghans who live in Communist-controlled cities are hostage to the behavior of the mujahidin. The dependence of the countryside on food supplies from urban areas (an ironic reversal of the usual situation) gives cities additional insurance against mujahidin attack.

It is difficult to come up with a word or phrase that describes accurately the Soviet policy. Usually the word "pacification" is used. This is correct, since the Russians' first goal is to stop the fighting. But pacification suggests an end to resistance, and even the Soviet Union does not hope to achieve this within the foreseeable future. Local commanders who make private deals with a nearby Afghan Army post, or who form self-defense units, are not pacified in the sense of accepting communism or modifying any of their traditional religious and social values.

The Latin phrase "modus vivendi" is defined by Webster's as a "manner of living or of getting along or a temporary agreement in a dispute pending final settlement." This seems closest to describing the immediate aim of the USSR and the Kabul government. Webster's defines the phrase "live and let live" in much the same way: "to do as one wishes and let other people do the same."

To me, this seems to be the most fitting description of Soviet policy. The Russians are trying to bring about an acceptance of live and let live. And the policy is succeeding. The International Institute for Strategic Studies in London reported that Zabihullah's death and a government amnesty "resulted in the virtual dissolution of his band, once 1,000 strong." The report said many of his former followers along with defectors from other groups had joined a Kabul-sponsored "self-defence" force.

The struggle in Afghanistan is laced with paradox; it is a war, but the Russians are not trying to win a military victory. Unlike Vietnam, where the United States escalated its forces in a vain attempt to win on the battlefield, the Soviet Union has steadily maintained its occupation strength at about 118,000 men. In 1986 it even conducted a token withdrawal of 8,000 men.

The Russians appear to believe that time is on their side; that a new generation of Afghans can be weaned away from Islam and traditional Afghan values. In the meantime, they consolidate their hold over urban areas and major transportation lines, denying any significant or permanent victories to the mujahidin.

But the Russians also have their weaknesses—particularly the low morale of their soldiers who are sent to a comfortless country to face a guerrilla enemy who fights with mines and shots in the dark. They do not even have the abstract justification of taking part in a struggle to defend the motherland. Moscow has always excused its intervention as an effort to protect a fraternal socialist government against a foreign capitalist effort to destroy it. Soldiers sent to Afghanistan are said to be performing their "internationalist duties." It is not a compelling reason for a conscript to risk his life.

The Revolt at Mattani

In May of 1985, while I was in Mazar, a prison uprising erupted at a Jamiat-i-Islami base at Mattani, in Pakistan's tribal territory. Early reports said that Russian soldiers held captive there seized control of part of the camp and demanded to be taken to the Soviet embassy in Islamabad. Both the Peshawar-based parties and the Pakistani government were so successful in blacking out the news that the first reports came from Moscow, where the Pakistani ambassador was handed an official protest against the detention of Soviet soldiers on Pakistani soil, along with a demand for the return of the bodies, which Moscow put at twelve. The Pakistanis replied with a flat denial that any Soviet soldiers were detained within Pakistan.

But in Peshawar authoritative mujahidin sources told me that some

Afghan Communists, also held at the camp, had instigated the revolt. In the disorder that followed, according to these sources, the Russians and perhaps some of the Afghan Communists entrenched themselves in an area used to store munitions. Professor Rabbani, the Jamiat leader, went to the camp to negotiate but without success. Shooting began and the munitions exploded, killing from nine to twelve Soviet soldiers and twelve Afghans. My informants were not sure whether the Afghans were prisoners held with the Russians or were part of the attacking force.

I pursued the subject. Mujahidin leaders, as well as relief workers and others who monitored the Afghan situation, estimated the numbers of Russian prisoners in mujahidin hands at from 100 to 200. Speaking off the record and not for attribution, they conceded that about half of these prisoners, that is, from 50 to 100 men, were held on Pakistani soil—in several of the large resistance camps in tribal territory as well as in similar camps in Baluchistan Province. Some authoritative mujahidin sources told me that Russian defectors were so well integrated in resistance ranks that they could wander freely with their Afghan companions through the streets of Peshawar, where they could easily pass for Tajiks from northern Afghanistan, since Afghan Tajiks are often fair-skinned, with blue or gray eyes and a general appearance similar to that of many of the Russian soldiers sent to Afghanistan. If the Soviet defectors are stopped and questioned by the Pakistani police, the fact that the defectors do not speak Urdu or Pushtu, the languages most commonly heard in Peshawar, is not necessarily a giveaway; thousands of Uzbeks, Turkmens, and Tajiks from Afghanistan don't speak these languages either.

I decided to take another trip into Afghanistan to find out more about Russian prisoners. After the Mattani incident, the parties were cautious on the subject of prisoners anywhere near Pakistan, but they had no reservations about discussing prisoners held in the north. I wanted experience with some party other than Jamiat, with whom I had traveled both to Jegdalek and Mazar. Two others—the Harakat-i-Inqilab and the Hizb-i-Islami—were strong in the north. I put in my request with both of them, concentrating on Harakat. The Hizbi, as it is generally called, accepted the fundamentalist belief that the United States and the Soviet Union were equally opposed to the Islamic revolution. It seemed unlikely that this party would want an American trailing along with its mujahidin.

A Talk in the Atrium

I told spokesmen of both parties that I needed an interpreter with a good command of English and said I would pay whatever was considered a more-than-adequate salary. I went to the Harakat office twice a week, only to be told repeatedly that an interpreter was hard to find and that my security presented serious problems. To my surprise, the Hizbi turned out to be more receptive. Qaribur Rahman Saeed, the Hizbi official who dealt with the press, came to Green's Hotel to say a convoy would leave for Baghlan Province the next day, on July 31. Was I interested? I was. Saeed returned in a few hours with a former agriculture student at Kabul University, a young man who would be my interpreter.

We were sitting in the restaurant in Green's Hotel, where we could not speak freely, but from the few sentences I was able to exchange with the interpreter, his English seemed adequate. When he said he had family obligations, and his mother was sick, I assumed he wanted to be assured that he would be well paid. I said I would pay 1,000 Pakistani rupees ($62) a week, double the wage for an educated person in Peshawar.

In the center of Green's is an atrium open to the sky, with plants and flowing water at ground level, designed to cool the interior in the days before air conditioning. Now the atrium serves another purpose: those with a need for secrecy, of whom there are many in Peshawar, can talk in whispers there without being overheard.

Saeed and I went to the atrium. He said there was a large Hizbi camp somewhere in Baghlan Province, north of the Hindu Kush, with fifteen or sixteen Russian prisoners. I could also go further north to Chardara in Kunduz Province, where he said the Soviets had slaughtered hundreds of old men, women, and children. The trip north would take about three weeks. Then I would have two weeks to talk with the prisoners and the survivors of the Soviet atrocities, and the return trip would take another three weeks—a total of eight weeks.

I was prepared for just such last-minute notice. My travel gear was packed and I had enough Pakistani rupees to buy a horse and pay my other expenses. Saeed said I would spend the night at a Hizbi safe house in Peshawar, in case anyone was watching me, and that we would leave from there early in the morning.

The Virtue of Patience

I was taken to a dimly lit room with an overhead fan stirring the stale, hot air and sat for an hour until Saeed arrived to report bad news: the interpreter said it was impossible for him to leave his mother. But Saeed said he might be able to persuade someone else to go with me. This would be a former Kabul University student who had spent a few months in London, where he was sent by Hizbi to improve his English.

As Saeed left to find the man, I told myself to be patient and just relax. I had already notified the American consulate and telexed the *New York Times* of my imminent departure. The worst that could happen now was that I would have to rescind these notifications and go back to nagging Harakat for a trip. Then Saeed returned beaming with pleasure. The man had agreed.

He joined us as we set out in the morning. His name was Qadrutullah Arif, thirty-two, a slim man about five feet ten, with a full black beard and wide eyes. We quickly agreed on a fee. I said I was grateful that he was coming on a long trip with such short notice and suggested 1,200 rupees ($75) a week. He accepted without discussion.

Saeed hired a new white jeep for the trip, thinking it looked official and would keep the police from stopping us. But just before the wide Kohat valley, where the highway twists to the top of a pass, we found that the police were inspecting all vehicles. As a plainclothes officer approached us, Saeed gave me the usual instructions: say nothing. The officer asked me who I was and where I was going. I remained silent. He talked to Saeed and then repeated the question to me. I remained silent. Saeed got out, and as he and the officer talked further, Arif told me I should say I was a doctor going to treat a recently wounded mujahid at Arfat, a place I had never heard of. The policeman returned, told me to get out of the car, and asked me again where I was going. I said I was a doctor going to Arfat. He asked why I had not spoken earlier. I said I was just doing what my companions told me to do. Meantime, my bag and camera case were being searched.

In about ten minutes we got back into the jeep and drove off. Saeed was laughing. He said the policeman had asked for a bribe of 5,000 rupees, which he had flatly refused, saying they were poor mujahidin and never had so much money. When the policeman asked for my passport, saying he had not found it in my bag (it was in a small inner pocket in the camera case), Saeed had told him it was kept in the Hizbi office.

We stopped at Parachinar for lunch and a long visit at a Hizbi office.

Thunder and heavy monsoon clouds hovered over the mountains of Afghanistan. Rain poured down in the early afternoon as we started for Teri Mangal, turning the normally dry riverbeds into muddy torrents. The drivers of buses and cars clustered on the banks, waiting for the water level to drop. Saeed had said the convoy would leave Teri Mangal in the afternoon, and when we came to a river where the water was racing furiously, I worried about getting there in time. Again, I told myself to relax and let come what may. The jeep now proved its worth. The driver geared down and slowly worked his way through the flood, lurching over hidden rocks with the water lapping over the fenders.

Dirt, Diarrhea, and Diamonds in the Sky

Our commander for the journey north was Fazl Rahim, a man in his early thirties, of medium height, with a soft smile and a thick black beard. He was the brother of one of the three Hizb-i-Islami general commanders for Baghlan Province. Fazl Rahim was waiting for us; the convoy would leave in an hour. Arif hurried to buy a horse and I sat amid the mud and ruins of the burned Teri Mangal bazaar, my thoughts of what lay ahead overlaid with all-too-fresh memories: the dirt and diarrhea, the fleas and greasy food, hard ground for a bed, hours of riding a horse, legs aching from constriction. And above all, the boredom and loneliness of endless hours among people whose language I did not understand. Only six weeks had passed since I had left all that.

Arif found a horse for the equivalent of $250. Then there was a final detail to settle: What would I be called? Arif suggested Jan, pronounced like the English name John. I agreed and later was told it meant "dear." Soon I was riding up the steep trail to the last border post, on past the wrecked tank and the ruins of the German-aid wood factory. I was later to discover that three Arabs were in our convoy. One of them, inspired by the jihad, began a long, clear recitation from the Koran. As I felt the cool air of Afghanistan and listened to the cadence of the chanting, the clatter of hooves against stones, and the shouts of men prodding their animals forward, I thought that I had good memories too from my other trips, of high mountains and wide desert plains, clear streams and bejeweled night skies, the comradeship of long marches and shared meals.

As we approached the Afghan Army post at Jaji a few hours later, we heard shouts of "Allah Akbar" (God is great) and saw tracer bullets streaking through the night: The local mujahidin were staging a routine harassing attack against the post. Amid the rattle of guns and the explosion of shells, men in our convoy led the horses into a ravine and spread their blankets to sleep until the attack ended, which it did in about an hour. Then we were on our way again.

We stopped shortly before dawn at a string of four teahouses. Because of the dangers of air attacks during the day, we would rest there and start again late in the afternoon. Heavy clouds and distant thunder marked the route ahead. Rain began to fall as the animals were loaded to resume the march. Then someone fired warning shots: A roaring wall of water was filling a narrow ravine next to the trail and spreading across terraced fields. Our horses, already loaded, were led quickly to a village on high ground about a quarter of a mile away. But two other groups only had time to lead their animals away; their heavy loads were left to be covered by the water.

The mujahidin, with their cheerful acceptance of setbacks, searched for bits of dry wood for a fire to make tea. When the waters began to recede, the men of the other groups took off their shirts and shoes and waded into the muck to drag and lift their equipment to firm ground. They made a game of it, laughing when someone fell into the water and rose black with mud.

I was surprised to find people living in the village where we sought shelter. The usual impression is that the entire border area has been depopulated to a depth of twenty to forty miles and only empty ruins are to be seen along the traveled routes. But here was evidence of Afghan tenacity in the face of daily danger: while some leave, others remain to preserve the collective hold on homes and land. Small locks on the doors of vacant houses further demonstrated that those who went to Pakistan expected to return some day.

When the villagers noticed a foreign visitor they brought tea and bread. Since the road ahead was probably deep in mud and blocked by swollen streams, it seemed reasonable to spend the night here and wait for the ground to dry out. But when I asked Arif if we were staying he said: "We don't know these people. We can't sleep among them. They know that commanders who have just come from Pakistan carry a great deal of money and have many valuable guns. They might kill us while we sleep." I had forgotten the intense suspicion with which the Afghans regard one another.

So we set off again late in the afternoon, the animals slipping in the mud left by the retreating waters. When we crossed and recrossed a torrent, Arif took off his shoes and waded over the sharp rocks, leading my horse by the reins. But I soon regained my confidence as a rider, and when we turned up a side valley I told Arif to walk with the men along a narrow trail higher up on the valley side while I continued with the other horses and mules along a riverbed.

The cinch of my saddle was loose and, as I guided the horse through the waters, I felt I would slip off. But that, as it turned out, was not the main hazard. Suddenly, as the last light was disappearing, a heavily loaded packhorse in front of me sank into a mire of dirt and river stones so saturated with water that it was like quicksand. Before I could turn my horse aside it too began to sink. I looked ahead at the pack-horse. Its forelegs had sunk so deeply that only its chin rested on the ooze and panic filled its eyes. If it sank any deeper, it would drown. My horse too sank to its belly. I pulled at the reins to get it to firmer ground while trying to keep my balance on the slipping saddle.

There were shouts and a rush of activity. One young man grabbed the first horse's head while another grabbed its tail. They began to work the animal free. Left to ourselves, my own horse and I managed to work our way to safety. Arif appeared and guided me in the darkness for about a mile to a rest house—actually just a large canvas stretched over poles. There was hot food, and a pile of burning logs, and we settled in for the night.

Youth Must Serve

The next day I talked with the young man, still a boy really, who had helped rescue the horse. He was one of nine men hired with their horses to carry our munitions and supplies. He said he was fifteen and his name was Ali Khan.

"I didn't go to school," he said. "My father died when I was twelve and I had to earn money to help support my mother and three brothers, who are younger than I am. I went to Kabul to sell potatoes from the back of a donkey. A Communist there tried to cheat me and I hit him with my stick and I think I blinded him. I had to leave Kabul so I took up this work and now I have two horses. There isn't a lot of money in this. I could get another job or go to Iran to work. But we have started our jihad against the Russians and even small children must take part. That is why I started at my age. God is with us and we are sure we will make the Russians leave our country."

I also tried to talk with the Arabs but had little success. The previous day, while we were waiting for the flash flood to recede, I heard one

Ali Khan, fifteen, who said, "God is with us. We are sure we will make the Russians leave our country."

of them speaking English to Arif, asking who I was and what I was doing in Afghanistan. But when I questioned the man, he would not talk about himself or his companions, other than to say his name was Abdullah and that they were on a mission to study the jihad.

I never had a chance to find out more about them. They were traveling with another Hizbi group that was on the trail just ahead of us. I guessed they were Wahhabi fundamentalists from Saudi Arabia. Abdullah, while describing their interest in the jihad, said Islam was the last and hence the most perfected of the religions revealed by God. That is a common fundamentalist assumption. Later, in the few times the two Hizbi groups traveled together, I saw the Arabs gathering the mujahidin for fervent group prayers.

Another night's journey brought us to Dubandi. The towers and long wall of a large fort atop a hill testified to its strategic site on an ancient trail. Tank tracks and rusting Soviet ration cans testified to its continuing military value. The area was controlled by a Harakat unit under Commander Ahsan Gul, a man of about thirty, who had a sharp nose and deep-set eyes. He wore a green turban and a double cartridge belt strung over his chest. He said he started with a hunting rifle and had been fighting for seven years.

"I have 200 mujahidin," he said. "They stay in our bases for two months and then are relieved. To get food, we send elderly people to Kabul. They bring back flour, rice, sugar, and whatever else we need. Last year the Russians put down a helicopter commando force at two places and then sent tanks to try to capture Dubandi. They held it for three days but we sent a force to their rear and the tanks had to retreat. We shot down a helicopter with an antitank RPG-7. Our mujahid was high on a ridge and fired down on it."

I asked about his relations with other groups. "There is no difference between the political parties," he replied. "We help any commander who comes here and we send someone out as a protection against ambushes on the road ahead."

We were now approaching the Logar desert and the Kabul-Gardez road. Six weeks earlier I had been with Brigadier Safi in Baraki, on the other side of the desert. Because of the danger, we then went west to Charkh, where Alphonse and our small party crossed the desert at a narrower point.

It was still a dangerous place. For several days the enemy had had ambush units in place and many mujahidin groups were waiting for the trail to open. Ahsan Gul said he had agents inside Afghan Army camps, to warn of the enemy's movements, and scouts out in the desert to guard against an ambush. He said they reported that the way was now clear.

The different groups, which were scattered and hidden in ravines or under trees, gradually assembled at a canyon called Kafirdara (Place of the Unbelievers), a reference, perhaps, to a pre-Islamic archaeological site.

About 400 men wearing every possible variation of costume and turban clustered in an area 50 feet wide and 200 feet long with 150 horses, mules, donkeys, and camels. The canyon walls, 50 feet high, seemed to provide good security, but Ali Khan said it was not as safe as it seemed. He said he was with a group that had been ambushed near Kafirdara just seven months earlier, with six mujahidin "martyred" and sixteen animals killed, though none of his horses or people.

"You're only fifteen," I said. "How many times have you been ambushed?"

"Three times," he replied. "The ambush near here was the first. The second ambush was four months ago. We all escaped. But then, about two months ago, I lost three horses in an ambush."

"What happens if one of your horses is killed?" I asked. "Does the man who has rented them pay you for the loss?"

"Oh, no," he said. "We must pay for ourselves and the horses and if a horse is killed that is also our responsibility."

Ghostly Shadows

The men had been wandering about, meeting old friends and kissing, embracing, and gossiping. As it grew dark they separated into their individual units and the long column snaked silently across the desert, each man listening intently for the distant sound of an armored car or tank that could signal an attack.

A three-quarter moon rose at midnight, sending long shadows of men and animals across the white, saline soil and revealing the evidence of past attacks: a mass of eight horse carcasses, the bones of horses and camels, scattered packs and bits of clothing and shoes, and every now and then a pile of rocks with one, two, or three pennants marking the graves of men who had not made it across. Once, as our group passed through a deserted village, a shot broke the silence and the men scattered to firing positions in ditches and behind walls. It turned out that someone had fired his gun by accident. We had to gallop and run to catch up with the column.

After we passed the Kabul-Gardez road, our pace slowed and the cohesion of the march deteriorated, some groups sitting down to rest, others to sleep, and some pressing on. At dawn our group straggled into Baraki. I remembered the town from the two days I was there with Brigadier Safi. It had never been bombed or strafed, although it was a major stopping-off point for the mujahidin.

Arif had a rash on his hands and arms and we went to a shop to buy an ointment. Mohammed Gul, the English-speaking owner, had converted an eight-by-twenty-four-foot container used for shipping goods by sea into a store where he sold medicines with labels from Pakistan, Iran, China, Korea, and several European countries. He said he bought the container in Kabul and trucked it to Baraki. I asked Mohammed Gul how he explained why Baraki was not bombed.

"There are no mujahidin bases here," he said. "There are also a lot of spies here. We suppose they tell the Russians how many mujahidin pass through and what they are carrying and so we are left in peace."

Although a few houses seemed new and some were being repaired, many had vacant windows and collapsed walls. Baraki was crumbling through neglect. Thanks to some forgotten foreign aid program, it had once enjoyed what was for Afghanistan the luxury of water piped to outlets in the streets. All that remained of this system was an occasional cement post to support a pipe, which sometimes had parts of a faucet still attached. Once Baraki also had a municipal trash-collection system, and alcoves for receptacles had been built neatly into the sides of houses to leave room for traffic on a narrow lane. But now there was garbage everywhere. The bazaar on the outskirts of the town, which obviously had developed to service the hundreds of men passing through, was the usual collection of ramshackle shops lining a muddy street.

The bullet-riddled minibus I had seen on my earlier visit to Baraki was gone. Now I saw a fairly new, bright yellow taxi from the streets of Kabul, about two hours' drive away. It was a strange war, I thought, where someone could hire a taxi to go back and forth from one side to the other.

The next leg of our trip was by night, to cross the Kabul-Kandahar highway. The Hizbi group with the three Arabs was traveling just ahead of us, under Commander Ghulam Rabbani. He had been delayed at Dubandi and traveled in the same long line that we did to Baraki. To regain time, he set out late the same day. His arms and munitions were piled on a large Soviet flatbed truck. His men rode standing up in the back of another Soviet truck. Arif said both vehicles belonged to a local Hizbi commander in Baraki, who had captured them about a year earlier. Our own party set out the next day in two vehicles hired from the local Harakat commander. Apparently, though there were no mujahidin bases in Baraki, all the parties had offices in the town.

Our animals had been sent ahead. Fazl Rahim, Arif, and I squeezed into the front seat of a German truck and the men rode in the rear. The truck was in good condition—the dials on the dashboard actually worked. The driver, Bismullah, managed briefly to hit a respectable speed of thirty-five kilometers an hour on the rutted road. In about two hours we stopped within a few kilometers of the highway. Bismullah was paid the equivalent of 43 cents for each of the men in our group, who, as I now counted, totaled forty-eight. The driver of a second truck carrying the munitions was paid separately.

A Game of Charades

Now came one of the most curious examples of live and let live I ever saw in Afghanistan. Ahead of us, the highway crossed a bridge over a deep ravine. Next to the bridge was a village. Militia ostensibly loyal to Kabul controlled the village and guarded the bridge. No mujahidin could approach in the daytime, when Soviet and Afghan Army convoys passed along the highway, but the militia tacitly allowed the mujahidin to cross the highway at night, when there was no Communist traffic. Even so, there were certain rules. The mujahidin, as well as their animals and supplies, had to circle around the edge of the village. A truck could go straight through, but only such vehicles as could normally travel in Soviet-controlled areas. This eliminated captured Soviet vehicles and others without legal license plates.

Our party loaded its equipment onto the animals and led them off on a shortcut straight across some hills. After dark, the rest of us piled into a decrepit American truck with Kabul license plates. We drove for about fifteen minutes, got out again, and filed silently along a path by a side wall of the village. At two places we were offered drinking water as a gesture of goodwill. The empty truck, meanwhile, went through the village, turned onto the highway, and went on for five minutes before stopping to await our arrival. On foot, we silently crossed the highway, walked into the countryside, and then turned back to the highway where we rejoined the truck. There, the unruly streak that is always present in the mujahidin asserted itself. They struggled for positions as they scrambled into the truck, with angry shouts. Then I heard shots.

I grew tense. Arif had kept me safe in the middle of the group as we passed by the village. We were about thirty feet from the truck when the shooting started. I thought that if there was a tank or armored car in the village we could be attacked within minutes. But Arif was not worried. "They're like children," he said, referring to the mujahidin, and told me to sit quietly by the side of the trail until order was restored. It was only later that I realized that there had never been any danger of attack and that our whole clandestine trip past the village had been a charade, acted out with Soviet complicity by both the government militia and the mujahidin.

It was nine o'clock when we got back into the truck. We rode for twenty minutes along the highway with headlights blazing, maneuvering around mine holes in the road, passing the skeletons of tanks and other vehicles pushed off to the side. Then we turned off onto a dirt track and stopped for dinner near the destroyed ziyarat of a saint called Shah Qalandar Baba. Before the driver let our group get back on the truck he lined everybody up to count heads and collect fares. For the first time I got a good look at him. He was the same man who had tried to squeeze extra money from our party on my earlier trip, by pretending there was a weak bridge on the route back to Pakistan. Schooled in deception, he guarded against being cheated himself and now he was careful to get his fare, the equivalent of $1.25, from each passenger. I also discovered why there had been a fight for space on the truck. Others had joined our group, so that sixty men were squeezed into the back.

After an hour's travel we reached Beksamun, where we spent the next day waiting for the animals to arrive and to rest. I asked Fazl Rahim why the mujahidin did not simply destroy the highway bridge where we had played out the elaborate charade the day before.

"We could destroy that post and the bridge," he agreed. "But the Russians would destroy all the villages in the area and drive the people to Pakistan as refugees. Then they would install their own post. We need villagers to grow food and give us shelter."

Toward the end of the next day we passed through a gorge with firm rock walls, where once there were plans for a hydroelectric dam. Just beyond it was Tangi Saidan, with several teahouses near a small river. Here Ali Khan and the other horse men were paid off. It turned out to be an elaborate process. The verbal contract called for payment of the equivalent of $6.75 for a local unit of weight that equaled fifteen pounds. But there was only a hand scale—borrowed from a merchant—to do the weighing. It was two trays strung from the ends of a stick, like the scales of justice in classical sculpture. Since the space on the round plate of the scale was limited, only one can of ammunition was weighed. Then all cans of a similar size were counted, multiplied by the weight of a single can, and a total determined. Since a box of mortar shells was too large for the scale, one shell had to be weighed, then a figure arrived at for an entire box, and this, in turn, was multiplied by the number of boxes. And so on for several kinds of mines, tubes containing antitank grenades, and separate bundles of rocket charges for the grenades. There was no way to weigh a bulky mortar tube plus its base plate or a heavy 12.7-mm Dashika with its large tripod. A dispute over estimating those weights lasted an hour.

Finally it was all worked out. Nine men had supplied seventeen horses to carry about one and three-quarter tons of arms and munitions. In the eight days since we had left Teri Mangal they had fed the animals and paid personal expenses, and they would have to spend another eight days returning to Pakistan. For all that, the bill was only $1,855, or $109.12 per man. If a horse was lost or injured, they would have to bear the loss themselves. As Ali Khan said, there was not much money in the business.

Again, Shia versus Shia

A large passenger bus arrived the next afternoon. We climbed aboard for the next stage of our journey and spent the night at a teahouse along the way. The next morning we reached Tillim Jai, a major junction of mujahidin trails and truck routes leading in several directions to the east and west as well as north and south. We were still following, in the reverse direction, the route I had traveled south with Brigadier Safi. I remembered Tillim Jai as an undistinguished marshy valley. Now there was a difference.

At the outskirts of the town, a man who appeared to be a Hazara stood in the middle of the road holding a Kalashnikov. He turned out to be from Nasir, the pro-Khomeini Shia group. Both Fazl Rahim and Arif got out to talk, but when a mujahid with an antitank rocket launcher also got out, the guard ordered him back into the bus and pulled the door closed. Beside the road was a building with sandbags on the roof. Three heads and the barrels of three guns appeared over the rim of the sandbags. Farther along the road, on a bit of high ground, a Dashika was pointed in our direction.

Fazl Rahim and Arif went down a slope to where several men were sitting on rugs spread beside a stream. Tea was brought and it was an hour before they returned. Arif said the Nasir commander had asked for our identification and party affiliation but not for money or munitions. Arif also said that farther along the road we would pass posts manned by Harakat-i-Islami, a Shia group that was allied to the Sunni parties in Peshawar.

There had been no such checkpoints when I passed this way with Brigadier Safi only six weeks earlier. That meant that struggle among the Shias, and the influence of the pro-Khomeini forces, was spreading east to the lower and easier passes through the Hindu Kush, where the Shias are numerous but still in a minority.

As Arif had been warned, we were stopped at two Harakat-i-Islami posts. The Shia commanders here complained of the danger they faced from Nasir and asked for ammunition. Fazl Rahim gave the first commander a tin of 250 Dashika cartridges, but refused either money or ammunition to the second, telling him to go to the Hizbi office in Peshawar if he needed help. I asked him why the parties tolerated feuding Shia groups, particularly the pro-Khomeini Nasir party, on their main supply lines.

"If we fight with them we will not be able to fight the Russians," he replied. "After we have forced the Russians out we will deal with these separate parties."

We changed to a truck in Tillim Jai and reached Kalu late in the afternoon. I was beginning to understand how the road system worked. The route was divided into sections, each under the control of a single commander or an alliance of commanders. In this manner the business was distributed among party sympathizers while, simultaneously, a commander could exercise a degree of control over who and what passed through his area. For each section there was a fixed rate for passengers and freight although there seemed to be no relationship between the rates in different areas. For instance, we were charged $2.50 per person and 25 cents per fifteen pounds of freight for the bus trip from Tangi Saidan to Tillim Jai, which involved an overnight stop, but about $3.35 per person and 40 cents per fifteen pounds for the truck from Tillim Jai to Kalu, a journey of only four hours, including long waits at checkpoints.

Ripe Fruit, Rotting Camels

The face of the war changed north of the Kabul-Kandahar highway. South of the highway, the villages were badly damaged, fields were abandoned, and irrigation canals were destroyed or had collapsed for lack of care. We traveled at night because of the threat of air attacks. But the Hazarajat was virtually untouched by war. We rode openly by day. In the fields farmers were harvesting their crops, driving horses and bullocks in circles over piles of wheat, and pitchforking the trampled stalks into the air to winnow the chaff from the grain. Apples and peaches ripened in ancient orchards, and children chased goats and sheep in the hills. The few villagers I had time to talk with showed me ruined houses and bomb craters but conceded that the damage was two or three years old. Now, they said, they were mostly left in peace.

But the road was not entirely safe. We passed a few destroyed trucks along the way. The driver who took us to Kalu, twenty-three-year-old Mohammed Hassan, had another truck destroyed by a helicopter last year. He carried us in an old International Harvester truck with no hood over the engine and no glass in the windshield. He said a cousin bought it for him in Kabul for the equivalent of $5,000 and that he was able to get diesel fuel from Kabul for 10 cents a liter.

"I began as a helper to learn to drive and now I have this business," he said. "It's dangerous but what else can I do?"

Just a little beyond Kalu, at the entrance to a narrow gorge, a stench arose from the rotting carcasses of eight camels and a horse. Camels are not good for travel in war-torn Afghanistan because if they are frightened they bunch up and refuse to move, instead of scattering as horses would. But refugees, especially those who were nomads, favor them because they can carry a heavier load and are easier to feed and care for than horses. Mohammed Hassan said a helicopter had attacked a refugee group here a few days earlier. The camels failed to move quickly enough and were destroyed, along with a horse that was caught among them. I would learn later that there was a special reason for So- viet planes to attack nomads: vengeance.

We had been traveling all day and I expected to spend the night at Kalu. Instead Fazl Rahim hired about twenty donkeys to carry the mu- nitions and we walked through the gorge, passing the hot springs and the river that disappeared underground, and reached Sheshpul at mid- night. Still we did not sleep. Fazl Rahim hired another truck that carried us to Doab, where the exposed pastel walls of the ruined hotel and the abandoned bazaar had reminded me before of a scene from a science fiction movie. We arrived early in the morning, had something to eat and short naps, and were off in another truck at noon, passing through Barfaq, where I had the long talk about schools with Bos Mohammed Khan, and continued on to Tala. Two more trucks took us to a collection of houses where we finally had a night's rest. Then it was back into the truck for a jolting ride through narrow, rock-strewn gorges and grind- ing up hills to the sprawling, dusty village of Kamirak.

When we rested the next day the mujahidin slaughtered a goat, but the meat had a strong smell and I could not eat it. They brought me hard-boiled eggs instead. The diarrhea attacks had resumed and I con- soled myself with the thought that the discomforts would some day fade into memory, but the truth was that my bodily functions were a constant preoccupation.

I was also depressed over the purpose of my trip. It had been twelve days since we left Peshawar. I wanted a clear idea of what my program would be and asked Fazl Rahim about Russian prisoners. To my sur-

A file of donkeys carrying arms and ammunition across a desert plateau in Baghlan Province.

prise, he said there were no prisoners in Baghlan. I said Saeed, at the Hizbi office in Peshawar, had told me of a camp with fifteen or sixteen prisoners. Fazl Rahim said he knew of no such camp. I felt I was living through my experiences in Mazar all over again, wandering in northern Afghanistan with no clear idea of what I was looking for. I had already written a series for the *New York Times* about the trip to Mazar, and I needed to explore some new aspect of the war to make this second trip worthwhile.

By now a mujahid who had been riding my horse while we traveled by truck had caught up with us. We left Kamirak the next afternoon, moving in a file with twenty-two donkeys across the low hills of a desert plateau, with winds whipping columns of dust into the air. That night we would cross the strategic highway that runs from the Soviet Union to Kabul, via the Salang Pass tunnel. An above-ground pipeline paralleled the highway, carrying aviation fuel, diesel fuel, and ordinary gasoline that were pumped at separate times through the single pipe. It was the most heavily guarded road in Afghanistan, patrolled day and night. The mujahidin had often attempted to sabotage the pipeline but never managed to disrupt the flow for more than half a day or so.

"They Will Try to Capture You"

We came to the outskirts of Dahana Ghouri shortly before dark. Arif gave me his turban to wear and took the Chitrali hat with the rolled brim that I found more comfortable. He told me to pull my blanket over my head and sit quietly by the side of the road: The Russians had learned that three Arabs and an American were going to cross the highway. "There are many spies here and they will try to capture you," he said.

For whatever reason, the enemy patrols were alert. No groups had been able to cross the highway for several nights and there was a jam of waiting mujahidin. Horses were in short supply. The first groups had already set out by the time Fazl Rahim found villagers who would agree to take us across the road with their camels. Just then, orange parachute flares shot into the black skies ahead of us. Machine guns rattled and shells exploded in the distance. Word came that there had been an ambush and there would be no further attempts that night to cross the highway. Our camel drivers led us across fields to a village to wait until the next day.

The group that had been ambushed was the Hizbi party led by Ghulam Rabbani. They had been traveling a day ahead of us, and were toward the front of the jam of men and animals waiting to cross the road. The first part of Rabbani's group actually crossed the road, but the animals and supplies were still on the highway when the flares were fired to light up the field of fire. The men escaped without casualties, including the three Arabs who were traveling with Ghulam Rabbani, but the munitions carried so laboriously from Pakistan had to be abandoned.

The villagers who had the camels now refused to take us across. Instead, a fourteen-wheel German truck—supplied, Arif said, by the local Hizbi commander—was brought to load both Fazl Rahim's and Ghulam Rabbani's groups for an attempt to cross the highway somewhere else. But enemy soldiers were also patrolling these other areas and the attempt had to be put off for another night. The two Hizbi groups now separated for greater safety.

When Fazl Rahim first discovered the shortage of animals he sent a message to his brother asking for horses to carry the munitions. His message was garbled in transmission, and only three horses were sent.

Fazl Rahim decided to leave most of the munitions in a friendly village to be retrieved later.

We set out the next night on a little-traveled trail miles away from the usual crossing point. The route began up a rocky slope that was so steep the hooves of the horses slipped on the smooth boulders. My horse fell on its side, but I managed to jump clear and found a rock to stand on to remount. At the top of the slope we filed silently within 200 yards of an Afghan Army post before moving down toward the highway. Then we froze. A searchlight stabbed the darkness. A Soviet armored car patrolling the pipeline had halted and its light was sweeping the sides of the road to detect possible saboteurs. After a breathless ten minutes, the armored car moved on and we started again, moving parallel to the road. But then a light flashed in the other direction. The road was monitored by pairs of armored cars moving in opposite directions, and the second car was coming toward us. We froze again. I didn't dare get off the horse in case I couldn't mount again quickly. The armored car stopped and swept the side of the hill with its light. I lay flat against the horse's neck. I could almost feel the light moving across me and I could see the long shadow cast by the horse. But the car moved on and we ran and trotted across the road to the safety of hills on the other side.

We went on through the night and at dawn were back in an active war zone. Jets bombed some distant target and artillery shells could be heard exploding over a hill. Arif said he was feeling sick. I gave him the horse and walked with several men who brought me, late in the morning, to the ruins of New Baghlan, once a fashionable (for Afghanistan) suburb of Baghlan city, now shattered and empty.

I could not find either Arif or Fazl Rahim. Instead I was befriended by Mohammed Khalid, a young commander who spoke some English, which he said he learned while studying agriculture at Kabul University before the war. With a sporadic rattle of machine gun fire around us, he showed me the sights of New Baghlan: where the enemy had posts and where the mujahidin dug trenches to besiege and exchange shots with them. He also led me to Ghulam Rabbani, the Hizbi commander whose supplies were lost in the ambush while crossing the highway. Rabbani arranged for me to be reunited with Fazl Rahim.

A Disappearing Defector

A guard of four men was assembled just before dark. "And there is our Russian," Mohammed Khalid said, as if it were the most ordinary thing in the world. He pointed to one of the guards. "He has joined our jihad."

I looked at the man. He had a fair, freckled face, reddish hair, pale blue eyes, and large ears. He wore a turban and Afghan clothes and had a Kalashnikov slung over his shoulder. I shook his hand and my spirits rose. The long and tiresome trip now had a focus. Here was a Russian, not just a prisoner but a defector fighting in the ranks of the mujahidin. I started to ask Mohammed Khalid about the man but he said I must leave immediately.

It was the kind of journey I hated the most: at night, on foot, across rough fields, and on the edge of slippery irrigation channels. When I obviously could not keep up, a man put a strong arm under my right arm to prop me up and almost dragged me along. After about two hours the guard was changed and the Soviet defector disappeared into the night. After another three hours, when I was nearing exhaustion, we came to a village where I was taken to the house of Amir Rasul, the brother of Fazl Rahim, who showed me to a bed with a flat spring and a mattress for the most comfortable sleep I would have on the entire trip.

The next day there was the sound of shelling in the distance. Arif was still missing. I was put into a captured Soviet jeep and sent to a house in a narrow canyon, where I had nothing to do except sleep and eat a large lunch of chicken pilau until the jeep came to take me back in the evening. It was boring, but apparently they felt I had to be hidden in a safe place away from the combat zone until Arif showed up.

When I returned, Arif was at Amir Rasul's village, which was called Turani. He said he had been too sick to travel and spent two days resting in a village along the way. I told him about my discovery of the Soviet defector in New Baghlan, saying I would like to return there the next day to question the man.

"There are no Russians in Baghlan," Amir Rasul said when Arif asked him about the defector.

"But I saw one on the way here," I insisted. "And Saeed in Peshawar said there were fifteen or sixteen Russian prisoners in Baghlan."

"He was mistaken," Amir Rasul insisted. "There are no Russians in Baghlan." He also said it was not possible for me to return to New Baghlan. Arrangements had been made for me to leave for Kunduz to talk to people about Soviet atrocities. However, Arif now held out some hope. He said there were two Russians, back toward the south, in the mountains leading to the Salang Pass, and we could search for them on the return journey to Pakistan.

My depression returned. I would be on my way back to Peshawar before I would know if the trip would be productive. But there was nothing I could do. Amir Rasul was obviously trying to be kind and I told myself, as I had since the start of the journey, to be patient and hope for the best.

Defectors and Believers

．．．．．．．．．．．．．

8

There are many handicaps in reporting about Afghanistan, of which the dangers, the distances, the difficulties of travel, and the differences in food and language are only the most obvious. Once these are dealt with, a reporter still faces the task of what to look for and, even more difficult, of understanding what he finds. When Amir Rasul said there were no Soviet prisoners in Baghlan, it did not mean I had no story. It meant I would have to find it.

I left Peshawar with no understanding of the life of Soviet prisoners in Afghanistan. I had a picture of a camp with barbed wire. Instead, I found defectors and converts. I discovered that the mujahidin could not maintain prison camps because the Russians, with their control of the air, would either drop a helicopter commando force to capture the camp or drop bombs to wipe it out. Moreover, the mujahidin lived and traveled in small groups. A prisoner would have to be guarded and the mujahidin would have to move frequently to avoid Soviet search parties.

A Soviet soldier could be kept only if he did not try to escape and would, in fact, resist rejoining Soviet forces. Since Islam infused the lives of the mujahidin, the only way a foreigner could live among them for any length of time was by becoming a Muslim. In their eyes, conversion made a person meritorious. It also clearly branded him as a traitor to his country and uniform. A man who prayed and fought with the mujahidin would be under no illusions about the fate that awaited him if he came again under Soviet control.

Eventually, I learned that there were four options for disposing of Soviet soldiers who came into mujahidin hands: kill them, convert them, send them to Pakistan, or exchange them for mujahidin prisoners. Several accounts of prisoner exchanges had been published in Peshawar and I assumed it was an ordinary event. But I discovered that exchanges touched a sensitive ideological nerve. My first hint of this came earlier in the trip, while I was traveling with Fazl Rahim. I mentioned exchanges and received an unexpected reply.

"They are our enemy," he said. "We do not want to make agreements with them. We should not even talk with them."

This was an example of the dogmatic zeal that marked the Islamic revolutionaries of the Hizb-i-Islami. Other parties might deal with the enemy to save the lives of some of their comrades, but not the Hizbi.

"This Is Where My Mother Died"

Amir Rasul was the first of many commanders I met who embodied this ideology. He was called amir because he was one of three Hizbi general commanders for Baghlan. His full name was Mohammed Rasul Jadid. He was forty, with a thick black beard, high cheekbones, and deep-set eyes. His father had been a member of Parliament. He studied agriculture through the twelfth grade and still spoke some of the English he had learned twenty-two years earlier from Peace Corps teachers. He said he was an agricultural officer in Baghlan before the war and started to fight the Communists as soon as Taraki seized power. He said his father was arrested because of this, and later died in prison, and that one of his brothers was now in prison in Kabul.

A month earlier, he said, forty of his relatives were killed when dozens of Soviet tanks and batteries of howitzers and mortars had shelled Turani in an attempt to destroy his base. He took me on a tour the next day.

"This is where my mother died," he said, standing in the doorway of a ruined house, fingering a bit of rattan with blood stains on it. "And there is where my sister was martyred," he continued, pointing to a nearby house. The village was a jumble of bricks and mud, with walls toppled into lanes and black, jagged trees etched against a blue sky. The stench of decaying animals buried under the rubble hung in the air. At one point Amir Rasul picked up an unexploded shell and carelessly tossed it on a heap. He pointed to piles of expended heavy machine gun cartridges and a scattering of Soviet rations, including small aluminum cans from Bulgaria marked in English as once containing a mixture of grape and apple juice. The Soviet tanks had parked at this point, he said,

Mohammed Rasul Jadid, left, and his brother Fazl Rahim in the ruins where forty of their relatives died. "We are happy if we kill the Russians," Mohammed Rasul said, "and we are also happy if we lose our relatives or ourselves in the way of God."

and fired directly into the village until a mujahid worked his way forward and drove them away, disabling one tank with a rocket. Although civilian casualties were heavy, Amir Rasul said only four of his mujahidin were killed and that the survivors escaped after dark by crawling through irrigation ditches.

The Soviet and Afghan Army forces occupied the village for three days. Amir Rasul showed me a small hospital that outwardly seemed little damaged. Looking through the windows I could see piles of wooden beds. He said the enemy had sowed the building with mines and booby traps and no one could go inside even now. They had also planted mines with delayed action fuses. Seven members of a family, picking through the ruins of their house after the Soviets left, were killed when a mine exploded beneath them. The tour ended at the edge of the village, where rocky mounds marked the graves of the dead. Amir Rasul said the Russians poured something on the bodies to hasten decay; many were badly decomposed and had to be hastily buried in mass graves.

"There is a mother and two children and there are two brothers, my cousins," he said, pointing to graves. I asked why so many members of his family were concentrated in what was undoubtedly a perilous place and why women, in particular, were not moved to a safer place.

"They were doing their jihad with me," he replied. "We are Muslim people and we are fighting for the cause of God and our Prophet, peace be upon him. The Afghan nation has a glorious history. Our fathers and grandfathers have never been under the control of a foreigner. Our God says if a foreigner attacks you, you must fight. For that reason we are willing to give the lives of our fathers, mothers, sisters, and ourselves. We are fighting for God and nothing else. We are happy if we kill the Russians. We are also happy if we lose our relatives or ourselves in the way of God. In both cases that is good for us."

I left my horse with Amir Rasul, and Arif and I, with two armed escorts, left that night on foot, taking only a few clothes, medicines, and the camera bag. At dawn we reached Sheikh Jalal, once a major pilgrimage spot. We rested in a mosque whose thick pillars supported a wide, high ceiling. It could easily accommodate a thousand men for prayer. The walls of the long room and the surfaces of the pillars were covered with elaborate, many-colored drawings of stylized plants and flowers. The colors were so bright and the patterns so intricate that the display suggested an ancient Egyptian tomb, but without the pictures of humans or animals that would offend Muslim sensibilities about graven images.

From there we went by bus and horses, provided by a local commander, to Narin, skirting a large Afghan Army garrison. The next day we traveled in a captured Russian truck across dusty plains to a town with the euphonious name of Ishkamish. And now, nineteen days after leaving Peshawar, I had the first real hope that the trip would prove fruitful. Arif said a commander traveling just one day ahead of us had a Soviet defector in his ranks.

Invading the Soviet Union

The next day we went for lunch with Bashir Khan, one of the three Hizbi general commanders for Baghlan and a man who organized raids into Soviet Tajikistan. His full name was Bashir Ahmad Shadadyar. He was twenty-eight, with a small pointed nose, gray eyes, and an intense

Bashir Ahmad Shadadyar, who conducted raids into the Soviet Union.

stare. He had studied engineering at Kabul University where he was known as a Young Muslim activist. Within days of the Communist coup in 1978 he fled to Pakistan, and three months later helped organize the growing resistance movement in southern Afghanistan. In 1982 he returned to his home province of Takhar, bordering the Soviet Union, and from there launched his invasion of Russia.

"There is a twelve-kilometer stretch of the Amu River where the mountains come down on both sides," he said. "It was always a place where people crossed back and forth. The people on both sides of the river are Tajiks and dress and look alike. At the start of our action we brought them 300 Holy Korans and other Islamic literature. Our mujahidin floated over on goat and cow skins and used a wooden raft to carry the Holy Korans. Then we decided on military action. We sent mujahidin across many times and they mined roads and killed Russian officials. I went myself once and stayed for a week."

Bashir's private war ended in 1984. After trying several times to destroy him, using only Afghan Army forces, the Soviets finally committed their own tank and infantry units to the battle. They encircled his base area and slowly closed the ring. He said 600 of his 700 mujahidin were killed in the operation, along with 2,000 villagers, and that thirty-two of his commanders were still in jail in Takhar. The blow did not weaken his will to fight. He brought the remnants of his forces to Pakistan to rest, resupply, and gather recruits. Bashir said he recruited 300 men, trained them in battles in Logar and Kunar provinces in the south, and was now ready to distribute more Korans and renew his raids across the border.

I asked if he really expected to pose a threat to a huge nation like the Soviet Union. He insisted that he could be effective.

"This is military strategy," he said. "When you are attacked you attack the base of the enemy to make him withdraw. I think if we attack the Russians inside their own territory maybe they will leave our country more quickly. The people there are Muslims. They have told my mujahidin they are ready for jihad but do not have enough equipment. If the mujahidin of Afghanistan are able to give them enough food, arms, and ammunition they will start their jihad as soon as possible. If I can start an Islamic struggle maybe they will become organized and start a revolution inside their own country."

A door opened behind me and a man with bandaged eyes began talking rapidly and vehemently in English as he was led out. He had been listening and thought I was casting doubts on Islam and the jihad.

"Listen to my commander," he said. "Look at me. I lost my sight fighting in Logar. When your soldiers were wounded in Vietnam they returned to the United States feeling something bad had been done to them. But I am not sad. I cannot see but I am happy. We are Muslims and we believe if we are killed or lose our lives it is for our God and He will give us a happier life after we are dead. The Russians don't know this. They think they can impose their beliefs on people by force, but you heard what my commander said. Even after so many years the people of Tajikistan are still Muslims and will not accept the Russians." Arif said the man had been a teacher for many years in Pakistan and that was why he spoke and understood English so well.

We left the next morning in a high-sprung, four-wheel-drive Soviet pickup truck. The Hizb-i-Islami was preparing a major attack on the Kunduz airport, one of the most important Soviet bases in the north. That was why Bashir had come north with his men. It was a bit of luck for us, since we could travel with Sayed Hamidullah, the Hizbi general commander for Kunduz Province, who was on his way to supervise the raid.

It turned out to be the most uncomfortable trip I ever made in Afghanistan. The driver's compartment was over the truck's motor, with room for the driver on one side of the protruding engine and a passenger on the other. We were four. Arif perched on a cushion atop of the motor, I squeezed next to him, trying to keep my legs free of the gear shifts, and Sayed Hamidullah sat next to me, with one arm out the window for a bit more room. I was thrown against sharp pieces of metal as the truck lurched violently in all directions, bouncing me up and down on the rim of the crude passenger seat. Fortunately, the truck often broke down or got stuck, so there were intervals between the periods of torture.

First we stopped to change a tire. We stopped again to take out and tinker with the entire gearshift assembly. Next the distributor had to be fixed. Then the truck slipped off the side of a dirt slope and came to rest on its front axle, one wheel dangling in the air. Cases and sacks of ammunition were unloaded, the truck was propped up with rope and poles, and the earth was rearranged. The truck was pushed, pulled, lifted, set right, and reloaded.

Late in the day the driver maneuvered the truck through cliffs up a rocky gorge so narrow that, at times, there was only a foot to spare on either side. If we ran into a big rock and could not get over it, I thought, that would be the end, since we could neither go around it nor go back. Sure enough, we were blocked. We got out and climbed to a plateau above the gorge. We had only six mujahidin with us, not enough to push or lift the truck from such a tight spot. But we discovered about twenty other mujahidin resting at the top. I asked Arif if we could persuade them to help.

"We can't do that," he replied. "They are Jamiat. We do not trust them." But the Jamiat commander solved the problem by volunteering assistance. Laughing and running, his men scrambled down into the gorge and within fifteen minutes the truck came chugging to the top. I stayed above and did not see how they accomplished this, but I imagined they had to lift the truck over the obstacle.

Mohammed Asjab Gul and the Seeds of Civil War

It was mostly downhill from there on. We spent the night at a mosque. The next morning we entered what was left of Khanabad. Once, Khanabad was a major city of northern Afghanistan. But the mujahidin captured it early in the war and ever since the city had been bombed and shelled almost every day. The population moved to farms and villages spread across the adjacent plain. Only mujahidin haunted the ruins and deserted gardens. We were taken to the courtyard of an abandoned house where Arif said there was an important man I must meet. He referred to him as amir and said he was the chief judge for the four northern provinces of Baghlan, Kunduz, Takhar, and Badakhshan.

Maulvi Mohammed Asjab Gul was fifty-two. His sedentary life and years in prison had taken their toll. He was fat, with heavy jowls and gray whiskers that grew high on his cheeks. He wore thick glasses. He moved slowly, holding his back as if it pained him. He wore a cartridge belt and pistol over his shoulder—more as a symbol than a weapon, since he obviously was not a fighter. As another symbol, one of his bodyguards lugged around a cumbersome 82-mm recoilless rifle (actually a small cannon). I never saw anyone with shells for the gun, but it was an expensive weapon and it demonstrated his importance. When I asked his history, he said he had studied in Afghanistan and Lahore, Pakistan, taught in a *madrasa*, or Islamic seminary, in Peshawar, and returned to Afghanistan to teach at a madrasa in Khanabad. He said his struggle began in the reign of King Zahir, long before the Communist coup.

"The Shah was not Muslim," he said. "He let Daoud do un-Islamic things. He did not put Communists in jail, only Muslims. The Communists don't believe in the Prophet, peace be upon him. They live like animals in the streets and never think of their future existence. I was always preaching against the Shah. I led a demonstration against him in Khanabad in 1970. The chief of police pretended to be a Muslim and called me to his house, claiming he wanted me to write sacred words on a paper to make an amulet for the protection of his son. Instead, he arrested me. But the people were upset and he could only keep me in jail for five days.

"Then Daoud ousted the Shah and took power himself. In 1974, a group of maulvis burned down a cinema house and took control of Khanabad for two days. I was arrested again and this time I was in jail

Maulvi Mohammed Asjab Gul: he smashed tobacco boxes as un-Islamic.

for six years. While Daoud was still in power I was allowed a separate room and books to continue my studies. But afterward my books were taken away and I was put in a small room. When the Russians invaded and put Karmal in power, I was watched more closely and guards began to insult me. Other guards, who were Muslims, thought I would soon be killed and warned the mujahidin. That was in 1980. One day a man came to the prison to cut wood. Really, he was a mujahid and he planted a mine by the wall. At a certain time, the mine exploded, the wall came down, and most prisoners escaped. But I couldn't move quickly enough. However, a soldier came a few days later and took me out."

Arif had good news. He said the commander who had the Soviet defector was in Khanabad and we would now go with the Maulvi to meet him. The Maulvi ponderously mounted a horse and I got onto another. We rode to a grove beside a wide, swift, irrigation stream where mats and embroidered pillows were spread on the ground. About twenty elderly men, apparently the elite of the area, stood as the Maulvi arrived and shook his hand. No one sat until the Maulvi had lowered himself to a pillow in the center. Green tea, flavored with cardamoms, was poured into glasses heaped with sugar. The Afghans dislike solemnity and the Maulvi and the men were soon laughing and joking.

As a mujahid filled the glasses, the Maulvi suddenly reached into the man's vest pocket and withdrew a small, round, metal box used to hold chewing tobacco. He put the box on the ground, borrowed a Kalashnikov, and smashed the box with the butt of the gun, sending bits of the mirrored cover flying into the air. Everybody laughed and the man whose tobacco box had been destroyed grinned sheepishly.

"I am against all things that are not Islamic," the Maulvi said. "The Holy Koran forbids drugs, and tobacco and cigarettes are types of drugs. I will not have them in my presence. But really, smoking or chewing is not important. We can solve all these things. For us, one thing alone is important: Islam. We want Islamic rule and Islamic law in Afghanistan. We will get rid of the Russians and the Communists and then we will look at all others. If they stand in the way of Islamic rule we will treat them the way we treat the Russians."

It was a concise and chilling statement of the fundamentalist belief that this was not just a war of national independence but a struggle to create a pure Islamic state. Here, I thought, were the seeds of civil war. I asked what he meant by Islamic rule. The question seemed to pose a problem. Arif and the Maulvi discussed it for several minutes and others interjected their own ideas.

"The Amir says it would take too long to tell you what is meant by Islamic rule," Arif finally replied. "He says if you want to know you should join us and become a Muslim. The people say they will give you a wife and garden and you can live here." As Arif spoke the Maulvi smiled, shook his head as if to say yes, and raised his hands before him in prayer, inviting me to join him.

"But I can tell you what Islamic rule means," Arif continued. "We will have justice. People who own land lawfully can keep it but if a man has enough to eat he must share with his neighbors. The Holy Koran says that out of nine measures, one measure is for the poor. In the case of goats and sheep, one out of forty is for the poor; cows, one out of thirty; camels, one out of twenty-five. If the rich pay this they can live in peace and they will not be hurt."

Vladimir Semyonov, Alias Faiz Mohammed

There was a stir as another group of mujahidin arrived. Finally, twenty-two days after leaving Peshawar, I talked with my first Russian. Arif called him Faiz Mohammed and said he had become a Muslim. He was fair-skinned with blue eyes and wore a denim vest over his Afghan clothes and a blue skull cap. The translation was laborious, since he had been with the mujahidin only two months and did not speak Dari, the predominant language. Mohammed Tajuddin, a mujahid who had been a student for three years before the war at Kabul Polytechnic, where Russian was obligatory, translated haltingly into Dari and Arif then translated into English. "Faiz Mohammed" kept looking down, avoiding eye contact, apparently still feeling uneasy in his new surroundings. The final result was a series of short answers to my questions:

"My name is Vladimir Semyonovich Semyonov. I am twenty-one years old. I come from a town 150 kilometers south of Moscow. I worked on the railways. I was conscripted when I was eighteen and trained in the city of Ashkhabad for six months. Then I came to Afghanistan, to the air base at Kunduz, where I was a soldier with the tank force. I was put in a post with twenty-five soldiers. The treatment was bad. They rotated twenty of the soldiers out but left five of us there, and we did all the work. The officers said we should never allow ourselves to fall into the hands of the Afghans. They said if we thought we would be captured, we should pull the pin on a grenade and blow ourselves up. But I planned to escape with an officer and another soldier who had contact for a long time with the Afghans who lived near the airport. I left with the officer but the other soldier did not come and the officer went back for him. They did not return, and I think they were killed. The officers said we would be fighting Americans, Chinese, and Pakistani soldiers. But since I have been with the mujahidin I have not seen any of these, and I have only seen weapons captured from the Russians. I think the mujahidin of Afghanistan are fighting against the Russians like the partisans fought against the Germans." He referred, of course, to World War II.

Arif ended the interview and we soon left with the Maulvi for a distant house. That night there was a display of deadly fireworks from

Vladimir Semyonov, "Faiz Mohammed," who said the mujahidin were fighting the Russians like the partisans fought the Germans in World War II.

the Kunduz air base about six miles away. Three separate salvos of rockets soared like tracer bullets into the night sky, separated with a shower of what looked like sparks, and soon the explosion of the warheads churned the ruins of Khanabad. The weapon was a BM-21, firing a salvo of forty rockets containing four and a half tons of explosives.

Several commanders arrived after breakfast to talk with the Amir. Arif said they reported that three other Russian defectors were in the Khanabad area and that someone had been sent to locate them. That was hopeful. I asked about what else I might do, suggesting a trip to the Soviet border on the Amu about fifty miles away. Arif said such a journey would have to be made at night because of intense Soviet surveillance and would take four days each way. I didn't feel I had that much time to spare. I asked when we would go to Chardara to talk with survivors of Soviet attacks on villages. Arif said it would be too dangerous because of the plans to attack the Kunduz airport, which was in the same direction.

Now we left the Maulvi, traveling for several hours along the crumbling and breached remains of a wide, concrete-lined irrigation canal built many years ago with American aid. We finally came to an isolated farmhouse. Arif said it was the safest place for me because there were no nearby mujahidin groups to attract attention. I slept there the next three nights. In the daytime Arif shifted me to as many as three different places for lunch or tea to confuse spies. Preoccupied with planning for their attack, the mujahidin were putting me aside for a while.

Gennadi Tsevma, Alias Naik Mohammed

Finally Arif reported that another Russian had been found and we set out at dusk for the mountains on the other side of the wide Khanabad plain. I had no flash for my camera and was worried that it would be dark when we met him. But then, as mysteriously as these encounters always happened, the defector suddenly appeared on the trail with a group of mujahidin. I got my pictures and we went to a base at the foot of the mountains.

This Russian too had converted to Islam and had been given the name Naik Mohammed. His real name was Gennadi Anatolyevich Tsevma, and he came from the town of Donetsk in the Ukraine. He was twenty-one, with wide eyes and reddish hair falling in bangs over his forehead, under a striped turban. He had been with the mujahidin for two years and spoke fluent Dari. He said he had been trained as a tank and armored-car driver for three months and was then assigned to the Kunduz airport. He said his contempt for Soviet officers and their abuse had led him to defect eight months after he arrived at Kunduz:

"They were always hitting us and being cruel. If a soldier wasn't willing to fight the mujahidin they would drive a tank over him. I had no contact with the mujahidin. But I heard about Taj Mohammed—all the soldiers there knew about him."

He referred to a Kazakh who defected from Soviet forces at the Kunduz airport in 1980 and fought for several years beside mujahidin of Harakat-i-Inqilab. Arif said no one there knew Taj Mohammed's Russian name. He said Taj Mohammed had married an Afghan woman and had a son by her, but later was killed in a fight with Soviet troops.

Tsevma continued: "Early one morning, I took my Kalashnikov and came out to the highway in front of the base. There was a tank and guard,

Gennadi Tsevma, "Naik Mohammed," fourth from left. The Russian officers told him that if a Soviet soldier was killed, the Russians would kill civilians.

but no one stopped me. I walked slowly to the nearest village and saw an old man saying his prayers. He was frightened and picked up two stones and threw them at me to chase me away. I signaled to him, no, and that I wanted to go with him. He took me to a house and kept me safe. Then the mujahidin came and took my gun and took me to Khanabad."

I asked about reports that Soviet soldiers sell their supplies to the mujahidin. "That's true," he replied. "They don't get paid enough, even to buy cigarettes. They sell petrol and ammunition. They steal guns from a storeroom and sell them. They use the money to buy hashish.

"None of the soldiers who come here want to fight against the mujahidin," he continued. "They're conscripted and sent by force. They're told they will fight against Americans, Chinese, and Pakistanis but I have seen no soldiers except the Afghans. I'm happy here with the mujahidin. I once went with a group to bring supplies from Pakistan and spent some time at Teri Mangal."

"If you were in Pakistan, why didn't you try to escape and seek political asylum?" I asked.

"I left to join the mujahidin, not to ask for political asylum," he replied. "I met two other Russians in Teri Mangal and they didn't look for political asylum either."

"There are reports that Russian soldiers kill civilians. Do you know about that?" I asked.

"Yes, the officers told us if a Soviet soldier is killed we must kill civilians," he replied. "They said if even one bullet was fired at us from a village we must go there and kill every man, woman, and child." When I asked if he had seen that happen, he said no and that the "Red Army" was responsible for such incidents. I assumed he meant professional soldiers rather than conscripts like himself.

Back to Ishkamish

Arif said I should hurry now, and we left for a mujahidin camp about two hours away. I was soon asleep there. During the night there was a repeated whoosh of rockets being fired not too far away but I just rolled over and went back to sleep. Arif woke me before dawn, saying the rockets were the start of the attack on the Kunduz air base. I would have to go back to the isolated farmhouse. That night more rockets were fired. In the morning Arif said Bashir Khan had planned to lead a ground attack in coordination with the rocketing, but that spies had alerted the enemy and Bashir had cancelled his part of the action. Arif said there was a threat of Soviet counteraction and we would return to Ishkamish.

That meant I had to give up any hope of meeting survivors of the reported Soviet atrocities in Chardara. I had spent four weeks in travel with little to show for it, only insubstantial interviews with two defectors and a vague promise that one or two additional defectors might be found on the way back to Peshawar. My resolve to be patient and hope for the best was becoming frazzled.

It was the holiday of *Id-al-adha* (The Feast of the Sacrifice), when Muslims bathe and put on new clothes, or at least clean clothes, sacrifice animals that are later eaten in family feasts, and then participate in large group prayers. Arif was away during the morning for prayers and visits and returned to take me to a mujahidin camp for lunch. Platters were heaped with the meat of a slaughtered cow. I was depressed at how little I had accomplished and was also sick with diarrhea. I just picked at the tough and strong-smelling meat. Arif urged me to eat. "It has been killed in the name of God," he said. "It will make you well."

Late the next day we crammed ourselves with Sayed Hamidullah into the Russian pickup truck and set out for Ishkamish. This time the headlights failed and we stopped for the night while the driver fixed them. The next day we got stuck in a sand trap and had to commandeer a pair of bullocks to pull us out. We made it easily through the narrow gorge but ran out of gasoline not far from Ishkamish and had to send a man on horseback for a jerry can of gas to complete the trip. There was a river nearby, and I managed to get in a cool wash and a swim before we started again.

Soviet Vengeance

Along the way I had asked Sayed Hamidullah about the killing of civilians in Chardara. According to refugees interviewed in Peshawar, the massacre was so bad that people loaded carts with the bodies of old men, women, and children and carried them to Kunduz city to demand that the Communists make the Russians stop the slaughter. Other commanders I had asked traced the killings to an incident in December 1983, when a Soviet general was killed. But they told different versions of the story. Since Sayed Hamidullah was the Hizbi general commander for Kunduz, I felt his information was the most accurate.

"It was in late December, just before the Christian New Year," he said. "A high-ranking Russian general from the Kunduz base went out in a tank or armored car with six other officers. They were drunk and ran the vehicle into mud and got stuck. Four officers got out with their weapons and went to a nearby nomad camp to ask for help. But the nomads killed them for their weapons, dumped their bodies into a river, then went to the tank or car and killed the general and the two other officers, and took their weapons. The nomads also stripped the vehicle of its heavy machine gun and whatever else could be carried away. They did something with the bodies of the general and the other officers, struck their tents, and disappeared.

"The Russians found the four bodies in the river and started a search for the body of the general and the two others. The general was a relative of some high-ranking Communist in Moscow so they had to recover his body. They dropped leaflets over a wide area, offering large rewards for information. But the bodies were never found. The Russians were furious at what must have seemed to them to be defiance. They sent ground parties into the three villages closest to the area and killed 560 men, women, and children, deliberately using cruel tactics— bayonetting women in their bellies and burning children before the eyes

The bazaar at Ishkamish, where merchants sold Turkish cooking oil, "Moon Rabbit" underwear from North Korea, and an orange drink from Holland.

of their parents. They thought they could force people to tell them what happened. But of course the people did not know. The terror spread wider and wider. Finally, the Russians accepted the fact that the officers had been killed by nomads. Ever since then their planes and helicopters have bombed or machine gunned any nomad camp they see."

Arms and Economics

I asked Sayed Hamidullah if it often happened that Soviet soldiers were killed for their weapons. He said it happened but no one knew how often; mujahidin commanders were not told of such killings since the villagers believed the commanders would take the guns.

Later, when Arif and I were sitting in the Ishkamish bazaar, having tea and huge plates of sweet yellow grapes, I asked the merchant how much a nomad or a villager would get for a Kalashnikov. As usual, a crowd had gathered around me and when Arif translated the question

I received several answers. The average buying price worked out to $1,100, figuring that a merchant would resell the gun for more than that. I wanted to translate this into local purchasing power and asked the price of sheep, cows, and horses. It worked out that if a villager killed a Soviet soldier and stole his weapon he would get enough money to buy thirty to thirty-five sheep, or twelve cows, or four horses—enough to make a man rich by village standards.

The Ishkamish bazaar had the wide variety of goods available in most towns, including Turkish cooking oil with vitamins added, "Moon Rabbit" underwear from North Korea, an orange drink from Holland, small oil lamps from Germany, and three kinds of strong, heat-resistant glasses from France, used for drinking tea. A Mercedes fourteen-wheel truck, so new that it did not have a dent or scratch, was parked on the muddy street. I was never able to understand how the mujahidin economy could support expensive trucks like this one and the one we used when we were trying to cross the highway on the way to Baghlan. Arif asked the people sitting around us who owned the truck, but they said they did not know.

Religion and American Aid

Maulvi Asjab Gul was in Ishkamish and a mullah invited local leaders to share an elaborate meal with him. It was the customary Afghan setting, in a courtyard with trees, a flowing stream, and a garden with bright marigolds and phlox. One of the commanders made the mistake of taking out his little round box for a pinch of chewing tobacco. The Maulvi seized and smashed it. He also saw one of the small aluminum spittoons, shaped like an hourglass, that the tobacco chewers pass around. He threw it high over a wall.

The Maulvi greeted me warmly and soon was repeating his questions about religion. He wanted to know my beliefs on life after death. He said life on earth was short and asked if I was not concerned about what would happen to me through eternity. I said I was a member of the Protestant sect of Christians and as such I believed that an individual was allowed a degree of freedom in matters of religious faith. He said the Communists thought like that but that the Word of God was clearly written in the Koran. Later, after the mujahidin performed their ablutions and assembled for the midday prayer, he motioned me to come to the first row and join in. I thanked him and stood silently in the rear, as I always did on such occasions.

He was not alone in asking questions. Bashir Khan also posed a few. "I have heard that the American government spends hundreds of millions of dollars to help the mujahidin. Why are you doing that?" he asked.

I said I did not work for the government and could not give him an official reason. But it was obvious that we did not like the Russians, and the thinking was probably that any help to the mujahidin would hurt the Russians.

"You are a Christian nation," he said. "There are Christian nations who also do not like the Russians. I have read about Poland. That is a very Christian nation and it is being persecuted by the Russians. You are not giving guns and ammunition to them but are giving arms to a Muslim nation. Why is that?"

I said I could not explain why. Perhaps, I said, it was because Christians in nations like Poland and Hungary had brief revolts against the Russians and then stopped fighting, while the Afghans are fighting year after year and thus could put weapons to use.

"Or maybe it is the other way around. They can't fight because you don't give them weapons," he said. "I think the Russians and Americans want to divide the world just as you have divided Europe. People feel you are active in Afghanistan because you want to divide this country, with the north going to Russia and the south under American influence."

Usually I tried to end such discussions quickly to minimize misunderstandings. But I could understand why Bashir felt it was strange that we were helping a Muslim country and ignoring Christian countries equally subject to Russian domination. I said the superpowers had to be careful about confrontations because of the danger of a nuclear war that could destroy the world. I said the United States was also constrained by its allies in Europe, who were worried that they would be the first to be destroyed if the United States and the Soviet Union began to fight. The reasoning seemed to be drawing a blank. The Maulvi, who had been listening, brought the discussion to an end with a comment that made everyone laugh.

"The Amir says give us the atom bomb and we will drop it on the Russians," Arif translated.

Aleksandr Levenets, "Ahmad." "If a soldier is killed, someone will try to steal his rifle and sell it to get money for hashish," he said.

Aleksandr Levenets, Alias Ahmad

It was time to start for a meeting with a third Soviet defector. Arif said it would take place at a secret munitions storage area to the south. We left in two trucks packed with mujahidin guards for our first stop, Falool, about two hours away. The Soviet Army had twice sent a tank force to capture the hidden depot but could not get past Falool. Huge shell holes in the walls of buildings gave evidence of the ferocity of the attacks. The next day brought relief from the choking dust of the road. We had a gentle breeze and clear blue skies as we rode horses high into the mountains, twisting through narrow, rocky ravines that were impenetrable to tanks. The munitions were hidden in caves and holes, invisible from the air.

We were sitting in the afternoon outside a mud and stone hut that blended into the mountain when Aleksandr Yuryevich Levenets walked down a trail. He had a slight beard and mustache, short hair, brown eyes, and wore black Afghan clothes with a small turban. He had been converted and given the name Ahmad. He said he was twenty-one, from the town of Melovatka in the Ukraine, and that his grandfather lived in Canada but he did not know exactly where. He said he had been with the mujahidin for eleven months and was now assigned to one of the Dashika antiaircraft guns that ringed the base. The interview went easily with the help of Mohammed Tahir, who had studied Russian for four and a half years at the Belorusssian Polytechnic Institute in Minsk.

"I was in school to the tenth grade and played a lot of sports and became a driver," Levenets said. "I was conscripted in April 1983 and was trained for three months in Azerbaijan. We went by train to Termez on the Afghan border. At first we were told we were going into Afghanistan by bus, but it was too dangerous and we were sent by plane to the Kunduz air base. I was there for three months. I had a friend from my village named Valery Kuskov. We were treated badly and Valery said we should escape. When we talked to some others about this, they said the mujahidin were far away and we could not reach them. But then we were sent north to Abadan," he continued, referring to a large Soviet base on the Amu River near the Afghan city of Sher Khan Bander.

"I had a fight with another soldier and was put in jail for fifteen days. When I was released I was made a driver. One day there was something wrong with the car and it would not start. An officer told me to get it. I told him it would not go, but he was drunk and insisted that I must bring it to him. When I told him again that it would not go, he went with me to the car and when I showed him it would not start he got angry and we had a fight. He called another soldier to beat me. My hand was hurt but I was not allowed to go to the hospital. Valery came to my tent. He was also in trouble because he was the driver of a car that was in an accident. We talked about what we could do and he went away. He came back in the evening and said, 'Come, let's go to the mujahidin.'

"We left the base and started walking along the highway to a bridge over a river where there was a guard post and two tanks. We went around it and came to a deserted village and stayed there at night. Valery could speak some Dari. In the morning we found a shopkeeper who gave us some watermelons to eat and said the mujahidin were three hours away.

But when we walked in the direction he pointed out, we soon met them and they took us to their base."

"Were there many soldiers like you who did not like the life in Afghanistan?" I asked.

"No one wants to be in Afghanistan," he replied. "If they were told they could leave they would not wait for a truck or a plane but would walk 10,000 kilometers back to their homes. Everything was bad at our base. We had to work all the time and did not even have a chance to wash our clothes. The dining hall was dirty and there was a bad smell. If a soldier was hurt or wounded, he was given first aid but was not sent to a hospital and put in a bed. Every week, someone tried to escape."

"What about the stories of soldiers selling their supplies?" I asked.

"They sell petrol and ammunition to get money to buy hashish. If a soldier is killed, someone will try to steal his rifle to sell it to get money for hashish."

"There are also reports of killing civilians. Do you know about that?" I asked.

"They can't find the mujahidin so they kill civilians. Our officers said we must go into a village and kill all the people and animals—sheep, horses, even dogs and cats. But I thought it was the mujahidin who were fighting against us, not elderly people and dogs and cats."

"How has your life been with the mujahidin?" I asked.

"Compared to being a Soviet soldier I am happy here. Our officers warned us that if we joined the mujahidin our noses and ears would be cut off and we would be killed. But I have been with the mujahidin and find them very kind."

Valery Kuzkov, Alias Mohammed Yusuf

When Levenets first mentioned his friend Valery Kuskov, Mohammed Tahir said he would tell me more about this man later. While Levenets went to get something to eat Tahir told me Kuskov's story:

"We called him Mohammed Yusuf. He was twenty-two years old. We decided to separate the two Russians when they came to us so they would have to speak Dari all the time and learn the language more quickly. Mohammed Yusuf told many stories about Russians who escaped from their bases. He said once three soldiers tried to find their way out of the Kunduz base but got lost and turned back. On the way one lost his rifle. When they returned the man who lost his rifle was executed. The other two were sent to jail for life.

"Mohammed Yusuf said that another time a code clerk could not be found. Announcements were made over loudspeakers surrounding the camp telling him to think of his family and friends at home and come back and that nothing would happen to him if he returned. Mohammed Yusuf said no one ever found out what happened to that man. When he told us the story we asked the people who lived nearby but they said they knew nothing about him. Perhaps he was killed for his gun.

"When Mohammed Yusuf joined the mujahidin he was always asking to take part in operations, especially in planting mines along the highway from Kunduz to Abadan. He also wanted to attack the Kunduz air base. He said the mujahidin did not have maps but he knew the safe routes through the mine fields and he also knew the roads inside the base. He said if we could make ten Russian uniforms he would lead a group inside the base to capture officers or plant mines. He also said he would stand by the road with mujahidin dressed as Russians and would stop a tank or car and capture the men inside.

"Sometimes, he would be very sad and would cry. We asked him what was the matter and he said he was thinking of his family and how much he missed them. We told him he could return to the Russians any time he wished. We said he joined us of his own will and could leave of his own will. We said we could guide him to within 300 meters of the base and leave him there. But he said no. He took part in many actions with us. One night last March a Russian and Karmal force surrounded a group of mujahidin near Koochi in Chardara District. They were bombed and strafed by helicopters and Mohammed Yusuf was martyred along with four mujahidin."

"How is it," I asked Mohammed Tahir, "that you spent so long with the Russians and now you are with the mujahidin?"

"I was doing well at the Polytechnic Institute in Minsk," he replied. "It is a big school with 500 to 600 students from thirty-three different countries, including the Middle East and Latin America. The largest contingent, about 200 students, was from Afghanistan. I came home last year for a holiday. I had only one year left to complete my education in auto mechanics. I had a passport and a visa to return. But one of my uncles came to me. He asked me: 'Why are you studying in Russia when your cousins and many of our relatives are in the jihad?' I put aside my passport and left immediately to join the mujahidin."

His answer was suggestive. The Soviets believe they can create a new generation of Afghans by sending young men to the Soviet Union for education and indoctrination. But as Mohammed Tahir indicated, the pull of family loyalties and family honor among Afghans remains a powerful force.

Tolerating Intolerance

The Maulvi was still with us. Since the mujahidin had to escort me from Ishkamish to the munitions base, they apparently decided they might as well make the trip an official inspection tour, so the Maulvi came along. This meant we remained an extra day so that proper hospitality, including a large meal with several local commanders, could be offered to the Maulvi. It also meant additional opportunities for him to smash chewing tobacco boxes and to prompt me to see the error of my ways. His moral nagging never bothered me. He acted the way the people expected and wanted him to act. I had long since resigned myself to the fact that the Afghans are intolerant of all beliefs different from their own, especially different religious beliefs. To live among them, one had to tolerate their intolerance.

A small earthquake shook the ground as we sat drinking tea after dinner that night. The Maulvi asked me what caused the earth to shake. I said a new understanding had developed in recent years and began to talk of plate tectonics and the movement of continents floating on molten rock beneath the earth's surface. Arif laughed so hard while he was interpreting that he had to stop. He said he never heard anything so absurd in all his life.

"The Amir will give us the proper explanation," Arif said.

The Maulvi had an attendant who followed him everywhere, carrying a worn leather briefcase containing his papers. Now the Maulvi asked for his case, took out a Koran, and began reading and chanting a section on the creation and destruction of the earth. The room was crowded. There was instant and complete silence and the men listened reverently as the Maulvi improvised a lecture that lasted for about fifteen minutes. When he finished, the silence continued as if no one wanted to be the first to break the mood of deep reverence.

Illiterate Spies

Back in Falool the next morning, we said our farewells to the Maulvi and others who had been with us for ten days. We would now return to Amir Rasul in Turani. We left by truck with a commander and small escort. The truck broke down a few hours later at the village of Burkeh, only half a mile from an isolated Afghan Army post. We were so close I could see the flag flying above it. The commander said there were about 100 Afghan Army soldiers at the post and that they had to be supplied by helicopter two or three times a week.

At the time I could not understand the value of such a post for the Kabul government. The mujahidin said there were several others like it throughout Kunduz and Baghlan. Kabul had to force recruits into uniform, but here it let them sit idle, wasting the use of helicopters just to supply them. The only apparent purpose of the post was to show the flag and to be able to claim that Kabul was represented in rural areas.

Later, in Peshawar, a mujahidin military analyst explained the value of these isolated posts. He said they were vital to the Soviet and Afghan Army intelligence system. With rare exceptions, the people in the countryside are illiterate, including those who are paid or otherwise induced, possibly by threats to relatives living under Communist control, to serve as spies for the Kabul authorities. If the spies had to travel to some distant city to deliver their reports, it would take days for authorities to receive messages. A post within easy walking distance meant that verbal messages could be received at night and radioed to a Soviet base. Then jets or a helicopter commando force could be sent to attack a mujahidin convoy or camp the next morning.

Our people could not get the truck working and we went by another truck, loaded with wheat, to Narin for the night. On the way north from Turani, we had gone by truck to Narin. Now, for reasons that Arif would never explain, we left Narin by foot on a different route. After only two hours we stopped for lunch at the house of a commander Arif had known in Peshawar, and that meant more hospitality and a long lunch. Then we walked for less than an hour to another village where we waited an hour for a new escort of two men and a donkey.

I was angry at Arif. Almost five weeks had passed since we left Peshawar. The days were slipping by and my stamina was ebbing. I said I should not be forced to sit for hours, bored and listening to a language I did not understand, just so his friends or local Hizbi commanders could display the virtues of Afghan hospitality. I said we should travel on our own, if necessary, joining with any group going in our direction. But Arif shared the Afghan fear of traveling alone, even in what was ostensibly mujahidin-controlled territory. He felt safe only if he was with a Hizb-i-Islami force. This was to become a recurrent disagreement that soured our relations for the rest of the journey.

It was after nightfall when we arrived at Turani. There we were told that an enemy tank force had been put into position on the main Baghlan-Kunduz highway about three miles away, and might be planning an attack. To underscore the danger, three mortar shells thudded in explosions not far away as we had dinner. Before dawn, four trucks assembled to evacuate us and Amir Rasul, with his entire force, to a safer position back through a narrow valley to the elaborate mosque at Sheikh Jalal for the rest of the night.

The Defector Who Got Away

Back in Turani the next morning, I asked Amir Rasul again about the Soviet defector I had seen when I arrived at New Baghlan three weeks earlier. Again he replied that there were no Russians in Baghlan but that I could go look for myself. We left at dusk with a guard carrying an old 303 rifle. When we saw three Soviet tanks parked by the side of the highway, we walked parallel to the road until it was completely dark. Finding a clear space, we hurried across.

The rattle of machine gun fire and sporadic single shots sounded as we entered the empty streets of New Baghlan. The mujahidin were playing their nightly game of harassing enemy posts and the Afghan Army soldiers were returning the fire. We were stopped by sentries and shown into a room with blackout curtains drawn across the windows. There, to my joy, was the very man I wanted to meet—Mohammed Khalid, who spoke English and had showed me around New Baghlan when I first arrived, pointing out the Soviet defector.

"Of course there's a Russian here," he said. "I will bring him to you tomorrow." I turned to Arif, saying this confirmed what I had said all along.

At the moment though, Mohammed Khalid had something else on his mind. He had written a long message for the Afghan soldiers at a nearby government post, calling them traitors in the pay of nonbelievers who would suffer in hell for their un-Islamic actions. He went outside and with a small battery-operated Japanese loudspeaker to amplify his message he read it to the soldiers.

Ten minutes later, a large mortar shell exploded in a lane about fifteen feet from us, shaking the house and sending a blast of air that billowed the curtains into the room and showered us with dust. Luckily, the deadly shrapnel was absorbed by a thick mud wall separating the house from the lane. The mujahidin normally pay little attention to the sounds of rifle fire and exploding shells around them, but now the room grew silent and tense. If the gunners changed, by just a hair, the trajectory of the next shell, there could be a direct hit on our house. The gunners did alter their fire, but in another direction, and succeeding shells fell farther and farther away. Mohammed Khalid returned, grinning broadly. "They heard me," he said.

The next day I got the bad news about the Soviet defector. Mohammed Khalid said he was sorry, but that the Russian who was once in New Baghlan had been sent elsewhere. Where, he did not know. Apparently, as I had long suspected, Amir Rasul did not want the existence of the Soviet defector to be known and, overnight, Arif had conveyed the official line. I was annoyed. If they had said at the start that a meeting with the defector could not be arranged, for security reasons or whatever, I would have been saved a great deal of effort. But perhaps they felt it was wrong to give a flat "no" to a guest.

I told Arif I wanted to return to Turani and waste no more time. He said we could not cross the highway by daylight and that Amir Rasul had arranged interviews with three Hizbi commanders. They had nothing of value to tell me and the meetings only added to my aggravation.

Discord and Depression

We returned after dark to Turani and I awoke the next morning depressed and sick. In addition to the endless diarrhea, I now had a cold and a rising fever. My blanket had been stolen a few weeks earlier. Then a mujahid had unrolled my sleeping bag and used it for taking a nap. In the process he broke the zipper, so I could never close it again, and bequeathed me a tribe of fierce and hungry fleas. To cap it all, my horse got hurt in a fight with another horse. It limped and had open wounds on its flanks where the other horse had bitten it.

Perhaps because I was feverish, I didn't try to curb my annoyance. I told Arif that we were wasting time and that I had only eight weeks for the entire trip. He reminded me that he had agreed to accompany me without notice and that he had been building a house for his family when Saeed came for him.

"There was mud on my hands," he said. "I was told that the Hizb-i-Islami needed me and I came. You keep saying: 'We must go, we must go.' But we cannot travel if we do not have mujahidin. Someone will come up to you on the road. They will see you are a foreigner and think you are rich. They will tell you to put your camera and money on the ground and then they will shoot you."

I realized I had been too outspoken and, for the hundredth time, told myself to be patient; I was undoubtedly as strange and annoying to them as they were to me. Amir Rasul and Fazl Rahim came after lunch to say goodbye and gave each of us a suit of pants and shirt, made by a village tailor, as farewell gifts. They had heard of our disagreement.

"You are our guest," Amir Rasul said. "Although you are not a Muslim I treat you with all the care and regard that I can. I did not lie when I said there were no Russians in Baghlan and you have seen this for yourself. We have made inquiries for you and we know you will be able to find one or possibly two Russians with Commander Salim near the Salang Pass." Commander Salim was the Hizb-i-Islami commander who harassed the Soviets on the northern side of the Salang Pass. I felt better with Amir Rasul's promise that I would meet at least one more defector and replied that I appreciated his help. We set off and spent the night at Sheikh Jalal.

An Afghan host honors and demonstrates his regard for a visitor not only by the way he greets him but also by the way he bids him good-bye. It is routine to escort a guest through the door and on to an outer gate. A more important guest might be accompanied to the end of the street or to the last house of the village. In turn, a guest demonstrates that he is unworthy of such honor by stopping, for instance, at the end of a street to insist that the final handshake and embrace should take place here and no farther. Arif, who prided himself on the elegance of his manners, sometimes took ten minutes to bid farewell, with his host insisting he will go farther and Arif saying no, no, this is far enough.

The next morning Arif decided my horse was too badly injured for the hard journey ahead and exchanged it plus the equivalent of $110 for a horse that seemed much stronger. In the afternoon Amir Rasul and Fazl Rahim arrived in a captured Soviet jeep for more farewells and gave us the jeep and six escorts to start our journey back to Pakistan. A mujahid followed on my horse.

That night we reached Badamdara, commanded by Amir Habibur Rahman, who was about forty-five and had high cheekbones, narrow eyes, and a paisley silk or rayon scarf around his shoulders. With time running out, I was determined to ask every commander I met about Soviet defectors. He knew of one.

"We had a Russian two years ago," he said. "He was a driver who ran away after an accident in which a Russian officer was killed. He was afraid he would be punished. We had him for six months and he became a Muslim, but the villagers complained that the Russians would bomb any place they thought he was staying. We had to keep moving him. Finally, we gave him to the Jamiat-i-Islami and they took him to Pakistan. We heard he was at the camp where the explosion took place and some Russians were killed."

The next day Habibur Rahman gave us a new escort of six men with American World War II bolt-operated rifles and we climbed into the mountains. We were moving south, about ten miles east of the highway that ran from the Soviet border to Pul-i-Khumri and on to a huge Soviet base at Qiligai, then over the Salang Pass to Kabul.

It was night when we arrived at Commander Salim's base, hidden in a narrow ravine. The few men there said Salim and the bulk of his force had recently attacked a convoy on the road to the Salang Pass, destroying many vehicles, and were now camped somewhere else. They also said, laying my lingering doubts to rest, that they would send for the Soviet soldier, who was not far away.

Nasratullah, Otherwise Anonymous

Outside the cave where we spent the night, a small stream fell over a cliff into a pool, where the next morning I washed myself and rinsed out some clothes. As I was hanging them on a branch to dry, a man walked down from higher in the ravine, alone and carrying a Kalashnikov. It was a few moments before I realized that he was the defector we had been expecting.

Nasratullah would not give his Russian name or say where he came from, only that he was Ukrainian. He had a prominent nose, large, wide-set eyes, brownish-black hair worn long over his ears, a slight mustache, and a pointed beard. A lot about him begged explanation. Arif said he had been a lieutenant in the Soviet army, but he said he was twenty-three and had been with the mujahidin for three years and seven months. That would mean he was about nineteen when he was in the army, too young to have been a lieutenant. However, Arif said Nasratullah helped the mujahidin to plan many operations and that Commander Salim trusted him. That was obviously true, since he walked freely carrying a weapon.

As we talked, he chain-smoked Soviet cigarettes with long, hollow holders that Arif said could be bought in some Afghan bazaars. "I volunteered to go to Afghanistan," he said, "to see what kind of war it was. But when I arrived at Qiligai I worked as the assistant to the commander of a tank and bus repair unit."

He said he defected only a month after he reached Qiligai. I asked him why. "I came here for fighting, but they gave me a job at the base. And they were killing civilians, even burning them with flame throwers. Once I saw them with binoculars running over civilians with their tanks in a village near the base.

"The soldiers are always thinking of ways to escape. While I was there, I heard of two who tried to run away. One got away, but the other, who was behind, was shot and killed by the guards. The officers said another soldier who escaped was killed for his gun by the villagers living near the base. We have a radio here that we captured in a raid on the highway. I listen to the conversation between the Russians. About a year ago they talked about a soldier who was captured after escaping. They said the officers put a mine under him and exploded it to kill him.

"One day I left the base and said to the guards I was going swimming in the river. I was not in a fighting unit and had no gun so they did not stop me. Really, I wanted to find a way out. The next day I left again and crossed the river. The next morning I met a man and used my hands to ask him where I could go. He was a mujahid and took me to his group only twenty minutes away."

I asked if he had taken part in fighting against his former comrades. "Yes," he replied, "five times. I use a recoilless rifle."

"You've been with the mujahidin for a long time," I said. "What do you think Russia's chances are for winning this war?"

"The Russians can't win because the Afghans are not fighting them face to face," he replied. "They are fighting a partisan war and keep changing their bases and withdrawing when they are attacked. In addition, the mujahidin are fighting for their country and for Islam."

"What are the Russians fighting for?" I asked.

"For Babrak Karmal," he said, laughing. Then, without being asked, he told a story of how the Russians were anxious to find him.

"They know I'm here and want to capture me or kill me. Last year Sultan Ali Kishtmand sent a message through the villagers," he said, referring to the Afghan prime minister. "It had in it a letter in Russian that was supposed to be from my father. It said he was waiting for me near Qiligai and wanted to see me. But we have a special sign in our family that we put on letters. The letter didn't have the sign so I knew it was false and they were sitting in ambush waiting for me there."

"If the Russians know exactly who you are and where you are, why don't you want to be photographed or give me your name?" I asked.

"The KGB knows about me, but maybe my family and the police in my town do not know. Maybe they have been told I have been killed or that I'm missing. If my name is published and my picture is shown, then everyone will know about me and maybe my family will suffer."

Nasratullah left after lunch, as did the men who had escorted us from Badamdara. The next morning a single man guided us past stretches of gnarled pine up and down the mountains. It was not until nine that night, when I was shivering with the cold of the high altitude, that we reached Mohammed Salim's camp at Kundipe village and the warmth of a wood stove. Salim was twenty-nine, with a round face, gray eyes, a pointed nose, and a small, pointed beard. He had studied hydro-electric engineering for four years at Kabul Polytechnic where, despite the obligatory study of Russian and exposure to Soviet indoctrination, he became an anti-Communist activist and had to flee to Pakistan soon after Taraki's coup. I asked about his main target, the highway leading south and the tunnel through the Salang Pass.

Salim said the mujahidin had managed several times to send their own men in the convoys passing through the tunnel, men disguised as drivers of civilian trucks. He said they planted mines that destroyed hundreds of vehicles. The tunnel was built for two-way traffic, he said, but was so badly damaged now that only one-way traffic was allowed, passing in opposite directions on alternate days. He said the Russians were so afraid of night attacks that traffic was limited to the hours between seven in the morning and four in the afternoon.

"There are many thousands of Russian soldiers at the Qiligai base," he said, "but only a few of them take part in fighting. If they do, and meet resistance, they will withdraw. Even their top commanders don't want to fight. They are always sending us messages asking for a truce."

Defectors: What to Do with Them?

I asked Mohammed Salim about defectors. "The ordinary soldiers are bored," he replied, "and are made to do a lot of manual work just to keep them busy. We must be aware of why they come to us. They don't have enough money so they try to sell petrol or other supplies just to get money to buy cigarettes. Because they are so bored, however, it's really hashish they want, to pass the time. Then they leave their bases because they are in trouble and fear punishment, not because they want to fight in our jihad, so we can seldom have complete confidence in them. What can we do with them? If we offer to exchange prisoners the Russians will capture our fathers and brothers in the bazaar and use them as hostages to make exchanges. In addition, we shouldn't have any agreements with the enemy.

"Should we kill them? If we do that, no more will try to escape and that's not what we want. We want to make trouble for the Russians and to encourage their soldiers to escape. But how can we keep them? Our fighting units are small and have to keep moving. If spies say there is a Russian with them, they will be bombed even more. So most commanders simply send them to Pakistan.

"We did that once. About six months ago we captured a Russian who was selling petrol from his tanker truck to small boys. The Russians do that. They think they will be captured or tricked if they deal with grown men. But the boys are usually mujahidin too, no matter how old they are. These boys told us of the place and time when the Russian was selling petrol. He foolishly left his gun on the seat of his truck as he filled the cans brought by the boys. One of our men got his gun and others captured him. We called him Islamuddin and tried to teach him about Islam. But he would not listen and was always trying to get hashish from the villages, so we sent him to Pakistan."

Arif was suffering from diarrhea and was feeling the strain of walking in the mountains. I suggested we buy a horse for him and, with Salim's help, we bought one for $235. Salim also gave us new escorts and we set out at one in the afternoon, following the contours of the mountains and climbing higher and higher. It grew colder and the vegetation diminished. We started a descent after dark and it was not until 10:30 that we reached our destination for the night.

In the morning I discovered we had slept in a cave in a ravine that was barely twenty feet wide. It was the rear base for a unit that frequently attacked the road from Qiligai to the Salang Pass. We also discovered that there was little food for the horses and that Arif's horse was sick with diarrhea.

We now had to cross the highway, which meant that we had to go by night. Late in the afternoon we crossed a wide plain. Arif exchanged his turban for my hat and also gave me his blanket, telling me to cover my head and face and not to speak to anyone. As usual, he did not explain why these precautions were necessary, but I assumed we were approaching a region controlled by government militia. We came to a large town, circled around its edge, plunged through a large stream, and rose into hills on the other side. Arif again told me to cover my head with the blanket, which I had allowed to slip, because we were passing an Afghan Army post. It was well after dark when we approached the highway, where the lights of a convoy were still winding down from the Salang Pass. We waited until the road was clear and then hurried across.

Sulfiq Finder and His Tricks

We had reached the Walyan district and the camp of Sulfiq Finder Mohammed, whom we met the next morning. He was fifty, illiterate, and a butcher by trade. His beard was gray but he had the wiry build and flat stomach of a man half his age. His shirt and trousers had been darned, and he wore an old brown sweater with holes in it. He said that when the Communists came to power he gave up his butcher stall in the Walyan bazaar and gathered nine men with hunting rifles, pistols, knives, and axes to attack government offices. He was now famous for his daring, cunning, and fierce hatred of the enemy. He displayed scars from battle wounds on his arms and hands and said two of his five sons had been killed, along with fifteen other relatives. He said two of his surviving sons were fighting with him and that the fifth, still a child, would join the jihad as soon as he was old enough. As we sat drinking tea, Arif said other commanders and their men, who were listening to us, wanted Sulfiq Finder to tell me about his exploits.

"Last year," he began, as the others smiled in anticipation, "a Russian general sent me a letter through a villager. He said he would release two of my men if I would agree to a truce. I sent back a letter saying I agreed. The men were released the next day. Right away I attacked a Russian post and killed some Russians and destroyed a tank.

"Then about nine months ago a Karmal general sent me a letter saying he wanted to establish two defense posts along the highway to Salang. He thought he would get praise from the Russians and that I could be easily persuaded because I am not educated. He said the posts would be good because he would promise not to attack the villagers and they would be safe. I sent him a letter saying I might accept and that I would meet him at a certain place to talk about it. I said he should come without weapons, but I knew he wouldn't do that. I sat in ambush on the way to that place and captured him along with three other Karmal officers who were with him. The Russians offered to exchange him for

Sulfiq Finder, left, and Aleksei Olenin, "Rahmatullah." They were like father and son.

three or four mujahidin prisoners and sixteen Kalashnikovs. I didn't listen. The Kabul general and other officers were put under the ground." By that, he meant they were executed.

Aleksei Olenin, Alias Rahmatullah

We were waiting for the Russian defector who, Arif said, stayed with a unit in the mountains. Sulfiq Finder said his men had captured the Russian three years earlier while he was selling gasoline from a tanker truck. During the first three months, he said, the Russian tried to escape several times and there were plans to send him to Pakistan, but now he was a good Muslim and had been given the name Rahmatullah. He finally arrived, wearing jogging sneakers and a blue zippered jacket with a BMW patch over his Afghan clothes. A light mustache drooped at the corners of his mouth and his hair was cut in bangs over his forehead. He said he was twenty-three and his name was Aleksei Ivanovitch Olenin.

"I come from the town of Otradny in the Russian Republic," he said. "I studied for ten years and was conscripted when I was eighteen. I trained for three months and then they sent me to Qiligai as a driver of a truck carrying water. I also drove a tanker truck sometimes and once made a journey carrying ammunition south to Kabul and Jalalabad.

"There are thousands of soldiers at Qiligai and a lot of times they have nothing to do. Half of them smoke hashish. The officers get drunk on vodka. The soldiers are paid in rubles and if they want to buy from the Afghans they need local currency, so they sell petrol, ammunition, and anything else they can find. I was there for about a year. One month after I arrived a soldier escaped because he lost his rifle during an engagement. He thought the officers would think he sold it and would punish him. After he escaped the officers made an announcement that if soldiers left the base and were captured by the mujahidin their noses and ears would be cut off. But later four or five escaped at one time. An announcement was made over the loudspeakers that they were missing and that other soldiers should bring them back. We never heard what happened to them.

"After I joined the mujahidin I heard other stories. About a year ago a soldier contacted the mujahidin. He said he would kill his officer and escape with his weapon. A small boy was sent to guide him, but when he came out the boy was afraid and ran away. The boy said the Russians came and surrounded the field where the soldier was hiding. Six hours later he tried to sneak away and was recaptured. I heard he was killed.

"Last year a Russian who joined the mujahidin told me about another soldier who escaped and was recaptured. He was put in a room with a mine under it and was killed when the mine exploded. Later the soldier who told me that story was also recaptured. They killed him by running a tank over him in front of all the soldiers. I heard that from a member of the militia who was a secret mujahid." Nasratullah had also told a story about a recaptured defector being blown up with a mine. I asked Olenin about this, but he said he did not know if the two stories referred to the same incident.

I asked about his life with the mujahidin. "Sulfiq Finder treats me like a son and I call him father. At first I couldn't eat rice, but now I'm used to it. It was also difficult to walk in the mountains but now I can do it easily. Until last year I was moved around to check on Russian posts and take part in operations. But now I stay in a rear base. All the Russians know I'm with the mujahidin. If a spy informs them I am in a village it will be bombed so I stay away not to make trouble for the villagers."

Abdul Sattar, one of the commanders who was listening, told a story to confirm how anxious the Russians were to capture or kill Olenin. "A cousin of mine in the Anderab Valley was put in jail by the Russians," he said, referring to a valley next to the more famous Panjshir Valley. "I went there to see what I could do. A Russian officer knew I had close relations with Sulfiq Finder and sent a message through the local militia. He said my cousin would be freed if I would bring Rahmatullah to him or if I would just kill him and bring his head. He also said he would give me a lot of money. I sent a message back saying I would do that, but first he would have to kill the man who was head of the Communists in Anderab. Nothing happened after that and my cousin is still in jail."

Defectors and Drugs

Olenin went to eat and I asked Sulfiq Finder about Soviet soldiers' using drugs. "I have told shopkeepers that if Russians come to them to buy hashish they should tell me," he replied. "About ten months ago a Russian who could speak some Dari asked for heroin. He was sent to one of our men who did not wear a beard like the mujahidin and looked like an ordinary person but he had a pistol under his shirt. He told the Russian he would get heroin in another village and the two of them got into a local truck, in the front with the driver, and went to that place. But the Russian said he would stay in the truck and the heroin should be brought to him. Our mujahid tried to persuade him to get out. When he wouldn't, the mujahid tried to take out his pistol and capture him. The Russian stopped him and they fought. Other mujahidin pulled the Russian to the ground. He shouted, 'Why are you doing this? I am your friend.' They shot him right there and left his body for the Russians to find.

"Just about three weeks ago a Russian officer asked for heroin in the bazaar. We decided we would capture him alive to use in exchange for some of our men who had been taken prisoner. The Russian came to the meeting place in a truck and one of our men asked him what he wanted to buy. We tried to get him to come down from the truck. He became suspicious and reached for his weapon. We had mujahidin hidden and when he made that move they shot him. They left his body with the truck so the Russians could see how he died."

I was surprised at Sulfiq Finder's reference to an attempt to capture a Soviet soldier for a prisoner exchange, since he seemed adamant about dealings with the Russians. Even among Hizb-i-Islami commanders, and one as fierce as Sulfiq Finder, some flexibility apparently existed.

Testing a Prisoner

We left the camp of Sulfiq Finder in the afternoon and traveled up a valley for only an hour to the camp of Maulvi Mohammed Nasrullah, a Hizb-i-Islami judge and administrator. He too told a story of an attempt at a prisoner exchange: "About two years ago there was a close fight and a Russian soldier was captured after he ran out of ammunition. His name was Victor and he said he came from the Urals. We told him about Islam but he did not want to become a Muslim. We could not keep him and, when we heard a well-known commander had been captured in Parwan Province, we sent him there in case they could make an exchange."

We were going to Parwan and I made a note to ask about this. Since Maulvi Nasrullah was a judge and could speak with authority, I asked if Islamic law allowed prisoners to be killed.

"The Holy Koran says that when a prisoner comes into your hands you must offer him Islam," he replied. "If he accepts, you must treat him as a brother. But it may be some time before an unbeliever realizes his errors. There are some who might say they accept Islam, but speak falsely. Once there was a Russian wandering around out of his mind because of drugs. We captured him and he said he would be our friend and would accept Islam. We wanted to test him and gave him a Kalashnikov and took him with us on an operation. However, we altered the firing pin so the gun could not shoot a bullet. Then our men, as if by chance, left their guns to one side to see what he would do. He raised his gun to shoot them and pulled the trigger. The mujahidin got their own guns and killed him."

We spent the night and all the next day at Maulvi Nasrullah's camp, hoping he could find mujahidin to escort us to Parwan, but no one was willing to make the long and arduous climb over the mountains. The Maulvi could only give us one mujahid to take us to another commander two hours up the valley, where we spent the next night.

Horse Trading

Arif's horse still had bad diarrhea: its head hung far down and its eyes were half closed. There was blood on its lips. The commander at our new camp found a boil on the roof of its mouth and punctured it with a knife. He said horses got such boils if they are not fed regularly. Arif decided he needed a new horse and the commander summoned a villager, who brought a small horse for an exchange. Arif said our horse was larger and would recover if it was allowed to rest for ten days and eat fresh grass. Since there were large pastures nearby, this did not seem a problem. Without lengthy bargaining a deal was struck for a new horse in exchange for Arif's sick horse plus $90. But the villager came back a few hours later to cancel the exchange, saying the horse would not recover as easily as Arif claimed.

So Arif was left once again with a sick horse. However, we sat around the rest of the day without finding escorts and the villager returned the next morning. He said the commander ordered him to go through with the deal because we were guests of the Hizb-i-Islami and needed a good horse for the road ahead. He made the exchange anew, but this time asked for, and got, $110.

He also brought along a friend who thought my horse, although its ribs were showing and it had saddle sores, would recover with rest and good food and could be used in his business of hauling wood. He offered a smaller horse that was more fit for travel. I agreed. I had only a pack pad as a saddle and no stirrups and I found it easier to balance on a smaller horse.

We were camped beside the only trail up the valley. Four days had passed since we arrived at Walyan and we had traveled barely ten miles. We still hadn't found escorts, but I urged Arif to make a start, pointing out that we now had fresh horses and that small groups, and even single individuals, passed by almost every hour. It seemed perfectly safe. He did not reply, but a few hours later he said the commander told him that five refugee families, traveling all the way to Pakistan, would leave early in the morning. We would go with them.

About three in the morning we heard the shuffle of their feet and the bells of their camels and saw their swinging kerosene lamps. We quickly joined them. But soon after dawn Arif said that because of the danger of an air attack we would camp by the trail until night. Again I went through my litany of the need to press on. After about an hour, as other travelers continued along the path, someone apparently convinced Arif that there was no danger, and we set out again.

After another hour we halted once more, this time near some merchants who had stopped to make tea. They laughed when they saw us. Arif said they knew about the sick horse we had exchanged and now reported that the horse had dropped dead during the night.

I felt sorry for the villager who made the exchange because the commander wanted to do us a service and now had a heavy loss. But sentimentality is not an Afghan trait. Arif said it was the man's own fault: he should have known better than to accept a sick animal.

The merchants had several donkeys and were carrying several dozen long, thin rolls of printed cloth, labeled as being made in Indonesia. They set out at noon. I said we should go with them; Arif insisted once again that it was not safe to travel by day. I said it was difficult for me to travel by night. An hour later, as I sat brooding and obviously very upset, he agreed to start.

We were in the high ranges, bleak desert with icy streams, just the two of us in an immensity of silence. The horses trudged slowly in the thin, cold air. Ahead loomed a wall of rock. At its base we caught up with the merchants, huddled in a circle of rock built as a wind shelter. A donkey was sick and one of the men offered to act as a guide across the mountains if we would carry some of their rolls of cloth on our horses. We agreed and began the ascent up a tortuous trail to the Walyan Pass. After an hour my horse was stopping for breath every few minutes. Arif dismounted and told me to get off too. The air was so thin that every step was exhausting. The pass was a little short of 15,000 feet, as I discovered when I later consulted a map in Pakistan.

We rested for fifteen minutes and began the almost vertical descent. Fortunately there was still some daylight. The guide led my horse as I slipped and fell on loose gravel, sometimes sliding down ten or fifteen feet at a time. Then it was pitch black. I climbed on the horse, grasping the front of the pack with one hand and the back with another and gripping with my knees. Nevertheless, I fell off twice and Arif and the guide had to lift me back on. We went through woods, forded streams, clattered on rocks, and lurched and bobbed for hours of worry and agony. It was almost midnight when we reached a tent that was our guide's home. His wife put brushwood on a fire to make tea and heated some kind of sweetened wheat meal for a quick supper. I opened my sleeping bag on the ground outside the tent and was asleep within minutes.

The next morning, with more persuasion, Arif agreed to start by ourselves. That evening he found a Hizbi mullah, who gave us dinner and a place to sleep until about two in the morning and then sent his son to accompany us to the wide Ghorband valley.

Exchanging Prisoners

We were now south of the Salang Pass and about sixty miles north of Kabul. We turned west and, just as the sun was setting, arrived at the base of Commander Mohammed Sabir of the Jamiat-i-Islami. It was the only time in the entire trip that Arif was willing to spend the night with any group except his own Hizb-i-Islami. Commander Sabir was twenty-five, heavily built, fair-skinned, and slightly sunburned, with light brown eyes and a thick black beard. He said there was a large Soviet base at Pul-i-Mattak, about twenty-five miles to the east. It protected the route from the Salang Pass to Kabul.

When Arif mentioned that I was not eating much, Sabir produced a meal of boiled eggs, fresh tomatoes, boiled potatoes, small onions, and soft, freshly baked bread. My appetite returned. Over tea, I asked him about two of the alternatives for dealing with Soviet prisoners: killing them or exchanging them.

"You must understand," he said, "that—in any war—if prisoners are killed it's generally when they are first captured: in the heat of battle. But here, Russians are rarely seized in battle, for two reasons. First, Russian soldiers seldom leave their tanks or armored personnel carriers. Battles in the open are left to Afghan government soldiers. Second, the normal tactic of any guerrilla fighter is to fall back when attacked. We do that too, because the Russian and Kabul troops have better and heavier weapons. Since we do not advance toward the enemy, we are rarely able to capture them.

"But sometimes the Russians patrol on foot and those who do come into our hands in this way are generally killed if we can't do anything else with them. I'll give you an example. Two years ago the Russians were making a sweep through mostly deserted villages near the Salang highway. Some mujahidin were hidden in one of the houses waiting to prepare an ambush when eight Russians came in and put their guns in a corner to smoke hashish. After a while our men took their guns and captured them. But there were so many of them, and so many other Russians in the area, that they could not take them away so they killed them.

"Prisoner exchanges don't happen often but there was one three months ago. We captured two Russians who were supposed to be guarding the pipeline but really they were stealing petrol. They shot holes in the pipeline so the petrol came out, and sold it to young boys. One filled the cans and the other took the money. We found out about this and some of our mujahidin dressed in old clothes, like villagers, and hid their guns under their blankets. The Russians had their Kalashnikovs over their shoulders. Our men came near and seized them. We kept them three weeks and tried to teach them Islam but they wouldn't listen. At the same time the villagers came to us and said it was causing danger for them, keeping the Russians here. They were being bombed by jets and asked us to get rid of them.

"We wanted to help the villagers so we said we would exchange the Russians for one of our best commanders. He was Mohammed Aman, who was captured with three of his men. They were held in Pul-i-Charkhi prison in Kabul. The villagers went to the Russians and worked out how the exchange would take place. Our men took up an ambush position on one side of the highway, at a place where the villagers usually cross. Karmal troops and militia and one Russian adviser were on the other side. The villagers walked between the two groups. We didn't trust the Russians. We said they must send over Commander Aman and the three mujahidin first. They told the villagers that one mujahid had died but they had Commander Aman and the two others. They sent them across and then we sent the two Russians."

I asked what condition Commander Aman was in after being imprisoned at Pul-i-Charkhi.

"He said he was beaten and tortured with electric shocks to his testicles," he said. "He could not hear in one ear and could not speak clearly. The two mujahidin said they were tortured too. They said the third man died under torture.

"We also captured a Russian about six weeks ago. We were sitting in ambush when he came walking along the road with his Kalashnikov over his shoulder. He was a Tajik who was looking for us. He said he was a Muslim, but Russians took away his Holy Koran and were going to punish him for having it. We kept him with us for a while and gave him the name of Allah Mohammed. Then we sent him to the Panjshir Valley where he is doing his jihad with Commander Massoud."

I asked about Soviet soldiers selling things to get money to buy hashish. "The Russians used to sell their Kalashnikovs but now they sell only ammunition, rocket grenades, and mortar shells," he said. "There is a shop near Pul-i-Mattak where they go to say they want to buy hashish. We tell boys to make the exchange with them. One boy has done this so often he has learned some Russian."

Arif discovered that a major Hizbi commander, Abdul Wahed, was nearby and we went to meet him the next afternoon. He was thirty-four, with a round face, full cheeks, and a large beard. He was an anti-Communist at Kabul University but was never arrested and later taught in a rural primary school. He fled to Pakistan after the Communist coup and, like many other Hizb-i-Islami commanders, he fought first in the south and then joined the war in the north, his home area. To my complete surprise, Abdul Wahed said the Hizbi was operating a small, intact hydroelectric dam and power system. He took us on a tour, showing irrigation canals running from the dam and the pylons and electric boxes for distributing power to houses and shops. He said the Hizbi collected revenue from 600 meters and got necessary spare parts from Kabul, or had items made to order in Peshawar. As a teacher, he was equally proud of the school system. He said they had three schools up to the ninth grade and an intermediate school up to the twelfth grade, including a library of several thousand books. No children were in classes—he said there was a three-month holiday so the boys could help their families with the harvest—but the buildings were in good repair and some boys were around the intermediate school.

The Ransom of Padshah

Commander Wahed said the Hizbi had a ruling board to supervise party affairs and that he was one of the members. The next morning, when we sat quietly, I asked the end of the story we heard from Maulvi Nasrullah about the Russian named Victor who was captured and sent to Parwan for use in a possible prisoner exchange.

"There was no need for him," Abdul Wahed replied. "An arrangement was already made to exchange two other Russians. Victor was sent back to Baghlan but on the way, as he passed near a government post, he tried to escape. The men who were guarding him shot and killed him."

I was surprised at his mention of an exchange of two Russians. As a party official, I thought he would be totally opposed to dealings with the enemy. I asked what happened.

"The commander who was captured was very active and very popular with his mujahidin," he said. "They called him *Padshah* (King). About two years ago he was doing an operation against the Bagram air base when he ran out of ammunition and retreated to a cave with twelve of his men. A spy told where they were hidden and the Russians fired some gas into the cave. The mujahidin were killed and Padshah became unconscious. When the Karmal troops saw him they beat him with their rifles and wanted to kill him, but the Russians said he was an important commander and they took him to their own jail at Bagram to keep him from more harm.

"Padshah's father and his mujahidin wanted to free him so they looked for a way to capture Russians for an exchange. One day, some children came and said two Russians from Bagram had come to their village to pick mulberries and the mujahidin went there and seized them. Soon, the Russians offered to exchange them for Padshah and the mujahidin, of course, agreed. The Russians and the mujahidin took up positions two kilometers apart. Some villagers went to confirm that Padshah was there and the exchange was made. This was about three months after he was captured. For a while he was out of his mind from the gas and the way he was beaten when he was captured."

"Martyrdom Is Our Victory"

I said I did not understand why this exchange took place, since other Hizbi commanders told me it was wrong to make agreements with the enemy.

"That's true," he replied. "The Hizb-i-Islami is against any agreements. We started our jihad for the cause of God. If anyone kills Russians that is his victory. If he loses part of his body, that is his victory. If he is captured or martyred, that is his victory. All this we accept as part of the jihad. If we agree to exchanges, the mujahidin will not be doing their jihad. It will be bad for discipline. They will think their lives are not in danger. The best way is to fight and not to agree to exchanges. If Russians are captured by the mujahidin they must be made Muslim or be killed."

"Then why did this exchange take place?" I asked.

"All of the other commanders and the entire board of the Hizb-i-Islami in Parwan were against it. But we did not interfere. Afterward, it was decided to punish the mujahidin who did it. Their arms were taken away and they were told, 'You cannot be mujahidin. Return to your villages.' They were very angry and joined the government militia but we could not help that."

"What happened to Padshah?" I asked.

"He had nothing to do with the exchange. It was his father who started it. After he got well he returned to his jihad. Last year, he was martyred along with two mujahidin in an operation against the Russians. Martyrdom in the name of God is our victory."

After lunch I discovered another example of an intact transport system linking Communist- and mujahidin-controlled territory. We were taken to a road junction where there was a bus stop, complete with a window where passengers could buy a ticket for a trip to Kabul that would take just three hours. Two old yellow buses packed with old men, women, and children passed while we were waiting. A yellow taxi also came by, with baggage piled high on its roof.

A truck loaded with mujahidin also stopped. They told Arif their group had two Russians at a base about two days away. A week earlier, I would have jumped at the chance to have talked with the Russians but now my strength, both of body and mind, was almost depleted, and I declined. I just wanted to get back to Pakistan.

It took eleven days: first by truck, then by foot over a pass so high the horse could not carry me, then down into a desolate valley where there were drops of human blood on the rocks and a cluster of rotting camels from a nomad caravan that had been bombed. We traveled on to a point on a road only eight miles west of the Kabul suburb of Paghman. Arif's family lived nearby in the village of Narkh, and he insisted on visiting them.

This had been the subject of another recurrent disagreement. Arif had first mentioned such a visit when we were still back in Kunduz. I said I would not mind a one day stay, but he said he had not seen his family for almost two years and would have to remain with them three or four days. It was now almost eight weeks since we left Peshawar. I said I had to get back quickly or I would be reported missing and people would start thinking I was dead, as they did when I was delayed on my return from Mazar-i-Sharif. He said a short visit was impossible and that he had to take part in prayer ceremonies with many branches of his family. As it turned out, the Russians solved the problem.

Running the Soviet Blockade

About three o'clock in the morning, after only one day of family ceremonies, Arif woke me and said we would have to leave. Mujahidin agents had reported that the Russians were planning a major attack. The horses were readied and Arif and I rode away, passing women and children who were also leaving for the safety of the surrounding mountains. Soon after dawn, we looked back in the direction we had come and saw jets on bombing and strafing runs to clear the way for a ground attack.

It was part of a major Soviet and Afghan Army move to disrupt mujahidin supply lines, and we kept running into their roadblocks. We were traveling south and crossing in a reverse direction the same area we had traversed at the start of our journey. First we went toward Beksamun, intending to go the next day to Baraki, the town that had never been attacked. Now we learned that Baraki had been bombed and we retreated to Tangi Saidan, the place where we paid off the men with the horses on our way in from Pakistan. We spent all the day in a field a half mile away as MiGs bombed and strafed Tangi Saidan, killing six mujahidin and wounding several others. We left in a hurry when we got word that a commando force of Afghan Army troops had been put down nearby.

Now, to Arif's relief, we met and joined Commander Razar Khan, a Hizbi commander from Bamiyan Province who was going to Pakistan with about a dozen men. That night we passed through the narrow gorge where a hydroelectric dam had once been planned, and spent the next day hidden in a grove of apricot trees while jets bombed targets a few miles away.

We started at four in the afternoon for a night crossing of the Kabul-Kandahar highway, stopping for dinner at a small irrigation dam. But as we approached the highway flares shot into the sky, and people came running back, shouting that the Soviet forces had an ambush party there. We turned aside and headed into the mountains, climbing a 9,000 foot pass to cross the highway by a different route. Razar Khan kept us going at a steady pace through the night, but as dawn neared we were still in the mountains. He began to trot the horses and the men had to run to keep up.

The highway is in a wide valley. If we were caught there by daylight we would be easy targets for the jets and helicopters that were now on constant patrol. We didn't make it in time to cross that night. At seven o'clock, with the sun well in the sky, we hid the horses under the trees of a small village and crowded into a mosque where the exhausted men were soon asleep. They had walked and run for eleven hours and never once complained.

Some men in the village were unhappy with our presence. When jets passed overhead, they came into the mosque and demanded that we leave, saying the village would be bombed if we remained. Razar Khan simply told them we would stay. We could see the highway and a procession of tanks, armored cars, and other military and civilian vehicles creeping west, apparently to take part in some attack.

The stop illustrated again the difference between the countryside by day, when the Russians ruled the skies, and by night, when their planes were grounded. As we watched the convoy from our half-destroyed village, it seemed that we were alone except for a few farmers. But when we set out after dark, about 100 men appeared from where they had taken cover and crossed the highway with us.

Originally, Razar Khan planned to travel via the Logar desert and Dubandi to Teri Mangal, which is the shortest route to Pakistan. Now Arif said we would go instead to Miram Shah in Pakistan. That was the crossing where, entering Afghanistan with Abdul Wahab's convoy, I had been threatened by the plainclothes officer with the bullets draped over his shoulder. I was so tired I hardly cared what happened, as long as this journey came to an end.

Arif said the next leg of the trip would be easy; we would go for about eight hours across a wide plain, rest for the night, and cross the Zurmat plain the next day. But at midnight, when we tried to stop at a village, some elders refused to give us the key to the mosque. They said the Russians were active in the area and would attack the village if they heard we were there. Arif said the people knew that a foreigner was traveling with the group and thought this made our presence especially dangerous. I could hear both Arif and Razar Khan using the word "*Musulman*." I gathered they were accusing the elders of being bad Muslims for not granting hospitality to a party of mujahidin. Finally, Razar Khan shouted something in an angry voice, jerked at the reins of his horse, and led us away.

There was no moon and no one in our group knew the way. We went to another village a short distance away, hammered at doors, and found an old man who agreed to guide us, if we gave him a horse to ride and paid him $12. We crossed the Zurmat plain, with the lights of Gardez on our left and with Afghan Army flares shooting into the black sky to guard against a night attack. We started so late that we had to travel the last two hours in full daylight, but there were no MiGs on patrol and we made it safely. This time it was a thirteen-hour night of relentless walking for the mujahidin. But again, no one complained.

After two more nights of travel we came to the valley with the teahouses where Abdul Wahab's convoy had spent a day, and where Ziahullah angrily searched the Harakat man. Now the teahouses were empty. The area had been attacked a few days before and several mujahidin groups and some refugees had scattered to the surrounding hills where they could take cover. As we crossed the valley to some trees on a hillside, I was reminded again of how Afghan customs and habits persist.

Horse Care, Afghan-style

Several times during the trip Arif had told me not to let my horse eat or drink while I was riding it. Often when we halted for the night he tied the reins high on a tree so the horse could not lower its head to nibble on grass or straw at its feet. But I felt sorry for whatever horse I was riding. They all were in miserable condition, and when Arif was not near I allowed them to eat and drink as they pleased.

Now as we forded a stream I allowed my horse to drink. Arif saw me and was furious. He ordered me off, jumped on my horse, and galloped back and forth. I vaguely recalled something I had read in J. P. Ferrier's account of his Afghan journey in 1846 and I looked it up when I got back to Peshawar: "They make their horses gallop after drinking, as they say, to warm the water in the stomach of the animal; were this neglected, they affirm that the hide would swell after the saddle is taken off, and in a short time fall away from the flesh at this spot. It is this belief that induces them to keep their horses saddled and without food for four or five hours after a journey if only of half an hour."

When we reached the hillside several mujahidin built a fire to roast ears of corn that they stripped from a nearby field. Two farmers saw them and came running, brandishing their hoes as weapons. Razar Khan intervened to calm them. Arif said the farmers complained that mujahidin came every day and stole the corn they depended on to carry them through the winter. Razar Khan gave them some money to placate them. They took the money but did not seem happy. It was another instance of tension between the mujahidin and local people.

With the end of the journey near, Arif decided to settle something that was bothering him: more money. During the past week he had recalled several times how his visit to his home village had been cut short. Now he mentioned it again. He also brought up another point. He said we agreed on 1,200 rupees ($75) a week, but that was as an interpreter, and as it turned out he also had to care for the horses. I suggested 1,400 ($87.50) but he still seemed unhappy and we settled on 1,500 ($97.75), a very large sum by Afghan standards.

The next night we crossed the final ridges and arrived at the border at dawn. I sat on the ground huddled under a borrowed blanket, wearing Arif's turban to make myself as inconspicuous as possible. But the precautions were unnecessary: It was too early for the border police to be at their posts, and without further trouble we hired a pickup truck and rode into Miram Shah. Arif parked me in the basement of a restaurant while he waited for the horses to arrive. They were in such bad condition that he sold both of them to the restaurant owner for $185. Then he bought bus tickets for Peshawar. It was not until long after dark, October 2, 1985, that I was back at Green's Hotel.

The next day when I called the *New York Times* to report my arrival, Annie Zusy, the editor who handled my stories, said she was especially glad to hear from me because an American newsman had been reported killed in the Kandahar area of southwest Afghanistan. I had been gone so long she had thought I might be the casualty. The man who was killed was Charles Thornton of the *Arizona Republic*. Four months later I would be back in Afghanistan, searching for his body.

Right now, however, I wanted only to rest, write my stories, and return to New York to see my wife. Arif came to Green's the next day. The trip took nine weeks and one day. I multiplied 1,500 by nine, added something for the extra day and came to a round sum of 14,000 rupees, or $875, and we parted as friends.

I had hoped for the best and so it happened. A series of stories on the Soviet defectors and the mujahidin commanders, with their fierce resolve to fight the Communists no matter what the cost, made the front page of the *New York Times* for three successive days.

Afghanistan Is Not Vietnam

....

9

Most of Afghanistan hibernates during the winter. The arid country-side provides little fuel to heat mud houses and people huddle in their thin blankets, so ill-nourished and thinly dressed that it is a strain to go outdoors even for a few hours. Outdoor activity is especially dangerous for the mujahidin: they leave tracks in the snow and, without the cover of leafy trees, can be easily spotted from the air. In addition, tanks and armored cars can maneuver over dry and frozen ground in pursuit.

I needed rest and returned to New York in November 1985. That March Mikhail Gorbachev had emerged as the new Soviet leader. Two weeks before my return home, President Ronald Reagan met Gorbachev in Geneva. Among other things they discussed Afghanistan. Mr. Reagan and his aides were reported to have come away with the impression that Gorbachev wanted to solve the Afghan problem.

I went to Washington to talk to government and military officials and scholars, who reiterated what I had heard earlier from American and European diplomatic sources in Pakistan: no end of the war was in sight. The UN-sponsored negotiations were seen as a Soviet propaganda initiative, with Moscow playing for time to educate a new generation of Afghans who would give them a reliable surrogate army and political and administrative cadres to run the government.

However, the Reagan administration decided to put Gorbachev to the test. In December the United States agreed to act as a guarantor for a "comprehensive and balanced settlement" to be worked out by a United Nations mediator.

With that a series of events unfolded. In March 1986 Gorbachev told the 27th Communist Party Congress that "counterrevolution and imperialism have transformed Afghanistan into a bleeding wound," and said he hoped for a negotiated settlement of the conflict by the end of the year. At the beginning of May, Babrak Karmal was removed as general secretary of the ruling People's Democratic Party of Afghanistan. His replacement, who used the single name of Najib, said he sought a government of national reconciliation. In mid-May the Soviet Union, for the first time since the UN-sponsored peace talks began in 1981, put a plan for a troop withdrawal on the table. In August Gorbachev announced that six regiments, or about 8,000 men, would be withdrawn by the year's end. In January 1987 Najib proclaimed a six-month unilateral cease-fire.

But simultaneously the Afghan Army became stronger and bolder, raiding out from its urban bases to destroy mujahidin strongholds and establish scores of small posts for interdicting mujahidin supply routes. The Soviet Union appeared to believe it was approaching the negotiations from a position of strength, not weakness.

No Stalemate, No Quagmire

A flaw in much of U.S. thinking about Afghanistan is that when the Russians talk of withdrawing their troops, Americans think of the Vietnam scenario: the United States was bogged down, sinking deeper into a quagmire. Years passed. No light at the end of the tunnel. When America escalated its forces, the Russians and Chinese escalated their aid. Stalemate. At the front, troops were demoralized; at home, there were antiwar riots. The solution: negotiate a face-saving formula to get the United States off the hook.

Now the scenario for the Russians in Afghanistan: another stalemate. Troops are demoralized, selling their equipment and using drugs; there is said to be concern about all those body bags returning home; there are reports of draft evasion and an increasing use of drugs in the Soviet Union itself as veterans return home. Afghanistan is an economic burden; the Soviet Union needs every ruble it can spare to prepare for a technological war with the West.

But the analogy fails for many reasons. Vietnam was 10,000 miles from the United States. Afghanistan is contiguous to the Soviet Union and shares ethnic and linguistic ties with Soviet Central Asia that cannot be ignored. In Vietnam the United States, with its emphasis on body counts and the capture or loss of strong points, had short-term goals, and the public and politicians grew impatient when these goals were not achieved. But Moscow has long-term objectives, and the Soviet military and political infrastructure has patience. With a controlled press and submerged public opinion, the government has all the time it requires to fight a drawn-out guerrilla war.

Equally important is the difference in the nature of the resistance. In Vietnam the United States faced a monolithic guerrilla force skilled both in war and politics. But in Afghanistan the Soviet Union faces disparate groups who fight among themselves for weapons and prestige and who, even if they were better armed and better led, would still lack the modern political skills needed to solidify military gains by establishing local governments in liberated areas. With such an enemy, the Russians can see a gleam of victory in the darkness of the tunnel ahead.

Finally, there are the political costs. In admitting its mistake and withdrawing from Vietnam, the United States created no adverse effect on America's relations with its allies and friends. But for the Soviet Union even to hint at a retreat under pressure from a Western-supported Islamic insurgency would be seen primarily as weakness, not realistic statesmanship, with the risk of a profound reaction throughout the Communist world and in Soviet Central Asia as well.

Did the Kremlin Make a Mistake?

A discussion of whether the Russians might abandon Afghanistan should begin with the question: How and why did they get involved in the first place? Some have said the 1978 coup by Nur Mohammed Taraki and Hafizullah Amin was an accident with no Soviet backing. Others said the Soviet Union was following the Czarist thrust toward warmwater ports or, in a modern context, that they seized Afghanistan to threaten the West's oil reserves in the Persian Gulf.

The accident thesis surfaced within weeks of the Communist coup of April 1978. Louis Dupree, then regarded as the foremost American scholar on Afghan affairs, called the coup a "blunder" and wrote a letter to the *New York Times* saying it was "unjustified" to describe the new government as Communist.

This view was refuted when Amin himself disclosed that there had been ten rehearsals for the coup and as more was learned about PDPA leaders and their close, almost daily, prerevolutionary contacts with the Soviet embassy. The most telling evidence was the Soviet-inspired moves, beginning in 1976, to unify the Parcham and Khalq Communists into a single party. This was when Mohammed Daoud was trying to break away from the Communists, who helped him seize power in 1973. Obviously, as early as 1976 the Russians were preparing to swallow Afghanistan.

With the Soviet intervention of December 1979, the "tar baby" thesis was proposed—so-called because, as in the Uncle Remus stories, it seemed that every time the Russians touched Afghanistan to try to pull themselves loose they got stuck even tighter. First, the theory went, because of the ties of ideology, Soviet leaders had no choice but to embrace the adventurist Taraki-Amin coup. Then, when their blundering protégés began to falter, they had to intervene—almost impetuously— to prop them up.

But this ignores another Soviet option: dump the PDPA and allow Afghanistan to revert to its previous status as a buffer state.

There is no evidence that Gorbachev is willing to do this. Instead, when he speaks of withdrawal he refers only to the 'limited contingent' of troops sent to Afghanistan in December 1979. He does not speak of a weakening of Moscow's absolute control of Afghanistan's future.

Sovietizing the Afghans

The strongest evidence that Moscow has no intention of abandoning Afghanistan is its attempt to sovietize the Afghan state and Afghan society. Molding a new Afghan man in the Soviet image began with education. The curriculum of Kabul University was reshaped to include Marxist-Leninism in all its faculties. Russian replaced English as the compulsory foreign language. Now, more than half the teaching staff are from the Soviet Union or East Bloc countries. The Koran, Islamic theology, and Arabic grammar, once taught five hours a week, are now taught one hour a week. A new department of Latin American literature has been created: the history of the Cuban revolution is taught. Books are translations of Russian, Uzbek, and Tajik texts. In any given year 10,000 Afghans are studying in the Soviet Union and Eastern Europe, including several thousand children from seven to nine years of age, who are sent for as much as ten years of schooling.

Children's nurseries are patterned on the Soviet style. Boys and girls are enrolled as "Vanguards of the Saur Revolution" and are taken to the Soviet Union for visits of three to six months to learn Soviet life-styles.

Afghan nationalism has been weakened by stressing the ethnic diversity of Tajiks, Uzbeks, Turkmens, Hazaras, and Nuristanis. Internal propaganda among these minorities stresses the need for them to struggle to free themselves from Pushtun domination. They are given the right to educate their children in their mother tongues. In the future, Afghans may have to speak Russian as a national language to communicate with one another.

Afghan television duplicates Soviet programming. Newspapers and government publications mimic *Pravda* and Soviet information organs. The Afghan government mirrors the Soviet Union. Power is held by the PDPA, whose apparatus includes a central committee, politburo, and secretariat, with Babrak Karmal's successor, Najib, serving as general secretary. As in Moscow, there is a nominal parliament—called the Revolutionary Council—whose president fills the ceremonial role of head of state. Similarly, the courts are organized according to Soviet practices and laws are direct translations of those in force in the Soviet Union. The ministry of interior, in Soviet style, has its own armored and commando units. KHAD also has its own combat units as well as its army of spies.

According to Western diplomats in Kabul and scores of Afghans who have defected from high-ranking civilian posts, Russian advisers control every department of the government. Given the bureaucratic nature of Soviet society, approval must be sought from Moscow before even routine actions.

Defense Becomes Offense

Some have said the Soviet invasion was necessary to protect the Soviet Union from Islamic militants who would attempt to subvert the traditionally Muslim peoples of Soviet Central Asia. But this is an odd argument, because it was the actions of the Soviet Union that led to the growth of Islamic militancy in Afghanistan. Previously, religious orthodoxy, although always strong in Afghanistan, had never played a predominant part in government affairs. In fact, during the constitutional era of the 1960s, the influence of orthodox teachers was weakened, as evidenced by the expansion of female education and the appearance of a growing number of unveiled women on the streets of Kabul.

More to the point, military strategists point out that Moscow's goals may be simultaneously defensive and offensive. In their view, what could be justified on defensive grounds, such as the denial of Western listening posts or missile-launching pads in Afghanistan, would also stand as a projection of Soviet air power over the Arabian Sea and the Hormuz Strait at the entrance to the Persian Gulf. To a strategist, an incremental expansion of power, justified as defensive and without any immediate further objectives, might prove beneficial in some unforeseen future crisis. And perhaps it may not be so far in the future. Afghanistan, sharing a border with Iran, may prove of enormous value in manipulating the inevitable struggle for power after the death of the Ayatollah Khomeini.

In a larger context, the invasion can be seen as the culmination of an overall activist policy that began with the joint Soviet-Cuban intervention in Angola in 1975, followed by direct support for the revolutions in Ethiopia and South Yemen and the use of the Vietnamese proxy for the invasion of Cambodia.

Negotiating a Way Out

And yet, since the early days of the invasion, the Soviet Union has cultivated the image of being a reluctant guest on Afghan soil, claiming troops were sent only after the new Democratic Republic of Afghanistan (DRA) made several requests for help.

What would become a long effort to test Moscow's willingness to end both its occupation and its political dominance of Afghanistan began in May 1980. The Organization of the Islamic Conference—whose members range from Western-leaning Saudi Arabia and Pakistan to Moscow-leaning Algeria, Syria, and Libya—proposed four principles:

1. The immediate and unconditional withdrawal of the Soviet forces from Afghanistan.

2. The restoration of Afghanistan's independence and sovereignty and nonaligned character and respect for its Islamic identity.

3. The rights of the Afghan people to choose freely their own form of government and their own social and economic system.

4. The voluntary return of Afghan refugees to their homes in Afghanistan in conditions of honor and safety.

In September 1980 Pakistan took the issue to the UN General Assembly, where the four principles, with an added proviso to guarantee noninterference in Afghanistan's internal affairs, were accepted as a framework for negotiations.

In February 1981 the foreign ministers of the Nonaligned Movement, meeting in New Delhi, produced a significantly altered version of the principles. They eliminated all reference to a restoration of Afghanistan's independence, respect for its Islamic identity, and the rights of the Afghans to choose their own government and social system. Instead, they called only for the withdrawal of foreign forces, the creation of conditions of security and honor to enable refugees to return home, and reciprocal guarantees of nonintervention and noninterference.

The Nonaligned Movement formula thus echoed the Soviet propaganda position: it eliminated any direct reference to the Soviet invasion of Afghanistan and equated the Soviet presence with foreign aid to the resistance forces.

The reference to Afghan rights of self-determination was dropped despite the fact that annual resolutions passed by the General Assembly—by increasing majorities that reached 122 to 19 with only 12 abstentions in November 1986—called for the right of Afghans to choose their own government.

Nevertheless, it was the Nonaligned Movement's set of principles that became basis for a United Nations' mediation effort. Kurt Waldheim, who was then UN secretary general, appointed Javier Pérez de Cuéllar (who is now secretary general) as the negotiator, with the title of personal representative. In April 1981 Pérez de Cuéllar began separate talks in Kabul, Islamabad, New York, and Geneva. Nothing much happened until the summer of 1983, by which time Diego Cordovez of Ecuador had replaced Pérez de Cuéllar as personal representative and "proximity talks" had evolved in Geneva.

They were so named because the foreign ministers of Pakistan and Afghanistan met in separate rooms, with Cordovez shuttling between them. Newspaper reports explained the configuration of the talks by saying that Pakistan did not have diplomatic relations with Kabul. In fact, Afghanistan has an embassy in Islamabad and consulates in Peshawar and Quetta. Pakistan has an embassy in Kabul and consulates in Jalalabad and Kandahar. There are normal trade relations, telephone and telex communications, and a daily bus service between Peshawar and Jalalabad.

The reason Pakistan resisted face-to-face meetings was to symbolize the lack of legitimacy of the DRA regime. But it was a futile gesture. The talks were a diplomatic victory for Kabul and Moscow.

In 1980 the Organization of the Islamic Conference had met with a delegation of the Peshawar-based resistance parties while Kabul boycotted the meeting. Now the situation was reversed: the resistance parties were excluded and Kabul had gained recognition. When and if a settlement was worked out, it would be signed by the existing government in Kabul and this same Communist government would be accepted as the legitimate entity for carrying out the agreement.

The Soviet Union, Iran, and China, which share borders with Afghanistan, were invited to take part in the negotiations. Moscow said it would send observers. In practice, it is Moscow who dictates what the foreign minister of Kabul says. China refused outright to participate, implying that it did not want the United Nations or any other third party involved in its quarrels with the Soviet Union. However, since Beijing did not specifically object to the negotiations, it is believed that China will not impede any settlement approved by Pakistan and the United States, both of which are on friendly terms with China.

Iran said it would not attend the talks but wanted to be informed. It can be expected that as long as the Ayatollah Khomeini rules, Iran will denounce any settlement that does not establish an Islamic government and will continue to nurture pro-Khomeini Shia separatists.

Testing Moscow's Intentions

After the death of Brezhnev in November 1982, and the search by Andropov for some way to lighten the burden of Moscow's ties with the Third World, speculation resurfaced that the Russians were sinking in a Vietnam-style quagmire and wanted to call it quits in Afghanistan. But Andropov himself left no doubt that a troop withdrawal would not mean Soviet abandonment of the DRA. In April 1983 he reminded a West German reporter that the Soviet Union shared a long border with Afghanistan. "And so," he said, "in assisting friends, we at the same time think of ensuring the interests of our security." After assessing Soviet intentions, the United States decided that there had to be some allowance for the right of Afghans to choose their own government and the negotiations were broken off.

Andropov died in February 1984 and was succeeded by the equally frail Konstantin Chernenko, who died in March 1985. He was succeeded by Mikhail Gorbachev, a protégé of Andropov. Gorbachev revived his mentor's efforts to invigorate the Soviet economy, cut red tape, and reduce the cost of maintaining Third World client-states. Signals of a desire to withdraw from Afghanistan were flashed at the Geneva summit.

By then Cordovez had reduced the negotiations to a series of four "instruments" or proposals:

1. The voluntary return of refugees.

2. Mutual nonintervention and noninterference.

3. Guarantees by the Soviet Union and the United States of a negotiated agreement.

4. The interrelationship of the first three instruments to the withdrawal of Soviet troops.

The last point came to mean an exact timetable for the withdrawal of Soviet troops, whether the withdrawal would occur simultaneously with the end of outside aid, or only after aid had ended, and some way of monitoring both the withdrawal and the end of outside assistance. Nothing was said about free elections.

Agreement on the first two instruments had been reached early in the talks. On point three, the Soviet Union had agreed to act as a guarantor but the United States had not. Washington began the test of Gorbachev's "new thinking" by also agreeing to act as a guarantor, thus advancing the proximity talks to the fourth and crucial point: a timetable for the withdrawal of Soviet troops.

In December, when U.S. Deputy Secretary of State John Whitehead announced that the United States would act as a guarantor for a "comprehensive and balanced settlement," he emphasized that this did not represent a change in American policy. "Without provocation, certainly without invitation," he said, "the Soviet Union simply invaded a nonaligned, nonmenacing and independent country." He accused the Russians of attempting "to obliterate Afghan cultural values" and charged that, rather than being just advisers, they "now either directly make or are deeply involved in every major political, military or social decision." He said the only lasting solution was a negotiated settlement that "gets Soviet troops out of Afghanistan and permits the Afghan people to determine their own destiny."

In May 1986 Moscow presented a four-year phased withdrawal timetable and hinted that the pullout could start simultaneously with the end of outside aid. The time frame was obviously too long, but it was assumed that this could be whittled down in further meetings.

A Challenge to Washington

The United States had been presented with a challenge. It had apparently assumed that the Soviet Union would never really present a plan to withdraw its troops. It assumed that the Russians felt that large numbers of their soldiers were needed to prevent the Communists in Afghanistan from being slaughtered in a matter of weeks.

But were the Russians so weak? To the contrary, they apparently believed that they had a flexible strategy—countering resistance strengths and playing upon their weaknesses—to ensure the eventual victory of a Marxist-Leninist state. Their propaganda within Afghanistan only asks that the fighting stop and that the people accept a hybrid government, with the Communists in control of the cities and transportation links, and local autonomy in the countryside—in short, a normalization of the status quo.

With their capacity for intrigue and limitless funds, the Soviet "advisers" who would remain after a formal troop withdrawal could be expected to sow discord among tribal and ethnic factions for whom selfishness, greed, and lust for power are historic cultural traits. Local leaders would be tantalized with offers of help against their enemies. Even if they did not openly take arms to fight their fellow Muslims, there would be the temptation to receive the money and guns and then sit idle in an uneasy peace until the future clarified.

Thus the assumption that a negotiated troop withdrawal would be followed immediately by the collapse of the Communist regime is doubtful. I asked a high-level American diplomat in Islamabad, "What would the American attitude be if the Communists could survive in Kabul without Soviet bayonets?" His answer was simple: "The United States cannot install a government of its choice in Kabul."

"Comrade Doctor" Najib

In practice, just the opposite happened: it was Gorbachev who installed a government of his choice in Kabul, in the person of Najib. The new leader's original name was Najibullah, but the ending, referring to Allah, was dropped as unsuitable for a pure Communist. From both the Afghan and Soviet point of view, Najib combined all the attributes needed to rule Afghanistan. He was an early member of the Parcham Communists, whose major strength is in the north. But he was a Pushtun from the south, like most Khalqis. He was born in 1947 near Gardez in Paktia Province. His family belonged to the Ahmadzai tribe, whose homeland straddles the Pakistan-Afghanistan border. The Ahmadzais are Koochis, also known as Powindahs—a large nomadic group with distinct cultural traits. For instance, Koochi women are not veiled or narrowly segregated.

Najib's father was a civil servant in the Department of Transport in Kabul and then was sent to Peshawar as an Afghan trade agent. Najib went to primary school in Peshawar and speaks Urdu, the national language of Pakistan, although with a heavy Pushtun accent. Since his father was stationed in Peshawar, Najib continued to visit and travel in Pakistan during his university years, developing a knowledge of Pakistani culture and politics. He also speaks English. He graduated in 1964 from Habibia College (actually a high school) in Kabul, where English was mandatory.

In 1965 Najib entered the medical college of Kabul University. The degree course lasted six years, but the university was often closed by strikes during that time and Najib took ten years to get his degree. Associates address him as "Comrade Doctor," but there is no record that he ever served in a medical capacity.

According to his official biography, he joined the PDPA in 1965, the year of its official formation. When the party split he joined the Parchamis, led by Babrak Karmal. According to mujahidin sources, both the Parchamis and Khalqis had a three-man liaison committee that met regularly with the KGB resident in the Soviet embassy in Kabul. Najib was one of the Parchami members.

When the Russians manipulated a union of the two factions as a prelude to the 1978 coup, Najib was appointed one of four Parchamis on the joint central committee. When the Khalqis, under Taraki and Amin, seized total control and exiled Karmal and other leading Parchamis, Najib became ambassador to Iran. Then, when the Khalqis were dismissed, Najib joined Karmal·in Prague.

He returned to Kabul five days after the Soviet invasion and was immediately appointed head of KHAD with the rank of brigadier general. As part of his duties he visited Moscow ten times and East Germany twice over a period of five years. He became a member of the PDPA politburo in 1982. Initially, according to mujahidin sources, Najib was assigned three personal Soviet advisers, increased to five in 1983. With their help, he made KHAD the most efficient—in fact, the only efficient—government organ. He created a pyramid of five directors who controlled various departments in the civil and military administration of each of Afghanistan's twenty-nine provinces. Their main functions, besides overseeing the army and government, were to recruit and train agents, organize and supply village militia and self-defense forces, infiltrate mujahidin groups and the leadership in the many refugee camps in Pakistan and, above all, to infiltrate the resistance party structure in Peshawar.

In December 1985 Najib left KHAD and was appointed as a secretary of the Central Committee. Thus, while sending signals to President Reagan about a willingness to withdraw Soviet troops, Gorbachev was implementing plans to reinvigorate and strengthen the PDPA. Early in May Najib replaced Karmal as chairman of the Central Committee. For the next few months Karmal retained the honorary title of president, but that too was taken away in November and Karmal disappeared from public view, officially on the grounds of poor health.

Najib toured the cities and military bases attempting to breathe new spirit into an army and civilian administration left moribund by red tape and the jealousies and infighting of the Parchamis and Khalqis. He said it was time for workers to lay down their tools and students to put down their pens to join in the fight to defend the motherland. Seasoned Communist officials were transferred to military duties and politically connected deferments for the children of party elite were ended. There was even an attempt to distribute better-fitting uniforms to the rank and file.

Najib, in a series of sometimes contradictory speeches, interviews, and party manifestoes, announced his agenda to: "strengthen the armed forces and improve their fighting ability . . . intensify the struggle . . . stop the bloodshed and establish peace and tranquility . . . secure the frontiers and reinforce and consolidate the armed forces . . . decisively crush the last counter-revolutionary bands imported from abroad . . . democratize the social fabric . . . broaden the political and social base . . . strengthen the principle of collective leadership . . . carry out a policy of national reconciliation."

"National reconciliation" was a facade. In 1985, even before Karmal was ousted, the regime convened a council of nearly 1,800 "elders" to consult on national affairs, and later assembled 3,700 frontier tribesmen in an effort to encourage the growth of regional militias. In early January 1986 ten nonparty individuals were added to the Council of Ministers and fifty-six others were added to the rubber-stamp Revolutionary Council. A year later seventy-six "representatives of workers, peasants, handicraftsmen, intelligentsia, clergy, traders and other social groups," most of them said to be non-Communists, were added to the council. The appointments coincided with the arrival of a large contingent of foreign journalists invited to Kabul in mid-January 1987 to observe the start of a six-month cease-fire. Najib told the reporters that national reconciliation "did not mean the destruction of the state and the defeat of the party."

A Body for Ransom

·············

10

When I returned to Peshawar in February 1986 I found a major expansion in humanitarian aid for Afghanistan. But, simultaneously, Doctors Without Borders had closed its clinics, and for the first time since 1980 none of its doctors and nurses were working in Afghanistan.

Also, more signs of Moscow's carrot and stick policy: Soviet commandos and an invigorated Afghan Army had started a drive to smash mujahidin bases and disrupt their communications. As for the carrot, a leading mujahidin commander had defected in Kandahar Province—bringing with him a knowledge of resistance bases throughout the southwest.

I decided to go to Kandahar, once Afghanistan's second largest city but now reportedly devastated by constant fighting. I also wanted to locate the body of Charles Thornton, the journalist who was killed the previous August. It took a few weeks to arrange the trip. Meantime, I looked into the medical story.

Foreign Medical Groups in Peshawar

In contrast to its covert, though ill-concealed, supply of weapons and other military aid, the United States approved $15 million for well-publicized medical assistance inside Afghanistan. Most of the money went for three programs to train Afghan paramedics to work in areas controlled by the mujahidin. One, called International Medical Corps, was organized by Dr. Robert Simon of Los Angeles; another, called

Freedom Medicine, was organized by Gay-LeClerc Brenner, an American lawyer from Hawaii; and the third, called Medical Training for Afghans, was jointly organized by French and Belgian humanitarian groups that had long been active inside Afghanistan.

The pioneer in sending medical aid into Afghanistan was the Swedish Committee for Afghanistan, funded by the Swedish government and by donations from the Swedish public and from humanitarian groups and individuals in Norway, Holland, West Germany, and the United States.

A similar distribution of medicines, although on a smaller scale, was organized by the Norwegian Medical Committee, funded with some government money but depending mostly on help from religious groups and private individuals. Two American organizations, the Committee for Free Afghanistan, based in Washington, D.C., and American Aid for Afghans, of Portland, Oregon, also supplied medical and other aid to be taken into Afghanistan.

Growing Arab Influence

Eight French humanitarian organizations worked inside Afghanistan. The four largest were Doctors Without Borders (*Médecins sans Frontières*), International Medical Aid (*Aide Medicale Internationale*), Doctors of the World (*Médecins du Monde*), and Franco-Afghan Friendships (*Amities Franco-Afghan*). In addition, a major German organization—the German-Afghanistan Committee—established a dozen hospitals, and two small and secretive Norwegian and British groups sent medical teams for brief trips into Afghanistan.

Most of these organizations as a matter of policy worked with several of the political parties. However, Doctors Without Borders restricted itself to the Islamic Society of Professor Burhanuddin Rabbani. Then, in November 1985, there was a crisis. Professor Rabbani informed Dr. Juliet Fournot, who administered the group's work in Afghanistan, that because of diminished security it was no longer possible to send female doctors or nurses into Afghanistan.

Dr. Fournot suspected that the influence of Arab fundamentalists lay behind the order. There were many signs of an increased Arab presence in Afghanistan. I found a Syrian Arab at Zari and encountered three Arabs of unknown nationality on the trip to Baghlan. On February ll, 1986, a week before I returned to Peshawar, two Arabs, identified as

Kuwaiti, were killed when a mujahidin force was bombed in Ningrahar Province. It could not be determined if they were observers or were fighting on the side of the mujahidin.

Arab fundamentalist opposition to Western organizations working with the Afghans was underscored by an article published in September 1985 in *Arab News*, a Saudi-financed newspaper in London. It made factual errors, but its thrust was clear.

"In the absence of effective work by Islamic scholars," the article read, "Christian missionaries are exploiting the situation. There are 90 Swedish clinics, 116 French doctors, in addition to clinics run by American and German Red Cross Societies. Over 500 missionary workers are employed in the Peshawar refugee camps. These societies and organizations try to Christianize the Afghan children and to weaken the morale of the mujahidin. Moreover, they amputated several slightly wounded Muslim warriors. In 1984, these clinics amputated more than 3,500 mujahidin without any evident reason."

"A Country That Is Partially Mine"

Dr. Fournot was in her early thirties. She lived in Afghanistan as a child, and obtained her medical degree, specializing in dental surgery, in 1979, the year of the Soviet invasion.

"I spoke the language and I had very strong feelings," she said. "I wanted to assist a country that is partially mine." I asked about closing the clinics.

"There were several problems, particularly with women doctors," she replied. "One was the cultural problem. For the Afghans, just to see women is provoking. They are not used to women except inside their homes as wives, mothers, or sisters. But there were other things—the manipulation by others to separate the Afghans from Western groups. Some of the manipulation comes from the Kabul regime, by KHAD, accusing the doctors of being spies and the women of being prostitutes. But the real instigator was some Arab groups who objected to our presence. They were coming from countries such as Algeria, Libya, Syria, and Palestine."

"These are countries linked with the Soviet Union," I said. "Were these Arabs in favor of the Communists?"

"No, they were against their own governments. They were Wahhabis," she said, referring to the ultraorthodox Islamic fundamentalists.

"They accused us of trying to convert the people to Christianity and turning women into prostitutes.

"Then there was a problem of Afghan politics. The Jamiat-i-Islami, the group that we work with, was often attacked by the Hizbi-i-Islami, who raised the question of women doctors in an attempt to discredit the Jamiat-i-Islami.

"So the Jamiat-i-Islami was put in a difficult position. They asked us not to send women because it would please the Arabs. But we decided we would not send any doctors because, in our mind, the women and children need medicine the most. The few Afghan doctors are males, so the presence of foreign women doctors is even more valuable than male doctors.

"We make conditions for offering our assistance. We must have a good and large facility, assured security for our group and our patients, good logistics to bring in medicines, and maximum access to patients, including women and children.

"We recognize that the presence of women causes problems. The Kabul regime is very skilled in making propaganda on points the Afghans will believe. They try to spread lies about the doctors, including myself. My father was an engineer working in Afghanistan. The Kabul regime searched the old police registration cards and found my name and the years I stayed there. They published a story in the *New Kabul Times* about a trial that was supposed to have happened. It said Miss Fournot was arrested in 1968 on a bus between Kabul and Jalalabad carrying something like twenty kilos of drugs. The story explained why there was no trace of the incident. It said the Ministry of Foreign Affairs and the Ministry of Justice agreed to suppress the facts in order not to harm good relations between France and Afghanistan. But they made a big mistake because they did not know my age. I was only twelve years old at that time."

"She Must Not Make Trouble"

I also asked Laurence Laumonier, of International Medical Aid, about the banning of women. Dr. Laumonier, thirty-two, was a specialist in gastroenterology with a private clinic in Paris. Over a five-year period, she had worked eighteen months at various clinics in Afghanistan and was the first woman doctor to work inside. In June 1980, only six months after the Soviet invasion, she went to the Panjshir Valley with

Dr. Laurence Laumonier, who said volunteer doctors were doing the job of journalists in telling what the Russians were doing in Afghanistan.

two female nurses to join the most prominent Jamiat commander, Ah-mad Shah Massoud.

Her experience was another example of both Russian disinforma-tion and the bitter infighting between the Jamiat and the Hizbi. The Russians spread reports that Massoud was keeping European prosti-tutes in his camp. The Hizbi used this as evidence to prove that Mas-soud was not a good Muslim. Because of this pressure, after Dr. Lau-monier left, Massoud never again allowed foreign women doctors or nurses to work in the Panjshir.

"We must not forget that there is a confrontation between Muslim and Western culture," Dr. Laumonier said. "A woman inside must be a doctor or a nurse and nothing else. She must not make trouble. I think there have been two or three stories of conduct that was not acceptable by Afghan standards. Among ourselves, as Westerners, we have to send women who understand the Afghan culture, to be sure they will respect it. It's not like the way we live in Europe. Some women don't know how important it is to be a good woman.

"But I think security was the real reason for the ban on sending women doctors. The war has increased a lot. The Afghans are afraid a woman might be captured by the Russians. Remember what happened when they captured Augoyard." She referred to Philippe Augoyard, a twenty-nine-year-old pediatrician from Rouen who was captured near Baraki in January 1983. He was sentenced to eight years in prison in March for aiding "counterrevolutionaries," but was released in June after he denounced foreign doctors as spies on Kabul television.

"If the Communists take a woman, the mujahidin are afraid they will oblige her to make bad propaganda about women and men in Afghanistan. In an Islamic culture, that could be a disaster.

"But we have not seen any change in the mentality of the mujahidin or of the Afghan people. When I went into Afghanistan, the women and men knew I was from a different culture. They accept this difference without any problem if I respect them in their culture. The real fact is that the Afghans much prefer to have Western women doctors going inside because they know we will treat their wives, their mothers, and their sisters."

Dr. Laumonier had a rhetorical question: "Do you know why we have to be in Afghanistan? It's not only for medical reasons. Journalists are not doing their jobs. The doctors were the first to tell the world what the Russians were doing. But where are the journalists? They make excuses: It's too difficult; it takes too long; they won't be able to earn enough money. So we go and we return to France or some other place and we tell people what it is like. We give them information they can't read in newspapers or see on TV."

This thought was echoed by Anders Faenger, a former journalist who headed the Peshawar office of the Swedish Committee for Afghanistan. Faenger was not particularly upset at the closing of the Doctors Without Borders clinics. The Swedes had always believed it was better to use scarce foreign resources to create an Afghan medical system.

"Sure," he said, "there are some circles—mind you, I don't say governments—who spread stories about foreigners who are acting as missionaries and trying to convert people. The Afghan leaders are under pressure from Islamic militants in Pakistan and throughout the Arab world. They see this as a part of a worldwide holy war and they don't think Europeans and Americans should play any direct role in it. They would like to ban all foreign medical workers, men as well as women. But what difference would it make? The Western humanitarian help inside Afghanistan is marginal compared to what Afghans do, even though the Westerners are better qualified. The Afghans themselves want Afghan doctors. Foreigners are a lot of trouble. They have to give them the best food and hospitality. Security is more of a problem. If an Afghan doctor is killed, so what? But it is a great disgrace, in Afghan eyes, if a foreign doctor is captured or killed. There is also the increased danger. Foreign doctors attract bombs.

"The major importance of Western doctors inside is publicity—talking to the press. A doctor is the most humanitarian of all people. Doctors risk their lives and what they say is trusted because the doctors want to help people and not to use them for propaganda purposes. That's the big thing. The presence of foreign doctors has given a big push to the Afghan cause in the media."

To Quetta

I arranged to go to Kandahar with Pir Gailani's National Islamic Front and flew to Quetta, in Pakistan's Baluchistan Province, for our departure. I checked into the New Lourdes Hotel in the old cantonment area. Why it was called New Lourdes I could never find out. Like the small tanks and old "25 pounder" artillery pieces that decorated street crossings, the New Lourdes was a relic of the days when Quetta was an outpost of the British Empire, overawing the local Baluchis and guarding the roads to Afghanistan and Iran.

In colonial style, the hotel was a collection of adjoining single-story rooms, most with their own small verandas, that opened onto unroofed paths. It was designed for the heat of summer when it never rained, with high ceilings in the rooms to allow the heat to rise and small windows to keep direct light to a minimum. But now, in winter, guests had to light small gas heaters to drive away the constant chill, and when it rained, as it did at least every second day, they got wet running from their rooms to the central dining hall for a meal of soggy rice and bony chicken or mutton. Pink paint peeled on the walls, and the pipes were balky. To take a shower (there were no baths) I had to hammer and twist at the faucets to fill a pail with hot and cold water and then use a large plastic cup to pour the water over my head.

I did not want to advertise my arrival in Quetta by walking in the streets and, despite the lack of comforts, remained in my room, except to make contacts and discuss my trip. Just five weeks earlier the Afghan government had released an Australian couple who had been kidnapped by Baluchi tribesmen outside Quetta, taken to Kabul, and held for seven months as hostages to obtain the release of their chief from a Pakistani jail. The Australians had been working on a World Bank project in Pakistan. The fact that Baluchis could use a jail in Kabul as a parking space for innocent persons was an indication of the reach and influence of the Kabul government.

United Nations officials took armed guards when they traveled outside Quetta. Pakistanis were not safe either. Just a few weeks earlier, marauders from across the border had raided a Pakistani public works road camp, killing one man and kidnapping three others.

Esmat: Liquor, Smuggling, and Defection

The raid was attributed to Esmatullah Muslim, the most celebrated and important resistance leader to join the Communist cause. It was said that he staged the raid on the road camp to seize hostages as bargaining chips to get back a Mercedes car and other valuables being held by the Pakistani government.

By now his name had been shortened to Esmat: the honorific references to God and Islam were dropped as no longer appropriate. He was the son of a chief of the Achekzai branch of the Durrani tribe. Esmat was stationed in Kandahar as a major in the Afghan Army when the Russians invaded. True to his honor, he rose against them and became one of the most important resistance commanders in the southwest. But he was far different from the religious leaders who assumed control of the resistance movement in Peshawar. Esmat was a product of the Westernized, Pushtun elite. Although a mujahidin commander, he drank heavily and lived lavishly on profits from the sale of weapons and tribute levied on smugglers.

He tried to form his own party and to disarm other groups, leading to open battles in 1984. In early 1985 an Achekzai tribal *jirga* (assembly) rebuked Esmat as much for his un-Islamic life style as for his independence. Then there was a quarrel over the distribution of covert arms received from the West. Esmat was said to have paid a large bribe to receive most of the weapons, but got none. He disappeared, then surfaced in Kabul, where he was rewarded with a seat on the Revolutionary Council and a trip to Moscow.

In 1986 Esmat was back in Kandahar, commanding a border force said to number 5,000 men. Previously the mujahidin could move freely from their bases in Baluchistan Province. They could even drive, without too much risk, from the border city of Chaman to the outskirts of Kandahar. Now the direct route was blocked and Esmat was living high—drinking heavily and richer than ever from gun selling and smuggling. Such things did not bother Kabul. The Communists only wanted to stop the mujahidin; anything else was not their problem.

Chaman: Where Smugglers Thrived

I was able to get away from Quetta in three days. My contact was Abdul Qadir, a nephew of Pir Gailani, the leader of the National Islamic Front. Abdul Qadir said that a commander named Haji Abdul Latif would take me to Kandahar. We left on February 17. Abdul Qadir sent us off in his jeep, saying the police would recognize the vehicle and not stop us.

We passed through dusty refugee camps the size of small cities, with populations ranging up to 100,000. There were snow flurries as we continued, ascending a narrow, twisting road through the barren mountains to the Khojak Pass, where half-ruined British fortifications are memorials to forgotten skirmishes. Then we zigzagged down to Chaman, the gateway to the wide deserts of southern Afghanistan.

The Chaman bazaar was full of Japanese cameras, watches, and electronics; small refrigerators and air conditioners from Europe; and textiles and clothing from the Far East. As a landlocked nation, Afghanistan is allowed to import in-transit goods, duty free, through the Pakistani port of Karachi. Most of the imports are simply taken a few hundred yards across the border and then smuggled, a few hours or a few days later, back into Pakistan, the original cartons still unopened.

In Chaman I was more nervous than ever. Jacques Abouchar, the French journalist captured in 1984, had been kept for three days in Chaman hotel before crossing into Afghanistan. But Haji Latif knew what he was doing. We stopped briefly in Chaman and then drove a few miles farther to his house, hidden behind a high wall.

Prison, Sporting Life, and Holy War

Haji Latif was the only commander I met who was older than I was. He was seventy-five, twelve years my senior. People called him Haji Baba and I did too. *Haji* is an honorific bestowed on those who make the *haj*, or pilgrimage, to Mecca. *Baba* means grandfather. It is a term of respect: age and a gray beard are automatically honored by Afghans. People even called me baba. My Afghan name for this trip, incidentally, was Gul Mohammed, meaning Flower of Mohammed.

Haji Abdul Latif, seventy-five: prison, sporting life, and the holy war.

as my interpreter on the journey to Jegdalek. It was chosen by Abdul Qadir in Quetta.

Haji Baba had an unkempt grizzled beard, soft, watery eyes, and a full mouth of white teeth, which he frequently displayed in wide grins and guffaws. He was always telling stories and jokes and kept the people who flocked to his side laughing and entranced.

When I asked about his history he said casually—as if it were an ordinary incident in a man's life—that he had spent twenty-one years in prison, from 1941 to 1962, for killing an enemy. Murders for revenge or honor are accepted, even considered mandatory, under the Pushtun code. Often tribal and local authorities try to mediate an agreement on compensation, called blood money, to avoid the domino effect of one revenge killing leading to another. Haji Baba said that after the killing he fled to Pakistan, where a conciliation offer, enclosed in a Koran, was sent to him. He assumed this was a holy contract, but when he returned to Kandahar, his native city, he was arrested, tried, and sent to prison. He said his wife died while he was prison, and that on his release he had opened a small hotel in Kandahar, married again, and had four sons, the oldest twenty-three, and three daughters.

My translator was Ghulam Jilani, twenty-two. He had just finished his college studies but had not yet taken his final exams. Jilani's family had been civil servants and landowners in Urozgan Province, adjacent to Kandahar. This was his first trip to Afghanistan since his boyhood.

He volunteered details that Haji Baba had overlooked. He said Haji Baba's second wife had died. The old commander then took a young woman as his third wife. His youngest daughter was only eight months old. And, Jilani said, people were not sure that Haji Baba was sent to prison for a single murder—he might have killed two or three men. As for the small hotel, Jilani said Haji Baba actually staged dog fights and bird fights between cocks or quails and, with his charm and conviviality, was famous as a sportsman throughout southwest Afghanistan.

I asked Haji Baba when he had visited Mecca. With customary insouciance he replied that he had never made the pilgrimage. "People liked me and just started calling me haji," he explained.

I grew to like him too. His lack of pretense was disarming and his humor, even when I did not understand what he said, was infectious. We left his home the next morning in a Toyota pickup truck with the words Ghazi Haji Abdul Latif lettered on the door. Ghazi, someone who kills an enemy in a fight against infidels, was another honorific. We drove northeast, paralleling the border, crossing another ridge of moonscape hills flecked with snow, and dropped down to a small valley where the last Pakistani post was several hundred yards off to one side, as if it were there to monitor mujahidin traffic but not control it in any way.

For the next hour we followed the course of a stream in a valley about half a mile wide, crossing and recrossing water up to the axles, until we came to Haji Baba's camp in an area called Shin Narai. It was a staging area for all parties, with similar camps tucked away in canyons at the sides of the valley. We stayed there two nights, waiting for two more pickups to join us with supplies. Haji Baba had vehicles and arms, but said money and food were scarce. Our invariable meal was bread and potatoes cooked in too much oil, with raw onions for flavor.

"I Want to Die"

The next morning, an hour after sunrise, I walked with Jilani and a few of the men into the hills, where they intended to shoot birds for target practice. The sky was a cloudless, pale blue; the gray and beige ground was frozen and crackled under our feet; the sun had not yet burned the hoarfrost from the pink budding plants. Ice at the edge of a stream twinkled like crystal and the air was crisp and so clear that every rock and ridge was etched in fine, delicate lines. Jilani was rapturous: "The air is beautiful. The sky is beautiful. The stones are beautiful. The mountains are opening their arms to welcome us."

The birds were few and too far away to present much of a target. The Afghans, for all their wanton killing of wildlife and felling of trees, are fond of nature and the outdoors. A man named Roshan spread on the ground a long wide cloak with a bold pattern of vertical purple and green stripes and we sat on it, chatting idly.

The major topic was an incident that had happened two days earlier. A mujahid had fled to Pakistan after killing another mujahid at a nearby camp. I remembered the man who had been killed at Zari and asked why such things happened. Jilani said the men are idle in the camps and get into arguments. He said there had been a similar killing five months earlier. I was surprised.

"Does it happen so often?" I asked.

When Jilani put the question to the men sitting with us, they laughed. One picked up his gun and waved it. "They say everyone has a gun," Jilani translated. "If there is a serious quarrel, Afghans use guns to settle it."

Roshan, who was about twenty-five, with fair skin, brown eyes, brown hair, and a wisp of a beard, told a long story of a time in Urozgan Province when his group was pinned down by an ambush and bombed and rocketed from the air. He said shrapnel went through his thigh and he lay unconscious on the ground for three hours. It was three weeks before his commander could arrange transport to take him to Quetta. Although there are Red Cross and Saudi Red Crescent hospitals in Quetta specifically to care for the war-wounded, he was taken to a municipal hospital.

"They're all Communists there," he said. "They wanted to cut off my leg. I was in great pain, but my commander would not let them. He carried me by truck to Peshawar and there they saved my leg. I don't like to be wounded. The next time, if I am hit, I want to die."

Earlier I had not noticed anything wrong with him. Now when he got up and walked, I saw he had a slight limp.

Memorial Tattoos

It was at Haji Baba's base camp that I saw the man who held his hand over a fire to prove his courage. And I saw still another example there of the stoic Afghan acceptance of death, pain, and suffering.

When I arrived at the camp I was greeted warmly by a mujahid named Nur Mohammed, whose nickname was Lalwan. He was about twenty-three, sturdily built, with a wide grin and long black hair that almost touched his shoulders. His father owned an auto body shop in Chaman. Lalwan had been to school through the tenth grade and knew a bit of English.

When he took off his jacket I noticed that his arms were covered with tattoos: flowers, a fish, a bird, a butterfly, a heart, a knife, and words, some in Arabic characters, others in English. One word was Kent. He could not get cigarettes and tattooed the name of the American brand that he missed.

Several years earlier, Lalwan had been captured and spent five months in Kabul's Pul-i-Charkhi prison. He was tortured, as are all prisoners in Pul-i-Charkhi, but not badly and spent most of his time in a cell with several others. That was when he got a needle and ink and passed the time tattooing himself. The other words in English were the names of young men who were in prison with him: Azia, Kadir, and Naim. I asked what happened to them. Lalwan said they were tortured a lot and were martyred.

Lalwan was unaffected by the ordeal. He was the life of the camp.

The men cleared ground for a game called rope and circle. Two teams of two men stood in the circle. One pair used a rope to whip the legs of other pair. The second team could retreat outside the circle, but the object was for them to leap into the air and try to touch either of the opponents with a foot. Once this happened, the rope was exchanged and the other side got to do the whipping. It was an exhausting game and, being Afghans, they played rough, laughing all the while. Different men entered the ring, but Lalwan played all the time.

Then there was wrestling. The men began with their chins resting on each other's shoulder and their arms wrapped around each other's waists, gripping the cords of the trousers at the small of the back. The object was to trip an opponent or to lift him and drop him on the ground. Again Lalwan was ever-present, either as a wrestler or leading the cheers of encouragement for a friend.

Prisoners Without Bars

There were two Afghan prisoners at the camp. One worked as the camp's cook and the other was his assistant, carrying water from the stream, peeling potatoes, and washing dishes. This was my first experience with Afghan prisoners in a mujahidin camp, aside from defectors who were soon released.

Earlier, just before crossing the border, we had stopped for tea at a small Pakistani eating house. Nearby two men were working under a jacked-up pickup. Jilani said one of the men was a prisoner. The man later got out from under the truck and walked around. He didn't seem to be under constraint, but when I asked if we could question him Jilani said we were still in Pakistan and I should not call attention to myself.

Now, at Haji Baba's camp, I asked to talk with the prisoners. The cook had been held for five months. He said he was forced to join the Afghan Army and had never fired at the mujahidin. Under Islamic law there is an automatic death penalty for a Muslim who attacks other Muslims in a jihad. But Haji Baba had never convened a court.

Jilani said Haji Baba intended to take the cook with us to Kandahar and release him there. The other prisoner was a difficult case. He wore a grease-stained field jacket with the hood constantly pulled over his head. He had a heavy stubble of beard and kept his eyes fixed on the ground as Jilani and I questioned him. He was captured eight months earlier—oddly, for the second time. The first time he was freed but promptly rejoined his regiment, where he was a second lieutenant, and went into battle again. He was slightly wounded and recaptured. He admitted he would join his regiment again if he were freed.

"What is there here?" he asked. "There is nothing to eat and I sleep on the ground. In Kandahar there is plenty to eat and drink and the rooms are comfortable." His bold answer incensed Jilani, who wanted to take a gun and shoot him on the spot. But Jilani was a student who had never seen battle or the inside of a prison. Haji Baba and many of the mujahidin had seen both, so the prisoner was kept alive and used as a servant.

Changing Allegiances

The mujahidin in the southwest were not as fragmented or as suspicious of one another as those in northern and central Afghanistan. There was also more evidence that, whatever the claims of the political leaders in Peshawar, their strength within Afghanistan depended largely on the whims of individual commanders and which party supplied the most guns and money.

The pickups of two other commanders were parked at Haji Baba's camp. They were carrying munitions and supplies to their bases in Urozgan. One, named Nur Mohammed, belonged to the Revolutionary Movement of Nabi Mohammadi. He complained that he had to buy his ammunition from his party office in Quetta. The other, Mohammed Omar, said he used to belong to the same party as Haji Baba but had switched.

"My enemy was in the National Islamic Front," he said. "He kept telling lies about me so now I am with the Islamic Party."

In Quetta, I had seen Abdul Qadir review a pile of papers in his office, turning them over one by one and putting questions to three men sitting before him. When he finished I asked what the business was all about. Abdul Qadir said the papers were applications from local commanders who belonged to other parties but now wanted to switch to the National Islamic Front. The three men were area leaders who knew the applicants and hence could judge whether they should be accepted.

Alarms, False and Real

We left Haji Baba's camp in the afternoon. Our driver, Shahzada, commented on wrecks along our route: a captured Soviet jeep had been rocketed by a helicopter six months ago, but the occupants jumped out when they heard the sound of the motor overhead and escaped safely; an ambulance was destroyed by a bomb two years ago, and a commander, his wife, and children had been martyred. Shahzada said he had been driving trucks for four years. I asked if he had ever been hit.

"I have lost four trucks," he said. "I have never been hurt but thirty-nine mujahidin have been martyred in my trucks." He also said his only two brothers had been killed in the jihad along with two of their sons.

We crossed some hills and came to a steep winding gully where a convoy of two dozen trucks, pickups, and jeeps formed for the night's journey. We started across a wide plain but halted only half an hour later. The sun was just setting, and someone toward the beginning of the convoy thought he saw a reflection of light from metal: perhaps an ambush. The mujahidin jumped down from the trucks and pickups and advanced in a wide skirmish line, moving forward eagerly, holding their weapons ready and scanning the horizon. Haji Baba joined them, trotting forward, calling instructions, and waving his arms for them to spread out. I joined him although I had a hard time keeping up: the vehicles would be a target if helicopters started rocketing and Haji Baba would know better than I what to do if we were attacked. It was a false alarm and the vehicles came to pick us up. Headlights were forbidden. Some men had gone so far and so fast that it was an hour before we found them all in the dark. It seemed the danger was over and I dozed in the front seat of a pickup, squeezed between Jilani and Shahzada. Then I awoke to excited shouting. We were at the edge of the glare of a parachute flare.

Shahzada gunned the motor to get out of the light, turned off the road, and parked in the shadow of an abandoned building. As he turned I looked through the side window and saw the red flash of a rocket hitting the ground about 100 feet back along the road.

More rocketing and bomb explosions followed but we could see no fires, meaning that all of our vehicles had escaped. We waited an hour and then continued. A little after midnight we came to a large community hall where we were given milk and bread. In the distance were more flares and the sound of bombs; the enemy pilots were still searching for the convoy.

"Life Was Not Bearable"

Just before dawn we came to a village and went to a mosque to sleep. When I walked around in the morning, I saw Haji Baba's three pickups and the two belonging to the Urozgan commanders parked under nearby trees. The rest of the convoy had scattered. Two old villagers brought Haji Baba, Jilani, and me tea and bread. This, and a similar offering in the afternoon, would be our food for the day.

One of the men, Aziahullah, who had a white beard and white turban, said this was Kalach village. "There used to be ten families here, with many wives and children," he said. "Now there are four, and only the old people. All around us, everyone has left for Pakistan." He gave the names of seven deserted villages nearby.

"Our ancestors for many generations lie buried here," he continued. "Once we had fields of wheat and potatoes and orchards of almonds, mulberries, and apricots and gardens of grapes. We had hundreds of sheep and goats and rugs and good houses. Now all the irrigation canals are destroyed and we get water from the river only part of the year. When the mujahidin came and stayed in the villages, the Russians bombed every day. Life was not bearable."

Just before dusk we joined the other vehicles that had similarly come out of hiding. The major event of the night's journey was crossing the Arghastan River, where the water lapped over the hood of the pickup and we worried that a motor failure or some hidden rock would strand us as a target for the next day's helicopter patrols. But we made it to Arghandab, about ten miles north of Kandahar, and spent the night there.

Arghandab is a general name used by the mujahidin for a wide area around a large, American-funded dam, built as part of the irrigation schemes along the Helmand and Arghandab rivers. The dam was controlled and closely patrolled by the Afghan Army, with some Soviet advisers. The mujahidin controlled the surrounding countryside, including several large villages.

The next morning Jilani and I, with Haji Baba and a few men, continued in a single pickup to a ruined house near Kandahar. Two mujahidin came running out, shouting greetings and firing their Kalashnikovs into the air. Another came with a light machine gun and added to the uproar. Haji Baba grinned. "Enough, enough," he said.

About an hour later, as we were having tea, shells exploded around us. The air was full of dust; the explosions were so close that some mujahidin went to a shelter under the house. I joined them and came out when it grew quiet. A mujahidin showed me two large, jagged pieces of shrapnel that had hit the wall of the compound. "They know Haji Baba has arrived," he said.

Riding the Rear of a Motorcycle

We moved later in the day and kept moving from place to place for the next week—to present a moving target and also because Haji Baba had to meet his commanders, who were scattered in a twenty-mile radius around Kandahar. He also had to decide how to divide the guns, ammunition, and mines he had brought from Pakistan.

The country is a flat, desert plain with no trees for cover. Motorcycles were the best way to travel. They could go straight across the hard desert soil and could be hidden in a shallow ravine at the sound of a helicopter or jet.

The first time I mounted one, the driver sped away, showing off in Afghan style and testing the mettle of his passenger. When I grabbed him around the waist, he shouted for me to let go. Jilani, who was riding on another motorcycle near me, said the driver needed to be free to keep his balance. I learned to stay on by gripping the seat, especially when we hit rocks or an irrigation ditch dug across the road. I found it easiest if I relaxed. The main danger was if the motorcycle itself slipped on the desert soil, as it did once during a tight curve around a ditch that suddenly appeared. But then we were not going fast and I had only a slight cut.

Every day, particularly in the early morning or late evening, we heard the sound of explosions, the whoosh of rockets overhead, and the rattle of machine guns. It was impossible to determine where the fighting was or what were the targets. Haji Baba said the early morning sounds were Afghan Army posts coming awake and shooting off a quota of ammunition to demonstrate to distant officers that they were always alert. The evening sounds were mujahidin attacking posts and the posts replying. The sounds during the day were routine shelling and rocketing of villages according to a preordained pattern. It was a terror tactic to drive people from their homes.

Kandahar was an example of a classic antiguerrilla concept: if the guerrillas are fish that swim in a sea of civilian support, the way to eliminate them is by draining the sea. As I moved with Haji Baba from camp to camp, I did not see a single village that was not severely damaged. Many were completely abandoned. Suburbs that once must have had populations of 10,000 or 15,000 were deserted: substantial two-story buildings were shattered hulks. It was rare to see a farmer working in a field.

Haji Baba, who spryly hopped on and off the back of a large, captured, Soviet motorcycle—beard blowing in the breeze, grinning broadly as if he were on a holiday—heard complaints from his commanders of not enough food and ammunition. He also mediated the endless petty quarrels within his party and with other parties. At times the different parties were sheltered in ruined houses only a few hundred feet apart. But despite bickering, they insisted that they fought the enemy shoulder to shoulder.

"All the commanders in the struggle will meet to make a plan," said Mullah Qarim, a stocky man in his early thirties with a thick black beard. He said he was a teacher in a religious school in Kandahar when the Communists seized power in 1978 and he had been fighting ever since. He was with Mohammadi's Revolutionary Movement.

"The commanders will agree to attack a post," he continued. "First my group will attack and then another and so on. Sometimes we go to the main road to attack convoys. We want to attack the air base but that is difficult. An area five to ten kilometers wide around the air base has been mined and is dotted with defense posts."

He referred to what was once known as Kandahar International Airport, located ten miles southwest of the city. It was built with American aid and opened in 1962, ostensibly as a refueling base for flights across Asia. There are hints that the United States secretly planned the airport as a possible strategic American base in the event of war. In any case, its runways were much too large for regional traffic and it was bypassed by international civilian flights when larger planes with greater fuel loads came into service. It turned out to be a gift to the Soviet invaders: they made it their major air base in the southwest.

"We need food," Mullah Qarim added. "That's our main shortage. I go to villages and ask for donations. But so many commanders do this, and so many people have fled to Pakistan, there isn't much food to be had."

One day we stayed with Fateh Khan, in his early twenties, who said he used to be with the Islamic Party of Yunis Khalis but now was with Haji Baba in the National Islamic Front. Fateh Khan was in charge of distributing the guns and munitions brought by Haji Baba. He traveled by day, using a high-sided cart pulled by a small tractor. The idea, apparently, was that helicopter pilots would take the tractor to be a farm vehicle and would be less inclined to attack it.

Fateh Khan said he had twenty men and was still building his group. I asked about casualties and medical treatment.

"In the past five months, four of my mujahidin have been martyred," he replied. "Others have been wounded, I don't know how many." With that, men from the inevitable circle of listeners volunteered to display their scars—on a neck, an ankle, a chest, or a leg—or missing fingers or toes. One man took off his turban to show a deep crease on his head. Some displayed scars of several wounds.

"We don't have medicines," he continued. "We have to go to Quetta. But it costs 50,000 Afghanis [$420] to hire a truck to take a wounded man to a hospital there. The man must stay here until we can find the money. That can take a week, maybe two weeks. If a man is badly wounded, he dies." He said this without a trace of emotion. To die in battle was an accepted fate. Often, after a man was killed, his small identification photo was added to a framed picture of martyrs hanging in the unit's headquarters.

I asked Fateh Khan how he could raise so much money. "There's only one way," he said. "We must sell guns. We don't sell the guns that are given to us by Haji Baba or others. But if we capture a gun, it belongs to us. A Russian Kalashnikov in good condition can be sold for 120,000 Afghanis [$1,000]. We need transport. I can buy a Japanese motorcycle in Chaman for 95,000 Afghanis [$791] and I would still have money to buy food and blankets for my men."

I asked Fateh Khan if he captured prisoners and, if so, what he did with them.

"If a Communist shows his face in Kandahar we will capture him," he said. "We will bring him before a court and if he is guilty we will shoot him." He showed a mound of earth near his base, saying it was the grave of a Communist who had been executed.

I asked what the man said at his trial.

"He said he was a good Afghan. He said what he was doing was good for Afghanistan." Hearing this, a mujahid went over and stamped on the grave.

That night, two mullahs joined us for dinner. One said his name was Issa, which means Jesus Christ, who is ranked as a prophet in Islamic belief. Mullah Issa said he had sat on many Islamic courts. I asked him about the death sentence.

"It is our belief," he replied, "that it is better to kill one Muslim who fights against other Muslims in the service of the unbeliever than it is to kill ten unbelievers like the Russians."

A City of Ruins

"I will show you that I control Kandahar," Haji Baba said one day. Previously we had been circling the outskirts of the city. Now six motorcycles lined up for Haji Baba, Jilani, and me and a complement of guards. The drivers gunned their motors. We were off in fine Afghan style, although hardly the way one would expect to enter a city under Soviet control. Haji Baba, of course, had not lived to be seventy-five by being foolish, although he enjoyed a bit of recklessness. He had sent a large force ahead of us and they stood guard near the Afghan Army posts to make sure we were not attacked.

Before the war Kandahar had a population of 120,000. Now, according to mujahidin estimates, only 30,000 remained. Those loyal to the Communists lived in a small section guarded by thousands of Afghan Army soldiers. There were some Soviet soldiers and advisers in the city, controlling the civilian administration. But the bulk of Soviet strength was at the air base, where security was greater.

Haji Baba said the Russians and the Afghan Army considered most of Kandahar a free-fire zone: if attacked, they avenged themselves with bombs and shells. As we moved through the city, I could see the result. Wide avenues were deserted, with storefronts only gaping holes. What were once modern schools or government buildings were twisted and cracked slabs of precast concrete. Hulks of Soviet tanks lay buried in rubble. In one narrow street, where there were still some occupied houses, a tank blocked most of the way. It was now a plaything for children to clamber over.

Several of the larger bazaars were still active, with merchants selling food and canned goods amid bomb-pocked walls. One shopkeeper said flour for bread cost the equivalent of $1.85 a pound, or more than a day's wage for a laborer. He conceded that the poor went hungry.

Our procession of motorcycles created excitement everywhere. When I took pictures, dozens of boys crowded before the lens and followed me wherever I moved. Lest we attract shells we could not stay in one place more than a half hour. We were especially careful passing some streets where there were Afghan Army posts. We followed the routes used by residents, who solved the problem by digging a ditch across a road and throwing up a rampart so they could pass without being seen.

We were in and out of Kandahar in four hours. The next day, Haji Baba said the Russians were told that an American and a Pakistani—

meaning Jilani—were in the city and had sent patrols to look for us a few hours after we had left.

A Mission That Failed

While wandering with Haji Baba, I had been looking for the body of Charles Thornton, the only American reporter, and the third Western newsman, to die in Afghanistan. The others were Staale Gundhur, twenty-five, a freelance Norwegian cameraman killed during fighting in June 1982 near Farah, in the western province of the same name; and Raffaele Favero, thirty-eight, an Australian cameraman who died during a bombing attack near Urgun in Paktia province in October 1983.

Thornton, fifty, had been married with two teenage sons. He was a medical reporter for the *Arizona Republic* of Phoenix. He was accompanied by Peter Schlueter, twenty-nine, a photographer for the same newspaper. They traveled with two medical volunteers, Dr. Judd Jensen, an assistant professor of neurology at the Rush Medical College in Chicago, and John Moughan of Miami, a nurse with military paramedic experience in Vietnam. The object of the mission was to survey possible sites for a hospital to be built in Afghanistan with the cooperation of Haji Habibullah Akhund, an Afghan religious leader whose headquarters was in Quetta.

The mission was initially sponsored by Dr. Robert Simon, but Dr. Simon subsequently received U.S. government funding to establish the International Medical Corps school for Afghan paramedics in Peshawar. The U.S. State Department—worried about being openly tied to the mujahidin struggle—inserted a stipulation into contracts that no part of the money would be used to send American citizens into Afghanistan. The sponsorship of Dr. Jensen's mission was then transferred to American Aid for Afghans, of Portland, Oregon.

The four men passed through Peshawar early in August 1985 and arrived in Quetta on August 8. Nothing was prepared and they entered Afghanistan only on September 2. They were going to the base of Mullah Malang, a well-known Islamic Party (Yunis Khalis) commander at Chinartoh, in Urozgan Province. But instead of taking the direct route, Haji Akhund led them on a circuitous route through the southern Hazarajat, where they were delayed by fighting between the rival Shia and Sunni groups. As a result, it took them sixteen days to reach Chinartoh.

After the tragedy Dr. Jensen, Moughan, and Schlueter returned to the United States via Islamabad where, between planes, they held a news conference that I attended.

Dr. Jensen said his mission was to "help choose a location and design for a 100-bed hospital." He said Haji Akhund told him he had been promised such a hospital by "other American doctors who had been in the area earlier this year." However, he said he rejected the idea of a large hospital "as too exposed and too dangerous" and said he ended up by treating villagers in outdoor clinics.

Schlueter said he and Thornton had told Haji Akhund from the start that because of the long delays they could stay only two weeks in Afghanistan and that they gave him money for separate transport. Schlueter said they left after only one night to meet their deadline. Moughan said he joined them because he was "fed up with Afghan disorganization." Jensen decided to remain another month to treat villagers.

Thornton, Schlueter, and Moughan set off in a pickup truck with six of Haji Akhund's mujahidin. It was the night of September 19. They traveled south and reached the area of Shah Wali Kot, about thirty miles northeast of Kandahar. Moughan told the news conference that the mujahidin were warned that helicopters had put down a blocking force earlier in the night. However, when a truck came safely from the opposite direction, the driver thought the way was clear.

It was a trap. The truck with the three Americans was struck by ground fire, and then helicopters with bright searchlights raked over the ground with rockets and machine gun fire. The survivors said a Soviet commando force was landed by helicopter to press the attack.

Schlueter, without knowing what had happened to Thornton and Moughan, left the area and spent ten days near Kandahar trying to get transportation. He said he then walked for three days to a mujahidin camp near the border, where he got a ride, arriving in Pakistan on October 1. Moughan helped drag away a wounded mujahid and then made his way back to Chinartoh. Two weeks later he returned with Dr. Jensen to Quetta.

"The *Basmachi* from Arizona"

Another version of the story came from Tass and *Pravda*. The four were called CIA agents who trained the *basmachis* to use surface-to-air missiles, such as the one used to shoot down a civilian transport plane near the Kandahar airport on September 20, killing fifty-two people, including seven women and children. The Basmachis were Muslim resistance fighters in Central Asia in the early 1920s. However, the Russians gave the name, which is of Turkic origin, a pejorative meaning and translated it as "bandits."

The Russians claimed that the Americans were killed in the crossfire of a battle between two basmachi groups. Further, the Soviet news agencies say that a bag belonging to Thornton, containing a camera, films, and a diary, was recovered from the scene. They allege that some of the pictures show Thornton "with a gang of counterrevolutionaries, helping to unload antiaircraft rockets" such as the one used to shoot down the plane. One picture, which has been widely distributed by Kabul propaganda organs, shows a man wearing a black turban standing near men handling long metal ammunition cases. Schlueter, in a later telephone interview, confirmed that the pictures were authentic but said the scenes were innocent. He said they were taken on a dull day when members of the party helped the mujahidin unload ordinary mortar shells from a truck just to help pass the time.

Tass, in an English-language broadcast late in October, gave quotations from the diary in which Thornton is said to have given his Afghan name as Abdul Gaffar. At one point he wrote: "I am glad that all is behind me and I will soon be home." Tass ended with the comment, "This is the last entry in the diary of the basmachi from Arizona."

Schlueter and the others were told that Thornton's body had been partially burned and was put in a mass grave with the bodies of three mujahidin who died in the attack. They were also told that it was not possible to recover Thornton's body because the enemy had dropped mines over the area and it was under constant enemy surveillance.

With this information, I expected to photograph the usual Afghan grave of a pile of stones. Then I met Haji Baba in Quetta. He said the body had been removed by Haji Akhund, who was demanding a hospital and other medical supplies before he would release it.

Perilous Pictures

Nevertheless, I told Haji Baba I wanted to take pictures of the site. He said it was dangerous—the area was in clear view of an Afghan Army post—but I could go at night. I said I must go by day to take pictures. Always obliging, Haji Baba arranged for motorcycles to take me and Jilani.

The drivers hid their guns under the blankets and told me to take off my glasses and keep my blanket over my head, with only my eyes

Stripped wreckage of the pickup in which American journalist Charles Thornton was killed.

showing. Not a single person or animal was in sight as we raced along a rutted dirt road—a sure sign of potential danger. Once, when the drivers heard the sound of a helicopter high overhead (how they could do this over the roar of the motorcycle engines was beyond me) we ducked into a ravine, threw brown canvasses over the bikes and lay in shadow. At another sound we simply parked in the shade near a stream lined with trees and waited.

When we reached the scene, a few glances assured me that there was no grave. The drivers remarked several times that we could be seen through binoculars from an Afghan Army post at the base of hills about a mile away. They also pointed out that walking around and taking pictures with no blanket covering my head, I would easily be recognized as a foreigner, especially since spies had undoubtedly long since reported my presence in the area with Haji Baba.

I worked as quickly as possible. Just before we left, I picked up several casings of AK-74 ammunition. These are smaller (5.45 mm) than the standard AK-47 ammunition (7.62 mm). The bullets have a hollow core and flatten out when they hit a target, causing more serious wounds. The AK-74, also known as Kalakov, was a new weapon, issued only to Soviet officers in Afghanistan. The casings confirmed that the Russians took part in the attack.

We went a few miles and were still on the empty, exposed plain when the bike that Jilani was riding sputtered to a halt. The drivers tinkered with the motor, pushed the bike, and got it started. But it came to jerky halt a few hundred yards farther. It was out of gasoline. Jilani got on my bike, with me wedged firmly between him and the driver, and we set off, arriving in Arghandab in time for lunch.

Although I was not conscious of it at the time, I must have been rattled by the prospect of a trip to the scene where Thornton was killed. The motorcycles had arrived that morning without prior notice and I did not take time to check my cameras before leaving to make sure they were loaded. When we returned after taking pictures of the wreck scene, I put the cameras aside until two days later, when we made an equally precipitous start for the motorcycle parade into Kandahar city. Halfway into the tour of the city I stopped to change film. I opened a camera for color film and discovered it was empty. I opened the other, for black and white, and it was empty too: I had lost most of my picture opportunities inside the city. Worse yet, I had no pictures of the scene where Thornton died.

I still had time to take pictures of Kandahar to make up, partially, for what was lost. When we finished for the day and returned to our temporary base, I gave Haji Baba the bad news: I had to return to the wreck scene to take the pictures again. He hesitated. Kind man that he was, he did not denounce me as an idiot, as well he might have. He only reminded me of the danger and asked if I was sure this trip was necessary.

One of the men who took us the first time refused to go again. Haji Baba found another man and we made the return trip two days later. The area was just as ominously deserted as before, but we encountered no helicopters and I worked faster. We got the job done quickly.

Where Is the Body?

All the while I had been asking people about Thornton's body. One man said all the bodies had been covered with dirt and rocks and then the bodies of the mujahidin were removed for burial in their home villages. Thornton's body, he said, was put under a flat stone but animals had pushed the stone away and eaten the body. Perhaps that was a story floated by Haji Akhund.

Haji Baba said I could ask the son of Haji Akhund. He gave us a single motorcycle, and Jilani and I squeezed on the back for a trip of about an hour.

We were greeted by Mullah Mohammed Shirin, who was about thirty, with fair skin and long black beard. He was associated with the Islamic Party of Yunis Khalis. After Thornton's death, the Khalis leadership in Peshawar denied any connection with Haji Akhund or the tragedy.

Mullah Shirin said the body was removed twenty days after the ambush and was kept somewhere nearby, but he would not let me take a picture of where it was kept. Haji Akhund's son, about twenty, arrived a short while later, adding nothing to my knowledge. They both said I must talk to Haji Akhund himself, who was in Quetta.

I told Haji Baba I wanted to return to Pakistan as quickly as possible. By then, his vehicles had returned to Chaman, but he went off on a motorcycle and several hours later a messenger came saying that transport had been found and we should join him at Khoja Mulk. This was a large village with a string of shops along a wide and deep irrigation canal. It was the center for mujahidin activity in the Arghandab area and dispatch point for traffic to Pakistan. We left after dark, in a convoy of three pickups and a motorcycle.

Haji Baba and another passenger rode in the cab of one of the pickups while Jilani and I crowded into the back with eight others, including a woman with a baby under her long robe and a child on her knees. After a few hours the convoy halted at the sound of a helicopter overhead and the flash of rockets before us. We sat for an hour waiting for things to clear. We went on a few more hours and then stopped again when there was bombing off to our right. It was hard to understand what the target could be since there was only empty desert in this region. Just after we crossed the Arghastan River there was more bombing. At this stop people brought us bread.

We spent part of the night and all the next day in one of the deserted villages near Kalach, where we had stayed on the incoming journey. The next night we continued straight through to Haji Baba's house near Chaman. Here we paid the fare, about $41 a head. Haji Baba said he had not expected to hire a truck. I paid for him and two of the passengers who were his mujahidin as well as for Jilani and myself—a total of $205. As Fateh Khan said, when we discussed bringing wounded to Quetta, it was expensive, by Afghan standards, to hire a truck.

Daylight disclosed that the husband of the woman with children in our pickup was a young mullah, with a white turban and heavy beard. He was going to a refugee camp. We gave him some money for food.

Haji Baba, tireless, hired a taxi and within an hour we went on to Quetta, arriving about noon. Two and a half days from Arghandab to Quetta was good traveling. It was February 24. The trip had taken only one week.

Haji Akhund's Version

It took Jilani two days to find Haji Akhund. His headquarters was a two-story house in a modern section of Quetta. He was a small, thin, gray-bearded man who talked excitedly and kept showing pictures and unrolling long scrolls of signatures. My questions were answered by a stocky, middle-aged man who may have been a merchant. He spoke English and, from some of the things he said, it appeared that he had lived in California. He did not give his name, saying that was not important.

He said Haji Akhund had studied and lived in Saudi Arabia and then came to Quetta to head a group called the Alliance of Muslim Clergy, Mujahidin and Refugees. Its function was to distribute alms from Afghans living abroad, principally in Saudi Arabia. The spokesman claimed that Haji Akhund was accepted as the spiritual leader of all Afghans in Kandahar and the surrounding provinces as well as those in refugee camps. That was what the scrolls of signatures that Haji Akhund kept unrolling were designed to prove.

"It was very dangerous when they went to Chinartoh," the spokesman said. "They spent sixteen days to get there from Pakistan because Haji Akhund was very careful. Then they said they had to go back. Haji Akhund explained to the gentlemen, 'You came so far from America to see what is going on here, so you have to stay here some days to look at everything and find out what is happening.' But they stayed only one night and said, 'We are leaving because our time has expired.' Haji Akhund told them, 'I am the only one responsible for your security. So you have to follow my instruction.' But they did not.

"Haji Akhund would not consent for the doctor to leave so early. He was trying to show the doctor a place in Chinartoh to establish a hospital. There was one truck ready, but it was only going someplace to get gasoline. Haji Akhund told the journalist, Mr. Charles, to stay in the place where he was assigned—to stay with the doctor. But Mr. Charles went with the truck. He and the other gentlemen left spontaneously, without permission.

"Dr. Simon promised Haji Akhund a hospital and many other things, like medicine and other aid. He has received nothing. A gentleman who is our representative in California has been in contact with Dr. Simon to find out what's happening and why he keeps silence. So that's why they did not let you take the photographs of the dead body. Haji Akhund wants an explanation. When Dr. Simon is no longer silent— when he explains what he intends to do about his promise of a hospital, medicines, vehicles, and other things—the question of the body will be no problem."

Dr. Simon's Reply

Before publishing my story, the *New York Times* called Dr. Simon to include his comments. Dr. Simon said he had been approached in California by a representative who described Haji Akhund as "an authoritative figure" with control over Kandahar Province and with mujahidin support. Dr. Simon said the representative asked for aid in setting up a medical clinic.

"We told him we would be happy to set up a clinic," Dr. Simon told the *New York Times*. But, Dr. Simon added, the team that went into Afghanistan found that Haji Akhund's group had "zero control over the area and lied to us about the mujahidin under their control. So consequently we told them we will not follow through with a medical facility. We decided to pull back from the area."

Dr. Simon called Haji Akhund "a religious lunatic holding a body."

"We have no intention of meeting his demand," he said. "We intend to ignore it entirely."

The Lessons of Thornton's Death

For anyone who considers traveling with the mujahidin, the tragedy of Charles Thornton had several lessons. Most important of all, foreigners must work through the established political parties in Peshawar. None of the Americans involved in the tragedy had contacts with the established parties. Neither had they made any attempts to consult with

European organizations with long experience in providing medical aid inside Afghanistan, particularly the French groups and the Swedish Medical Committee. Thus no one could vouch for Haji Akhund or evaluate his ability to plan an undertaking as major as a large hospital.

Further, there were no Afghans with influence over Haji Akhund who might be persuaded by Western governments or groups to bring pressure on him if something went wrong. Humanitarian organizations and experienced journalists know that the Islamic Party of Yunis Khalis is actually a loose amalgam of strong local commanders who act on their own. Thus after the disgrace—in Afghan eyes—of Thornton's death, the Khalis organization in Peshawar simply denied any connection with either Mullah Malang or Mullah Shirin.

Foreign diplomats and humanitarian workers are well aware that all Afghan organizations exaggerate their importance and the numbers of their followers. If Haji Akhund's representative in California did this, it should not have come as a surprise.

To an American, an offer of a 100-bed hospital is obviously conditioned on security, the availability of water, fuel and transport for staff, medicines and patients, the size of the community to be served, and above all on the support that will be received from the Afghan sponsor.

To an Afghan, as the case of Haji Akhund showed, a promise might be taken as a contract, with all else mere details to be smoothed out as the work proceeds.

The tragedy also suggested lessons for individual travelers. Again, individuals must travel only with those whose authenticity and abilities can be verified. Invariably, this means working through the Peshawar-based political parties, all of whom are well known to foreign diplomats and humanitarian organizations.

There must also be a single agenda and proposed length of a trip. This was the fatal flaw in Thornton's group. Dr. Jensen was on extended leave from his work in Chicago, but Thornton and Schlueter had a deadline. Moughan, apparently, also had motivations that differed from Jensen's.

Haji Akhund claims he objected when the three insisted that they must leave. But, as far as he was concerned, they were excess baggage: Dr. Jensen was the reason for the trip. Haji Akhund felt he had no obligations to the others and let them go.

I have often complained about the irresolution of a commander or group and fretted at the restrictions imposed on me. But I never attempted to travel without experienced and responsible guides. When I tried to travel alone with Alphonse, when returning from Mazar-i-Sharif, I knew the dangers I faced. I was well aware of the Afghan sense of honor and responsibility for a guest—especially a foreign guest. Anyone who removes himself from the protection of his host does so at great risk.

A Victory Garden: Opium

....

11

Before we parted Haji Baba gave me a message: "Tell the world we are willing to fight but our stomachs are empty. With their planes and bombs the Russians want to chase everyone out. With no one here to grow food we will have to stop fighting."

That was my impression too. The mujahidin I saw had little food and no amenities. They were poorly dressed and wore crude, locally made leather sandals with rubber soles cut from auto tires. For another opinion I talked with Zia Mujaddidi, a former professor at Kabul University who earned a meager living as the Quetta representative of several Western news agencies.

"The whole country is torn to pieces," he said. "The mujahidin must engage in illegal activities to get arms, ammunition, food, and clothing to make fighting and living possible."

I thought he was referring to smuggling but he said he meant opium. "Most of the opium comes from the northern part of Helmand Province but it's grown all over," he said. "The commanders sell it to the Iranian market and come here to buy arms from the parties and other supplies. Where else can they get money? They will do anything for their men."

I asked Zia if it was possible to go to Helmand Province. He said the trip would be difficult to arrange: much of the southwest is thinly populated desert where it would be easy for Soviet or Kabul forces to put down a helicopter commando to capture a foreign traveler.

But after I returned to Peshawar an opportunity presented itself. Dr. Karl Freigang of the German-Afghanistan Committee was planning to tour the southwest to look for a site for a hospital. He was willing to take me, saying the trip might take two months and that I must go where he went and return only when he returned. From the length of the trip, I assumed he planned to go all the way to Herat but, for security reasons, did not want to say that openly. He also said I could not bring my own interpreter. Karl, as he preferred to be called, said the Afghan who would act as his interpreter spoke German, which he had learned while studying in Kabul. This man—who for reasons that will become clear later I will call Iqbal—was also a paramedic. Besides interpreting he would dispense medicines and keep records. Thus Karl would have to interpret for me, a severe handicap since I could not expect the doctor to drop his medical duties when I found someone I wanted to interview. Still, it was a rare opportunity.

I joined Karl in Quetta at the end of April. He said we would leave for Afghanistan in a few days. This gave me time for another meeting with Zia Mujaddidi. He was pessimistic and extremely critical of the leadership in Peshawar.

War Widows: Prostitutes and Beggars

"The United States gives money," Zia said, "but it goes for the personal interest of individuals. The political leaders were not made by the Afghan people and they are not respectable among Afghan society. The struggle is a profitable business for them. The mujahidin call them shopkeepers."

"If supplies are short, and the leadership is as corrupt as you say, can the war be won?" I asked.

"Oh yes," he replied. "But it might take generations and generations. The Afghans have patience, a great deal of courage, and endurance to go on fighting. And they really enjoy it. They love it. A mujahid does not ask much for himself. A man says, 'OK, take care of my family. I only want to be sure that after I die my wife will not become a prostitute.' Men join the resistance and leave their families to the mercy of God. I know of wives of mujahidin who are beggars on the streets of Quetta. When you ask them, they say, 'My husband is in the jihad.' This is horrible. What can we do?

"The mujahidin must have help. If they are beggars, taking from the people, their honor is lost. Seven years ago the mujahidin were called angels and were respected as saints. When a mujahid walked the streets, old men collected the dust from his footprints and kept it in their houses as sacred. One old woman told me a story: 'My chickens got sick. Their heads were shaking and they were about to die. I took the dust from the footprints of a mujahid and put it in a bowl of water. The chickens drank from that water and they were cured.' Now, a mujahid has to knock many times on a door. An old man will come out and will look at him in a hateful manner and will close the door. His wife will ask, 'Who was that man?' He will say, 'Those sons of such and such were at our door again.'

"We believe we must fight, but how can we without food? The Russians have destroyed the *karezes*. The land has dried up and no one can grow food." A *karez*, an ancient system of irrigation, is a series of shafts dug into the soil and linked underground to form a tunnel that drains water from the base of mountains to fields as much as a mile away.

"The Russians want the people to run away or stop fighting. Either way suits their purpose. Recently elders and tribal leaders were called to a meeting in Kandahar. They were told that if the mujahidin stopped their attacks on the city and the highways the Russians would go home."

"Jihad Enterprises"

I heard much the same story from Habibullah Karzai, whose father was a senator and chief of the Populzai tribe, one of the largest tribes of the southwest. Karzai, about five feet ten, with a deep voice and a cultivated command of English, served in the Afghan foreign office but was dismissed when Daoud seized power. Then, when the jihad took shape, he thought the new political leaders were trying to manipulate his tribal authority for selfish reasons. He now sits out the war in a large, well-furnished house in Quetta and seldom travels either to Peshawar or Islamabad.

Karzai's exile is indicative of the deep political changes that have occurred in Afghanistan. All of the great khans and rural aristocrats who once were the bridge between Kabul and the rural areas have gone abroad or live in Kabul. The power vacuum has been filled by an amalgam of village chiefs, mullahs, and local landholders, all of whom are mujahidin commanders or otherwise active in the jihad.

Karzai was caustic about this new leadership. "I call it jihad enterprises," he said. "Most are in the resistance for what they can get out of it. Out of every ten commanders, six are in the field for themselves and the other four are getting weaker. People know what is going on. They know that commander so and so had a little land before the war or was a shopkeeper but now has a big house in Quetta and two cars. Or maybe he has a business that deals in smuggled goods. He spends most of his time in Pakistan but still calls himself a commander.

"Thousands of men who could be fighters sit idle. Fathers do not want to send their sons. They say, 'If my son is killed, no one will even give me money for a coffin. Why should I send my next son?' If a man loses his life, who will look after his family?"

I asked him about Soviet offers of peace if the people stopped fighting.

"That's true," he said. "But they also offer war. They attack once or twice a month, particularly around the big cities. They have three objectives. One is to weaken the mujahidin, to force them to expend their ammunition and to push them away from the city. If the mujahidin have less ammunition they will not be able to attack. Secondly, the Russians want to capture men and force them into the Afghan Army. Thirdly, they want to take revenge for attacks on themselves and, at the same time, intimidate the people so they will not help the mujahidin.

"Their other policy is to make it seem that the Kabul government is no threat. Party leaders and ministers come from Kabul and make speeches asking people for their cooperation. They say: 'If you help us to have a little bit of calm around Kandahar and other major cities, the Russians will withdraw from Afghanistan. We will be glad and you will be glad. We will not distribute the land and we will act according to your suggestions.'

"Some of the people, with very little food, have lost confidence in the future. They're in trouble with day and night bombing. These people say: 'We will cooperate but if we do the mujahidin will punish us. First you must push them back.' And that's when the Russians come in with the first part of their policy. They attack and push the mujahidin back. Then the local people might take guns from the Communists to keep the mujahidin away and maintain the peace."

This was the clearest exposition of the Russians' carrot and stick policy I had heard.

Our Group Assembles

Karl Freigang was fifty-five years old, five feet six, stocky, and had gray hair and a gray beard. He wore Afghan clothes with a large striped turban perched on the top of his head. He had two vehicles: a Toyota pickup with room for three passengers behind the driver and a British

Land Rover with the rear fitted as an ambulance, with padded benches along the sides and built-in compartments for medicines.

Ruth Buser, a Swiss nurse, helped with the medicines. This was Ruth's first experience outside Europe. We also had two commanders: Mohammed Mussa Alukot, of Hekmatyar's Islamic Party, and Ahmad Akbar, of Gailani's National Islamic Front.

The fact that the two commanders were from parties that elsewhere were hostile indicated the relaxed political atmosphere of the southwest. Local commanders along the way would supply additional guards.

The usual arrangement was for Karl and one driver, whose name was Ismael, to sit in the front seat of the pickup and Ruth, Mussa, and me to sit behind them. Most of the room in the rear bed of the pickup was taken up by large galvanized tin trunks filled with medicines and two steel drums of diesel fuel. Akbar rode with the other driver, whose name was Islam, in the front seat of the Land Rover, and Iqbal rode behind in the ambulance portion, which was also crammed with medicines.

Prisoners and the Curse of Shin Narai

We left Quetta on April 23, following a route that bypassed Chaman, crossed into Afghanistan, and followed the river to the Shin Narai area. We stayed at the camp of Saleh Gul, a distinguished-looking Gailani commander with a graying curly beard, wavy black and white hair, and a whitish karakul hat tipped on the side of his head.

Saleh Gul took us to the nearby camp of a Sayyaf commander where, to my surprise, we were shown eighteen Afghan prisoners hobbled by leg irons. To walk they had to lift the irons by pulling on a chain that reached to their hands. They appeared to be healthy, standing erect and looking at me with as much interest as I looked at them.

Our guides said the prisoners were captured three or four years ago and that four of them, who stood in front of the others, were officers. We were also told that Islamic courts had spared their lives because they had not taken part in fighting, but did not set them free because they had not defected from Communist service. As we left, the prisoners and the men who accompanied us smiled and bid each other farewell, as if friendships had developed.

That night I slept in a house on a hill while Karl and the others stayed with the vehicles in the valley below. Long after dark there were

Manacled prisoners at Shin Narai: their lives were spared because they had not taken part in fighting.

shouting and lights and people moving about. When I joined Karl in the morning, I saw blood-stained bandages.

It was another instance of what appeared to be the curse of Shin Narai—men sitting idle and then fighting and killing each other. Karl said two men were brought in with bullet wounds. He gave them emergency treatment and sent them to a hospital in Pakistan. Their companions said the men were good friends and they did not know what caused the argument.

We left the area late the next afternoon, joining a convoy of sixteen vehicles for a night journey, and spent the next day out of sight in one of the deserted villages near Kalach. Another night brought us to the suburbs of Kandahar, where we stayed near the ruins of what had been Mussa's home. The area was under continual shellfire. We passed craters ten feet deep and fifteen feet wide and could smell the decaying flesh of animals. Twice we passed graves of men. Instead of the usual

fluttering pennants, they were marked with large white cloths with ex-
cerpts from the Koran written on them, stretched between two poles.
Mussa said that was the way the Shias marked their graves.

We had lunch at a camp where Karl hoped to find an East German
who had defected to the West and had come to Afghanistan to fight the
Communists. We were told he had become a Muslim and had gone to
Quetta to be circumcised before his marriage to an Afghan woman.

Instead, we met an Arab from Saudi Arabia who was also fighting
on the side of the mujahidin. He was tall, with a heavy beard and a
bright blue turban. He said his name was Jalaluddin and that he had
received some money for pocket expenses from a doctor at the Saudi
hospital in Quetta. He would not let me take his picture.

The Atrocity at Sosnay

Before I left Quetta Zia Mujaddidi told me he had received a report of a terrible atrocity near Khoja Mulk: the Soviets had killed two
dozen children in revenge for an attack on a convoy. He said this happened just a few weeks earlier. Ahmad Akbar repeated the story, saying
twenty-five children had been bayoneted to death.

I had been to Khoja Mulk with Haji Baba; it was a large village
along an irrigation canal in the Arghandab area. Karl agreed that it
would be important to try to document the incident. We set out before
dawn to drive there, but a helicopter buzzed over our heads and Mussa
and Akbar ordered our drivers to take cover. They said we had to remain hidden for the rest of the day.

However, I was allowed to wander around and discovered a large
field of pretty purple, red, and white flowers. It was an opium field almost ready for harvest. Apparently I had come on the trip at the right
time. Mussa said opium was planted in the winter to flower and be harvested in a one-month period in spring. "With the money they get from
opium," he said, "the villagers can fight until all the Russians go out
from our country."

I was still anxious to investigate the atrocity report. Mussa and Akbar now said the killings had not taken place at Khoja Mulk but at a
village called Sosnay, five or six miles away. I said I would walk, but no
one would go with me. Finally, late in the afternoon, Mussa said we
would go in the pickup with the driver Ismael and four local mujahidin
as guards.

The countryside was deserted: no place to be riding in a pickup

At a clinic in Kharkrez: nurse Ruth Buser, left, Dr. Karl Freigang examining a patient, and Iqbal the dispenser and interpreter.

during daylight. After a while Ismael parked the truck under some trees and Mussa and I got out to walk. I had my blanket draped over my head. Two mujahidin, with guns hidden under their blankets, walked 100 feet ahead of us and the other pair guarded the rear.

Mussa could speak a few words of English. We passed one collection of houses and then another. He said, "Sosnay, Sosnay, all Sosnay," and held up seven fingers. He meant that there was a string of seven settlements along the road and they were all known as Sosnay.

The houses were set fifty feet away from the road, with abandoned fields in between. The soil of the fields was chewed up and flattened by fresh tank tracks. Several of the houses and walls in the villages were shattered or had large holes. Obviously a column of tanks had come along, avoiding the road in case it was mined, and fired point blank into the houses as they passed.

We crossed a field to one group of houses. An old man came out and took us to a graveyard where there were two new graves for adults and three small mounds for children.

"Women," Mussa said, pointing to the adult graves. "Children," he continued, pointing to the small graves. "His family," he concluded, pointing to the man. There was nothing else to see and we turned back.

Apparently there were no mass killings—no bayoneting of children. But, I thought, what is an atrocity? When something terrible happens, and women and children are killed, the Afghans try to attract attention by talking of bayoneting children. But the simple facts were enough. The Afghan Army or the Russians—no one knew who was in the tanks—came along and fired at random into civilian houses. Women and children were killed. Wasn't that an atrocity?

With Afghan stoicism, two men were repairing a wall shattered by a tank shell; one man was on a ladder and the other man was throwing mud up to him. This was their home, and they would not be driven away.

Pains, Real and Imaginary

As darkness fell we set out for the mountains that rose to the north and went about thirty miles over a good dirt road to Kharkrez, Akbar's home and base. Karl said he would hold his first clinic in the morning. The interiors of houses are too dark and rooms are generally too small for medical work, so the clinic had to be outdoors. Karl said he needed a secluded space and chose a walled vineyard.

Kandahar is famous for its small, green, sweet grapes, which are dried for raisins. The vines are grown on mounds of hard earth about three feet high and thirty feet long. A field may comprise about 100 of these mounds with a path down the center. Irrigation water flows into one end of the field and spreads in the hollows between the mounds, watering the base of the plants. The vines, extending over the tops of the mounds, grow rapidly in the bright and constant sun. After harvest the plants are pruned down to the gnarled and ancient stems. Now, as winter ended, they were just beginning to come to life again.

A tall building used for drying the grapes was at the end of the field, with a cleared space before it. There a canvas was spread on the ground and medicines were set out. The routine of life seldom changes in an Afghan village; watching a foreign doctor at work is a treat to be recalled for years to come. The wall around the vineyard was soon covered with spectators, the boldest of whom gradually infiltrated the mounds of earth and edged closer and closer to a point where a mujahid guarded the final open space. When the spectators became too numerous, the guard shooed them back behind the wall and the process started all over again.

Karl insisted that the patients, except those who had something wrong with a leg or foot, strip to the waist. When they peeled off layers of jackets, shirts, and undershirts, I saw that almost all were wearing triangular or square charms hanging from strings around their necks— a few words from the Koran encased in cloth or leather. The charms were blackened by years of dirt and body oils. Some men wore two or three. Children wore more. Infants carried in their fathers' arms might wear a half dozen.

Some men also had blue tattoos of lines or dots or a number of dots in a circle. One man had circles tattooed around his nipples. Karl said the tattoos were to cure psychological pain or anxiety.

A few had dirty cloths wrapped around their waists. Karl said women tied these on husbands or brothers as a mystical protection against evil and that the men never discarded the cloths.

Magic was medicine and medicine was magic. About half the patients had nothing wrong with them. The routine was for a man to come forward, sit on the ground before Karl, and say what was wrong. Iqbal would then translate into German.

"Here is a man who says he has pain here and here and here," Karl said, pointing to the man's chest, back, and stomach. "This is the famous disease of Afghanistan. It's called pain-all-over. They are not sick, they just want to see a doctor. I don't like it but I must give them something so I give them multivitamin tablets." He also distributed aspirins and antacids and the patients went away content.

There were also serious and sometimes pathetic cases: a five-year-old boy with pneumonia in his left lung, a four-year-old boy with an ear infection, an old man shaking violently from Parkinson's disease, another old man with his left eye blind from glaucoma, a middle-aged man whose bronchitis had turned to emphysema. Many had eye and skin infections. Boys had scabies and ringworms. For some, Karl could do much: simple infections respond quickly to modern medicines. For others, like those with Parkinson's disease or emphysema, and several with severe tuberculosis that required a long course of treatment, he could do nothing.

Afghans consider injections the best of all treatments. Local doctors—or those who call themselves doctors—inject painkillers into every patient who comes to them, using the same needle over and over again. I once saw a "doctor" dip a needle into a glass of hot tea to clean it before use.

To the delight of all, Karl also favored injections. He gave one man four injections, two in the upper part of his chest and two in the lower part. After he gave another man four injections in the chest and then two in the back I asked what he was doing.

"You're surprised, aren't you?" he said, laughing. "You don't see this in America. Americans think this is something like voodoo. But it is well proven in Europe, especially in Germany. It's nerve therapy—something like acupuncture—only based on a scientific knowledge of the nervous system. We inject a mild sedative into the nerve endings and the influence spreads to the whole body. It treats the whole body and not just an isolated symptom. It can last twenty-four hours or it can last for a lifetime."

An old man with thick glasses hobbled forward. Karl took one look and sent him away. "He's filthy. They're all filthy. They never wash or bathe," he said. "Tell him to wash his legs and come back." The man left and returned several patients later. Karl felt and manipulated his knees.

"This is against all the rules of medicine in Europe or America," he said. "Washing in cold water is not enough. I should sterilize the knee and should have sterile gloves and a sterile area to work in. But, you see, he can hardly walk and I can help him."

He had the man lay on his back with one knee bent. He braced the man's leg against his own body and jabbed a needle deep into the knee. All the while Karl kept talking.

"First I give him an analgesic and then a form of cortisone. You have to find the right spot or else it will be very painful. If I would try to do this in Europe they would put me in jail. This hygienic situation is terrible."

When Karl finished the man stood up, tested his knees gingerly, and immediately noticed the pain was gone. He laughed, showing a mouth full of crooked teeth, and walked away.

"You see, he's happy," Karl said. "He's been in daily pain for years. Should I not help him?"

The clinic ended when the sun was directly overhead and the shade disappeared. After lunch and a nap, a clinic for women was held in a room off a courtyard. A mujahid stood guard at a gate and the women, hidden under their dirty and ragged cloths and often carrying a child and guiding one or two others, disappeared inside.

The clinic did not end until after sunset. Karl said he treated thirty patients: seven with serious ailments and all anemic. "They have a child every year. If they don't, their husband will take a second or third wife. One woman said she was thirty-five and had twelve pregnancies. Only five of the children are living. I gave multivitamins and iron pills to all of them."

Early the next day he began another clinic. One of the patients was a boy in his teens with a small patch of tuberculosis on one eye. Karl bandaged it and thought that it might heal if the boy kept the eye closed, to give it rest, and took penicillin tablets for a few weeks. An old man received an ointment for the beginnings of trachoma. Another old man had a prostate weakness and could not control his elimination. Nothing could be done for him.

One boy, fifteen, giggled and lowered his head when Karl told him to take off his shirt. Karl said that if he did not want to take off his shirt he should go away. The boy looked around to see who was watching and then draped his blanket over his head and slipped out of his shirt. Karl told him to stand up and put his arms out and then cross his feet to see if he could keep his balance. "I'm doing this," Karl said, "because he says he sees spots before his eyes and keeps falling down. But I can't see much wrong with him."

The boy sat down and Karl asked him to stick out his tongue. The boy held his hand over his mouth in embarrassment and tried to suppress more giggles. "He's a homosexual," Karl said. "He's just very nervous. But he also seems to be anemic and probably has a severe case of worms." Karl gave him something for the worms and a handful of multivitamins and aspirins.

A man in his early twenties was deaf and dumb and dressed in rags. He showed a badly closed bullet wound on the back of his leg. "No one knows how he was hurt or who did this botched job. I could open the wound and close it properly, but I would need surgical cleanliness and I would have to keep him for aftercare. Now I can do nothing for him, poor man. This is why we need a hospital.

"But where can we find a place that is safe from Russian bombs? If you're a doctor you can't be hidden. People must know where you are, otherwise who will you treat? But if you're working like this it's only a question of time before they find you and bomb you. So we will stay here just a few days and then go somewhere else."

The clinic ended suddenly. The news, indeed, had spread that there was a foreign doctor in Kharkrez. A jeep arrived carrying a wounded man from twenty miles away. Karl hurried to a nearby house to examine him.

"He is a Koochi," Karl said, after talking to the commander who brought the man. "He was wounded a long time ago and they bribed a doctor in Lashkar Gah to treat him." Lashkar Gah is the Soviet-occupied capital of Helmand Province, about seventy miles southwest of Kharkrez.

"The Koochis are difficult," Karl continued. "He should have been taken to Quetta but he refused to go." Karl and Ruth removed several layers of dirty, blood-stained bandages, disclosing depressions in the skin oozing blood and foul-smelling pus.

"Whoever did this made a mess of it," Karl said. "He has osteo-myelitis, an infection of the bone. In Europe or America it is forbidden to close a wound until all the infection is removed. You might have to clean the wound two or three times, keeping it open until you're sure all the infection of the bone is removed. Now this is a disaster. The whole thigh bone is infected. He has to go to Quetta. Maybe they can put in an artificial bone replacement, but I think it would be impossible, even in Europe. They will probably have to amputate almost up to the hip."

All the while the man, who had a sharp face, long pointed nose, and long beard, looked at us with calm eyes. Karl cleaned the wound, bandaged it, and gave the commander penicillin tablets and aspirins and urged him to persuade the man to go to the Red Cross hospital in Quetta.

A walled garden next to three large poppy fields was found to provide shade for an afternoon clinic. The audience had already gathered and Karl chased them away, waving his arms and shouting in English, "Go away. This is not a cinema." They did not understand but moved back—although not far.

First the canvas was spread and then a thin mattress. As Karl sat cross-legged on a pillow, large ants swarmed over the canvas and one crawled up his leg. He brushed it away. "Work here is very difficult," he said.

A boy said he could not eat, but when he took off his shirt he showed a fat stomach. He got multivitamins. Another boy complained of aches in all his joints. "Just growing pains," Karl said, giving him aspirins.

A man in his early twenties had hands stained a deep brown from crushing marijuana leaves, marking him as a grower of the plant. Karl laughed and told Iqbal to write a prescription. "The man has worms and we have the medicine. But he has so much money from hashish he can buy his own medicine in the bazaar," he said.

An old farmer in rags said he had a headache and colds. "They don't know if something is wrong," Karl said. "You cannot let them go empty-handed but it is very tiresome." He gave the man aspirins.

A young man said that if he had to take off his shirt, he was not sick. "I think we have another homosexual," Karl said. The patient changed his mind and took off his shirt, after first draping his blanket over his head so that only Karl could see him. He said he felt bloated a few hours after eating. "If we had facilities, I could test him to see what was wrong, but now I can do nothing," Karl said. He sent the man away with antacid tablets.

A boy, fourteen, complained of a pain in his eye. "You see," Karl said, pointing to the boy's left eye, "the socket is empty. He's so young, but already he has been in battle. His eye was injured in fighting six months ago. A hospital in Quetta removed the damaged eye but did not give him a glass eye. He must return to Quetta for help."

A man in his late forties had large breasts. "He has a hormonal imbalance," Karl said. "He needs a specialist. I can't help him."

Another man had a dirty cloth wrapped around his waist. "I think he has a kidney ailment," Karl said after examining him. "His wife wrapped that cloth around him to ease his pain and I can't do anything better. I can only give him some pills that might help for a few weeks."

About ten patients received injections. One was a mujahid in his early forties with the scar of an entry wound in the middle of his right side and an exit scar on his back. Karl gave him injections on each side of both scars. "He says he still feels the pain of the bullet. This is psychological therapy. I'm giving him an analgesic and the pain will go away and maybe it will never return."

Opium: Forbidden but Necessary

In the afternoon we drove around to inspect several sites for a hospital. Karl admitted that sufficient people—an estimated 10,000 to 20,000—lived in a twenty-mile radius that would be served by a hospital, but said the area was too easily attacked by tanks from Kandahar.

We came to a Shiite village that was a depot for fuel brought from Kandahar. Diesel fuel cost $2 a gallon. Karl had the large drums in the back of the pickup filled to the brim: it might be some time before we found another depot.

I learned that the opium fields I saw earlier were owned by Ahmad Akbar, the National Islamic Front commander who was our host. Obviously it was a profitable crop: Akbar had a Toyota pickup and two Massey Ferguson tractors parked in a yard. With Karl as interpreter, I asked Akbar about opium.

"When there is an Islamic state," he said, "farmers will be forbidden to cultivate opium and hashish. It's allowed now only because the money is needed for the jihad. The parties don't give enough money and the mujahidin must grow opium to buy Kalashnikovs. And the people need money to buy food. It's easy to grow poppy but it takes a long time to grow wheat, and the Russians might burn the crop when it comes time for harvest. What's more, farmers don't have trucks to carry a heavy crop to market." I asked him where the opium was marketed. He said the Pakistan market was saturated and it all went to Iran.

After a women's clinic the next morning Karl counted the names in a logbook compiled by Iqbal and said he had seen a total of 119 patients in two and a half days. The medicines were packed, and shortly before nightfall we set off. We went only a few hours and spent the night at the small village of Nesh. From there on, security was relaxed and we traveled by daylight, with opium fields visible in every village we passed. At times, half the cultivated fields were flowered carpets of poppy.

By now Karl had admitted that he was carrying large amounts of medicine in the hope that he could continue to Herat. But when we came to the Helmand River, he saw at a glance that an extended journey was impossible: the waters were high and swift from the melting snows of the Hindu Kush. The only bridge—downstream at the American-built Kajaki Dam—was firmly in Soviet hands.

Deh Rawod, in Urozgan Province, is the name of a wide valley and also the collective name for twenty villages stretching for twenty-five miles along the left bank of the Helmand. We stayed at the southern end of Deh Rawod as guests of Kadai Nagar, an imposing Islamic Party commander with a large hooked nose, jet black beard, and wide-set eyes. He wore a sparkling white shirt with elaborate white embroidery known as Kandahari—a delicate white-on-white stitching that is a disappearing handicraft. He also wore a large gold wristwatch. Kadai Nagar was said to have 2,000 mujahidin under his control. During the expected ceremonial visit soon after we arrived, Karl interpreted as I asked about opium.

"People must have money to live," Kadai Nagar said. "Before, they were rich and could sell grain and fruit to Kandahar. Now that's not possible. Quite a few have fled to the mountains. Others remain here. They love their country and will stay here even if they are hungry. To eat, they must buy grain from Kandahar and Pakistan and poppy is a way both landowners and the landless can earn money. Poppy gives work at a time when labor is not required for other farm operations. If you examine the wheat crop, you will see it is only up to your knees and nothing is ripe on the fruit trees."

He said it took three men twenty-one days to harvest the equivalent of one acre of poppies. With dozens of acres under cultivation, even in a small village, that meant a great deal of work for the landless. He also said that with the irrigation system destroyed, crops were lost when there was not enough river water late in the year. But poppy matures in the spring, when water is plentiful from the melting snows, and thus a farmer is certain to get a return for his efforts.

Pressures on the Mind

Karl held clinics for the next two days. Villagers had the usual complaints of pain all over, along with a wide range of real ailments, including eye and skin infections, anemia, tuberculosis and bronchitis, stomach and bowel disorders, urinary disorders, and hernias.

Several times, when young mujahidin told of general pain, Karl had them hold their arms straight out, with their fingers extended stiffly. The tips of their fingers shook. "You see, it is nerves," he said. "Afghan culture says all men must be brave. But they are human beings and not all humans are brave. So they have to pretend. Their bodies are doing one thing and their minds are telling them something else. Even if a man starts out as brave, the constant war will be a strain on his mind."

An older man had a combination of mental and physical pain. "He has an old wound," Karl said after listening to the man's story. "He was struck in the shoulder by three bullets. He can't move his arm freely. Then, four months ago, his brother was killed in battle. Now he says the pain of his wound is much worse." Karl raised the man's arm and he winced with pain.

"It seems a nerve has been damaged. I will make an injection and we will see immediately," Karl said. He did and the man was able to raise his arm partly above his head. "You see," he continued, "there is more movement than he thought. If he could go to Quetta, perhaps a doctor there could operate to help the nerve. If he had help with what is bothering his mind, he might also take exercises and that would also restore some movement. That's what I mean by 'whole body treatment.' You must treat the mind and the body—and all of the body, not just a part of it. Now I can only give him an injection that will help him a little."

Treatment behind a Curtain

A women's clinic was scheduled for the afternoon. A room was cleared and a blanket was stretched across the middle so that only Ruth would see the unveiled women. She sat on one side of the cloth, using a stethoscope and a blood pressure instrument, and called out her findings to Karl and Iqbal, who sat on the other side. If Karl needed to probe or feel a woman, he could reach in with his hand, but he could only touch a woman's back or arms—never her chest.

"This has never happened to me before," Karl said at the end of the day. "I must respect their customs but I don't like it." During her examinations, Ruth had found a pregnant woman with a large abscess under her breast that had to be cut out. But surgical instruments and dressings had not been prepared so the operation was put off until the next morning. The men were told that the woman had an abscess on her arm.

She came the next morning and Karl removed the abscess. She was the only woman scheduled for treatment that morning, but the news had spread and fifty-three women showed up, some as early as six in the morning. Karl treated two who seemed the most seriously ill along with two girls. The rest were sent away. A men's clinic had been scheduled for that morning, and men had a higher priority.

However, another women's clinic was scheduled for the afternoon. But just before it started a commander reported that over 100 women had gathered. He said it would be impossible to establish an order for who would be treated first. He also feared there would be trouble if only some were treated by the day's end—there would be recriminations from those who were sent away. The problem was solved simply by sending all the women away and holding a men's clinic instead.

Ruth was furious. "The women are oppressed and ignored," she said. "Yesterday there was a woman whose toes were black and putrid. I had to leave the room for a while it was so horrible. Karl said it was a dry gangrene and that she needed surgery. She had to go to Quetta. But these men. Will they spend money on a woman? I think not. And these women. Would she go? I think not. The women are afraid to leave their homes."

Late that afternoon Karl arranged a photo session. "I made a speech in a Swiss school and the children donated money for children in Afghanistan," he explained. "We have found two children who can be helped if they are taken to the hospital in Kandahar. Men of military age can't show themselves, but the Communists will treat women and children.

"There is a boy who is eight years old with a painful growth on one of his testicles. It's a simple operation. I could do it if I had follow-up care. They'll cut off one of his testicles and he'll still be able to have children when he grows up. But if the parents wait, it will be too late. They are poor. I'll give money so a relative can take the boy to Kandahar and feed him for a week or so.

"There is also a girl who is eight. Her mother has tuberculosis. For the mother, it's too late: the pus is coming out of her broken spinal cord. But the child seems to have just the beginnings of TB in one lung. Her family has relatives in Kandahar. If someone takes her there, with money to pay for her food for a few months, she can get a course of penicillin and perhaps be cured."

When the children were brought by male relatives, Karl took several pictures. "I'll send these to the school in Switzerland," he said. "The children will be interested in knowing what happened to their money. Maybe they'll also learn about the terrible things that are happening in Afghanistan."

"I Wanted To Do Something Different"

I asked Karl how he started this work. He said that from 1966 to 1974 he was scientific director of a large German pharmaceutical company in Japan. He returned to Germany to work in a hospital and then practiced general medicine and nerve therapy in Moers, between Dusseldorf and the Dutch border.

"I wanted to do something different," he said. "I found that only speaking about injustice was not enough. You must also set an example. I saw a film on the terrible life in Afghan refugee camps in Pakistan. That gave me direction."

He said he received a grant from a German government agency

and spent most of 1983 working in the camps. He said the grant was not enough for all of his expenses and that the trip also cost $9,000 of his own money.

"I'm not poor," he said. "I told my wife and children they would have enough money to live just as if I were home. My wife knew I had to do what I felt necessary. She would have been happier, of course, if I stayed home.

"I found there were eighteen relief agencies helping the refugees and decided the real need was for Afghan doctors to work in Afghanistan. When I returned to Germany at the end of 1983, the German-Afghanistan Committee had recently been formed, mainly with the help of graduate students, teachers, and professors. I told the committee I would help to establish hospitals and if they would pay some of my expenses I would pay the rest. We agreed and I returned to Peshawar early in 1984."

The Swedish Committee donated half a ton of medicines and Mohammadi's Revolutionary Movement supplied mujahidin and arranged for packhorses, at Karl's expense. An Afghan doctor, Ibrahim Rashid, acted as his guide, interpreter, and assistant. Karl said he established three clinics in Bamiyan, Samangan, and Baghlan provinces. I had traversed this region while returning from Mazar-i-Sharif and again when going to Baghlan and Kunduz. I had seen the ruined tourist hotel at Doab, with its pastel-colored walls exposed to the elements. Now Karl told me how it was destroyed.

Doctors as Targets

"At Doab," he said, "I found this old hotel. I didn't know much about Afghanistan then. It seemed the perfect place for a clinic. There were many rooms and even toilets. The pipes were not working, but water could be brought from the nearby river. I was there only fourteen days when the Russian MiGs came. In five minutes they blasted the hotel with twenty-one rockets, not one of them landing more than fifty meters from the building. Under my normal schedule, I was supposed to be there treating the sick. But I had been delayed at another clinic in the north. When I arrived later in the morning I found the hotel in ruins."

Karl made two trips into Afghanistan in 1984, for a total of nine months. When he returned to Germany and told of his experiences, especially the bombing of his clinic at Doab, his lectures helped to swell the resources of the German-Afghanistan Committee. He returned to Afghanistan in 1985 for another nine months, expanding the chain of clinics to eight and the staff to fourteen Afghan doctors.

"Afghan doctors want to serve their country," he said. "It's only necessary to give them help. We pay our doctors $315 a month—about the same as they would earn working for a foreign agency in a refugee camp. But it's not money: The clinics give them a way to help their country win its freedom."

He said the Afghan doctors served for eight months, then returned to Pakistan to visit their families and receive additional training at the American-aided hospital and paramedic school that was established in Peshawar by French groups in 1985. "We have also had three German doctors and a German nurse at our clinics," Karl said. "They worked for three to six months."

One of his clinics, in Kunar Province, was destroyed by bombs during a Soviet offensive in 1985, with two paramedics killed. Another clinic in Ningrahar Province was also attacked, but it was located in a deep valley and escaped damage.

One Afghan doctor was killed. "He was Kazim Noori," Karl said. "Kazim graduated from a medical school in Jalalabad. Under the regulations, he had to work in a government hospital after he got his degree. He served for two years under the Karmal regime in a hospital in Ghazni. But at night he treated the mujahidin. He was put in prison twice, first for eight days and then for a month. He knew his double life was getting dangerous and he went to Pakistan. We worked together in Ningrahar Province for six months in 1985. At the end of that year, when I returned to Germany, he went to see his family near Ghazni. On the way back he was caught in an ambush and was killed along with eighteen mujahidin. He was a fine man. He left a wife and five children. Kazim said every Afghan had to be prepared to fight for freedom."

"This Nonsense War"

In the four winter months of 1985–86, Karl said, he gave a dozen or so television and newspaper interviews and delivered fifty slide lectures to high school and university students in Germany and Switzerland. He said the rooms and halls were always full.

"I try just to give the facts," he said. "They know nothing about Afghanistan. I don't criticize the Russians except to say they made this nonsense war. What does it bring? Nothing. The objective of ideology—

to bring people under communism—is not a good reason for killing people. I say our work is humanitarian and not political and that the destruction is comparable to that of Germany in World War II in proportion to the population.

"Naturally, there are more conservatives in the audiences than members of the liberal Social Democratic Party. But we also get young people from the very liberal Greens party. They are not anti-Russian but they agree we must finish the war as quickly as possible and stop this killing of innocent people. I tell them 90 percent of those who are killed are old people and women and children."

War-Weariness

After two days with Kadai Nagar, we went to the northern end of the Deh Rawod valley to the village of another Islamic Society commander, Daoud Khan. For most of the way we followed the river but once swung wide into the desert, avoiding an Afghan Army post, and circled back to the river about a mile north of the post.

There were tank tracks all along the way. Three months earlier, enemy columns had converged to destroy a mujahidin base on the other side of the river. It was called Islamdara, or the Fort of Islam. The mujahidin boasted that it was impregnable, but the combined action wiped it out in four days. Two columns supported by helicopter commandos attacked on the opposite side of the river and one column reached Deh Rawod as a blocking force. Having seen the tank tracks I expected to find ruins. Instead, all the buildings in Daoud's village were undamaged. Daoud was thirty-two, with light gray eyes, a prominent nose, and curly hair and beard. That night after our welcome meal, I asked him what had happened.

"The villagers knew the tanks were coming and went away to the mountains, taking blankets, food, and whatever else they could carry," he said. "The soldiers came and looted what they could find but they didn't destroy anything. When the villagers returned, they found they could move back into their houses."

It seemed a textbook example of how to fight a war that is both military and political: attack the guerrillas but leave the civilians alone because, eventually, you hope to win them to your side.

I asked Daoud how many armed mujahidin he had and how many were in the entire valley. He said he could raise 100 men but he had only twenty-three Kalashnikovs and three Enfield rifles, all of which he said he had bought in Pakistan. He said there were ninety groups in the Deh Rawod valley, with more than 5,000 armed men.

"With that many men, why don't you destroy the government post?" I asked.

"If we destroyed the post," he said, "the Russians would come and destroy our homes and food supplies and everyone would have to go to Pakistan."

"Do you attack the post? Do the men in the post ever attack you?" I asked.

"Sometimes we shoot at the fort," he replied. "But they don't shoot at us. They want to be our friends."

I knew Daoud hated the Communists. When they first seized power and arrested potential opposition leaders, Daoud's father, who was a member of Parliament, was arrested and killed. The peace arose from war-weariness. Mujahidin commanders had to accept an undeclared truce.

Opium Caravans

I asked Daoud how the poppy crop was sold.

"Dealers come from Iran with money in their hands," he said. "If a farmer thinks he can get a better price at the border, he can hire a camel for the trip. The price is much higher in Iran and the route is safer. The farmers go in groups with four or five camels, traveling at night by secret routes. They have their own guns, but if they need extra security they hire mujahidin with Kalashnikovs. It's not the Russians they worry about. It's robbers who are Afghans." He smiled broadly when he said this.

He said a camel could easily carry 350 pounds of opium along with a rider and supplies for the trip. I said that much opium would be worth $15 million to $20 million when converted to heroin and cut to 6 percent purity for sale on the streets of New York. Daoud said a farmer only received about $50 a pound, but that was still a fortune by Afghan standards.

Daoud said the caravans went to the town of Robat, on a triangle of land in the far southwest where Iran, Pakistan, and Afghanistan converge. Since the war, and the outlawing of opium cultivation and use by the Ayatollah Khomeini, Robat had become a busy town.

Zia Mujaddidi once visited it. When I talked with him in Quetta he said he had counted five bakeries, two butcher shops, and fifteen restaurants there. He said Robat had its own electric generating plant and was protected by a small army of mujahidin armed with Kalashnikovs, anti-tank rockets, and antiaircraft guns. The camel trains returning from Robat, he said, carried transistor radios, bolts of cloth, medicines, and other goods scarce in Afghanistan.

A Note of Triumph

A crowd of men gathered for a clinic early the next morning. Among them was a man who said he was 100 years old. He had thick white eyebrows that he combed to the side and was almost blind from cataracts. When Karl said he could not help him see again, the man said that he had two wives and needed something to restore his virility. Karl gave him an injection of vitamins.

Among the wounded children were a boy of six, who was blinded in his right eye by a bullet when his village was attacked, and a boy of nine, who was wounded when shrapnel struck his upper arm. A doctor in Communist-controlled Lashkar Gah had carelessly closed the wound before the bone was cleaned, and now the boy had osteomyelitis. His arm might be saved if he could be taken to Peshawar or perhaps all the way to Lahore in Pakistan for a bone implant. But the family was poor and Karl did not have enough money to pay for such expensive treatment.

There was also a girl of five with what appeared to be a light case of tuberculosis. Karl gave money to her uncle to take her to Kandahar for penicillin treatment and later took her picture to show to the school children in Switzerland.

A family came and camped near an irrigation ditch beside the house where we were quartered. Daoud said their little daughter was dying. The father carried in an inert child of four. Karl examined the girl and found she appeared to have a ruptured appendix. The child could not eliminate. Without facilities for an operation, it seemed the poisons would spread and kill her. Karl gave the girl an injection of a sedative and then a massive injection of antibiotics. Now he would just have to wait.

In the afternoon the medical team held a woman's clinic like the earlier one, in a room divided by a cloth. The room was on an open courtyard with no way to keep away spectators, including me. The women flocked like wraiths in black or brown cloths that were patched, torn, and stained with mud and dust. Sometimes bright embroidery appeared when the fold of a cloth worn by a younger woman blew open. Immature girls, not yet veiled, wore bright red cloths covering their hair and hanging down their backs and costumes of deep blue, pale green, and purple. All had silver bangles on their wrists and chains of silver coins about their necks.

So many came that Daoud had to act as traffic warden. The women squatted down, their eyes fixed on the door of the clinic, always edging closer to the door. If one moved, five would follow. Daoud waved his arms and told them to go back. When someone came out, several would dart forward and Daoud had to determine priority.

That afternoon and again after dinner Karl gave the girl with the ruptured appendix massive doses of antibiotics. The morning would tell the story. And it did. It was the single note of triumph of the whole journey. As we ate breakfast, the father brought the child in and stood her up. He said she was now eliminating. She took one look at the man who had been jabbing her with those needles and wailed in terror, retreating to her father's comforting embrace. Karl laughed. Ruth was overjoyed. Over her protests, Karl gave the girl another injection and we later saw her toddling about the courtyard as if she had never been sick.

Harvesting Poppy

The next morning we drove thirty miles north into a region of low mountains to examine possible hospital sites, but all the places were too exposed. We then went south and west to Sangin, once a major market town and control station for the Helmand irrigation project. The massive gates and a pumping station were in ruins, and only the shattered final 100 feet remained of what had been a bridge across the wide river. The bazaar was also destroyed along with a two-story hospital, a two-story intermediate school, and several smaller schools and government buildings. Here, as elsewhere, all of the investments of the 1950s through 1970s were wiped out.

We stayed with Ali Ahmad, a twenty-four-year-old Islamic Society commander whose father was said to have 1,400 men armed with Kalashnikovs. Ali Ahmad's family owned several hundred acres, much of it planted in poppy that was just being harvested.

Poppy plants grow to about four feet tall. The bright petals fall to the ground, revealing a green pod about the size of a golf ball. The pod is slit and thick gum oozes out. Men in a line were walking slowly through the fields, scraping off the gum with small serrated blades and putting it into a tin can strung around the neck of one of the reapers.

In a few days they would repeat the procedure on the same plants, harvesting each pod twice. A few weeks later they would collect the dried pods and remove the seeds for flavoring in cakes and drinks.

Ali Ahmad discussed the crop with the eagerness of someone who has recently found a way to repair the fortunes of his family farm. He said the opium could be sold for the equivalent of $45 to $55 a pound, depending on supply and demand.

"That's 100 times more than I can get from another crop on the same land," he said. "It's such a rich crop that everyone's taking it up. We need the money for the jihad. If a mujahid is sick or wounded, we must send money to his family. We must also feed our men and give them money for shoes and clothes. Where else can we get money?"

Hunting Fleas

At dawn the next morning when I awoke and looked out from my sleeping bag, Karl was sitting by the door of our room with his shirt off. He was examining its seams, looking for fleas. I did the same, turning my sleeping bag inside out and searching there. We had been doing this ever since we arrived in Afghanistan. With no privacy, Ruth could only watch us. She was in constant torment. Fleas seemed to find her delectable, and she was always scratching red bite marks on her wrists and ankles. All during the trip Karl had asked for pails of warm water so that we could bathe almost every day, and he arranged for our clothes to be washed. But Ruth's infestation never lessened. She said her body was covered with red marks as if she had measles.

Ruth was feeling the strain of the trip. Nothing seemed to be going right. After Karl found the way to Herat blocked by the high waters of the Helmand, he wanted to go northeast to Ghazni, but the two commanders, Mussa and Akbar, resisted. So did Iqbal and the two drivers. They all wanted to finish the search for a possible hospital site and return to Quetta.

Ruth was particularly upset at what was happening to the medical supplies. As we traveled, some of them were disappearing. We had to take mujahidin with us everywhere we went. Some of them perched on the luggage rack atop the ambulance but others rode inside, with Iqbal. The ambulance driver, Islam, also stopped to pick up stray travelers, because there was seldom a bus service and it was customary for anyone with space in a vehicle to offer a ride to others, especially men escorting women and children.

The Afghans are an inquisitive people. Few can read, so they open

Harvesting opium poppies. The crop is planted in the winter and harvested in the spring. After the petals fall, the pod is slit and a line of men walk through the field removing the gum with curved blades. The gum is put into a tin around the waist of one man and then collected into a large basin. A few weeks later the dried pods are harvested and the seeds used for flavoring.

packages to see what's inside. Ruth was always finding packages torn open or pawed over. She had to straighten out the mess. But what bothered her the most was that medicines were disappearing. Karl thought the drivers must be giving them to people in the villages.

In Afghan thinking, if a person has a lot, it is reprehensible if he does not give a small portion to those who have nothing. Karl told the drivers that some medicines were dangerous and that if children got them and put them in their mouths they could become seriously ill. The drivers denied they were responsible, but the disappearances continued.

Ramazan and Medicines

May 9 was the first day of the month of Ramazan, when Muslims must not eat or drink between sunrise and sunset. From then on, when Karl said a pill must be taken three times a day with meals, they reminded him of Ramazan and said they would take the pills at night. They even renounced their cherished injections, saying that taking liquid, even by means of a hypodermic needle, was forbidden during daylight hours.

In Sangin Karl found an Afghan doctor, Abdul Baqi, who had graduated from Kabul University. He had worked with American doctors at Lashkar Gah, the headquarters of the Helmand River project, and spoke English.

"We have no modern medicines and equipment," Dr. Baqi said. "The Communists don't allow medicines to be sold freely, in case they're taken to the mujahidin. Sometimes, the only way I can treat a serious injury is by amputating an arm or leg." He said he had done twelve amputations.

"Once, there was a woman," he said. "I had no surgical instruments. I had to find a saw with small teeth and use this to remove her leg."

Growing Poppy: An Islamic View

After three days at Sangin we crossed the Helmand by walking over mud flats and then riding in a crude metal boat propelled by two men who used shovels as paddles. A messenger had been sent ahead to prepare the way, and a captured Russian jeep was waiting on the other shore to take us to Musa Qala, about thirty miles to the north.

We were the guests of the Amir Nazim Akhundzada, who was widely regarded as the most powerful commander in Helmand Province.

He was linked with Mohammadi's Islamic Revolutionary Movement and was said—with undoubted exaggeration—to command 10,000 men, including 1,200 who had guns. As his name implied, he was the son of a respected religious leader, Akhund. Members of his extensive family were also large landlords, another example of the leadership that had assumed power under mujahidin rule.

When we paid our ceremonial call, the stately, long-bearded Amir was seated in a leafy bower by the side of a swift irrigation stream, surrounded by his followers. A large Koran was open before him and another Koran was on a small bookstand before a mullah. They were engaged in Ramazan meditations and were not to be disturbed except for brief courtesies.

A few days later we met Maulvi Mohammed Rasul, the Amir's older brother. He had a thick gray and black beard and large, watery eyes. He sat with a companion in the shade of an ancient tree, with a Koran open before them. In the fields, poppies were growing everywhere. Earlier several commanders had told me that growing opium was permitted by Islamic beliefs. Now I put the question to Mohammed Rasul—both a maulvi and a member of a landowning and hence poppy-growing family.

"Islamic law bans the taking of opium," he said. "But there is no prohibition against growing it. We must grow and sell opium to fight our holy war."

Because we could carry only emergency medicines with us across the river, Karl could not hold clinics. Instead Amir Akhundzada gave us transport, and for the next several days we probed valleys deep in the mountains, looking for a possible hospital site. Karl rejected them all as too open to bombing and a ground attack.

West of Musa Qala at Nauzad—where, again, substantial concrete buildings two stories high were in ruins—we found a man who could speak good English. He said his name was Azimi and that he had taught in a secondary school under the Americans at Lashkar Gah.

When he returned with us to Musa Qala, I asked if there were any schools there. He said there were Islamic schools, where boys were taught to recite portions of the Koran but usually not to read or write.

"Why not have modern schools?" Karl interjected. "When you have your Islamic government, who will build roads or do anything without education?"

"They do not think of that time," Azimi replied.

"You're a teacher," Karl said. "Why don't you start your own school?"

"The Akhundzada feels that children who learn writing and arithmetic will become Communists," he replied. Nothing happened in Musa Qala without the Amir's approval.

I wanted to get the answer for myself. When we paid a farewell call on the Akhundzada to thank him for his help, I said we had met Azimi and I wondered why a modern school could not be started, since a trained teacher was available. The Amir didn't speak of Communists; he put me off with the same answer I heard a year earlier from Bos Mohammed in Barfaq—they were busy with the jihad and had no time for other things.

We crossed the river again in the small metal boat and returned to Sangin, where Karl left a large supply of medicines with Dr. Baqi. The next day we continued to Akbar's home in Kharkrez. Karl was still trying to persuade Akbar and Mussa to go with us to the Ghazni area. They were reacting in the usual Afghan manner: too polite to say no, they said instead that they would have to consider the matter more.

Karl had never seen Kandahar so we went there. But significant changes had occurred since I had visited the city two months earlier. The Communists had built twenty strong posts around the city. Where previously I had roared into Kandahar on the back of a motorcycle during the day, now the mujahidin could only slip in and out by night, and even then only by twos and threes.

We drove at night to within a few miles of a still-occupied northern suburb of the city. I had gone through this area by daylight several times with Haji Baba as he visited his units around the city. Now we remained under cover all day with the constant sound of distant explosions and the whoosh of missiles overhead.

There did not appear to be any immediate danger outside the suburbs. But when we left one house to go to another, passing over open ground, a mortar shell hit the ground 500 yards away. Then another hit 200 yards away, and a third hit only 10 yards away. There was no doubt that the gunners were aiming at us. With our mujahidin guides leading the way, we ran and clambered over a wall to the safety of the high mounds of a vineyard.

That night I remained behind as Karl rode into the suburb on the back of a motorcycle. He saw nothing but did meet a minor government official who worked with the mujahidin at night. The next morning, as I gathered my belongings for our departure, I discovered my pocket tape recorder was missing. The mujahidin at the house said they knew nothing about it and we let it go at that.

A Mystery Solved

Ruth had remained in Kharkrez. When we returned there Akbar and Mussa finally gave a clear statement: it was impossible to go to Ghazni because of all the new enemy activity; we would have to return to Pakistan. Karl was not convinced that their excuse was valid, but he had to abide by the unbending rule that once a commander makes a decision it must be accepted.

That afternoon as Ruth and I were sitting quietly in the sun, Karl and the two drivers, Islam and Ismael, came up, all excited. The mystery of the disappearing medicines had been solved: Iqbal was selling them to merchants in the bazaars along the way.

Karl said Islam and Ismael had been walking through the small bazaar in Kharkrez and noticed, on the open stall of a pharmacy, several large packages of medicines still in their original transparent plastic wrappings. They summoned Karl and he confirmed, at a glance, that the medicines were his. The pharmacist said he bought the medicines from Iqbal. Karl bought them back at the price the pharmacist had paid—a tenth of the real value—and now had the evidence to confront Iqbal.

Iqbal was found and brought to the house, along with Mussa and Akbar. He flatly denied that he had been stealing medicines. Instead he blamed the drivers. With that, the men began to exchange punches and had to be separated.

A great deal of talk ended with the realization that nothing could be done at that time. It was a matter to be settled by Karl, Iqbal, and the German-Afghanistan Committee.

Except for the fact that several hundred people had received medical treatment, it had been a journey filled with disappointments. First, we had not been able to make the adventurous trip to Herat. Then Karl had failed to find an acceptable site for a hospital. Then Mussa and Akbar had refused to accompany us to Ghazni. And now this.

But Karl said he had learned from the experience: "We cannot build a complete hospital serving many people. It would be attacked by the Russians within one or two weeks. But we could build a mobile unit with a place for one or two doctors, an X-ray unit, and a laboratory. It could treat sixty to seventy patients a day. It would cost $10,000 to $20,000 a month, depending on the number of doctors and assistants, more if we had German doctors. I'm sure we could raise the money in Europe. Then we can treat civilians and also go to areas where there's fighting and a need for emergency care of the mujahidin and civilian wounded."

Karl said he would modify his ambulance and return in a few months to experiment with that technique. We drove to the outskirts of Kandahar where he left two large tin trunks of medicines with an Islamic Society commander who was reputed to be active both in fighting and in helping civilians. We then joined a convoy for the journey back to Pakistan.

The Soviet forces and the Afghan Army had increased their surveillance and bombing of traffic to and from the border. Traveling by night and resting during the day, after crossing the Arghastan River we had to swing wide to the east, passing through a portion of Zabul Province, then south to the familiar border crossing at Shin Narai and on to Quetta. It was May 23. We had been gone exactly thirty days.

Morals versus Expediency

Before parting Karl and I talked about opium. He had also seen opium being grown in the Ghazni area and had worked for six months in Ningrahar Province, the principal opium-growing area of Afghanistan. "Poppy is everywhere in Ningrahar," he said.

He had already considered the moral ambiguity of giving medical help to people who were growing opium that would eventually find its way into the veins of addicts in the West, including Germany.

"Everything has a positive and negative side," he said. "My work cannot be negative because we act for humanitarian reasons. But a negative result can occur. The commanders can use us as an instrument for improving their own power. I try to avoid this, but it's difficult. And I help people who grow opium. But as long as the war continues and the innocent people are hurt, it's not possible to make a moral judgment on the basis of opium alone. The Afghans only see good and nothing bad. They are not addicted and do not see opium as a problem. We have seen only two addicts during the whole time we've been here. Both cases were men who began using opium because they were in physical pain."

On the other hand, the Afghans saw many advantages to producing the crop: a short growing season in spring with a plentiful supply of water from the melting snows, and thus the certainty of production; a plentiful supply of labor, since workers are not needed in the spring for other crops; easy transport; a ready market; a high return; and the lack of other cash crops.

I flew to Islamabad to complete my research on opium production. A French doctor said he had seen poppy growing in Badakhshan Province in the northeast. A French journalist said he had seen opium fields in the Herat area of the northwest. Finally, an official of Pakistan's Narcotics Control Board said opium was grown in twelve of Afghanistan's twenty-nine provinces.

There was nothing new about opium cultivation in Afghanistan. Travelers reported seeing the crop 150 years ago. It was part of the traditional culture of the Pushtun tribes living on both sides the border. According to American officials, these tribesmen accounted for most of the prewar crop, estimated at 300 tons of opium a year.

What was new was the explosive growth in production following the Soviet invasion. These American officials estimated that the output for the 1985–86 harvest would be 800 tons, and said they expected output to keep expanding.

The American Dilemma

The Americans were unhappy with the link between opium growing and guerrillas armed with weapons paid for with American dollars. By way of mitigation, they said that the market was seeking the mujahidin, rather than the mujahidin seeking the market.

"There is no evidence indicating that the Afghan mujahidin freedom fighters have been involved in narcotics activities as a matter of policy to finance their operations," said a report prepared by the American embassy in Islamabad for a visiting delegation from Washington in March 1985. As evidence, the report said that the wholesale price of opium on the illicit market near the Khyber Pass jumped by about 300 percent, to the equivalent of $170 a kilo (2.2 pounds), just prior to the 1985–86 growing season. Officials saw this as an attempt by wholesalers to entice the Afghans into planting more opium.

But at the same time American officials were gloomy about the long-term implications. "It's a no-win situation," one narcotics official said. The officials said they feared that Afghanistan might become the world's largest sanctuary for opium cultivation. Governmental action within Afghanistan, they said, was ruled out because the Soviet Union and the Communist regime in Kabul had no incentive to interfere with a drug trade they saw as harmful to the United States, Europe, and the non-Communist nations of South Asia.

Narcotics officials said that even if a non-Communist government came to power, it would be too weak to stop poppy cultivation. "They would be the best defended poppy fields in the world," a Western reporter said.

American narcotics officials felt frustrated because the Pakistani government was having some success in bulldozing poppy fields and persuading farmers to switch to alternative crops. They feared these efforts—subsidized with American money—might be nullified by a sanctuary that included Afghanistan and the Pushtun tribal territories.

Their fears were justified. In December 1984 Pakistan sent tanks and paramilitary forces against Kukikhel tribesmen, whose homelands are in the semiautonomous Khyber Agency. Pakistani officials said most of the opium from Ningrahar Province was smuggled through or converted into heroin in the Landi Khotal area of the Khyber Agency.

About 100 houses were bulldozed, including the fortress-like stronghold of Wali Khan Kukikhel, the seventy-six-year-old malik of the tribe. Wali Khan fled to Afghanistan with many of his warriors. "Opium is our oldest crop and the mainstay of our agriculture," he later told a Pakistani reporter. "I maintain that Islam has not forbidden opium cultivation. The arbitrary ban has resulted from American pressure."

Kabul welcomed him as a valiant fighter against American imperialism, giving him guns and trying to enlist the Kukikhel tribesmen against the mujahidin in Ningrahar.

However, the quarrel was resolved two months later: Wali Khan and his men returned to his tribal territory and were given money to repair their forts and assuage their outrage. A tribal council was held and the elders said they were good Muslims who would not fight against the coreligionists.

The problem of opium cultivation and heroin labs was left unresolved. But at least there was one comforting lesson for the Afghan mujahidin: no matter how hard Kabul wooed the Pushtun tribes, any success would be temporary; the tribesmen might take money or guns for short term gains, but their greater and abiding loyalty was to Islam.

By chance, the *New York Times* published my opium report on the same day that Rabbani, Gailani, Mujaddidi, and Mohammadi were visiting Washington. (An account of their trip is given in chapter 12.) Professor Rabbani, who was taking his turn as chairman of the seven-party alliance, felt the story was a slur.

"Our movement is an Islamic movement," he told Bernard Gwertzman of the *New York Times*. "What we do is based on the tenets of Islam. According to our religion, the use, the growing, and the production of drugs is prohibited. We signed an agreement in the alliance according to which an order was given to all commanders that if they find individuals who grow these things, they should destroy them. There may have been some growing in some remote areas, but these were small cases and the article was wrong to generalize."

There was one other postscript to the trip. The following August Dr. Freigang and Ruth Buser returned to Kandahar Province to experiment with an ambulance equipped as a mobile hospital. They made several trips between Quetta and the vicinity of Kandahar city over a period of four weeks. Then on the night of September 15, they were traveling in a newly purchased pickup truck near two small mountains on the northwest side of the city. There was a warning that an ambush party was lurking nearby. Their mujahidin guards got down and walked ahead into the darkness to see if the road was clear. Unfortunately, the guards walked right past the ambushers, who were off to one side of the road. But then a commander with Karl and Ruth saw motion ahead and shouted for them to run. Their vehicle was sprayed by machine gun bullets but they got out just before it was struck by an antitank grenade.

Karl and Ruth climbed the steep side of one of the mountains and looked down to see the truck burning and Afghan Army soldiers dancing around it in triumph. Luckily no Soviet soldiers were present to establish discipline and to begin a search for survivors. Karl and Ruth were later rejoined by their guards and the party walked twelve hours to safety. They soon returned to Europe, where Karl's wife insists that he must not return to Afghanistan again.

Ghazni

············

12

Even though the ambush of Dr. Freigang's truck was ineptly executed, the fact that an Afghan Army unit was assigned to carry it out was significant. It illustrated Moscow's continued attempts to create an Afghan force that it hoped would someday be able to control the country without the help of thousands of Soviet soldiers.

The most revealing illustration of this invigorated Afghan Army was an April 1986 attack on the base of Commander Jalaluddin Haqani at Jawara, the staging area for mujahidin attacks in Paktia Province. After softening-up air attacks, Soviet and Afghan units moved from Kabul and Ghazni to protect the rear and flanks, and commando troops were landed from helicopters to seize the base. With thousands of mujahidin just across the border in Pakistan, it would have been too expensive for the troops to try to hold Jawara, and so they withdrew after a few days.

The mujahidin later admitted that they suffered 120 dead and more than 200 wounded and lost a great deal of equipment and ammunition. They claimed they counted 400 enemy dead and said other bodies were removed by the enemy when they withdrew. The mujahidin also claimed they captured 500 men and destroyed 17 helicopters and jet planes.

In questioning prisoners, the mujahidin found that only one of thirteen units that took part in the action was Soviet—the 40th Brigade based in Kabul. The others were Afghan units drawn from as far as Kandahar and Mazar-i-Sharif. It was assumed that these had Soviet advisers, but their numbers were minimal.

The attack demonstrated that the mujahidin were not safe anywhere, even just miles from their bases in Pakistan. They would have to expend more of their resources to protect themselves, giving them less to use in attacking the enemy. It also demonstrated that the war could be brought to Pakistan's doorstep. The Kabul government had long been instigating small, cross-border air attacks. At about the time of the Jawara raid, a series of bombings and minings of roads erupted in Peshawar and the tribal areas. One bombing took place at the Peshawar office of the government airline, another at a bus depot, and even one at Green's Hotel, shattering a plate glass window. I was away at the time.

Meantime, evidence accumulated that the mujahidin were growing weaker. In February Dr. Bahauddin Majrooh, whose Afghan Information Centre in Peshawar issued a monthly bulletin, interviewed Haji Mohammed Anwar Pilot (so named because he was an Afghan air force pilot for seventeen years before he defected in 1978) about the situation in Farah Province.

"Medicines are not available or found at prohibitive prices," Haji Anwar told Majrooh. "On many occasions, with nothing to eat, I and my mujahidin ate grass for several days. During the year 1985 the Russians carried out a large offensive against our centers. Our strongholds were destroyed, almost all of our military equipment was lost, and the mujahidin were scattered."

Another Peshawar news agency, the Afghan Information and Documentation Centre, reported in June that new Afghan Army posts were being installed in Kunduz Province, especially in the Khanabad area. "The mujahidin say they will face innumerable difficulties in their movement if the regime succeeds in establishing posts in the province," the report said.

Other reports reaching Peshawar told of houses being torn down in Mazar-i-Sharif and streets widened for a new ring of defense posts, of sixty new security posts built around Herat, and of a road under construction from the Soviet border to Faizabad, the capital of Badakhshan Province.

Communists also intensified attacks on supply lines. "Special commando actions at night against supply routes have become more frequent," read a Jamiat-i-Islami report in May 1986. "Lack of cooperation among different parties to keep the routes safe is serving the enemy purpose. In some areas, it takes twenty-five to thirty days of walking to take supplies to the fronts."

And another important mujahidin commander had joined the Kabul forces. Sarwar Nuristani had been a brigadier general and a member of Daoud's Central Committee. He was then sent as an attaché to the Afghan embassy in India. After the 1978 coup he crossed to Pakistan as a refugee and later entered the Nuristan region, where he became the commander of an independent mujahidin force. Toward the end of 1985 he surfaced as a militia leader, receiving arms and supplies by helicopter from the Kabul government.

Disunity and Possible Defeat

Amid this discouraging news, mujahidin political leaders continued their quarrels and jockeying for power.

Previously there had been two coalitions: one of the three traditionalist parties and one of the four fundamentalist parties. These coalitions were disbanded in May 1985 and a single, seven-party alliance was formed, called the Islamic Unity of Afghanistan Mujahidin, with the chairmanship rotated every three months among the party leaders. However, each party retained its name, treasury, and enlistment rolls: the alliance was merely window dressing for international appearances. A joint delegation was sent to the UN General Assembly in New York later that year.

What seemed to be the parties' near-suicidal urge to fight among themselves—to the extent of quarreling over the spoils of foreign humanitarian aid—was demonstrated in February 1986. Under the previous arrangement, the three-party traditional coalition had received aid to staff and administer a hospital in Peshawar. When this coalition was dissolved, the traditional parties simply divided the equipment and supplies three ways. At one point policemen had to be called in to mediate the distribution of motor vehicles.

Later a supply of medicines donated by a private American organization arrived at the Peshawar airport. An American doctor was asked to divide the consignment into three medically sound portions, one for each of the parties.

In May a group of elders met at the Nasir Bagh refugee camp near Peshawar to discuss the revived Geneva talks and the increased Soviet and Afghan Army military pressure. Dr. Majrooh published a report in his monthly bulletin:

> The elders . . . stressed that the time for separate organizations and leaders is over. They warned the leaders that if soon they did not find a solution in this direction their survival as leaders at

the head of separate organizations will become increasingly doubtful. They believed that the Afghan resistance could not be defeated
militarily, but if the situation stays as it is, it might be defeated politically by the disunity of the political leaders in exile.

That was the first time I had read or heard anyone devoted to Afghan
freedom use the word defeat.

Any semblance of unity among the seven parties crumbled in June
1986 when the leaders were invited to Washington to meet President
Reagan at the White House. Although the United States was by far the
largest supplier of arms and money for the resistance, only four resistance leaders showed up: Rabbani, Gailani, Mujaddidi, and Mohammadi. Khalis went on a pilgrimage to Mecca while Hekmatyar and
Sayyaf simply snubbed the president. Hekmatyar called the journey a
"blunder" that appeared to justify charges that the war was really a
struggle between the United States and the Soviet Union.

Again, the Shias

In July I decided to return to the Hazarajat. I wanted to get a better
understanding of the strength of the United Islamic Council, the traditional Shia party led by Sayed Ali Beheshti and Sayed Jaglan.

I made arrangements with Amin Wardak, the leader of a wealthy
clan with scores of members in Europe and the United States who regularly commuted back and forth to Afghanistan. Amin Wardak spoke fluent French and his base, about twenty miles north of Ghazni, was a fa-
vorite goal of journalists, providing an entry-level view of Afghanistan
with lots of color—scenery, animals, mujahidin with guns, and foreign
doctors—but not much else. It was in a region that the Russians ignored.

Early in the struggle Doctors of the World, one of the four principal French humanitarian organizations, had established a hospital
near Amin's base. With journalists going back and forth, it was well pub-
licized, yet it was the only foreign hospital in Afghanistan that was never
bombed. No one could explain why.

I was told that the trip would start through Miram Shah, where I
had the confrontation with the plainclothes Pakistani officer brandishing a gun. But Amin's representative in Peshawar—a brother who lived
part of the time in California—told me not to worry: hundreds of journalists and doctors had made the trip without mishap. He asked me not
write about how this was arranged and I agreed.

I left Peshawar in the evening of July 7, traveling with three doctors in their mid twenties—Joaquim Miro of Montreal, Patrick David of Reims, and Sylvie Croset of Somloire, France—and a nurse—Marine de Torsiac of Paris. While crossing tribal territory, Sylvie and Marine were shrouded in burqas, which they removed with great relief on crossing the border: Afghans only asked that foreign women cover their heads.

Jawara is an extended area of low canyons scoured out of riverbeds by flash floods. Jalaluddin Haqani's base was on a side canyon. We went by the entrance and did not see the damage from the April attack. Instead, we went to the same teahouse where Abdul Wahab and the Jamiat party had assembled for the trip to Mazar-i-Sharif. This area was untouched, demonstrating the depth of Soviet planning. The troops attacked Haqani's base without being distracted by secondary targets.

No Rest for the Weary

It had taken us a long night and all the next morning to get from Peshawar to Jawara. Now we had time only to eat and rest briefly. The medicines were packed on three mules and two horses, with an extra horse for riding. Sylvie rode the free horse and Patrick and I perched atop the baggage on the other horses. Marine had been to the hospital before and knew that it would be a hard and fast trip but, undeterred, she set out blithely on sneakered feet. She could speak some Pushtu and was our interpreter.

We stopped for dinner at ten o'clock that night. We had been going for twenty-four hours since leaving Peshawar, but we were only allowed to sleep until two the next morning and then continued until ten in the morning. It was a grueling pace. Once we went for an hour in pouring rain and then kept going while our clothes dried on our backs.

We started again at ten that night, reaching a camp near Allauddin just before dawn. I first saw Allauddin while traveling with Abdul Wahab and recalled a steep bank of houses rising on a mountainside above the road. They were occupied then, but now walls and roofs had collapsed and windows were empty.

The destruction had happened a few weeks earlier. This was the place where convoys changed to trucks for a ride of about an hour. A large Sayyaf party had piled their supplies on the road while waiting for trucks. Mujahidin transporting medicines to the Doctors of the World hospital were also waiting and with them were three French journalists, including Alain Chevalerias and a photographer whom I knew only as Dominique. Two jets appeared and rained bombs and rockets to destroy the medicines and the Sayyaf supplies, killing fifty animals. Alain and Dominique lost their photographic gear, except for two cameras around their necks.

The attack was sudden and accurate. Chevalerias believed there might have been a radio-equipped informer in the area who helped to spot the target. It was one more example of increased Soviet or Afghan Army efficiency and intelligence.

The Spirit of Free Enterprise

The jets came back every day the week after the supplies were bombed, destroying Allauddin. The innkeepers and truckers had made quick adjustments: teahouses were relocated a few miles away and the trucks were hidden in caves during the day.

In fact, the innkeepers were active all along the way. We had passed several teahouses destroyed by the flanking parties in the attack on Jawara. Now some were under repair and new inns were under construction.

We were roused at three in the morning and piled into a truck for the ride to Miran Jan, where we ate and then walked higher into the mountains, resting until the men and animals caught up.

Later we crossed a high pass and came to the familiar teahouse with the heads of wild mountain sheep on poles. We passed five new teahouses under construction. I assumed that the more heavily traveled routes to the east, passing close to Kabul, were being attacked more frequently and that innkeepers were responding to the increased traffic on this route.

Summer was the time for mujahidin to replenish supplies. Once I counted 187 men in a single group going south for arms. At another place I counted 43 loaded animals and almost 100 men going north.

We also passed two camels going south. I glanced at what they were carrying and then looked again. They were loaded with the shell of a Soviet helicopter chopped into pieces and now on its way to Pakistan for recycling.

We rested for only three hours and then started across the Zurmat plain. Large parties traveled only at night, but with just six animals and about a dozen men we went by day. Joaquim had twisted his knee and walked with a limp. He rode and I walked much of the way, not that I minded: it was uncomfortable on the packhorse and the skies were a clear blue and the winds cool. But soon it all became a blur. We went on and on, day and night, up one steep rise and down the other side, all the while gaining altitude, with short halts to eat and a few hours' rest.

Finally one night we were put in a large farm cart hauled by a tractor—jammed in with the sacks of medicines and ten mujahidin, with no room to stretch out and with knees and elbows in one another's backs or faces. The cart lurched and bounced, but we were so exhausted that we slept and woke the next morning to find we had crossed the Kabul-Ghazni road and were in the untouched Hazarajat.

There were fields of green and yellow wheat that would soon be ready for harvest and wide stretches of purple clover buzzing with bees. We stopped for breakfast at a house that had rows of hives and sat beside a sparkling stream drinking green tea flavored with cardamom, using newly baked bread to scoop up globs of golden honey.

After a rest, we walked for an hour and met Amin Wardak. He was in his early forties, about five feet ten, strongly built with wide clear eyes and a short beard. We piled into a farm cart pulled by a tractor and rode for two hours to a small, hidden valley where the doctors lived.

A Convert and a Captive

Another doctor at the quarters was Isobel Rodriguez. She had volunteered for service with Doctors of the World, but when the customary three-month term expired she did not leave. She had become a Muslim and had stayed another year working at the hospital without a salary and receiving only her food and a place to live.

She was five feet two, slightly built, with a somewhat feline face. She spoke English but answered questions in few words. Marine said Isobel's mother in Paris kept writing to ask her to come home. Marine had brought a package of foods and toilet articles from Isobel's mother to reinforce the pleas.

Isobel was a lonely figure, steeped in thought and the conflicting pulls of home and her adopted culture. When we arrived, and Joaquim moved to kiss her on the cheek, she drew back. Sometimes her eyes sparkled and her eyebrows raised as if she were conducting an inner dialogue. I saw her several times at prayer: standing in the open, a slim figure wrapped in a green cloak that covered her head and reached to

Sharif Garyagday, left, a Turkmen soldier captured while buying hashish near his post in Ghazni, with the mujahid who seized him, and commander Amin Wardak, right. The scratches on Garyagday's face were inflicted when he resisted capture.

her ankles, outlined against the blue sky, bowing, standing, kneeling, and standing again in the ancient ritual.

The next day a Soviet soldier who had been captured in Ghazni just two days earlier was brought nearby. He sat under a tree answering the questions of a Russian-speaking interrogator. He said he was Sharif Garyagday, twenty, from a suburb of Ashkhabad, the capital of the Turkmen Soviet Socialist Republic.

In the early days of the invasion, after antiwar demonstrations in the Soviet Central Asian republics, the Russians were reluctant to send recruits from these areas to Afghanistan. Garyagday was evidence that Soviet Central Asians were now being forced to perform their "internationalist duties" the same as everyone else.

"I was sent to Kabul in August 1984," he said. "There were Turkmens, Kazakhs, Uzbeks, and Russians in our group of 140 soldiers. I had no idea of Afghanistan when I came. I did not know where we were going or for what. After one day in Kabul I was sent to Ghazni and I spent twenty-three months in a post near the airport. There were twenty soldiers at the post. They all smoked hashish and five or six were drunk all the time. There was nothing to do except write letters or sit around joking. In two months we had just one newspaper."

There were bruises and scratches on his face. The mujahidin said that these were inflicted when they seized him and he fought to escape. He had been captured while buying hashish from boys near his post. After some time, the boys had lured him a little distance away to where several young and strong mujahidin were hidden.

Like the defectors I had interviewed in the north, Garyagday was bitter: "If we make any mistake or do not follow orders we will be killed. The soldiers are far from their families. Everyone is tired and wants to go home to see his father, mother, and brothers."

The interrogator said the Russians had come to Afghanistan and had killed many people. "Now, what shall we do with you?" he asked.

"It's true that if an Afghan is captured, they will beat him and kill him," he replied. "But I didn't kill anyone; please don't kill me. I'm a Muslim. The people here are like my brothers. I will fight the Russians and will give you good information about Russian tactics."

Amin Wardak, who was monitoring the interrogation, said it would be too dangerous to keep the man near Ghazni and that he would be sent to Pakistan. I later read an interview with him, confirming his safe arrival.

The Hazara Awakening

Amin said I could start for the Hazarajat in two days. The political awakening of the previously isolated Shia Hazaras began in the 1950s and accelerated in the 1960s when Hazara youth in Kabul were exposed to the new thoughts developing in Afghanistan and Iran. The revivalist and reformist ideas were brought to the Hazarajat itself in the 1960s, when Sayed Beheshti opened a madrasa at Waras that also taught public school students during their holidays.

After the Communists seized power and the Hazarajat declared itself independent, Hazara leadership coalesced. In September 1979 a council of elders and *mirs* (large landowners, the equivalent of khans) was held at Waras and elected Beheshti president of the United Islamic Council (Shura-yi-Ittifaq-i-Islami).

However the Shura was soon split by corruption, nepotism, and a hierarchic structure that prevented it from developing a popular following. Moreover, many of the Hazara youth had been radicalized in the

1960s and formed the core of the extreme Maoist Communists. To them, the Shura appeared to be a status quo instrument of the mirs and religious conservatives.

Almost simultaneously with the revolt in the Hazarajat, the Ayatollah Khomeini seized power in Iran. By the summer of 1982 the Khomeini revolutionaries were sufficiently confident to reach out to their fellow Shias. They found willing allies in the Hazarajat. First Sadiqi Neeli broke away from the Shura and, with help from Iran as well as from other discontented groups in the Hazarajat, put together a loose coalition that he called Organization for Victory (Sazman-i-Nasir). He tried to capture Waras but was driven off by Sayed Jaglan, the Shura's military commander.

In 1983 a new group—the Soldiers of the Revolutionary Guardians (Sepah-i-Pasdaran)—was formed to counter the nationalistic tendencies of Nasir and assure complete domination by Iran. Sepah leaders, as part of their claim to selfless sacrifice, refuse to give their names —as I discovered when I accidentally talked with a Sepah leader in Dara-i-Souf a year earlier. Because of this, their leaders in Afghanistan are unknown.

Since it is seldom possible to distinguish whether Nasir or Sepah is responsible for any action, their names are used together, although this masks their rivalry.

In 1984 Beheshti was driven out from Waras. Jaglan recaptured it some months later. But in 1985, perhaps because of the infusion of Pasdaran zealotry, leadership, and arms, Waras was lost again as Nasir and Sepah drove the Shura completely out of the central Hazarajat.

To the Hazarajat

Amin assigned one of his best men as an interpreter for the trip north. Kamaluddin, who spoke English with easy facility, had been in the struggle since the beginning and had studied guerrilla tactics with Ahmad Shah Massoud in the Panjshir. Two other mujahidin accompanied us. We started at an altitude of 9,000 feet. I was uncertain if I could manage the higher passes that lay ahead and asked Amin for a horse. He provided a strong black horse with a comfortable saddle and stirrups.

We soon climbed a pass about 11,000 feet high—an hour and a half of slow plodding. On the other side we were in Shia territory dominated by Nasir and Sepah. Kamaluddin said peaceful travelers from Amin's base were not molested and he did not expect trouble. We saw no signs of Nasir or Sepah soldiers along the way. However, at two small villages we saw recent graves marked by white cloths with phrases from the Koran written on them. Kamaluddin said these were graves of Nasir soldiers killed in clashes with the Shura.

We stopped to eat and sleep at a small village and got an early start in the morning. We were traveling along valleys never more than a half mile wide, with the bare sides of mountains—green, purple, rust, and black from bands of minerals—rising above us to peaks of up to 15,000 feet. Clear streams flowed through the valley floors, and on both sides the brown soil was carpeted with green and yellow wheat and patches of purple clover. Riding on a comfortable horse, feeling the slight breeze, and watching the colors unroll and the shadows cast by clusters of pristine white clouds in the blue sky was pure delight.

Courtesy at Fantasy Fort

In midmorning we passed the partially collapsed round tower of an old fort. Nearby was a new fort, with twenty-foot walls and a wide entrance gate ten feet high. Here again, the heads of wild mountain sheep were fixed on the four corners of a tower above the gate. It was both a fort and a house; I would see many like it as we went along. Rooms were built around the inner side of the walls, leaving an open area in the center for animals and for small rooms used for cooking and the other routines of female domestic life. Visitors were received outside.

Near a stream not far from the gate was a shaded, graveled space marked off by a circle of rocks. Kamaluddin and the mujahidin stood outside the circle until someone from the house came and motioned us to step inside. We did, and soon large felt rugs for us to sit on and bolsters for us to lean against were brought. Then came tea, bread, and bowls of fresh yogurt. The head of the family, who had a long narrow face, narrow eyes, and a black beard, came and sat facing us with three retainers slightly behind him.

He said the nearby ruined fort had belonged to the previous owners of the land. After they had disappeared, his family had come and built this fort. They liked it so much they called it Fantasy Fort. Kamaluddin was amused. "Fantasy Fort, what a strange name," he said.

We went on to the mouth of the valley where a high mountain loomed ahead, then turned west along another valley. Kamaluddin said we would make a wide semicircle and would not have to climb any more passes. One of the mujahidin had bad shoes and was bleeding at his heels. He rode the horse and I walked until late in the afternoon, when we came to the town of Khawat. There we boarded a sputtering yellow bus that barely made it up steep hills but eventually brought us to Jaglan's headquarters.

Sayed Jaglan

I had first heard of Jaglan from Rudy Senaeve, at the Doctors Without Borders hospital in Zari. He had blamed Jaglan's greed in continually asking for money and supplies until his demands became outrageous for the closure of a Doctors Without Borders hospital at Jagori, about sixty-five miles southwest of Narwar.

Jaglan's base was a cluster of former government buildings at the northern edge of the desolate Narwar desert, which glistened with salty or alkaline soil and had no trees or growth of any sort. We met him the next morning. He was in his early fifties, five feet four, with a pointed mustache and a tuft of beard. He was wearing a brown military jacket with a bandolier over it and a karakul hat. On his left pinky was an aquamarine ring, unusual because Afghan men seldom wear rings. He walked with swift, short steps as if he had much to do in little time.

His real name was Mohammed Hassan. Jaglan means a major in the army, but Kamaluddin said the leader now had the rank of general. Since all mujahidin officers are called commander, Kamaluddin kept referring to Jaglan by the awkward title of commander general.

"Nasir and Sepah are cruel people," Jaglan said. "Everyone knows that. They are killing people, burning their houses, eliminating the landlords. But they don't solve the problems of the people. By their tactics and actions we know they are not against the Russians. In fact, they are assisting the Russians. They want to divide Afghanistan. But we will fight them with the slogan of national unity. National unity means all the ethnic groups, Shias and Sunnis, Hazaras and Pushtuns."

He said the Shura was getting weapons through the National Islamic Front of Sayed Gailani and he was confident of victory because Nasir and Sepah had no roots among the people. "If the Iranian government does not support them or if the commanders of the other parties around the Hazarajat stop the flow of ammunition, they'll be defeated," he said.

Later, when I discussed the interview with Kamaluddin, he agreed with Jaglan: "Nasir and Sepah have never fought the Russians. I have seen captured weapons that came from Libya. They were not sent for use against the Russians but to help Nasir and Sepah in their fight against the Shura and the Harakat-i-Islami." He referred to the fourth Shia group, the Islamic Movement led by Sheikh Asaf Muhseni.

"Nasir and Sepah don't want the unity of Afghanistan," Kamaluddin said. "They don't even think of the motherland. They want to collect all the Shias into an international empire of the Shias. That's Khomeini's goal everywhere."

Dogs in a Mosque

Jaglan and Kamaluddin insisted that Nasir and Sepah used terror tactics. As proof I was taken to inspect the results of a raid by a commando force—in this case, clearly identified as Nasir—that in the summer of 1985 had destroyed the houses of Shura commanders in the Khawat area.

We were given a guard of Shura soldiers and a rickety bus for transport. Our guide was Qurban Ali, an elderly, slightly built man with a small gray beard who was an assistant to Jaglan until he was weakened by illness in 1984.

First we were shown a village with a destroyed house. "The commander general and his men were fighting the Russians in Wardak," Kamaluddin said. "But some remained behind as guards. This was the village of one of the commander general's best commanders and this was his home. He was killed here."

Nearby, charred marks on the ground showed where the village's store of brushwood, vital for the winter, had been burned. Then we were taken to a small mosque. Kamaluddin listened to a story and laughed.

"Nasir brought dogs into the mosque and fed them," he said. "They told the villagers: 'You allow the Shura to use your mosque as a place to rest and eat. Now you see what they really are. They are dogs. Should you allow dogs in a mosque?' The people are simple and uneducated. It was a lesson they will not soon forget."

We went on, twisting through steep valleys and up and down roads with slopes of 20 degrees, until we came to Qurban Ali's home. He said he was away when the raiders came and that they killed his wife, stole goods and money from a shop he owned, and exploded mines to destroy part of the outer wall of his fortress-like house. He showed us the new beams and doors and then took us to a small, traditional guest room with mats and pillows and fed us milk, curds, and fresh bread with butter.

In another valley the family of a commander who had been killed in earlier fighting had managed to flee before the raiders arrived and blew up the central gate and one corner tower of their fort.

Later a crowd of men in a village by a river pushed three small children toward me. "Nasir made them orphans," one said. "You must tell the world." Kamaluddin explained that the father of the children had been killed by the raiders, the family's belongings stolen, and their house destroyed. He said the children now lived on the charity of an uncle.

"There's a story the people believe," another man said. "If you fight against the Russians, Nasir will come and burn your house. They came to my land, took my property, destroyed my house, and went away with 100 of my sheep."

Another man said the Nasir raiders took him and several others with them as prisoners to their base in an isolated valley not far from Amin Wardak's headquarters.

"There were twenty prisoners to be used to exchange for Nasir men who might be captured," he said. "I'm an old man so they let me go in forty days. There were twelve of us in one room. Every night three men beat us, shouting, 'Shura is an American organization. We are Islamic fighters and you are devils. Jaglan is an agent of America. You are American agents.' Each time they said a sentence, a blow fell on us."

Sayed Beheshti

We stayed the night at that village. Late the next morning, after we inspected two more houses partially destroyed by the raiders, the bus left us at the edge of a cliff leading down to a steep valley. At the narrow end of the valley, behind huge boulders and rocks that had collapsed from the sides of a cliff, and guarded by fifty well-armed mujahidin, was the headquarters of Sayed Beheshti.

A pole topped by a brass crescent with streamers of colored cloth— the signs of a religious personality—marked the entrance to his room. Kamaluddin and our two mujahidin were asked to leave their guns outside. Beheshti was not there. Hussain Daoud, his principal aide, greeted us. He had narrow eyes and a thin beard and wore an embroidered red and white skull cap with red pompons hanging down over his forehead. I never ceased to be surprised at Afghan arrays.

Sayed Beheshti, Shia spiritual leader of the Shura party. "If one person remains, we will fight for independence," he said.

"We knew many of the commanders of Nasir and Sepah before the war," he said. "They were Parchamis, Khalqis, and Maoists. They pretended to change when the Communists were driven from the Hazarajat. They went to Iran for training and now have come back as Nasir and Sepah."

We all stood as Beheshti entered. He was fat, with heavy jowls and lips. He wore thick, black-rimmed glasses, a tightly wrapped black turban, a sweater, and a shawl over his shoulders. As he sat on a long cushion, with his legs stretched before him, he flicked a whisk to chase away the flies that always infest an Afghan room.

"The problem of returning to Waras is not important," he said. "Our essential desire is the unity of the Afghan nation and to make Afghanistan an independent Islamic country. When we started, we fought only as Afghans. But then Sadiqi Neeli wanted to make it a war against the Sunnis. He played this up. He wanted to create contradiction."

He then began a long speech. Kamaluddin listened and did not translate. When Beheshti fell silent, Kamaluddin said that "the leader," as he called him, thought it was important to make a general statement. It was, almost word for word, a speech I had heard many times before.

"If one person remains, we will fight for independence," Beheshti said in part. "We have fought against the Russians and their puppets for seven or eight years. We will fight against them until victory. If Pakistan and Iran help us without conditions we are glad. If they cut off weapons and ammunition it does not matter. This would help to create a good unity among the Afghan people."

Beheshti, like Jaglan, talked bravely. But it was obvious that the Shura had few soldiers or arms and was shattered and barely able to maintain itself.

Eager for Education

We walked back to Khawat, skirting a long, wide marsh that filled the valley and was thus another protection for Beheshti's home in the defile at the valley's end. Hussain Daoud had said as we waited for Beheshti that Jaglan had ordered schools to be rebuilt. As we returned the next morning to Amin Wardak, we stopped for an hour to look at a school.

The Sayed Mohammed Hassan General Primary School, named after Jaglan, was once a government school, a low brick building built on three sides around a courtyard. As we arrived on Saturday classes were not in session, but the administrator and two teachers were living in a nearby building. They said they had 125 students in grades one through six, and proved it by showing enrollment books with lists of names and boxes checked to show attendance. They said they had teachers for more children but did not have books.

"If we had materials we could open schools in Narwar and two other places to teach 500 children," they said. The school year extended from April to October. They said that in the winter, when farmers could not work their fields, adult literacy classes were held in mosques.

We resumed our return journey at about eight in the morning, stopped at Fantasy Fort for lunch, and spent the night in a mosque. The next day would be leisurely. Kamaluddin said we would stop in mid-morning to have a treat of fresh eggs cooked in fresh butter-oil.

We came to another village and I sat in the cool sun outside a mosque while stones were set up for a fireplace, brushwood was bought for fuel, a large pot was borrowed, eggs and oil were bought, and finally they were cooked. Shia rural villagers are less insistent than the Pushtuns on isolating their women. One woman came and asked if I was a doctor. Kamaluddin told her no. She pointed to my camera bag and said I must have medicines.

"You have so much, why will you not share?" she asked. Kamaluddin again said I was not a doctor. I began to open my camera bag to show there was no medicine inside, but he told me to stop—that it was not a good idea to display wealth.

When he went with the others to gather the provisions, he left his gun tilted against the wall next to me, saying this was a Sepah village. I said I didn't know how to use a Kalashnikov.

"It doesn't matter," he said. "They won't know that."

My diarrhea had returned almost from the day I started this trip and I was not eager for a plate of greasy eggs, but when the dish was cooked I was pleased to find I could eat what was set before me and fulfill the demands of politeness.

Do This, or Else

We went into the mosque for a short nap. Unlike the Sunnis, who are intolerant of graven images, the Shias hang pictures inside their mosques. There was a large picture of Khomeini and a poster showing a dozen Iranian leaders.

There was also a hook with several typed and cyclostyled notices on it: a striking example of Nasir or Sepah's efficiency. I had never seen any of the mujahidin groups within Afghanistan equipped with a type-writer, let alone a method of duplicating instructions.

Kamaluddin could not read Persian so I took one sheet and later had it translated. It was instructions from what was called "the base," reminding the villagers that quarrels were forbidden and warning against excessive wedding expenses. The notice threatened severe punish-ment—although it did not specify the nature of this punishment—if the ordinances were disobeyed.

The mujahid with the bad shoes was still limping. I walked and he rode the horse. Toward the end of the day, as we rounded a bend in the path, three burly men appeared, all cleanly dressed and with the appear-ance of being educated. One had a pistol in a holster over his shoulder. The others were not obviously armed, but perhaps had pistols under their long shirts. We exchanged the ritual greeting—"Salaam"—and passed without stopping.

"They were Nasir or Sepah," Kamaluddin said. "They just have to walk like that through the villages and spend a night at a mosque. If Nasir or Sepah is near, the villagers dare not speak their minds or give aid or shelter to the Shura. Now I'm sure people back along the way will have to say who we were and what we talked about. Just these questions will make the people more afraid that Nasir and Sepah will come and burn their houses."

I rode the horse when we came to the pass and was back at the doctors' quarters well before dinner. Sylvie was away at a village where, some months earlier, it had been discovered that 50 percent of the people had tuberculosis from infected cows. An elaborate program, involving the self-injection of penicillin, had been started and Sylvie was trying to persuade the villagers to maintain it.

A Toyota pickup with a hooded back was parked near the steep trail leading to the quarters. It had just been driven from Miram Shah for use as an ambulance. I was told that the route could be traveled by truck in three days, but it was dangerous and foreigners were never taken that way.

Joaquim, whose specialty was gynecology, planned to go with Marine in the ambulance the next morning to a village where a woman was reported to have a dead child in her womb. He said he had no facilities for a cesarean operation, but perhaps delivery could be induced.

Left alone, I rinsed out some clothes and, taking only my camera, walked to the hospital to visit Patrick and Isobel, who was staying there to be with a woman in-patient. I then walked another two hours to Amin's headquarters to see about my future program. Amin said I would stay the night there and leave the next day to visit the Ghazni area.

To Ghazni

I left a little before seven in the morning with only one mujahid, Jaybar, who was in his middle twenties and had a good command of English. Apparently Amin felt there was no immediate danger. We walked across a wide plain where apricot trees were heavy with fruit and men winnowed piles of yellow wheat. Twice we passed men digging wells and several times men repairing their houses. Not once did I see a bomb hole or any other indication of recent war.

We spent the night at a mosque, and the next morning climbed a low pass to a narrow gorge on the other side. This was Amin Wardak's forward base, commanded by his brother, Mustafa. Mustafa sketched a crude map showing the disposition of mujahidin forces around Ghazni. There were twelve "fronts," as he called them—different groups under separate commanders—including a Shura group. He said they were located in the mountains six to ten miles away from the city. The Russians had ringed Ghazni with new defense posts, he said, but I would be taken as close as possible.

With two additional guards, we left late in the afternoon and walked down the gorge to the plain before Ghazni, from where a captured Soviet command car took us close to the city. A local guide led us through a populated village to a low wall, where I was told to peek over at an Afghan Army post, with a tall television mast, 200 feet away.

"We go into Ghazni and plant bombs to kill the Communists," he said, "but they have sixty posts and many are only a few hundred feet apart, so we must go at night."

He then took us to peek at two other forts, one with a primary school next to it. He said Ghazni had radio and television programs and a school system, including three small colleges. He also said merchants could buy food and consumer goods in the city for sale in the countryside.

"They Leave Us Alone"

We passed children bringing in sheep and goats for the night. I remarked that it did not seem dangerous.

"We don't fight here, because the Russians would come and destroy the farmers' crops," Jaybar replied.

We walked back to the command car and returned to where we had picked it up. The local commander was Rahimullah Jan. "The Russians sweep through our district every week, sometimes twice a week," he said as we sat eating tea and bread. "But we know when they're coming so we go back to the mountains or we have secret hiding places. If they don't find anyone they go away. They don't steal anything or hurt people or destroy our houses."

We returned to Mustafa's base and left the next morning. As we crossed the plain, an old farmer who was sitting by the side of a stream drinking tea invited us to join him.

"The Russians leave us alone," he said when I asked about local conditions. "No one has left for Pakistan from these villages. But there is not enough water. I can grow enough wheat to feed my family but I also need money from my brother, who is working in Pakistan."

He said he bought sugar, tea, cooking oil, and other supplies from merchants who traveled back and forth to Ghazni. We later stopped at a village store, where Jaybar bought American cigarettes sold by the government tobacco monopoly. The store displayed, among other things, Soviet matches and a large bar of brown washing soap stamped "USSR."

It was another example of the policy of live and let live. The mujahidin had moved back to the hills and the villagers, posing no threat to the Soviet-dominated cities, were left in peace.

When we arrived at Amin's, I learned that the doctors were no longer at their quarters. Amin had heard on the radio that the French government had approved $300,000 for humanitarian assistance within Afghanistan, the first time France had made such a commitment on a government level. Amin, worried that Kabul might retaliate by attacking the hospital, had arranged for the doctors to stay in separate villages.

I was put on the back of a motorcycle to retrieve my knapsack and sleeping bag from the doctors' quarters. Isobel was at Amin's when I returned. For lunch we were driven to another village, where Isobel disappeared into the women's quarters. I managed to take a bath—my first in a week—in a secluded irrigation canal before we set off again on foot, with Jaybar as our guide. We spent the night at an isolated village—Isobel again staying with the women—and the next day Amin came to say goodbye. Marine and Joaquim also came in the ambulance. They reported, sadly, that the woman with the dead baby had died before they could reach her. With Joaquim there to translate from French, I finally had a chance to discuss the war with Amin.

"We Are Certain of Victory"

"The Russians control the cities and afterward they think they will control the countryside," he said, talking with his hands as if he were really French. "Our policy is to try to persuade the people to remain here to hold the countryside. That's why we have this hospital. Last year we had a French specialist for an agriculture program.

"We are certain of victory. The Russians thought we were people ruled by ignorant mullahs. But we have 5,000 years of a history of never being conquered. The Western people make the mistake of saying we have no unity. We fought the British and they also said we had no unity. But we defeated them. When we started we didn't have help from the United States or the Arab countries. Our jihad is not like the fighting in Nicaragua or El Salvador. If we find help or if we do not find help, we will fight because we have an Islamic idea and know God will help us."

Amin provided a horse and a mule for our return to Pakistan. He also provided an interpreter and the same commander who had brought me and the doctors from Miram Shah. His name was Mohammed Jan, but he was called Bajan. With a large mustache and a stubble of beard, he was famous among the many foreigners who visited Amin.

Isobel came from the house at the last moment with the palms of her hands dyed with henna, a form of decoration used by Afghan women. She was holding embroidered handkerchiefs as farewell gifts and her eyes were moist.

The trip was without incident. However, our horse just plodded along and Bajan kept trying to trade it. But the villagers asked for money in addition to the horse and he refused. Finally he got what looked like a strong horse. I asked Bajan why the villager had made the trade.

"Because he was stupid," he replied. Not so. A day later our new horse hardly walked at all. Bajan cursed it, kicked it, prodded its soft belly with a sharp stick, and threw rocks at it, but the horse would only take a few steps and stop. Bajan uncharacteristically even tried kindness. He bought some choice grain and fed it to the horse handful by handful. That didn't work either. The horse was turned over to one of the mujahidin escorts and the man patiently persuaded the animal to trail along hours behind us.

Isobel and I shared the mule. We were back in Jawara in five nights and four days, and after another night were back in Peshawar early in the morning of August 2.

Decades of War

13

For several years when I worked in Manhattan I often saw a man sitting at a small table at Park Avenue and 57th Street. He had a sign that read "Save the Whales," a large glass jar for contributions, and a sheaf of petitions that he invited passersby to sign. Day after day, smiling pleasantly, he apparently dedicated his life to the cause of the whales.

In Afghanistan an ancient civilization is threatened. The country has little natural wealth to attract the greedy, and a people who posed no threat to the outside and only wanted to be left in peace. The Afghans cultivated good relations with the Soviet Union and invited it to equip and train the Afghan Army.

Then, in the name of Marxism-Leninism, a tiny band of ideologues—no more than a few thousand—manipulated the military resources provided by the Soviet Union to seize the government apparatus in Kabul. When the Afghans rose to defend their society, as they had risen against the British in centuries past, the Soviet Union sent troops across the border to protect its new satellite.

As the Afghans continued to resist, schools, hospitals, factories, and roads were destroyed; deserted villages crumbled back to their original mud; a third of the population fled into exile; and bombs, hunger, and disease became the lot of those who remained.

Why is no one sitting on a street corner offering "Save the Afghans" petitions? Without slighting concern for the disappearance of an animal species, could not sympathy also be shown for the possible disappearance of an ancient way of human life?

Admittedly, aspects of Afghan society are unappealing to the West-

ern mind: the segregation of women, the suspicion of modern education, Islamic intolerance of other faiths, and the lack of even lip service
to the ideals of secular democracy. But can there not also exist an over-
arching concern for freedom and the right of a nonthreatening culture
and society to choose its own way of life?

Several responses have been suggested for the lack of Western
sympathy, none entirely satisfactory. The Afghans themselves often say
that a pro-Israeli and anti-Muslim bias is responsible. Americans suggest that the liberal intellectuals who allegedly dominate public opinion
fear that carping on the Soviet Union's invasion of Afghanistan would
bolster conservatives to the detriment of a domestic agenda ranging
from improved health care to banning nuclear energy.

The Jihad and Journalism

A frequent suggestion is that the press is responsible, which implies the dubious belief that the press creates public concern rather than
merely reflecting it.

Professor Alvin Rubinstein of the University of Pennsylvania, a senior fellow of the Foreign Policy Research Institute and frequent com-
mentator on Afghan affairs, wrote:

> The failure of the American media in reporting the story of the
> Soviet war in Afghanistan is a national disgrace. . . . The media
> cannot use the excuse that it lacks access. There are more than
> three million Afghan refugees in Pakistan's NWFP [Northwest Fron-
> tier Province], and the leading mujahidin groups are headquartered
> in Peshawar. All are available and eager to tell of their struggle.
> Moreover, opportunities exist for journalists . . . to accompany
> Afghan freedom-fighters into the war zone and to report on the
> situation in the cities, the mountains and the villages.

The criticism can just as well be turned on others. Afghanistan is a
mother lode of dissertations and theses waiting to be mined. What has
happened to all the Peace Corps and Fulbright scholars who went to
Afghanistan, learned Pushtu or Dari, and now are sitting at desks in the
United States? It is they who have the training and incentives to study
peoples, societies, and events at great length, not journalists who are
concerned mainly with the "news" of day-to-day events.

The fact is that scholarship, like journalism, has been institutional-
ized. The days are long past when a Margaret Mead could sail off to the

Pacific to launch her career and reputation after limited discussions with her sponsors. Now the funding is arcane and closely scrutinized, and a seemingly controversial subject has little chance for approval.

Similarly, the days of an adventurer-reporter like Richard Harding Davis, who made his own assignments to cover wars and the great affairs of state, have also passed. Foreign correspondents climb career ladders and are tied to a home office by an umbilical of telephones and lap-top computers. They are expected to cover a story quickly and move on.

To say that all the political groups are "available and eager to tell of their struggle" is only partially true. The political parties are divided, suspicious, and jealous. They claim to be fighting the same holy war, but there is no central location where a reporter can go for help. One party will not even give the telephone number or address of another party.

Peshawar is a stronghold of true believers. A reporter who manages to track down a spokesman for one of the parties is usually regaled with stale, self-serving stories of brave mujahidin and Red Army atrocities. No reporter wants to be an agitprop conduit, nor is he willing to risk his reputation with stories that cannot be independently verified. But he has to write something, if only to justify his travel expenses, and confines himself to bland, carefully attributed interviews or simple descriptions of refugees—stories that add little to what has been written many times in the past.

If a reporter seeks firsthand experience, his trip to Afghanistan takes a week to arrange, and then another two weeks to travel to and from depopulated areas close to the border. There, he will interview commanders who will tell him what his escorts want to be heard. After three weeks and a great deal of discomfort, he will have material for a few "color" pieces about people and geography with nothing significant about the progress of the war or the state of the economy.

But even such a short trip by a staff reporter is unlikely. In Afghanistan a reporter risks his life where there are no direct American interests and where, moreover, the United States specifically forbids its own employees, or those receiving government funds, to go. This is known as "deniability." The United States wants to avoid or deflect Soviet charges that America is directing the Afghan resistance movement. The presence of American citizens inside Afghanistan would weaken this deniability, particularly if an American is captured or killed, as illustrated by Moscow's charges that Charles Thornton was part of a group training mujahidin to use ground-to-air missiles.

In the circumstances, no editor feels he has a right to assign a staff reporter to go into Afghanistan or even to encourage a freelancer to travel on his own.

My own experience is an example. When I first offered to write for the *New York Times*, I said I intended to enter Afghanistan to gather material for a book. The newspaper agreed to accept articles based on my travels, with the clear understanding that my travels were voluntary.

When Thornton was killed in September 1985, I received both telex and phone instructions saying I must not enter Afghanistan again. As it happened, I had just returned from the long trip to Baghlan and Khanabad and did not intend to travel any more that year.

Early in 1986 I told my editor that I intended to make further trips into Afghanistan for research purposes even if I could not offer any material to the *New York Times*. Once again, since it was clearly understood that no inducements were offered, I was told that the newspaper would consider publication of material generated in the course of my travels.

With the constraints on staff reporters, major coverage of the Afghan war is narrowed down to a handful of freelance correspondents. This raises a new question: What is the news from Afghanistan? Certainly, the destruction wrought by the Soviet forces is a major part of the story. But there are other elements: How well do the mujahidin get along with the villagers? Does political disunity affect their fighting ability? How valid are their battle claims?

These are questions the Peshawar-based political parties do not want asked. There is nothing surprising about this. Nations at war seek loudspeakers and perambulating microphones, not someone who asks questions and looks for weakness.

I Am Boycotted

After returning from Ghazni in August 1986, I felt my trips were becoming repetitious: I was seeing and hearing, with slight variations, the same things. I decided to return home to see if several months of reflection would give me a new perspective. By then I had been in and out of Pakistan and Afghanistan for almost two years. People frequently asked my opinions. Since I, in turn, always asked questions of others, I willingly discussed what I had seen and what I thought. Since I did not like it when other people asked not to be quoted I never asked for anonymity.

Two days before I was scheduled to leave for New York, I was interviewed by a reporter from *The Muslim* of Islamabad, a newspaper that opposed American involvement in Afghanistan and demanded that Pakistan negotiate directly with Kabul to end the conflict.

In *The Muslim* I was quoted as saying that the "war was over in Afghanistan as no fighting spirit is left amongst the Afghan people who are eager to see normal life restored in their country." What I actually said was that I had traveled extensively in the southwest and in Ghazni and had seen no fighting, that war-weariness was spreading, and that I had encountered many areas where fighting had stopped.

Otherwise, except for a few outright errors, the article generally reflected my findings. I said the Soviet military were perfecting their tactics to interdict mujahidin supply lines and were building a new Afghan Army with a professional officer corps. I also said the mujahidin had failed to develop an effective strategy and were not demonstrating an offensive spirit, but were simply defending themselves. Further, I said that civilians complained that the presence of the mujahidin exposed them to bombing.

Some months later, in New York, I was told that Afghan political leaders were angry at me, because of both the article in *The Muslim* and my earlier article in the *New York Times* about opium cultivation in mujahidin-controlled areas. I discovered the extent of their anger when I returned to Peshawar in April 1987.

In the previous months the mujahidin had been supplied with American Stinger ground-to-air missiles and were claiming to be shooting down an average of one enemy aircraft a day. I planned to shop around among the political parties for a trip to the Kabul area to see if there had been any improvement in the battle situation and civilian morale.

Instead, I was boycotted. The mujahidin representatives I met so often in the past did not answer my telephone calls or respond to messages I left at their gates. My career as a reporter on Afghanistan had come to an abrupt end.

Is Increased Aid Self-Defeating?

I was not alone in questioning the efficacy of the resistance. In August 1986, almost simultaneous with *The Muslim* interview, a committee of American senators and congressmen heard that mujahidin might lose the war if they did not develop a unified strategy and receive more aid.

At a hearing of the Congressional Task Force on Afghanistan, Republican Senator Orrin Hatch of Idaho, who visited the border area the previous January, said: "The battles you hear about are Soviet initiatives to close the supply lines of the resistance from Pakistan. These battles are bad news."

Joseph Collins, a U.S. Army military expert, told the committee that without a change in the existing military balance, in ten or fifteen years "there will be an Afghan communist state with a small and not very significant insurgency."

Since I could not travel again into Afghanistan, I spent only three weeks in Pakistan, seeing old friends and asking what was new. The most obvious new development was the presence of dozens of new Americans in big new cars. There was a building boom in the University Town residential area of Peshawar to accommodate the newcomers.

The members of the congressional task force apparently hoped their pessimistic findings would generate support for increased military and humanitarian aid for the mujahidin. But journalists, humanitarian workers, and foreign diplomats in Peshawar and Islamabad pointed to the newcomers as evidence of too much aid, not too little.

In 1986, when I first surveyed American humanitarian aid, it amounted to $15 million. When I returned a year later, the cumulative sum had increased to $50 million. There were plans to open schools and clinics within Afghanistan, to supply farmers with seeds and fertilizer, and to send in tons of food and civilian necessities. All of this was to be carried out by working through committees representing the seven parties. The aid would then be funneled separately to each of the parties. To observers, it seemed an attempt to create a semblance of unity without the reality of unity.

Military aid was also increasing but without producing significant victories. Covert aid had reached a reported cumulative $1.35 billion, but the mujahidin were still fighting in the few regions where they had always fought—generally around Kabul, Kandahar, Herat, and a few other cities—while much of the rest of the country remained quiet.

Simply throwing taxpayers' dollars at a problem can be self-defeating. Amid unconfirmed reports of flagrant corruption, bickering, and ineffectual battles, an invidious analogy could be made between the mujahidin and the much-criticized anti-Sandinista contra guerrillas in Nicaragua.

All of the Afghan watchers I questioned agreed that the cornucopia of dollars was having a deleterious political effect—making it unnecessary for the political parties to resolve their differences. Instead, disunity was becoming stronger as they competed for the largess.

They also pointed out that a heightened American presence meant that the jihad was losing what Gulbuddin Hekmatyar had called its "originality"—the perception of being a struggle started by Afghans for Afghan Islamic values. The mujahidin no longer appeared to be innocent victims but, instead, were labeled as "American-aided guerrillas" or "American surrogates" in the superpower rivalry.

It's Not News When People Are Still Suffering

Otherwise, there was no "news" in the sense of moving the story forward or providing new insights. To say that people are still suffering, that bombs are still falling, and that refugees are still arriving is to say, in newspaper terms, that there is no story.

Yet, after an absence of six months, I seemed to see with fresh eyes signs of the appalling human cost of the war. Everywhere were men who were crippled and some who were blind. I visited a German volunteer organization in the basement of the sprawling, dirty, noisy Khyber Hospital on the main road leading north to the Khyber Pass. It had facilities to make 2,000 prosthetic devices a year and hoped to raise funds to hire more workers to increase production to 3,000 a year. The Red Cross also maintained a workshop that made another 500 artificial legs and arms. A German technician at the Khyber Hospital workshop said that even with these facilities the demand was still unfilled.

There were frequent newspaper stories of terrorist bombings in tribal territories and violations of Pakistani airspace and the bombing of border villages. In February 1987 the outskirts of Miram Shah were bombed, killing eighty people. Then in March planes from Afghanistan struck Teri Mangal, killing another eighty people, after which the mujahidin abandoned Teri Mangal as a staging point for convoys into Afghanistan. Even Robat, the smuggler's capital in the far northwestern corner of Afghanistan, was bombed twice.

According to Pakistani authorities, more than 300 civilians were killed in air attacks during the first three months of 1987, with a total of 1,000 air incursions—three times the rate of the previous year. There were also constant terrorist bombings in and around Peshawar and in the tribal territories. But it was surprising how calm everyone remained. I could remember bombings in 1984 that touched off large protest parades by opposition parties and demands that the government negotiate with Kabul to end the war and thus assure peace and tranquility. A few times, when bombs killed people in crowded parts of Peshawar, there was anger and attacks on Afghans, but after a few days all seemed to be forgotten.

When I went to Islamabad, diplomats and foreign reporters agreed that the Geneva proximity talks had played themselves out. The Soviet Union had reduced the timetable for a withdrawal of its "limited contingent" to eighteen months. Pakistan had said it was willing to accept a withdrawal of seven months, so there was a difference of only eleven months. But the issue, these observers said, was not withdrawal: it was the successor government. They said the United States and other Western countries, as well as Pakistan, Saudi Arabia, the Gulf States, and Iran, were convinced that Moscow would not allow the Afghans the freedom to choose their own government and return to an Islamic way of life. Without that, they said no agreement was possible.

These same informants said Najib's proclamation of a government of national reconciliation had failed: that he had not attracted a single major tribal leader or some other person of regional stature to the government, and the few leaders he had attracted had obviously been drawn for selfish reasons. They also said the attempts to threaten Pakistan had failed: that the air attacks had only increased the perception of Pakistan as a frontline state deserving the West's support.

Deaths and Disunity

I found Dr. Juliet Fournot of Doctors Without Borders in Peshawar. She said the misunderstanding with Professor Rabbani and the Jamiat-i-Islami been resolved. One reason for this, she said, was that commanders in Afghanistan had sent messages requesting European women doctors and nurses to treat their mothers, wives, and sisters. She said the hospital in Badakhshan had reopened and that the hospital at Zari might also be reopened.

Happily, I found that Dr. Paul Ickx was back, having gained twenty pounds since I saw him in Zari almost two years earlier. He was in Peshawar arranging for supplies for a new Doctors Without Borders hospital near Ghazni. He said the many groups surrounding Ghazni had achieved a new unity and that recently they had simultaneously attacked all of the enemy posts surrounding the city. He also had news from the north: the enemy post near Shulgara—the one Commander Abdullah had waved his rose at while telling me there was a truce—had now been captured by the mujahidin.

A few days later I again called on Dr. Ickx and found him with an old acquaintance from Zari. He was Mohammed Daoud, the commander I had thought resembled a young Fidel Castro.

"And how is Martin?" I asked, recalling the young commander I had grown to like so much. When I last saw Martin, he was testing mines and explosives to use as an urban guerrilla.

"He was martyred," Daoud said. "It was an accident with some explosives."

"And the other commander, Ziahullah, who also traveled north with me. What happened to him?" I asked.

"Martyred," Daoud replied. "He went into Mazar as a guerrilla and was caught in an ambush."

I was dismayed and asked Daoud if I could contribute to a fund to help their widows.

"They were not married," he said. "But this a great problem. We have more than 300 widows with children and no way to help them."

Later, Paul said the Jamiat in Mazar was still split by factional fighting and that for a while Commander Daoud himself had been made a prisoner by one of the factions. Daoud was in Peshawar for that reason: he was trying to get Professor Rabbani to settle the dispute.

I also learned of another factional dispute that led to the killing of a commander I met while traveling to the north to search for Soviet defectors. He was Mohammed Salim, who had the defector Nasratullah among his men.

Salim commanded Hizb-i-Islami forces on the north side of the Salang Pass. He spoke Russian, was a graduate of Kabul Polytechnic, and was one of the most skilled commanders in the north. Now he was dead: killed treacherously by another Afghan.

Since it reflected badly on the political parties, this news was suppressed in Peshawar. Instead, there were two sets of rumors. Both tied the killing to an attempt by the leading Jamiat commander, Ahmad Shah Massoud, to create a unified military and political structure for the entire northeast.

Massoud had organized a control board, consisting primarily of Jamiat commanders drawn from the five provinces of Badakhshan, Takhar, Kunduz, Baghlan, and Samangan. Commanders from other groups were invited to join with equal standing.

One version of the assassination was that some Jamiat commanders were opposed to any plan that would undercut their autonomy and killed Salim in an attempt to start a feud between Hizbi and Jamiat that would make Massoud's unity impossible.

Another version was that Salim wanted to join the unity but was killed by his own party members who opposed cooperation with Jamiat. Supposedly the assassins fled to Jamiat where they were welcomed by others who also opposed the unity.

Basmachis and the Warnings of History

The disunity and the lack of a political and military strategy have a disturbing historical analogy dating back to the Bolshevik seizure of power in Russia in October 1917. Soviet Central Asia, then known as Russian Turkistan, was the home of nomads and peoples who were conscious only of their local or tribal identity. Most of the region was under direct tsarist military rule except for the protectorates of Khiva (mainly an oasis between the Kara Kum and Kizil Kum deserts) and Bukhara, bordering Afghanistan.

The Bolshevik revolt encouraged minorities throughout Russia to seek more freedom. A handful of intellectuals in the Uzbek city of Kokand proclaimed an autonomous government of Turkistan. The Bolsheviks smashed the revolt, sacked the city, and imposed a food blockade that led to extensive famine. The resistance, known as the Basmachi movement, spread to the surrounding regions. In September 1920 the Red Army invaded Bukhara, and early in 1921 the Amir of Bukhara sought sanctuary in Afghanistan.

In November 1921 Enver Pasha, a Turkish army officer who called himself a representative of the Prophet, unified several of the scattered Basmachi bands. But, in attempting to fight a positional war against a reinforced and resupplied Red Army, he merely offered a weak and tempting target. In August 1922 Enver Pasha died in a cavalry charge.

Intellectuals spoke of Pan Islamic idealism and of Turkic revivalism, but individual Basmachis could not see beyond their clan, tribe, or village. What they sought bordered on anarchy: no government except local government. They made and broke alliances with each other and with the Bolsheviks. Some capitulated, some declared neutrality, and others roamed aimlessly, seeking targets of opportunity.

Mustafa Chokayev, who had been president of the provisional government of Kokand, described the Basmachi guerrilla leaders as "extremely crude and adventurously-minded" who "not only postponed the general aim of the struggle and failed to establish the unity of the front, but . . . were instrumental in dividing the country." He also called them "brave fighters for whom the whole meaning of the struggle was defined by the success they obtained in the battles of the day."

By 1923 the Basmachis were no longer a serious military threat. Ideology and the slow weaning of the people away from the Basmachis became the principal Bolshevik weapon. The Red Army maintained control of the cities, railroads, postal facilities, and other communications, while the peasants, who came to depend on the cities for food and other necessities, were left free, except for punitive military expeditions against Basmachi bands. The grim shortages of food and manufactured goods eased with Lenin's New Economic Policy. Peasants were given seeds and loans, and traders were allowed free commerce and were assured that private property would be respected. There were also concessions to Muslim institutions, including the reopening of mosques and the acceptance of Islamic law.

At the same time the Soviet government sought to isolate the Basmachis from foreign sympathizers. Peace treaties were signed with Turkey, Iran, and Afghanistan, where the reform-minded King Amanullah felt encouraged by the Bolshevik attacks on traditionalism. In 1923 Amanullah renounced official support for the Basmachis, although they continued to operate across the border.

There were isolated skirmishes until as late as 1933, but the Basmachis could not hinder the evolution of a Soviet society. Then, in the late 1930s, the same Muslim intellectuals who had helped the Bolsheviks create this Soviet society were swept into Stalin's labor camps or execution chambers and thousands of mosques were razed. A recrudescence of Basmachi-type resistance in World War II only brought more political and religious repression.

The similarities with the present day are apparent. But there are also significant differences. Where early Soviet propagandists could claim that the Basmachi movement was purely an internal problem, the Soviet troops in Afghanistan signify patent aggression. Moscow has been condemned by all Western governments as well as by noncommunist political parties and newspaper editorial writers. Even the Swedes, who are proud of their neutrality, send volunteers and government funds to help the Afghan resistance.

Afghanistan has long frontiers with Pakistan and Iran and cannot be isolated. Pakistan—facing what it views as a mortal threat from India—must cultivate the support of the United States and Saudi Arabia. As long as Afghanistan is an integral part of the global strategies of Washington or the Islamic strategies of Riyadh, Pakistan in particular has no option but to keep its border open for aid to the mujahidin.

Finally, Moscow has failed to heal the historic fissure between the Khalqis and Parchamis in its surrogate People's Democratic party of

Afghanistan. Visitors to Kabul say the ouster of Babrak Karmal in favor of Najib merely created a new clique of Karmalists within the Parchami faction.

Reason and Unreason in Afghanistan

People ask: What will happen next? They expect a rational answer based on observable or quantifiable facts, like how many guns does one side have and how good is their logistics. But the struggle in Afghanistan is irrational.

When I first began to travel among the Afghans I was skeptical and then annoyed at their constant claims to be fighting in the name of God and that God had promised them victory. It seemed to be an excuse to avoid the hard problems of leadership and strategy.

Then I saw the mujahid at Haji Baba's camp in Shin Narai who had put his hand in the fire to prove his bravery. On the surface it was a foolish, impulsive act. But I asked myself whether that wasn't what the entire nation had done—put its hand into a fire to prove its willingness to suffer for an ideal that was beyond the bounds of reason?

The more I lived and traveled among the Afghans the more I came to believe that any discussion of the jihad and the mujahidin must start with the irrational and work outward. The war is irrational because it is an authentic "people's war" that springs from the history, culture, religion, and traditions of Afghanistan. That's why it has no Tito or Ho Chih Minh and can never have one. The war arises from all of the people and not a single individual or ideology.

A people's war means the Afghans have a clear political objective with no need for commissars to teach them to think or how to act. They were an independent Islamic nation before the Communists seized power, and they want to return to that state.

They also have an easily perceived enemy. The Russian invaders and their local Communist allies are solely responsible for the atrocities and destruction that has harmed every family and village. It is obvious to all Afghans that the kafirs must be driven out and the martyrs avenged.

At the same time theirs is a moral and ethical war: fought according to Islamic codes that everyone knows and respects. This explains why there are no death squads or torture chambers.

Self-Preservation or Islamic Liberation

A philosophical question can be asked: Are the mujahidin like ants rushing around blindly to rebuild a ruined nest? To phrase it differently, are they the rear guard of a traditional society instinctively fighting for self-preservation?

James Morris, in *Heaven's Command*, a history of the expansion of the British Empire, wrote of the attempt at independence and quick defeat of the Metis, the half-Indian, half-French settlers of Western Canada in the 1860s: "It was a timeless tragedy, the intuitive protest of a people whose manner of life was doomed by the no less instinctive progress of an empire: a gesture from that older, simpler world, impelled by airier aspirations, and worshipping more fragile gods, which it was so often the destiny of the British Empire to destroy."

Is that what is happening in Afghanistan or are the mujahidin the advance guard of a Central Asian liberation movement?

Olivier Roy, the French scholar, recalls the Rif war of 1921–26, in which the French and Spanish destroyed the Rif Republic of Abdul Krim:

> The Afghanistan war may be compared with the Rif war which, although it appeared at the time to be just another tribal uprising, actually prefigured the liberation movements which were to come; it is not just chance that the Rif war involved the Muslim guerrilla movement which showed the greatest similarity with the Afghan resistance, and certainly very much different from the Basmachi of Central Asia. . . . It is necessary to see the war from the perspective of history, something which goes far beyond the mountains and deserts where men decided to engage in the struggle before starting to ask what their chance of success is.

If Roy is right, American hopes to force the Soviet Union to the bargaining table by increased attrition through quantum leaps in covert aid and by supplying sophisticated weapons like the Stinger missiles are baseless. Moscow could accept nothing less than complete victory, no matter what the cost.

Americans and Europeans are impatient—always pressing to resolve a situation and move on to something else. To a foreigner, it is remarkable how the Afghans can ignore the possibility of surrender or defeat and accept a struggle that may last far into the future.

"The Resistance Will Not Die"

Shamsuddin Majrooh was a cabinet member in Kabul in the 1960s and chaired the committee that drafted the 1964 constitution. In his late eighties he retains his vigorous mind and speech. He lives in Peshawar with his son, Dr. Bahauddin Majrooh. Soon after I arrived in Peshawar in February 1985, we had a long talk about the vanished days of King Zahir and Prime Minister Mohammed Daoud. Toward the end, I asked him about the prospects for mujahidin victory.

"The struggle will be a long process, and that will not be to our benefit," he replied. "Our resources will be exhausted, our human resources, economic resources, and food supplies. Gradually people will have to turn to the Russians for help. They will depend on the Russians just to get along in life, and the Russians, gradually, will be able to establish themselves in Afghanistan. But the resistance will not die, as long as help is available from outside the country, from Pakistan, Iran, and especially America."

"How long will the resistance last?" I asked.

"A long time," he replied. "Sometimes the Russians will grow strong, sometimes they will become weak. The resistance will also have ups and downs, but it will not die."

"But exactly how long?" I persisted. "Five years, ten years?"

"Oh no," he said. "It will be decades. More than decades. Many, many decades."

If the mujahidin do manage to keep the flame of resistance burning that long, the outcome of the struggle may not be decided by guns but by the force of world public opinion. With time, the mujahidin might gain what they now sorely lack: support from the Western public at large—the man and woman in the street—as distinct from governments, politicians, and a handful of doctors and other humanitarian workers.

Mikhail Gorbachev seems to value world opinion: he seeks agreement on strategic arms and says he will grant more human rights to his own people. But as long as the mujahidin fight on, stoically accepting death as their victory, they give the lie to the Soviet Union's claims to be a nation of peace and justice.

If the war goes on for decades, someone might even set up a table with a petition to "Save the Afghans."

Sources

·············

There are few sources for accurate, unbiased information about current conditions in Afghanistan. Against the paucity one book stands out: *Islam and Resistance in Afghanistan* by the French scholar Olivier Roy, who speaks Persian and has traveled widely in Afghanistan.

A monthly bulletin of the Afghan Information Centre, edited by Professor Bahauddin Majrooh, a former dean of the College of Letters of Kabul University, is the only regularly published English language summary of general mujahidin activities. A similar publication, the semimonthly report of the Afghan Information and Documentation Centre, was edited by Fazal Akbar, president of Afghanistan Radio from 1978 to 1980. This publication ceased in February 1987.

Both reflected the values and attitudes of the traditionalist mujahidin parties and depended mainly on reports, otherwise unverified, from commanders returning from the field.

Some of the parties, particularly the Jamiat-i-Islami, also published monthly reports of their activities.

Pakistani newspapers, given the political climate and the passions aroused by Afghan affairs, restricted themselves to summaries gathered from foreign news agencies.

In generalizing, I have been guided by the research of Olivier Roy. I have had extended conversations with Professor Majrooh and Fazal Akbar, with foreign humanitarian workers who have spent considerable time in Afghanistan, and with about a dozen Pakistani and foreign journalists and diplomats who have followed the conflict over a number of years.

For general information I consulted:

Bradsher, Henry, *Afghanistan and the Soviet Union*, expanded ed. (Durham, N.C.: Duke University Press, 1985).

Hyman, Anthony, *Afghanistan Under Soviet Domination* (London: Macmillan, 1984).

CHAPTER 1

Torture:

Extensive reports of torture in Communist prisons, particularly Pul-i-Charkhi, are in Afghan Information Centre bulletins 35, (February 1984), 41 (August 1984), 42 (September 1984), 46 (January 1985), 68 (November 1986), and 70 (January 1987). Also see Afghan Information and Documentation Centre, bulletins 52 (March 16, 1986), 54 (April 1, 1986), 62 (August 1, 1986), and 67 (October 16, 1986).

CHAPTER 2

Islamic traditions:

Canfield, Robert, "Islamic Sources of Resistance," *Orbis* 29, no. 1 (Spring 1985), 57–71.

Shahrani, M. Nazif, "Marxist 'Revolution' and Islamic Resistance," in M. Nazif Shahrani and Robert Canfield, *Revolutions and Rebellions in Afghanistan* (Berkeley: University of California Press, 1984), 27–57.

Early Afghan history:

Barni, Ziauddin, "Tarikh-i-Feroz Shahi," in Henry Elliot and John Dawson, *The History of India as Told by Its Own Historians*, vol. 3 (Allahabad, India: Kitab Mahal, reprint, n.d.), 183–88.

Yadgar, Ahmad, "Tarikh-i-Salatin-i-Afghana," in Elliot and Dawson, *The History of India as Told by Its Own Historians*, vol. 5, 29–30.

British period and Afghan cultural attitudes:

Ahmed, Akbar, "Pathan Society," *Journal of Area Study* (University of Peshawar, Peshawar, Pakistan), no. 13 (Winter 1983), 17–30.

Singer, Andre, *Lords of the Khyber* (London: Faber and Faber, 1984), 18–19, 153–57.

Spain, James, *The Pathan Borderland*, (Karachi, Pakistan: Indus Publications, 1985), 18–19, 32–35, 68–71, 135.

Daoud period:

Anwar Khan, Mohammed, "The Second Afghan Constitution, Part 3," *Journal of Area Study* (University of Peshawar, Peshawar, Pakistan), no. 4 (Winter 1979), 1–23.

Anwar Khan, Mohammed, "The Third Afghan Constitution, Part 1," *Journal of Area Study* (University of Peshawar, Peshawar, Pakistan), no. 5 (Spring 1980), 1–25.

Bauer, Peter, *Equality, the Third World and Economic Delusion* (Cambridge, Mass.: Harvard University Press, 1981), 86–134. Although Bauer does not refer to Afghanistan, his observations on the destabilizing effects of massive foreign aid are pertinent.

Communist history and Soviet invasion:
Anon. correspondence, *Central Asian Survey* 1, no. 4 (April 1983), 159–63.
Arnold, Anthony, *Afghanistan's Two-Party Communism* (Stanford, Calif.: Hoover Institution Press, 1983), 52–63, 91–98. I have followed Arnold in discussing the Soviet Union's involvement in the communist coup of 1978.
Arnold, Anthony, "The Stony Path to Afghan Socialism" *Orbis* 29, no. 1 (Spring 1985), 40–57.
Male, Beverley, *Revolutionary Afghanistan* (New York: St. Martin's Press, 1982), 13–67.

Growth of Islamic resistance:
Amin, Tahir, "Afghan Resistance, Past, Present and Future," *Asian Survey* (University of California Press, Berkeley) 24, no. 4 (April 1984), 373–99.
Anwar Khan, Mohammed, "The Third Afghan Constitution, Part 10," *Journal of Area Study* (University of Peshawar, Peshawar, Pakistan), no. 14 (Summer 1984), 1–20.
Broxup, Marie, "The Soviets in Afghanistan," *Central Asian Survey* 1, no. 4 (April 1983), 83–100.
Jansen, Godfrey, *Militant Islam* (London: Pan Books, 1981), 147–54, 172–76.
Roy, Olivier, *Islam and Resistance in Afghanistan* (Cambridge: Cambridge University Press, 1986), 69–83.

CHAPTER 4

Foreign military aid:
New York Times, June 19, 1986, January 13, 1987.
Washington Post, January 16, 1986.
Watson, Russell, "Insurgencies: Two of a Kind," *Newsweek*, March 13, 1987, 32.
"The Military Balance 1985–1986," International Institute for Strategic Studies, London, *Strategic Survey 1985–1986* (Spring 1986), 119.

CHAPTER 5

Travel accounts:
Bellew, Henry, *Afghanistan, A Political Mission in 1857* (Lahore, Pakistan: S. H. Mubarak Ali, Oriental Publishers, reprint, 1978), 25, 70–71, 107–8, 138, 305–7, 421, 458.
Ferrier, Joseph, *Caravan Journeys and Wanderings in Persia, Afghanistan, Turkistan and Beloochistan* (Karachi, Pakistan: South Asia Publishers, 1981), 276–85.
Masson, Charles, *Narration of Various Journeys*, vol. 1 (Karachi, Pakistan: Oxford University Press, reprint, 1974), 150–51.

Shia conflict in the Hazarajat:
Afghan Information Centre bulletins 27–28 (December 1983), 39 (June 1984).
Edwards, David, "The Evolution of Shia Political Dissent in Afghanistan," in Juan Cole and Nikki Keddie, *Shiism and Social Protest* (New Haven, Conn.: Yale University Press, 1986), 201–29.
Roy, *Islam and Resistance in Afghanistan*, 139–48.

CHAPTER 6

Doctors Without Borders:
Malhuret, Claude, "Report from Afghanistan," *Foreign Affairs* (Winter 1983–84), 426–35.

CHAPTER 7

Genocide:
The 1986 annual report of the UN Human Rights Commission said: "Continuation of the military solution will lead inevitably to a situation approaching genocide." *Pakistan Times*, February 28, 1986.

Changes in Afghan society:
Roy, *Islam and Resistance in Afghanistan*, 149–59.

Soviet tactics and defections in Mazar-i-Sharif:
Alexiev, Alex, "Soviet Strategy and the Mujahidin," *Orbis* 29, no. 1 (Spring 1985), 31–40.
"Afghanistan, Wearing Down the Rebels," International Institute for Strategic Studies, London, *Strategic Survey 1985–1986* (Spring 1986), 130–39.

CHAPTER 8

Taj Mohammed:
Winchester, Mike, "Guerrilla Theater, Holy Warriors Take the Stage," *Soldier of Fortune* (April 1987), 60–67, mentions and has a picture of the defector Taj Mohammed.

Horse care, Afghan-style:
Ferrier, *Caravan Journeys and Wanderings in Persia, Afghanistan, Turkistan and Beloochistan*, 384–85.

CHAPTER 9

Did the Kremlin make a mistake?:
Arnold, *Afghanistan's Two-Party Communism*, 99–114.
Bradsher, *Afghanistan and the Soviet Union*, 126–204.

Sovietizing the Afghans:
"Annexing the Afghans," *Soviet Nationality Survey* 2, no. 11-12 (1985), 1–3.
New York Times, January 15, 16, 17, 22, 26, 1987. This is a series by Philip Taubman, the Moscow correspondent of the *New York Times*, who visited Kabul with a group of Western correspondents.

Defense becomes offense:
Jones, Rodney, "Superpower Interests and the Geopolitics of Southwest Asia," *Defense Journal* (Karachi, Pakistan) 11, no. 1-2 (Spring 1985), 9–21.

Negotiating a way out:
Bradsher, *Afghanistan and the Soviet Union*, 265–70.

Fukuyama, Francis, "Gorbachev and the Third World," *Foreign Affairs* (Spring 1986), 716–31.

Noorani, Munawar, "Afghanistan Negotiations: Implications for the U.S. of an Impasse," *Journal of South Asian and Middle Eastern Studies* (Villanova University) 9, no. 3 (Spring 1986), 3–17.

Riaz, Mohammad, "The Elusive Peace," *Enquiry* (London) 3, no. 6 (June 1986), 8–12.

Rosenfeld, Stephen, "The Guns of July," *Foreign Affairs* (Spring 1986), 698–714.

Shahi, Agha, "Prospects of a Political Settlement of the War in Afghanistan," *Journal of Area Study* (University of Peshawar, Peshawar, Pakistan), no. 13 (Winter 1983), 1–15.

Testing Moscow's intention:
Whitehead, John, Address before the World Affairs Council, Washington, D.C., December 13, 1985.

Comrade Doctor Najib:
Afghan Information Centre bulletin 62 (May 1986).

International Institute of Strategic Studies, London, *Strategic Survey 1985–1986* (Spring 1986), 130–39.

No destruction of the state:
New York Times, January 16, 1987.

CHAPTER 10

Growing Arab influence:
Al-Rifat, Ahmed, "Afghan Mujahidin Fight to Defend the Honor of Their Faith and Country," *Arab News* (London), September 14, 1985.

Chevalerias, Alain, "The Radicalization of the Afghan Resistance," *Swiss Review of World Affairs* 35, no. ll (February 1986), 23–24.

Esmat:
Davis, Anthony, "A Fire in the Borderlands," *Asiaweek* (Hong Kong), June 29, 1986, 26–41.

Kandahar International Airport:
Bradsher, *Afghanistan and the Soviet Union*, 30, cites reports that the airport was built for American strategic interests.

Basmachi from Arizona:
Afghanistan, The Road to Reconciliation (London: Harney and Jones, January 1987). This includes the photograph of Thornton with ammunition.

Soviet Analyst, A Fortnightly Commentary 15, no. 2 (January 22, 1986), contains Soviet media comments on Thornton's death.

Tass English language broadcast, October 24, 1986, includes the "Basmachi from Arizona" reference.

Dr. Simon's reply:
New York Times, April 12, 1986.

CHAPTER 11

Rabbani's reply to opium article:
New York Times, June 19, 1986.

CHAPTER 12

Mujahidin weakness:
Afghan Information Centre bulletin 62 (May 1986) reports on Jawara, the Haji Anwar interview, and the remarks of the refugee leaders at the Nasir Bagh camp.
Afghan Information and Documentation Centre bulletin 62 (August 1, 1986) reports on Kunduz.
Eshaq, Mohammed, "The Present Situation in Afghanistan, June 1986," *Central Asian Survey* 6, no. 1 (1987), is a reprint of a report issued in Peshawar in May 1986.
New York Times, June 17, 1986, reports on the visit of the four party leaders to Washington.

The Hazara awakening:
Roy, *Islam and Resistance in Afghanistan*, 141–48, discusses corruption, the Shura being "cut off from the people," and the "collapse" of the Shura.

CHAPTER 13

Journalism and the jihad:
Rubinstein, Alvin, "Speculations on a National Tragedy," *Orbis* 30, no. 4 (Winter 1987), 605–6.
The Muslim (Islamabad, Pakistan), August 13, 1986.

Is increased aid self-defeating?:
New York Times, August 14, 1986.
"Insurgencies: Two of a Kind," *Newsweek*, March 23, 1987, compares the mujahidin with the contras and describes the mujahidin as "American surrogates."

Air attacks and the breakdown of the Geneva talks:
New York Times, February 28, March 25, 26, 1987.

Basmachis:
Bradsher, *Afghanistan and the Soviet Union*, 246–48.
Dickson, Keith, "The Basmachi and the Mujahidin: Soviet Responses to Insurgency Movements," *Defense Journal* (Karachi, Pakistan) (January–February 1986), 19–33.
Fraser, Glenda, "Basmachi-I," *Central Asian Survey* 6, no. 1 (1987), 1–73,

Disunity in Kabul:
New York Times, May 13, 1987.

Reason and unreason:
Morris, James, *Heaven's Command* (Harmondsworth, England: Penguin Books, 1979), 356.
Roy, *Islam and Resistance in Afghanistan*, 217–18.

Central Asia Book Series

Experienced eyewitnesses offer a reader special insight into events that most people cannot hope to see. And when it comes to writing about a foreign country in the throes of
change, outsiders may create the most compelling accounts for their own countrymen.
That is true partly because the keen outside observer can sustain an essential detach-
ment from his subject. He discriminates clearly between what is particular to the inhabitants of the region and those universal aspects of human behavior that he finds there.
For the author's own domestic audience, close communication also flows from the
unique capacity of both observer and reader figuratively to see the foreign culture
through the same eyes.

From the start of the Central Asia Book Series the editor has searched for firsthand reports from Central Asia by just such informed outsiders to the area as Arthur
Bonner, author of *Among the Afghans*. He is, in the full sense, a primary source of knowledge and insight from Central Asia.

Mr. Bonner's career as a journalist began in 1942 when he joined the *New York
Daily News* as a copyboy. In 1945 he moved to the Columbia Broadcasting System as a
radio news writer. He went to India in 1953 as a CBS cameraman and radio correspondent, reporting from every country in South and Southwest Asia, and also contributed
articles to the *Atlantic*, the *Saturday Evening Post*, the *Reporter*, and the *Wall Street Journal*. In 1960 he returned to New York as a television documentary producer and radio
reporter with added assignments in India, Africa, and Latin America.

In 1965 he left CBS to write *Jerry McAuley and His Mission*, published in 1967:
a pragmatic history of the life and heritage of the nineteenth-century founder of the
world's first Christian rescue mission for alcoholics in New York City.

He then joined the National Broadcasting Company as a television producer and
news writer for WNBC-TV in New York. He officially retired in January 1985, and a
few weeks later he boarded a plane for Peshawar to resume his career as a foreign
correspondent.

Mr. Bonner was born in Brooklyn, N.Y., and is married with three children.

The editor of the series invites writers to send for consideration manuscripts of original firsthand accounts, academic studies, reference works, and related writings concerning or from Central Asia.

GENERAL EDITOR
Edward Allworth,
618 Kent Hall,
Columbia University,
New York City 10027

ADVISORY EDITORS
Andras J. E. Bodrogligeti,
University of California
at Los Angeles, and
Richard N. Frye,
Harvard University.

Index

Muslim proper names are alphabetized last name first when both appear in the text.